Standard Catalog of

DUCATI

MOTORCYCLES

1946-2005

Ian Falloon

©2004 Ian Falloon

Published by

An imprint of F+W Publications, Inc.

700 East State Street • Iola, WI 54990-0001
715-445-2214 • 888-457-2873

Our toll-free number to place an order or obtain a free catalog is (800) 258-0929.

Library of Congress Catalog Number: 2004105222

ISBN: 0-87349-714-7

Designed by Jamie Griffin

Edited by Brian Earnest

Printed in United States of America

INTRODUCTION

With production spanning 60 years, and dozens of models, it isn't an easy task to catalog Ducati motorcycles. Compounding this difficulty is the absence of factory records prior to 1973, so the information on early models has required considerable research of period brochures, advertising material, parts lists, owners' and workshop manuals, and magazines. Every endeavor has been made to include all the motorcycle variants of the 1950s and 1960s, and if there are exclusions it wasn't deliberate. With considerable variation in technical specifications between brochures, workshop manuals, and owners' manuals for many models, I have generally selected workshop manuals in preference.

Only production motorcycles and catalog production racers are included in this catalog. Special factory racing models that were not freely available are not featured, and neither are unusual or obscure vehicles such as the ill-fated Girino of 1948, and 200cc Muletto of 1959 and 1960. As they were not produced in Bologna, the Spanish Mototrans singles are also not included, although those overhead-camshaft singles with Mototrans engines are featured because they were assembled in Bologna. There will always be some confusion over the exact correct specification for many Ducatis, especially early or late examples in a production series as there was often an overlap of components. Within the scope of this volume I have tried to include as much of this variation in specification as possible.

The organization of this catalog is in families and types of motorcycles, rather than as annual production. While current production emphasizes annual updates, the Italian production style highlights family groups that overlap from year to year. In the past, many models barely changed from year to year. Although production levels are much higher today, as a small company Ducati cannot afford to provide a new model lineup every few years. Instead, it concentrates on one family revamp at a time, and there is considerable annual carryover.

Many individuals have assisted in this project, and I would like to thank them all. Ludovica Benedetti and Livio Lodi at Ducati Motor assisted with press releases, access to motorcycles, archival material, and production data. Without access to Rob Klootwijk's incredible collection of brochures and advertising material many models may have been overlooked. Jeremy Bowdler, editor of Two Wheels magazine, and David Edwards, editor of Cycle World magazine, allowed the use of photos from their archives. Warren Lee of NFI, the Australian Ducati distributor, has always been most helpful and supportive. My good friend in California, Roy Kidney, provided more wonderful photos, as did another friend in Greece, Nico Georgeoglou. Many others contributed photos and information, or allowed their motorcycles to appear in this catalog. So thanks to Phil Aynsley, Philip Ayres, Gerolamo Bettoni, Rolf im Brahm, Alan Chalk, Tony Cottle, Jerry Dean, Brian Dietz, Leigh Farrell, Alex Finlay, James Feery, Fred Fitzgerald, Geoffrey Foord, Paul Frost, Ian Glover, Kai Higdon, Phil Hitchcock, Bill Irwin, Richard Kennedy, Dean Markham, Don O'Connor, Clayton Potter, Gerard Porter, Eric Reeves, Peter Shearman, Thorsten Schulze, Brendan Stephenson, Peter Sundberg, Paul Taylor, Fred Fitzgerald, Gregg Rammell, Phil Schilling, Neil Spalding, Heinz Tschinkel, Guy Webster, Jonathan White, Geoff Young, and in memoriam to one of the strongest supporters of my work, Bruce Finlayson.

I would also like to thank my publisher, and Ducati enthusiast, Bill Krause for embracing this project, and my editor at KP Books, Brian Earnest. I have written many books on Ducatis, but this encompasses them all, and I hope it will be of interest and benefit to all Ducati enthusiasts. Whether they be single nuts, bevelheads, Desmoquattro, or Testastretta fanciers. Finally, without the support of my lovely wife, Miriam, and the happy smiling faces of my two wonderful boys, Ben and Tim, this book would never have happened.

CONTENTS

MONTJUICH, LAGUNA SECA, SANTA MONICA

CHAPTER 7:

CAGIVA BELT-DRIVE TWO-VALVE TWINS

INDIANA

750 SPORT 1988-89, 900 SUPERSPORT 1989-90, 400 SUPERSPORT JUNIOR 1989

ELEFANT

900, 750, 600, 400, 350 SUPERSPORT, 900 SUPERLIGHT, FINAL EDITION

CHAPTER 8:

851 & 888

CHAPTER 9:

MONSTERS

600, 600 DARK, 620 I.E., AND 400 MONSTER (JAPAN)

CHAPTER 10:

916, 996, 998, and 748

CHAPTER 11:

SPORT TOURING AND MULTISTRADA

CHAPTER 12:

SUPERSPORT AND SPORTCLASSIC (FUEL INJECTED)

CHAPTER 13:

999 and 749

CHAPTER 1

PUSHROD OVERHEAD VALVE SINGLES

CUCCIOLOS

The Cucciolo was initially sold as a motor to attach to a bicycle. This is a T1 Cucciolo, with diagonal cylinder finning.

Ducati Motor

CUCCIOLO T1

Ducati came into the world of motorcycle manufacture almost by accident. Prior to World War II, Ducati was well known internationally as a manufacturer of radios and electronic equipment, and were the second largest company in Italy. Operating from a large modern plant in the Bologna suburb of Borgo Panigale, Ducati expanded throughout the 1930s, eventually employing 11,000 workers. Everything changed following the bombing of the factory in October 1944. Ducati virtually ceased to exist, and after WWII formed an alliance to produce a clip-on motorcycle engine, the Cucciolo, or Puppy, with SIATA (Società Italiana Applicazioni Techiche Auto-Aviatore), a Turin technical development company known for developing racing auto engines. From this humble beginning grew one of Italy's greatest motorcycle makes.

After the Armistice in 1943, a Turinese lawyer and writer, Aldo Farinelli, designed a prototype auxiliary engine that could be easily mounted on a bicycle. Against government directives, he had a prototype running by 1944 and nicknamed it the Cucciolo because of the high-pitched, yapping exhaust. It seemed an unremarkable design, but the immediate post-war period was a very opportune time to produce such a motor. It was easily installed in a bicycle frame, providing cheap and economical transportation, and, because it was a four-stroke, it was extremely economical. Fuel was a scarce commodity in post-war Italy, and Farinelli's little engine had the added bonus of good torque and two-speed gearing, allowing the bicycle to climb modest grades.

Farinelli's design was adopted by SIATA, and in July 1945, barely a month after the end of the war, they announced plans to produce the Cucciolo. Because it was the first new automotive design to appear in post-war Europe, demand soon outstripped supply and SIATA looked for a partner with more production capability. They turned to Ducati,, and in June 1946 Ducati also began to supply Cucciolo engines. At this stage Ducati was still called S.S.R. Ducati (Società Scientifica Radiobrevetti Ducati), and the distinctive SSR logo adorned all its products. These early Ducati-produced Cucciolo T1 engines were identical to the SIATA examples, with diagonal cylinder finning, and the 20-degree inclined forward alloy cylinder cast integrally with the narrow vertically split aluminum crankcase. A cast-iron sleeve was shrunk into the barrel, and the aluminum piston included two compression rings and one oil scraper ring. The steel con-rod ran in roller bearings, and the crankshaft was supported by two ball bearings.

The cylinder head design was unusual, with both the exhaust and intake facing rearwards. The two overhead valves were parallel, and operated by twin pullrods, rather than the usual pushrods, behind the cylinder and driven by a single cam in the crankcase. The rockers and valve springs were exposed, and the lubrication system didn't include an oil pump. Although only lubricated by gravity drip feed, engine life was exceptional, and the Cucciolo soon earned a reputation for outstanding reliability. On the T1, the single spark plug was inclined forward in the head. The flywheel magneto on 1946 models was also a SIATA, and the ignition advance was a moderate 24 degrees.

A gear primary drive drove a wet multi-plate metallic clutch, and a pre-selector allowed the pedals to shift gears. The pedals in a vertical position selected neutral, with the right pedal forward selecting first, and the left pedal forward selecting second gear. The clutch was operated by a lever on the left handlebar, with a hand throttle on the right handlebar.

The T1 engine was designed to attach to a bicycle frame, using the bicycle chain for a secondary drive, and included a 2-liter gas tank that fit above the rear wheel. Starting was by the usual moped method of pedaling while the engine was in gear, and the weight distribution was 55 percent on the front wheel and 45 percent on the rear.

With claims of 275 miles per gallon, the Cucciolo was so successful that production levels continued to increase during 1947, to over 240 a day, although at this stage the Cucciolo was still only available in Italy. By 1947, with more than 25,000 sold, Ducati assumed control of the entire manufacture and distribution of the Cucciolo, establishing an export department in Milan. So confident were Ducati brass that engineer Aldo Loria took one to New York in 1947. The Cucciolo didn't end up conquering America, but it was widely distributed throughout the world, and the most successful of all the post-war micromotors. The Cucciolo was also built under license by Rochet in France.

CUCCIOLO T1 1946-7

Engine	Single cylinder four-stroke, air-cooled	**Valve Timing (degrees)**	8, 32, 32, 8	**Clutch**	Wet multiplate
Bore	39mm	**Carburetion**	Weber or Dell'Orto 8mm	**Gear ratios**	12.5:1, 10.25:1
Stroke	40mm	**Power**	1.25 horsepower	**Weight (engine only) kilograms**	7.8 kg
Displacement	48cc	**Maximum revs**	5250 rpm	**Speed (1st gear)**	4-20 km/h (2.5-12.5 mph)
Compression ratio	6.25:1	**Ignition**	12mm spark plug, four-pole flywheel magneto with 2 Ducati coils	**Speed (2nd gear)**	7-40 km/h (4.5-25 mph)
Valves and valve actuation	12mm intake and exhaust, pullrod	**Lubrication**	Splash		

CUCCIOLO T2

For 1948, recently appointed chief engineer Giovanni Fiorio redesigned the Cucciolo engine, creating the T2. Most of the developments were aimed at improving the ease of manufacture, notably the inclusion of a removable cylinder. The cylinder finning was horizontal, and the cylinder bolted on via a four-stud flange to a new one-piece alloy crankcase. The revised cylinder head included

a forward-facing exhaust. The 14mm spark plug was positioned more centrally, and the carburetor size increased to 14mm. The crankcase now included an oil filler on the front of the engine, and the 6-volt, 15-watt generator was a Ducati. The 2-liter (3 1/2-pint) gas tank now came with attachments to mount on the frame front downtube.

In 1950 the T2 was updated into the T50, with the oil filler at the rear of the crankcase.

There were two versions of the T2, the Turismo and Sport. Also available to special order was a higher performance T2 Sport that included a slightly larger piston (creating a full 50cc), with the compression ratio increased to 8.9:1. A special 70/30 percent petrol-benzole fuel was required and with the ignition advance increased to 32 degrees the Sport delivered 2 horsepower at 5,700 rpm. When installed in a racing bicycle frame it was capable of nearly 40 mph. As early as February 1947 the Cucciolo was winning races in the Micromotore class, and the T2 Sport was the first of many special factory machines available for the privateer racer. An updated version of the T2 appeared in 1950, known as the T50. Apart from crankcase oil filler moved from the front to the left, there were developments to the clutch, primary drive, and carburetor. Most of these appeared after engine number 250500.

CUCCIOLO T2 1948-52

Engine	Single cylinder four-stroke, air-cooled	Valve Timing (degrees)	15-15, 25-30, 45-35, 0-20	Lubrication	Splash
Bore	39mm	Carburetion	Weber-Cucciolo 14/8	Clutch	Wet multiplate
Stroke	40mm	Power	Turismo: 0.8 horsepower Sports; 1.25 horsepower	Gear ratios	18.2:1, 10.5:1, high to low 1:1.735
Displacement	48cc	Maximum revs	5,500 rpm	Weight (engine only)	8 kg (17.6 lbs.)
Compression ratio	Turismo 5.5:1 Sport: 6.5:1	Ignition (degrees)	14mm spark plug, flywheel magneto with two Ducati coils, advance 25-29	Top speed	35 km/h (22 mph)
Valves and valve actuation	12mm intake and exhaust, pullrod				

CUCCIOLO T3

Another development of the Cucciolo T1 appeared during 1948: the T3. Fiorio bored the existing Cucciolo to 60cc, enclosed the exposed valves with grease lubrication, and installed a three-speed transmission. A foot gearshift was separate from the bicycle pedal cranks, which were still employed for starting. This engine formed the basis of the first complete Ducati motorcycle, but was initially displayed in an unusual three-wheeled machine called the Girino. This didn't make it into production, but in the meantime the T3 was prepared for racing by a number of private entrants. However, it was never as successful as the 50cc version because it was outclassed by the 65cc Moto Guzzi Guzzino.

CUCCIOLO T3 1948-49

Engine	Single cylinder four-stroke, air-cooled	Stroke	40mm	Gears	Three speed
Bore	43.8mm	Displacement	60cc		

Ducati Motor

The 48 of 1952-54 was more of a motorcycle than earlier Cucciolos, and included front and rear suspension.

During 1950 and 1951, Cucciolo sales declined, and in an endeavor to gain more publicity Ducati assisted Ugo Tamarozzi and Glauco Zitelli in a successful quest for world speed records. After achieving 49 records in four attempts, the Cucciolo was given a new lease of life as the 48. Sold as a complete motorcycle, not just a clip-on engine, the 48 engine combined features of the T2 and T3, in a pressed steel rigid frame. The 48 cc engine included the T3's enclosed valves with grease lubrication, and three-speed transmission. Starting was by lever. The pressed steel frame included a sprung parallelogram front fork, and incorporated a 4-liter gas tank. Under this sat a tire pump. A big advance over bicycle type Cucciolos were the double drum brakes. Although an unremarkable machine, the 48's primary appeal was its exceptional fuel economy, a claimed 90 kilometers per liter. There were also other variants of the 48, the type G and Type DG that were similar to the 48, but based on a bicycle-style tubular frame. Another variant was the Ciclo scooter, with valanced fenders and panels over the engine, but this was unpopular and short lived.

48 1952-54

Engine	Single cylinder, four-stroke, air-cooled	**Carburetion**	Weber 14mm	**Brakes**	Double drum
Bore	39mm	**Power**	1.5 horsepower at 5,500 rpm	**Weight**	41 kg (90.2 lbs.)
Stroke	40mm	**Gears**	Three speed	**Top speed**	50 km/h (31 mph)
Displacement	48cc	**Tires**	1.75 x 24-inch Pirelli	**Colors**	Light grey; black highlighting

The final Cucciolo was the 55, with the E having rear suspension.

The final development of the Cucciolo was the M55, released at the end of 1954. Still displacing 48 cc, and remarkably similar to Farinelli's near decade old design, the M55 was installed in a new pressed steel frame with moped-style leading link forks. The 55E (Elastico) had rear suspension, while the 55R (Rigido) had a rigid rear end. In some respects the M55 was lower specification than its predecessor, the 48. Although it featured a more efficient silencer instead of an expansion box, the engine made less power, and there was only a two-speed transmission. Neutral was controlled by the left handgrip, with an indicator to show which gear was engaged. As with the earlier Cucciolo, starting was by bicycle pedals. The transmission was via a single 3/16-inch chain with a shock absorber in the rear hub.

By the time the M55 was released the motorcycle world was changing. Motorcycle sales began to decline in the mid-1950s as a more affluent clientele moved towards affordable automobiles. Cheap basic motorcycles for transportation, such as the M55 suffered most, and sales never met expectations. By 1957, the Cucciolo had its day, but with over 400,000 produced it put Ducati on the map as a motorcycle manufacturer.

55E, 55R 1955-57

Engine	Single cylinder four-stroke, air-cooled	**Power**	1.35 horsepower at 5500 rpm	**Wheelbase**	1,090mm (43.6 inches)		
Bore	39mm	**Gears**	Two speed	**Height**	1,000mm (40 inches)		
Stroke	40mm	**Generator**	6 volt/12 watt	**Saddle height**	840mm (33.6 inches)		
Displacement	48cc	**Tires**	2.00 x 18-inch CEAT	**Weight**	45kg (99 lbs.)		
Compression ratio	6.7:1	**Brakes**	Double drum front and rear	**Top speed**	48 km/h (30 mph)		
Carburetion	Weber Type 14 MFC	**Length**	1,700mm (68 inches)	**Colors**	Light grey or red		

OVERHEAD-VALVE FOUR-STROKE SINGLES (60-125cc)

60

Faced with a proliferation of competition in the clip-on motor market, Giovanni Fiorio's 60cc T3 of 1948 led Ducati to consider the production of a complete motorcycle. Ducati had no experience in chassis manufacture, but many other manufacturers were developing special frames for the Cucciolo. One was a tubular steel frame with rear suspension by Caproni of Rovereto, a company primarily known for pre-war airplane manufacture. Ducati asked Caproni to supply frames for the first Ducati: the 60. This first appeared in 1949, but by May 1950 Caproni decided to produce its own motorcycle and the relationship ended.

The 1949 60 was very advanced for its day, and markedly different to the second type, introduced in March 1950. The first engine was essentially a Cucciolo T3 with pullrods, a revised bore and stroke, a higher compression ratio and slightly larger Weber carburetor. The Caproni pressed-steel frame included a telescopic front fork with coil springing and a cantilever rear suspension with a spring under the seat and two friction dampers. The bike ran on 22-inch wheels, and these included front and rear single drum brakes.

60 1949-50

Engine	Single cylinder four-stroke, air-cooled	**Valve type**	Overhead valve, pullrod	**Rear suspension**	Cantilever
Bore	42mm	**Carburetion**	Weber Type 15 MFC	**Weight**	44.5 kg (98 lbs.)
Stroke	43mm	**Power**	2.25 horsepower at 5,000 rpm	**Colors**	Dark red with gold pinstriping
Displacement	59.57cc	**Gears**	Three speed		
Compression ratio	8:1	**Front suspension**	Telescopic fork		

60 Sport, 65 Sport

By 1953, the 60 Sport was called the 65 Sport, but the overhead-valve engine was unchanged.

60 SPORT 1950-52, 65 SPORT 1953

Engine	Single cylinder four-stroke, air-cooled	**Carburetion**	Weber Type 16 MFC or Dell'Orto MA16B	**Rear suspension**	Swingarm	
Bore	44mm	**Power**	2.5 horsepower at 5,500 rpm	**Weight**	48 kg (106 lbs.)	
Stroke	43mm	**Gears**	Three speed	**Top speed**	70 km/h (43 mph)	
Displacement	65.38cc	**Generator**	6 volt/15 watt	**Colors**	60 S: Black frame, chrome tank with red panels	
Compression ratio	8:1	**Front suspension**	Telescopic fork		65 S: Dark red or green tank with chrome	
Valve type	Overhead valve, pushrod					

As soon as the 60 entered production, Fiorio had another engine on the drawing board—a 65cc engine with pushrod-operated overhead valves. Still ostensibly based on the Cucciolo, this engine would last for nearly two decades. The extra displacement came from a 2mm bore increase, and the power increase through an improved combustion chamber, and a larger carburetor. The cylinder head layout was unusual in that the intake was on the left, and exhaust on the right. Some features of the T3 were retained, notably the external permanent magnet four-pole flywheel, but a more modern feature was the incorporation of a vane-type oil pump. Starting was by a kickstart lever on the right.

Initially, the 65cc ohv engine was installed in the Caproni chassis of the 60 and called the 60 Sport. Soon after the demise of the Caproni connection, a new 60 Sport appeared, with the same engine in a new chassis. While the open pressed-steel frame and telescopic front fork was similar, the rear end included a swingarm with twin shock absorbers. This allowed a rack to be installed behind the sprung solo saddle. The 60 Sport was renamed a 65 Sport for 1953, and was identical but for new colors and paint scheme.

The first Ducati motorcycle was the 60 Sport of 1949. The frame was by Caproni and it only lasted a year.

Ducati Motor

65T, 65TL

With the release of the 98 in 1952, the 65 was initially relegated to the role of mundane workhorse. Also released for 1952 were the touring 65T and higher-specification 65TL (Turismo Lusso). The 65 Sport was discontinued for 1954, but two touring models continued until 1958.

For the 65T and 65TL there was a new pressed-steel open frame, similar to that of the 98, with a curved tubular section rear subframe. The rear rack was a simpler fitting over the rear fender, and the 65T and 65TL remained virtually unchanged over the next few years.

DUCATI 65T

l'utilitaria per tutti....

Ducati Motor

With its pressed-steel frame and rudimentary suspension, the 65T was the small-displacement workhorse in the Ducati lineup until 1958.

Ducati Motor

Although sold as a more luxurious model, the 65TL looked very similar to the 65L.

65T, 65TL 1952-58

Engine	Single cylinder four-stroke, air-cooled	**Valve type**	Overhead valve, pushrod	**Front suspension**	Telescopic fork
Bore	44mm	**Carburetion**	Weber Type 16 MFC	**Rear suspension**	Swingarm
Stroke	43mm	**Power**	2.5 horsepower at 5,600 rpm	**Weight**	54 kg (118.8 lbs.)
Displacement	65.38cc	**Gears**	Three speed	**Top speed**	70 km/h (43 mph)
Compression ratio	8:1	**Generator**	6 volt/15 watt	**Colors**	Most dark red
		Tires	2.00 x 22-inch Pirelli		

65TS

In 1955, the 65TS (Turismo Sport) became available, similar to the earlier 65 Sport, but in the T and TL running gear. The gas tank was reshaped, there was a dual seat, and low handlebars were complemented by a small screen. This was an extremely successful model, coinciding with Ducati's success in the Motogiro d'Italia that year, and was the best selling motorcycle in Italy during 1955.

Ducati Motor

One of the most successful models of the mid-1950s was the 65TS, which had a sporting lip on the headlamp and a small screen.

65TS 1955-58

Engine	Single cylinder four-stroke, air-cooled	**Valve type**	Overhead valve, pushrod	**Tires**	2.00 x 18-inch CEAT
Bore	44mm	**Carburetion**	Weber Type 16 MFC	**Front suspension**	Telescopic fork
Stroke	43mm	**Power**	2.5 horsepower at 5,600 rpm	**Rear suspension**	Swingarm
Displacement	65.38cc	**Gears**	Three speed	**Weight**	54 kg (118.8 lbs.)
Compression ratio	8:1	**Generator**	6 volt/15 watt	**Top speed**	70 km/h (43 mph)

CRUISER

Heavy and complicated, the Cruiser was an unsuccessful attempt by Ducati to break into the scooter market.

By 1950, with Cucciolo sales declining and Italy was under the spell of the scooter, Ducati decided it should enter the expanding scooter market. Not content to build a Vespa or Lambretta two-stroke clone, Ducati had Giovanni Fiorio design a new four-stroke engine. The company also commissioned an outside design house to style the bodywork, and no expense was spared in the Cruiser's development. Amazingly ambitious, it was the first four-stroke scooter, and the first motorcycle with an automatic transmission. Envisioned as a luxury model appealing to a new and more prosperous clientele, the Cruiser was decades ahead of its time.

Some of the Cruiser's engine design features came from the overhead-valve 65, although the included valve angle was reduced to 80 degrees. A single Dell'Orto carburetor mounted directly on the cylinder head, feeding downdraft into the cylinder. Initially, the engine produced 12 horsepower, but was later detuned to 7.5 horsepower due to a government imposed 50-mph speed limit for scooters.

A spare tire was fitted behind the engine, along with a large battery.

The horizontal engine was transversely mounted under the seat. A first for a scooter was the standard electric starter, and at a time when just about all cars and motorcycles used a weak 6-volt electrical system, the Cruiser had 12-volt electrics. The 45-watt dynamo powered a huge for the day, 32-amp hour battery. As a result, the Cruiser's lighting was exceptional and far superior to other motorcycles and scooters at that time.

Even more remarkable than the engine and electrical system was the gearbox. Running longitudinally under the seat, it was automatic with a hydraulic torque converter housed in an alloy casting that incorporated the swingarm pivot. A torque converter was an extremely unusual feature in 1952, and the system was essentially similar to that of the Moto Guzzi V1000 Convert over two decades later. Unfortunately, while commendable in endeavoring to make the Cruiser a user-friendly machine, the automatic gearbox was extremely complicated and the technology for such a vehicle in its infancy. Not surprisingly, problems with the gearbox resulted in numerous warranty claims. The gearbox drove the rear wheel via a short connecting shaft to a crown wheel and pinion. It was a clever design, also intended to provide ease of use with minimal maintenance.

The rear suspension was unusual in that it comprised a long arm connected to a cylinder with rubber inserts for damping, the unit positioned horizontally underneath the engine. The heavy swingarm/transmission casting worked like a fluctuating arm. The front suspension was a patented new type, similar to the swinging shackle scooter type, but with a single hydraulic shock absorber.

Although Ducati initially only admitted that the bodywork was designed "by a well-known car design company," it eventually transpired that it was completed by Ghia. Ghia was then, and now, better known for luxury cars, and the Cruiser's styling was unremarkable. It was the first of several misguided examples of involving an automotive styling concern in the design of motorcycles. Other features included a separate sprung seat for the rider, with a pillion seat behind, a single built in headlight above a front grill, and hinged side panels to allow access to the engine. A spare tire was located under the left hand panel, but the Cruiser was substantially heavier than its two-stroke competition and considerable more difficult to manhandle and put on its stand.

Released at the Milan Show in January 1952, the Cruiser was initially hailed as a highlight because of its technical innovation. With automatic transmission, electric start, crown wheel and pinion final drive, and a 12-volt electrical system, it should have been successful. But Ducati had no reputation for manufacturing scooters, was going against the established and successful Vespa and Lambretta, and

CRUISER 1952-54

Engine	Single cylinder four-stroke, air-cooled	**Valve type**	Overhead valve, pushrod	**Tires**	2.45 x 10-inch Pirelli
Bore	62mm	**Carburetion**	Dell'Orto	**Weight**	54 kg (118.8 lbs.)
Stroke	58mm	**Power**	7.5 horsepower at 5,600 rpm	**Top speed**	80 km/h (50 mph)
Displacement	175cc	**Gears**	Automatic	**Colors**	Blue and gray, red and gray
Compression ratio	7.5:1	**Generator**	12 volt/45 watt	**Number produced**	2,000

the Cruiser was seen as heavy and complicated. The fuel consumption of 95 mpg was comparable to that of the two-strokes, and the engine performance was inferior. More expensive, requiring more maintenance (oil changes and valve adjustment), and quickly earning a reputation for unreliability, the Cruiser was doomed. Although lasting until 1954, very few Cruisers have survived. Somehow, Ducati didn't learn from this experience, repeating the scooter debacle a decade later.

Until mid-1956 this "SSR" logo was still incorporated on brochures, and some motorcycles.

98, 98N

Ducati Motor

The 98 of 1952 was even more of a proper motorcycle than the 65.

Alongside the Cruiser at the 1952 Milan Show was a new motorcycle: the 98. Also designed by Fiorio, this was a descendant of the 65, but was more conventional in its execution. The overhead-valve four-stroke engine had a forward-facing exhaust, and rear carburetor, with an external oil pipe on the right to feed the valve gear.

The cylinder was inclined 25 degrees, and the two valves were set at an included angle of 100 degrees. The engine cases were restyled to smoothly incorporate the gearbox, which was initially still three-speed. The dynamo was also enclosed, in a vented cover, and the kickstart was on the left. Also new was the open spine-type pressed-steel frame.

With the heavy valanced fenders and substantial, but undamped, telescopic forks, the 98 looked more like a proper motorcycle than the 65. A small (10-liter) gas tank sat atop the frame spine. Apart from a different muffler, the 98 continued virtually unchanged into 1954. The similar 98N replaced the 98 in 1956, also with a solo seat, and still with a three-speed gearbox. For 1957, the 98N received a four-speed transmission, but was discontinued when the 98T was introduced as the solo seat model in 1958.

98 1952-55, 98N 1956-57

Engine	Single cylinder four-stroke, air-cooled	**Carburetion**	Dell'Orto MA16B	**Rear suspension**	Swingarm
Bore	49mm	**Power**	5.5 horsepower at 6,800 rpm	**Wheelbase**	1,240mm (49.6 inches)
Stroke	52mm	**Gears**	Three speed (four-speed from 1957)	**Seat height**	730mm (29.2 inches)
Displacement	98.058cc	**Generator**	6 volt/25 watt	**Length**	1,880mm (72 inches)
Compression ratio	8:1	**Tires**	2.75x17-inch Pirelli or CEAT	**Weight**	98: 72 kg (158.4 lbs.) 98N: 81 kg (178.2 lbs.)
Valve type	Overhead valve, pushrod	**Front suspension**	Telescopic fork	**Top speed**	98: 75 km/h (46.5 mph) 98 N: 80 km/h (49.6 mph)
Valve timing (degrees)	30, 69, 69, 30			**Color**	Gray

By 1953 the 98 lineup encompassed this 98 TL with passenger saddle and large engine protection bar.

Ducati Motor

More variations on the 98 appeared for 1953. In addition to the 98N were the 98T (Turismo), 98TL (Turismo Lusso), and a higher specification 98 Sport. The 98T received a restyled larger gas tank (now 14 liters), new handlebar, dual seat, and new colors, but the engine and running gear was identical to the earlier 98. The 98TL was based on the 98T, but with light alloy wheel rims, a higher, braced, handlebar, a different tank, and a two-piece saddle. The 98TL also had a large protective crash bar.

For 1956, the 98TL was restyled along the lines of the new 125, sharing the same tubular steel frame, but without the double front downtubes. The suspension on the 98TL was from the 98 SS, and the wheel rims were now steel. The engine specification was unchanged. Sharing the same frame was the 98 T. It now had a solo seat and rack and was a base model alongside the 98 N from 1956. From 1957, the 98 T also had the tubular steel frame and four-speed transmission.

The 98 TL for 1956 received a new frame, but retained the three-speed transmission.

Ducati Motor

98T, 98TL 1953-58

Engine	Single cylinder four-stroke, air-cooled	**Primary drive**	3.454	**Rear suspension**	Swingarm
Bore	49mm	**Gears**	Three speed, four speed from 1957	**Wheelbase**	1,245mm (49.8 inches)
Stroke	52mm	**Gear ratios (from 1957)**	1, 1.365, 1.85, 2.69	**Seat height**	762mm (30.48 inches)
Displacement	98.058cc	**Generator**	6 volt/25 watt	**Length**	1,890mm (75.6 inches)
Compression ratio	8:1	**Final drive**	2.706	**Weight**	80 kg (176 lbs.)
Valve type	Overhead valve, pushrod	**Tires**	2.50 x 17-inch, 2.75 x 17-inch	**Top speed**	75 km/h (46.5 mph)
Carburetion	Dell'Orto MA16B	**Front suspension**	Telescopic fork	**Color**	1953-55: Red 1956-58: Dark red and white
Power	5.8 horsepower at 7,500 rpm				

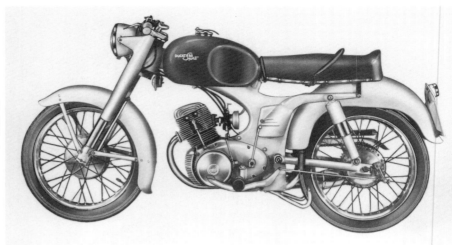

Ducati Motor

With the 98 Sport of 1953, Ducati produced its first true sporting motorcycle. The finning at the front of the sump was an oil cooler.

98 Sport 1953-58, 98 SS 1954-55

Engine	Single cylinder four-stroke, air-cooled	**Power**	1953-54: 6.8 (7) horsepower at 7,300 rpm	**Tires**	2.50 x 17-inch, 2.75 x 17-inch CEAT
Bore	49mm		1955-58: 6.5 horsepower at 7,000 rpm	**Front suspension**	Telescopic fork
Stroke	52mm	**Primary drive**	3.454	**Rear suspension**	Swingarm
Displacement	98.058cc	**Gears**	Four speed	**Weight**	75 kg (165 lbs.)
Compression ratio	9:1 (10:1)	**Gear ratios**	1, 1.365, 1.85, 2.69	**Top speed**	Sport: 90 km/h (56 mph)
Valve type	Overhead valve, pushrod	**Generator**	6 volt/25 watt		SS: 95 km/h (59 mph)
Carburetion	Dell'Orto MA18B (MB20B)	**Final drive**	2.706	**Color**	Black/silver

The first sporting Ducati, the 98 Sport, also appeared at the Milan Show in early 1953. Along with a four-speed transmission, the engine was uprated, the larger carburetor mounted on a longer intake, and attached to the front of the sump was a finned oil cooler. The gas tank was from the 98 TL, but the handlebars were lower, and the 17-inch wheels with light alloy rims included a full-width drum front brake. The Sport was an interesting variation on what had been a range of mundane motorcycles up until that date, but the 98 Super Sport that appeared in 1954 was even more so. The sculptured 14-liter gas tank was augmented by a small handlebar-mounted fairing and screen. The engine was further uprated and there was new suspension.

Because of the success of the overhead-camshaft Marianna, the 98 Super Sport only lasted until 1955, but the 98 Super Sport chassis and styling was inherited by the 98 Sport from 1956. The 98 Sport and 98 Super Sport were certainly the most attractive offerings of all the rather dull ohv models.

Ducati Motor

The 98 Super Sport was an attractive sporting model, but provided only modest performance.

The 98 TS was new for 1958. Its engine and frame were based on the 85. The flywheel was enclosed.

Although the overhead-valve singles grew to 125cc in 1956, and were downsized to 85cc in 1957, the 98cc engine continued in a new model, the 98 TS (Turismo Speciale), in 1958. In 1959, this became the similar 98 Bronco, which was a model produced primarily for the American importer Berliner who had gained distribution during 1958. The 98 Bronco was available in Italy, but as a Cavallino.

The 98cc engine was similar to that of the 85 models introduced a year earlier. To allow access to the valves and rockers there was a removable rocker cover, fixed by four fasteners. The cover also lacked the two-stroke-like finning of the earlier cylinder head. Also, like the 85, there was a reshaped right side cover, and an enclosed flywheel on the left, inscribed with a "DUCATI MECCANICA" winged emblem.

Both the new 98s shared a milder tuned version of the 98cc engine and the 125 tubular steel frame—also with a double front downtube. The styling of the 98 TS was very similar to the 125 T, and both received the unusual two-tone saddle for 1960. The 98 Bronco also included

this saddle, but with a smaller (13-liter) gas tank (from the 85 T and Bronco). The 98 TS and 98 Bronco's most significant feature was the fuel economy of 120 mpg, but by 1961 the 98s were struggling to find an identity between the 85 and 125. Despite this, the 98 Bronco was imported by Berliner until 1963.

The 98 TS engine differed from earlier 98s in that the rocker cover was easily removable.

98 TS 1958-60, 98 Bronco 1959-63

Engine	Single cylinder four-stroke, air-cooled	**Gears**	Four speed	**Wheelbase**	1,270mm (50.8 inches)
Bore	49mm	**Generator**	6 volt/28 watt	**Seat height**	750mm (30 inches)
Stroke	52mm	**Tires**	TS: 2.50 x 17-inch, 2.75 x 17-inch	**Length**	1,910mm (76.4 inches)
Displacement	98.058cc		Bronco: 2.75 x 16-inch	**Height**	960mm (38.4 inches)
Compression ratio	7:1	**Front suspension**	Telescopic fork	**Weight**	87 kg (191.4 lbs.)
Valve type	Overhead valve, pushrod	**Rear suspension**	Swingarm	**Top speed**	85 km/h (53 mph)
Carburetion	Dell'Orto ME16BS	**Brakes**	TS: 123 x 25mm	**Colors**	Most 98 TS: red and white
Power	6 horsepower at 6,800 rpm		Bronco: 116 x 25mm		Bronco: purple with bronze frame.

One of many models produced for Berliner was the 98 Bronco of 1960.

Ducati Motor

85 TURISMO, 85 SPORT, 85 BRONCO

After 1957, the lineup of production models expanded considerably. Ducati was enjoying a particularly buoyant period, and seemed intent on capitalizing with as many model variants as possible. Not only were the new overhead camshaft singles introduced, the pushrod overhead valve range grew to with more 125s, and in 1958, the 85. With several 65 and 98 cc models already available, the release of two 85cc versions seemed unnecessary. Although sold as budget models, as parts bin specials in some respects the 85s were more highly specified than the 98s. They featured the stronger frame of the 125, with double downtubes, and the 85 Sport was styled to mimic the 175 Sport with its distinctive jelly mold gas tank. The 85 Sport also had the front fork of the 98 S, and abbreviated sporting fenders.

With its solo sprung saddle and rear rack, and deep fenders, the 85 T harkened back to an earlier time, while the 85 Bronco was similar to the 98cc version, except for the smaller engine and 17-inch wheels.

The 85cc overhead-valve engine was a revised design, still with the external oil line on the right, but with a removable rocker cover that allowed for easier valve adjustment. Only the 85 Sport received a four-speed gearbox; the 85T and Bronco featured a three-speed. The problem with the 85 Sport was that, while it looked impressive, the performance was still very ordinary. During 1959, the 85 Bronco was the only ohv model offered in the United States.

The 85 T of 1958 received a revised engine and the stronger frame of the 125.

Ducati Motor

85 Turismo, 85 Sport 1958-60, 85 Bronco 1959-62

Engine	Single cylinder four-stroke, air-cooled	Power	T: 5 horsepower S: 5.5 horsepower	Brakes	116 x 25mm
Bore	45.5mm	Gears	T: Three-speed S: Four-speed	Weight	80 kg (176 lbs.)
Stroke	52mm	Generator	6 volt/28 watt	Top speed	85 S: 76 km/h, (47 mph) 85 T: 70 km/h (43 mph)
Displacement	84.55cc	Tires	2.50 x 17-inch		
Compression ratio	7.5:1	Front suspension	Telescopic fork	Colors	85 S: silver and blue, blue frame 85 T: red with white, red frame 85 Bronco: bronze and maroon
Valve type	Overhead valve, pushrod	Rear suspension	Swingarm		
Carburetion	Dell'Orto ME15BS				

With its distinctive jelly mold gas tank, the 85 Sport replicated the 175 Sport, but the performance left something to be desired.

Ducati Motor

One of the more desirable overhead-valve models is the 125 TV of 1956. Unlike earlier ohv singles, the 125 TV had a double-downtube frame and full-width brake. The headlamp was in a Triumph-like nacelle.

125 TV, 125 T 1956-60

Engine	Single cylinder four-stroke, air-cooled	Carburetion	TV: Dell'Orto ME20B T: Dell'Orto MA18B	Front suspension	Telescopic fork
Bore	55.2mm	Power	6.5 horsepower at 6,500 rpm	Rear suspension	Swingarm
Stroke	52mm	Gears	Four speed	Weight	95 kg (209 lbs.)
Displacement	124.443cc	Generator	6 volt/25 watt	Top speed	86 km/h (53.3 mph)
Compression ratio	7:1	Tires	2.50 x 17-inch, 2.75 x 17-inch	Colors	Red
Valve type	Overhead valve, pushrod				

Although the future lay with the new overhead-camshaft singles, before these made the production line, the pushrod overhead valve single grew to 125cc. The first 125s were the 125 TV (Turismo Veloce), and 125 T (Turismo), listed in the 1956 catalogue ahead of the four 98s, three 65s, and two 55s. The release of the 125 coincided with a boom year for the Italian motorcycle industry, and Ducati sold 10,767 motorcycles (3.5 percent of the market) in 1956. These were halcyon days, and it wouldn't be until 1992 that these sales would be matched.

There was little to externally distinguish the early 125 engine from the 98 of the same era, and it still incorporated

The 1956 125 T was a budget model without the double-downtube frame.

the external oil line on the right and finned cylinder head without a separate rocker cover. The 125 TV was the first

Ducati Motor

For 1958, the 125 T was updated with the double-downtube frame.

model to feature the tubular steel do uble-downtube frame, along with upgraded suspension and a full-width front brake. The headlight was incorporated in a nacelle over the top of the front fork, and today the 125 TV is considered one of the more desirable 125cc ohv singles. The 125 T was an economy model, with a spine frame without the downtubes, less sophisticated suspension, and smaller brakes. There were two types, one with a solo seat and rack, and the other with a dual seat (sella lunga). All included a 14-liter gas tank. For 1958, the 125 T received the double-cradle frame, decals instead of tank badges, and colors of bright red and white. As with all the ohv singles of this era, the 125s also featured a tire pump mounted on the chainguard.

125 AUREA

In 1958, the 125 ohv lineup expanded to include the sporting Aurea, with the 125 Bronco joining it in 1960. The 125cc ohv engine was redesigned, and the external oil line disappeared as there was a separate larger oil sump underneath the crankcase, similar to the overhead-camshaft singles. An engine breather tube ran up from the rear of the crankcase, and although there was still a flywheel magneto, a battery was added to power the lighting and horn.

This revamped engine was installed in a chassis similar to the 125 TV, but with the sporting 15-liter gas tank shaped like that of the overhead camshaft 125 Sport. Complementing this tank was a sporty headlight, cigar-shaped muffler, and from 1960, the distinctive two-tone saddle of this period.

Ducati Motor

The 125 Aurea of 1960 was another ohv single styled along the lines of the ohc models. The engine was redesigned to include the oil line internally.

125 AUREA 1958-62

Engine	Single cylinder four-stroke, air-cooled		Power	6.5 horsepower at 6,500 rpm		Wheelbase	1285mm (51.4 inches)
Bore	55.2mm		Gears	Four speed		Seat height	790mm (31.6 inches)
Stroke	52mm		Generator	6 volt/28 watt		Length	1,920mm (76.8 inches)
Displacement	124.443cc		Tires	2.50 x 17-inch, 2.75 x 17-inch CEAT		Height	910mm (34.6 inches)
Compression ratio	6.8:1		Front suspension	Telescopic fork		Weight	90kg (198 lbs.)
Valve type	Overhead valve, pushrod		Rear suspension	Swingarm		Top speed	86 km/h (53.3 mph)
Carburetion	Dell'Orto ME18BS		Brakes	123 x 25mm		Color	Metallic blue and gold, blue frame, blue seat

125 BRONCO

In 1960, the 125 Bronco joined the 98 Bronco as the base model in the U.S. lineup. Although the 98 finished in 1963, the 125 lasted through until 1966 with only minor developments. The general specification was identical to the 125 Aurea, but with a touring handlebar, smaller 13-liter gas tank and 16-inch wheels shod with knobby tires.

The 125 Bronco was one of the mainstays of the lineup in the U.S. during the 1960s.

125 BRONCO 1960-66

Engine	Single cylinder four-stroke, air-cooled	Power	6.5 horsepower at 6,500 rpm	Wheelbase	1290mm (51.6 inches)
Bore	55.2mm	Gears	Four speed	Seat height	790mm (31.6 inches)
Stroke	52mm	Generator	6 volt/28 watt	Length	1,900mm (76 inches)
Displacement	124.443cc	Tires	2.75 x 16-inch	Height	960mm (38.4 inches)
Compression ratio	6.8:1	Front suspension	Telescopic fork	Weight	91 kg (200.2 lbs.)
Valve type	Overhead valve, pushrod	Rear suspension	Non-adjustable twin shock swingarm	Colors	Candy red and silver, black and silver, dark blue and silver
Carburetion	Dell'Orto ME18BS	Brakes	123 x 25mm		

125 CADET/4, 125 CADET/4 LUSSO, 125 CADET/4 SCRAMBLER

The final pushrod overhead-valve Ducati single was the 125 Cadet/4 of 1967 and 1968. Many cycle parts were shared with the two-stroke Cadet (covered later), but the engine was still based on the earlier overhead valve unit. The bore and stroke were changed, as was the cylinder head design. The spark plug was moved to the right, and the two overhead valves were set parallel, rather than opposed as before. The electrical system was shared with the 160 Monza Junior, a flywheel alternator charging a 6-volt, 13.5 Ah battery. The double cradle tubular steel frame was similar to the 125 Bronco, and for 1967 the tires were a smaller profile 2.25 and 2.50 x 18-inch.

Alongside the Cadet/4 was an almost identical Lusso (luxury), with a better front fork and sporting headlight, and larger tires. The Scrambler featured a gaitered fork, high-rise exhaust pipe, and an engine protection plate. There were only minor changes to the Cadet/4 for 1968, including larger tires, new sidecovers, and a different paint scheme. These unremarkable overhead-valve models were short lived primarily because Berliner decided they weren't suitable for the American market.

Redesigned slightly, the 125 ohv engine lived on in 1967 as the 125 Cadet/4. The angular fenders and headlight were styling features of that period.

The Cadet/4 Scrambler resided alongside the 125 Cadet/4, but this was hardly a true off-road machine.

Phil Aynsley/Two Wheels

125 CADET/4 (SCRAMBLER, LUSSO) 1967-68

Engine	Single cylinder four-stroke, air-cooled	**Primary drive gearing**	3.000:1	**Rear suspension**	Swingarm
Bore	53mm	**Gears**	Four-speed	**Wheelbase**	1,160mm (46.4 inches)
Stroke	55mm	**Generator**	6 volt/28 watt	**Seat height**	670mm (26.8 inches)
Displacement	121.3cc	**Tires**	Cadet: 2.25 x 18, 2.50 x 18	**Length**	1,810mm (72.4 inches)
Compression ratio	8.4:1		1968 and Lusso: 2.50 x 18 2.75 x 18	**Height**	770mm (30.8 inches)
Valve type	Overhead valve, pushrod		Scrambler: 2.75 x 18, 3.25-3.50 x 16	**Weight**	72kg (158.4 lbs) Scrambler: 75 kg, (165 lbs.)
Valve timing (degrees)	30, 70, 70, 30	**Brakes**	Drum 118mm	**Top speed**	95 km/h (58.9 mph) Scrambler: 80 km/h (49.6 mph)
Carburetion	Dell'Orto ME18BS	**Front suspension**	Marzocchi telescopic fork		

Ducati Motor

Assembly of the Ducati overhead-camshaft engine required care and attention to detail.

In 1953, Ducati SSR was split into two divisions, with Ducati Meccanica responsible for motorcycle production, and Ducati Elettrotecnica the electrical division. Although operating independently, both were under the parent SSR company until 1956. Heading Ducati Meccanica was Dott. Giuseppe Montano, and while he was a government appointment, Montano was also an enthusiastic motorcyclist. He immediately saw the limitations of Fiorio's overhead-valve design for competition, especially when the 98s were so soundly beaten in the 1954 Motogiro d'Italia and Milano-Taranto by the Laverdas. Montano lured the great engineer Ing. Fabio Taglioni away from Mondial and commissioned him to design a new motorcycle capable of winning the 1955 Motogiro.

The result was the magnificent Gran Sport, later nicknamed the Marianna. This advanced design formed the basis of the all the overhead-camshaft singles through until 1974, and many of its design characteristics feature on the current engines. After the humiliation of 1954, no one could have predicted the success of the Marianna in the 1955 Motogiro d'Italia. The Mariannas were unbeatable, initiating a racing record that continues today. Taglioni's one-year contract was extended, and his association with Ducati would last four decades.

Gran Sport (Marianna)

The Gran Sport was hand built in limited numbers for racing and was extremely successful.

While the Marianna was subsequently developed into the Bialbero double overhead-camshaft racers and the magnificent desmodromic singles, it was also a catalogued model. Although it was only available in limited numbers, from 1956 there was a 100 and 125 Gran Sport, with a 175 in 1957.

The basis of the Gran Sport engine was its vertically split aluminum unit construction sand-cast crankcase. The cylinder (with cast-iron liner) was inclined forward 10 degrees and a single overhead camshaft was driven by a set of straight-cut bevel gears from the crankshaft. All the bearings were ball or roller, the crankshaft featuring full circle flywheels with a stepped crankpin (32mm on the rollers and 27mm at the ends). The forged steel con-rod included dual strengthening ribs around both the small and big-end, and a 14mm wrist pin, while the forged piston had three rings.

Incorporated in the crankcases was a four-speed gearbox, driven by straight-cut primary gears with a wet multi-plate clutch. There was battery and coil ignition with the points driven off the lower bevel gear on the right. On the Gran Sport the cylinder head was two pieces, with the two valves opposed at a wide 80-degree included angle. The valves were closed by exposed hairpin valve springs that were so prone to breakage that each rider was supplied a valve spring compression tool to facilitate quick replacement.

This engine was placed in a single-downtube tubular steel frame and was utilized as a stressed member. On the earliest Grand Sport, the engine was mounted to the frame by separate plates. The wheel rims were light alloy and the brakes magnesium Amadoro. To comply with Italian FMI (Italian Motorcycle Federation) regulations, there was also a generator, horn and headlamp. The three

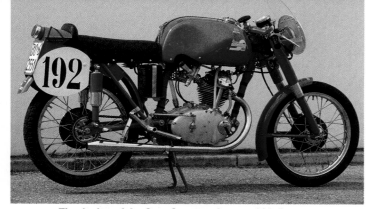

The design of the Gran Sport engine would influence overhead-camshaft Ducati engines for the next three decades.

versions of the Grand Sport differed in detail, with the larger models also receiving larger brakes along with 18-inch wheels.

The Gran Sport, particularly in 100 and 125cc versions, was incredibly successful between 1955 and 1958, and even after it was replaced by the F3 many riders in Italy continued to campaign the Gran Sport. As it was hand-built and produced in very small numbers for Italian racing, the Gran Sport is rarely seen today outside Italy.

100, 125, 175 GRAN SPORT

Engine	Single cylinder four-stroke, air-cooled	Valve diameter	100: 31mm inlet; 27mm exhaust 125: 33mm inlet; 29mm exhaust	Gear ratios	Four speed
Bore	100: 49.4mm 125: 55.25mm 175: 62mm	Carburetion	100, 125: Dell'Orto SS1 20C 175: Dell'Orto SS1 22.5C	Front suspension	Telescopic fork
Stroke	100, 125: 52mm 175: 57.8mm	Power	100: 9 horsepower at 9,000 rpm 125: 12 horsepower at 9,800 rpm 175: 16 horsepower at 9,000 rpm	Rear suspension	Swingarm with twin shock absorbers
Displacement	99.66cc			Wheels	100: 17-inch; 125 and 175: 18-inch
Compression ratio	8.5:1			Wheelbase	1,250mm
Valve actuation	Single overhead camshaft driven by a shaft and bevel gears			Dry weight	100: 80kg (176 lbs.); 125: (85kg (187 lbs.)
		Ignition	Battery and coil	Top speed	100: 130 km/h (80.6 mph), 125: 150 km/h (93 mph) 175: 155 km/h (96.1 mph)
		Clutch	Wet multiplate		

175 Sport, 175 T

The first production overhead-camshaft single was the 175 of 1957. This is the 175 Sport, with sculptured gas tank and dual muffler.

Unlike the Gran Sport, the production 175 engine had enclosed valves.

175 Sport, 175 T 1957-61

Engine	Single cylinder four-stroke, air-cooled	**Generator**	6v/40W	**Height**	960mm (38.4 inches)
Bore	62mm	**Battery**	6v/13.5Ah (SAFA 3L3)	**Seat height**	750mm (30 inches)
Stroke	57.8mm	**Primary drive**	2.522:1	**Dry weight**	Sport: 106kg (233.2 lbs.) T: 104kg (228.8 lbs.)
Displacement	174.5cc	**Clutch**	Wet multiplate	**Top speed**	Sport: 130 km/h (80.6 mph) T: 110 km/h (68.2 mph)
Compression ratio	Sport: 18:1 175 T: 7:1	**Gear ratios**	0.97, 1.18, 1.65, 2.75		
Valve actuation	Bevel gear-driven overhead camshaft	**Final drive**	Sport: 2.875:1 T: 3.066:1	**Colors**	Sport: gold frame, tank chrome and red, also blue and silver with chrome (1957), tank red and gold (1958-61) T: black frame, tank dark crimson
Valve timing (degrees)	44, 73, 73, 38	**Front suspension**	Marzocchi fork		
Carburetion	1957-59: Dell'Orto MB22.5B 1960-61: MB22B UBF24BS	**Rear suspension**	Three-way adjustable twin shock swingarm		
		Brakes	Drum 180mm front, 160mm rear	**Engine Numbers (five digits)**	175 Sport from 75001-79000 approx 175 T from DM175 00001-06000 approx
Power	14 horsepower at 8,000 rpm (12 horsepower at 7,000 rpm)	**Tires**	2.50 x 18, 2.75 x 18 CEAT		
		Wheelbase	1,320mm (52.8 inches)	**Frame Numbers (five digits)**	175 Sport: from 75001-79000 approx 175 T: from DM175 00001-06000 approx
Spark plug	1957-59: Marelli CW225A 1-60-61: Marelli CW250A	**Length**	Sport: 1,950mm (78 inches) T: 1,980mm (79.2 inches)		

The success of the Gran Sport was such that Taglioni was allowed to adapt his advanced single-cylinder overhead-camshaft engine for production. Most motorcycles of the period still featured overhead valves operated by pushrods, and while there was little to separate the ohv 98s and 125s from dozens of other Italian motorcycles available at the time, the overhead-camshaft 175 provided exceptional performance. The 175 was first displayed at the end of 1956 as the 175 Sport, and followed shortly afterwards by the 175 T, with a slightly detuned engine. This engine was soon produced with various capacities and as a number of different models.

Although the aluminum overhead-camshaft engine was based on the Gran Sport, the crankcases were now die-cast, and the cylinder head was in one piece. To keep the engine oil tight, the hairpin valves springs were enclosed. To reduce noise, the bevel gears and primary drive were helically cut. The sump held 2.4 liters of oil. The electrical system was 6-volt, with a small battery, and the ignition points were under a timing cover on the right.

The chassis, too, was based on that of the Gran Sport, with a single-downtube frame that utilized the engine as a stressed member. Setting the 175 Sport apart from other

Although the 175 engine was detuned slightly for the 1957 175 T, the performance was still outstanding for the day.

Phil Aynsley/Two Wheels

motorcycles in 1957 was the sculptured fuel tank. Designed purely to follow function, it featured arm recesses to allow a crouched rider to hug the motorcycle while gripping the clip-on handlebars. There were even eyelets in the tank to secure a chin pad for racers who really wanted to get their head down. Further emphasizing the sporting nature were light alloy wheel rims. The 175 T received a more

traditionally styled gas tank and deeper fenders, and there were the options of clip-on or high handlebars and a dual or solo sprung saddle . The very first 175 Ts also had 17-inch wheels shod with 3.00 x 17-inch CEAT tires, but during 1957 the wheels became 18-inchers.

There were detail changes to the 175 Sport and 175 T over the next few years. The 1957 silencer on both the 175 Sport and T was a single type, but for 1958 the 175 Sport received a dual silencer that it shared with the Americano. Starting in 1958, the front engine plates had four mounts instead of three, and the Sport gained a peaked headlight rim. The rocking gearshift pedal was reshaped and positioned higher. This year the 175 Sport featured a revised UB22.5BS2 carburetor, and from 1959 there was a tuning kit available that included a larger SS1 25A carburetor. In England, the 175 Sport was called the 175 Silverstone, and with the tuning kit was known as the 175 Silverstone Super. To further confuse the nomenclature, Berliner decided to call the 175 Sport a Super Sport in 1959, with a single silencer. There were a number of changes from 1960: all 175 Sports received the single Silentium muffler, and a number of 200 Élite components, including the carburetor. These final 175 Sports were really sleeved-down 200 Élites, or 200 Super Sports.

125 and 100 Sport

The immediate success of the 175 Sport and 175 T (they accounted for 25 percent of 175cc sales in Italy during 1957) saw a proliferation of overhead-camshaft models during the next few years. Only a year after the introduction of the 175, the 125 Sport and 100 Sport were offered. Styled with a pretty 17-liter gas tank, and running on 17-inch wheels with light alloy rims, these diminutive machines began a tradition of Ducati race replicas that continues today. In this case, the little Sports looked similar to the new 125 F3.

The engines differed to the 175 in a number of details, notably the sump was cast smooth, without finning, and contained only 2.100 liters of oil. The 100 and 125 were virtually identical, except the 100 had a flat, rather than peaked, headlight rim. The earliest examples of both had larger brakes and the 125 had gas tank badges, with the badges replaced by decals during 1958. Also during 1958, the brakes were reduced in size on the 125, but not on the 100.

As there was no export demand for the 100, it was discontinued in 1960, but the 125 Sport maintained a loyal following (in Italy at least) until 1965. In America the 125 Sport was marketed as the 125 Super Sport (with Sport decals), and in England, the 125 Sport was the 125 Monza. There was also a 125 Monza Super in 1960 and 1961, with a higher-compression piston and hotter camshaft. Until the end, the 125 looked very similar to the first version, even retaining the earlier "D"-type gas tank decals.

The sump and rocker covers were smooth cast on the 125. (Roy Kidney)

The 1957 125 Sport for the U.S. was bronze and maroon, with tank badges rather than decals.

Roy Kidney

125 Sport 1957-65, 100 Sport 1958-60

Engine	Single cylinder four-stroke, air-cooled	Ignition (degrees)	Points and coil; 18-20 static, 46-48 total	Seat height	750mm (30 inches)	
Bore	125: 55.2mm 100: 49mm	Battery	SAFA 3L3 13.5 Ah	Dry weight	125 Sport: 100.5kg (62.3 mph) 100 Sport: 100kg (62 mph)	
Stroke	52mm	Primary drive	3.000:1			
Displacement	125: 124.443cc; 100: 98.058cc	Clutch	Wet multiplate	Top speed	125 Sport: 112 km/h (69.4 mph) 100 Sport: 105 km/h (65.1 mph)	
		Gear ratios	0.97, 1.18, 1.65, 2.75			
Compression ratio	125: 8:1 100: 9:1	Final drive	125: 2.750:1 100: 3.066:1			
Valve actuation	Bevel gear-driven overhead camshaft	Front suspension	Marzocchi fork	Colors	100 Sport: blue frame, blue and silver 125 Sport (U.S.): metallic bronze and maroon 125 Sport (Europe): blue frame, blue and gold	
Valve timing (degrees)	125: 24, 40, 56, 22 100: 44, 68, 72, 41	Rear suspension	Three-way adjustable twin shock swingarm			
Carburetion	Dell'Orto UB20BS (MA18B)	Tires	2.50 x 17, 2.75 x 17 CEAT			
Power	10 horsepower at 8,500 rpm (8 HP at 8,000 rpm)	Wheelbase	1320mm (52.8 inches)	Engine numbers (six digits)	125 from 200001-208000 approx	
		Length	1910mm (76.4 inches)			
Spark plug	Marelli CW260N	Height	920mm (36.8 inches)	Frame numbers (six digits)	125 from DM125S (125S/1) 200001-208000 approx	
Generator	6v/40W	Width	580mm (23.2 inches)			

125 TS, 175 TS, 175 "Due" Selle

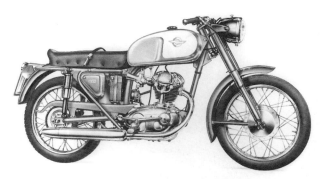

Ducati Motor

The lower-horsepower 125 TS was available for 1958, built primarily for the Italian market.

Ducati Motor

Among the many mundane models of the late 1950s was this 175 "Due" Selle.

New models for 1958 were the 125 TS (Turismo Speciale), and similar 175 TS. The 175 TS shared a lower specification engine with the 175 "Due" Selle, while the 125 TS was powered by a lower-compression version of the 125 Sport (although the cam timing was the same). They also had a smaller carburetor than their sporting brothers and the reduced power made them particularly sedate machines. The chassis of the TSs were similar, except the 175 had larger wheels. The 125 TS had a Marzocchi fork, and a new 17-liter gas tank with a black bakelite filler cap, while the 175 TS had an 18-liter tank.

In 1959, some TSs received the red and white studded seat of the 125 Aurea, and the handlebars were mounted on the top triple clamp. All these mundane touring models were built primarily for the Italian market and the 125 TS lasted until 1965. The "Due" Selle had universal tires and was intended for police or military use.

125 TS 1958-65; 175 TS, "Due" Selle 1958-60

Engine	Single cylinder 4-stroke, air-cooled	Generator	6v/40W	Wheelbase	1,310mm (52.4 inches)
Bore	125: 55.2mm 175: 62mm	Ignition (degrees)	125: Points and coil; 13-16 static, 41-44 total 175: 12-15 static, 40-43 total	Length	125: 1890mm (75.6 inches) 175cc: 1950mm (78 inches)
Stroke	125: 52mm 175: 57.8mm			Height	940mm (37.6 inches)
Displacement	125: 124.443cc 175: 174.502cc	Battery	SAFA 3L3 13.5 Ah	Width	680mm (27.2 inches)
Compression ratio	7:1	Primary drive	3.000:1 (2.522:1; 25/63)	Seat height	125: 760mm (30.4 inches) 175: 750mm (30 inches)
Valve actuation	Bevel gear-driven overhead camshaft	Clutch	Wet multiplate		
Valve timing (degrees)	125: 24, 56, 40, 22 175: 34, 56, 70, 24	Gear ratios	0.97, 1.18, 1.65, 2.75	Dry weight	98.5 kg (108 kg)
Carburetion	125: Dell'Orto UA18BS until #1500; ME18BS 175: Dell'Orto MB22B	Final drive	125: 2.875:1 175: (3.066:1; 15/46)	Top speed	90 km/h (118 mph)
		Front suspension	Marzocchi fork (125), Ducati fork (175)	Colors	125 TS; blue frame, blue and gold, red frame, red and silver
Power	125: 7 horsepower at 7,000 rpm 175: 11 horsepower at 7,500 rpm	Rear suspension	Three-way adjustable twin shock swingarm		175 TS, blue frame, blue and silver
		Brakes	Drum 158mm front, 136mm rear		175 "Due" Selle; black and dark red
Spark plug	Marelli CW225A	Tires	125: 2.50 x 17, 2.75 x 17 175: 2.50 x 18, 2.75 x 18		

175 and 200 Americano, 200 TS (Turismo Speciale)

During 1957 the Berliners began to assert their influence over Montano, and the first of many models designed purely for the American market appeared. This was the strange Americano, essentially a 175 T with high cowboy-style handlebars and a studded scalloped seat. There was a twin muffler, and the gas tank of the recently released 125 Sport. The shielded headlamp was from the 175 Sport, and the Americano came with a large crash bar, adorned with twin air horns (in addition to the usual horn under the carburetor.

Joining the 175 Americano for 1959 was the 200 Americano. The 200cc engine was basically a bored 175, and appeared on several new models introduced in 1959, also at the request of Berliner. Changes to both Americanos now included a single muffler, fewer studs on

Ducati Motor

For 1 year only, 1959, the 200 TS had the Élite gas tank. Subsequent 200 TS's were Americanos, with Bronco styling.

the seat, and no air horns. Both the 175 and 200 were visually similar this year, except for the shallower front fender on the 175. The 200 TS was also offered for 1959, not as an Americano, but with the 200 Élite sculptured gas tank. There was a deep front fender and single muffler. The 175 Americano and Élite style 200 TS were dropped for 1960, and the 200 Americano was styled more like the 125 Bronco, with a 13-liter peanut-style gas tank, and the red and white saddle. Titled the 200 TS Americano for 1960, the 200 TS continued into 1962, now with a white seat, before it was replaced by the 250 Monza. This year the 200cc engine was the revised 250 type, rather than 175.

One of the strangest overhead-camshaft Ducatis was the wild Americano of 1957, complete with studded seat and twin air horns.

175, AMERICANO 1957-60, 200 TS 1959, 200 TS AMERICANO 1960-62

Engine	Single cylinder four-stroke, air-cooled	Generator	6v/40W	Height	1,040mm (41.6 inches)
Bore	175: 62mm 200: 67mm	Primary drive	2.522:1	Seat height (mm)	800mm (32 inches)
Stroke	57.8	Clutch	Wet multiplate	Dry weight (kg)	118 kg (259.6 lbs.)
Displacement	175: 174.500cc 200: 203.783cc	Gear ratios	0.97, 1.18, 1.65, 2.75	Speed (km/h)	175: 110 km/h (68.2 mph) 200: 120 km/h (74.4 mph)
Compression ratio	7:1 (8.5:1)	Final drive	3.066:1		
Valve actuation	Bevel gear-driven overhead camshaft	Front suspension	Telescopic fork	Colors	175 Americano; bronze frame, tank bronze and red 200 Americano; red or blue with gold or silver, red and white from 1960
Valve timing (degrees)	175: 35, 65, 65, 35 200: 34, 56, 70, 24	Rear suspension	Three-way adjustable twin-shock swingarm		
Carburetion	Dell'Orto MB22B (UB24BS)	Brakes	Drum 180 front, 160 rear		
Power	175: 11 horsepower at 7,500 rpm 200: 17 HP at 7,500 rpm	Tires	175: 2.50 x 18, 2.75 x 18 200: 2.75 x 18, 3.00 x 18	Engine and Frame numbers	Shared with 175 Sport and 200 Élite
Spark plug	Marelli CW250A	Wheelbase	1,320mm (52.8 inches)		
		Length	175: 1,980mm (79.2 inches) 200: 2,000mm (80 inches)		

175 and 200 Motocross

Also intended primarily for the American market was the 175 Motocross, which was released in 1958. This was a much more successful rendition of the overhead-camshaft series. While the early examples were not particularly popular, the series grew in stature that by the end of the 1960s it represented the mainstay of production. Underneath the off-road exterior of the 175 Motocross was a 175 T, and the low exhaust pipe and front fender did little to disguise it. There was a frame extension and plate underneath the engine, and the larger carburetor included an air filter. The swingarm was also strengthened, and the rear subframe included additional bracing. The front brake was a conical type, and the wheels were 21

While the first 175 Motocross of 1958 wasn't particularly suited to off-road duties, it initiated a model range that would eventually be very popular.

and 19 inches. For 1959, the Motocross (or Scrambler in America) was available as 175 and 200, with a high-mounted front fender and longer suspension to improve the ground clearance by 2 inches.

175, 200 Motocross 1957-60

Engine	Single cylinder four-stroke, air-cooled	**Carburetion**	175: Dell'Orto SS1 25A 200: Dell'Orto SS1 27A	**Rear suspension**	Three-way adjustable twin shock swingarm
Bore	175: 62mm 200: 67mm	**Power**	175: 14 horsepower at 8,000 rpm 200: 19 horsepower at 7,800 rpm	**Brakes**	Drum 180mm front, 160mm rear
Stroke	57.8mm			**Tires**	2.75 x 21, 3.00 x 19
Displacement	175: 174.500cc 200: 203.783cc	**Generator**	6v/40W	**Wheelbase**	1,380mm
Compression ratio	8:1 (8.5:1)	**Clutch**	Wet multiplate	**Length**	2,060mm
Valve actuation	Bevel gear-driven overhead camshaft	**Gear ratios**	0.97, 1.18, 1.65, 2.75	**Seat height**	830mm
		Front suspension	Telescopic fork	**Dry weight**	175: 122 kg (268.4 lbs.) 200: 124 kg (272.8 lbs.)

200 Élite, 200 Super Sports, 200 GT (Gran Turismo)

By 1959, the overhead-camshaft engine had grown to 200cc in the Élite or Super Sport in the U.S.

As the Berliners demanded a larger capacity motorcycle, Ducati responded by boring the 175 and creating the 200. The first 200 was the Élite, and was essentially the same as the 1958 175 Sport but for the larger engine, deeper fenders, and steel wheel rims. The Élite had the 175 Sport dual muffler, and it was listed for the U.S. as the 200 Super Sport (available from January 1959). The U.S. 200 Super Sport featured a single muffler, abbreviated sporting fenders, and alloy wheel rims. Shared between all was the 17-liter sculptured jelly mold gas tank, but the 200 incorporated chrome panels on the tank to set it apart from the 175, along with specific tank badges.

During 1959 the Élite gained the sporting fenders and alloy rims, and continued until 1965 with few changes. Another 200 was available for 1962, the 200 GT, essentially

Chrome gas tank panels set the 200 apart from the 175.

similar and styled like the new 250 Diana. The gas tank was the new shape 16-liter (but with the earlier "D"-type decals), there were new side toolboxes, and the fenders were deeper than the Élite. Some had clip-on handlebars and other had a higher touring type. This period saw a proliferation of 200 models, and they differed between markets. In England the 200 Élite was the 200 Grand Sports, with a 200 Super Sports almost identical but for a single muffler and optional alloy wheel rims. Some 200 Super Sports this year also had the deeper fenders, and both the Grand Sports and Super Sports were available with an optional racing kit that included a hotter camshaft and megaphone. The 200 GT wasn't particularly popular but was still offered in Italy for 1963 before it was replaced by the similar 250 GT.

200 Élites after 1960 featured a revised engine, and the weight was up to 111 kilograms (240 lbs.). The power was unchanged but the top speed was reduced to a claimed 135 km/h. The 200cc engine was no longer an overbored 175, but a smaller 250. The cylinder head castings were different, and stamped either "A" for a 175 type, or "B" for a 250 type. There was also a new cast-iron 250 type clutch housing, with integral bearings, and a longer crankshaft and camshaft. The full circle crankshaft flywheels were no longer equal width and the main bearings went up in size to 30 x 62 x 16mm. As the 200 was never especially popular in America Berliner didn't offer the 200 Élite after 1962, concentrating on the 250. In England the 200 Élite was available well into 1966, although it was titled a 200 Super Sports by the British distributor, Ducati Concessionaires. By this stage the 250s had received a five-speed transmission and the 200 was obsolete.

Ducati Motor

The 200 GT was less popular than the Élite or Super Sport.

200 ÉLITE AND SUPER SPORTS 1959-65, 200 GT 1962-63

Engine	Single cylinder four-stroke, air-cooled	Battery	SAFA 3L3 13.5 Ah	Height	965mm
Bore	67	Primary drive	2.520:1	Width	580mm
Stroke	57.8	Clutch	Wet multiplate	Seat height	800mm
Displacement	203.783	Gear ratios	0.97, 1.18, 1.65, 2.75	Dry weight	Élite/SS: 111 kg (244.2 lbs.) GT: 115 kg (253 lbs.)
Compression ratio	7.8:1	Final drive	2.812:1		
Valve actuation	Bevel gear driven overhead camshaft	Front suspension	Ducati fork (31.5mm)	Speed	Élite/SS: 140 km/h (86.8 mph) GT: 135 km/h (83.7 mph)
Valve timing (degrees)	34, 56, 70, 24	Rear suspension	Marzocchi three-way adjustable twin-shock swingarm	Colors	Élite/SS: Gold frame, maroon and gold with chrome tank trim GT: Deep red frame, red with white tank trim
Carburetion	Dell'Orto UBF24BS	Brakes	Drum 180mm front, 160mm rear		
Power	18 horsepower at 7,500 rpm	Tires	Élite/SS: 2.75 x 18, 3.00 x 18 GT: 2.75 x 18	Engine numbers (six digits)	DM200 150001-157500 approx
Spark plug	Marelli CW250A GT: CW260N	Wheelbase	1,320mm	Frame numbers (six digits)	DM200 150001-157500 approx
Generator	6v/40W	Length	Élite/SS: 2,000mm GT: 1,990mm		
Ignition (degrees)	Points and coil; 18-21 static, 46-49 total				

FORMULA 3 MODELS

Roy Kidney

Although it looked similar to the 125 Sport, the 125 F3 was essentially a Gran Sport with enclosed valves.

125 Formula 3

With production of the overhead camshaft singles well underway, for 1958 the Formula 3 superseded the Marianna as a catalogued production racer. Offered initially as a 125 and 175 (and from 1960 as a 250), the F3 was still largely based on the earlier Marianna. The 125 F3 had Marianna sand-cast crankcases and, apart from the cylinder head with enclosed valve springs, was essentially identical.

Each version of the F3 featured different sand-cast crankcases, and they shared little with the production models. Inside the engine was a longer crankshaft, supported by two ball bearings in the sand-cast timing case and angular thrust main bearings. The con-rod featured the usual racing style dual strengthening ribs around the big and little end eye and there was a stepped crankpin (32-27mm) with longer (2mm) 3.5mm-diameter needle big-end rollers. There were also 20 rollers compared to 18 on the production model. The 125 F3 had a 16mm

125, 175, 250 FORMULA 3 1959-62

Engine	Single cylinder four-stroke, air-cooled	**Valve actuation**	Single overhead camshaft driven by a shaft and bevel gears	**Ignition**	Battery and coil (optional magneto)
Bore	125: 55.3mm 175: 62mm 250: 74mm	**Carburetion**	125: Dell'Orto SS1 20C 175: SS1 22.5A 250: SS1 29A	**Clutch**	Wet multiplate
				Gear ratios	Four speed
Stroke	125: 52mm 175, 250: 57.8mm	**Power**	125: 12 horsepower at 9,800 rpm 175: 16 horsepower at 9,000 rpm 250: 23 horsepower at 8,200 rpm	**Front suspension**	Telescopic fork
Displacement	125: 124.4cc 175: 174.5cc 250: 248.6cc			**Rear suspension**	Swingarm with twin shock absorbers
Compression ratio	8.5:1			**Wheels**	125, 175: 18-inch 250: 19-inch

Light and reasonably powerful, the 175 was the most successful of the F3s. It also came with twin-scoop Amadoro brakes.

The 1962 250 F3 had a large Oldani front brake, but was still handicapped by a four-speed gearbox. All F3s had sand-cast engines, and the dimensions varied between model.

wristpin and 107mm long con-rod, while the 175 and 250 had 18mm wristpin and 125mm long rod. Like the Gran Sport there was a four-speed gearbox, and straight-cut primary and bevel gears. Unique to the F3 were mirror image rocker covers, different camshaft covers and shorter camshafts than the production versions. As an indication as to how unique the F3 was, virtually none of the engine gaskets were interchangeable with a production ohc single. There were twin oil lines draining from the cylinder head and a tachometer drive from the camshaft bevel drive. The 250 cylinder head also came with bosses for desmodromic closing rocker spindles. Early F3s had 8mm rocker pins while the later ones had 10mm pins and the exhaust was retained by studs.

Although patterned after that on the road versions, the single downtube frame was quite different. Lighter and lower, with a lower steering head, shorter swingarm, and shorter forks, they also varied between models. All three F3s had different dimensions, the 125 with the lowest steering head, shortest 35mm forks, and 18-inch wheels had identical specifications to the 125 Gran Sport. The 175 was also a physically small motorcycle with a lower steering head than the 250, although the 175 frame would still accept the 250cc engine. The 175 also had shorter

35mm alloy forks and 18-inch wheels. The 250 F3 was a much larger, and heavier, machine, with special 35mm Marzocchi forks with steel fork legs and 19-inch wheels.

All F3s had racing specification brakes, with the 125 generally having a Gran Sport front brake. Some also had a twin-scoop Amadoro, similar but smaller to that on the 175. The 175 brakes were 180mm front and 160mm rear, while the 1961 250 F3 had a 200mm Amadoro front brake (for 1962 there was a 230mm Oldani). Despite their obvious race orientation, many F3s also came with complete street equipment that included a headlight, muffler, taillight, number plate holder, and centre-stand. Although the F3s were genuine factory racing machines they suffered through being too expensive for most privateers and were penalized by the four-speed gearbox. The 125 was essentially a Marianna of 1955, and the 250 too large and heavy, offering little advantage over a well-prepared Diana. In England, the 250 F3 was called the Manxman, but it was extremely expensive and found few buyers. As club racers in America generally liked to modify their machines, they enthusiastically adopted the Diana in preference to the expensive F3 and found it an excellent basis for a racing machine. Although they were listed for several years, production of the F3 was very small, with perhaps less than 100 of all types manufactured.

250 Diana (Daytona), 250 Monza

As Ducati was already successfully campaigning 250 racing machines, with the 250 F3 available via special order, it was inevitable the overhead-camshaft engine would grow to 250cc. The first production 250 was released during 1961, as the touring Monza and sporting Diana, with the engine incorporating the developments that had already appeared on the 200 Élite and 200 TS. This included new crankcase and cylinder head castings, a revised crankshaft with uneven flywheels and a 20mm

wide con-rod. There was a new clutch housing, and the clutch included 13 plates instead of 11 on the 200. The wristpin diameter was 18mm, and the big-end eye 39mm. The big-end roller diameter was 3.5mm with a 32mm crank-pin. There was always some confusion as to the actual power output of the new 250, with some brochures claiming an unrealistic 24 horsepower for the Diana, with 22 horsepower for the Monza. Accompanying these engine developments was a more powerful generator.

One of the classic narrow-case singles was the four-speed Diana. This is a 1962 example.

Roy Kidney

250 Diana (Daytona), 250 Monza 1961-64

Engine	Single cylinder four-stroke, air-cooled	**Primary drive**	2.500:1 (24/60)	**Seat height**	Diana: 750mm (30 inches) Monza: 800mm (32 inches)	
Bore	74mm	**Clutch**	Wet multiplate			
Stroke	57.8mm	**Gear ratios**	0.97, 1.18, 1.65, 2.75	**Dry weight**	Diana: 120 kg (264 lbs.) Monza: 125 kg (275 lbs.)	
Displacement	248.589cc	**Final drive**	2.647:1 (17/45)			
Compression ratio	8:1	**Front suspension**	Ducati 31.5mm telescopic fork (170mm wide)	**Speed**	Diana: 140 km/h (86.8 mph) Monza: 135km/h (83.7 mph)	
Valve actuation	Bevel gear-driven overhead camshaft	**Rear suspension**	Three-way adjustable twin shock swingarm			
Valve timing (degrees)	20, 70, 50, 30	**Brakes)**	Drum 180mm front, 160mm rear	**Colors**	Diana; blue frame, blue and silver Monza; blue frame, blue and gold with chrome panels	
Carburetion	Dell'Orto UBF24BS	**Tires**	2.75 x 18, 3.00 x 18			
Power	Diana: 19.5 horsepower at 7,550 rpm Monza: 16.4 horsepower at 7,200 rpm	**Wheelbase**	1320mm (52.8 inches)	**Engine numbers (on left crankcase)**	From DM250 80001-90000 approx	
		Length	2000mm (80 inches)			
Spark plug	Marelli CW250A	**Height**	Diana: 960mm (38.4 inches) Monza: 1040mm (41.6 inches)	**Frame numbers**	U.S. bikes didn't have a frame number as Berliner attached a foil tag to the frame with the same number as the engine.	
Generator	6v/40W					
Ignition advance (degrees)	Static 5-8, Total 33-36					

The chassis was similar to the 200, with the single-downtube frame featuring a 27-degree steering head angle. The Diana had a new 17-liter gas tank, and the side cover on the right provided for an air filter. The Monza retained the smaller 13-liter tank of the 200 TS, but also included a bellows tube for an air filter under the side cover. Both models featured abbreviated fenders, and the Diana had clip-on handlebars and narrower (2.25 x 18 instead of

While the 250 motor was similar to the 175 and 200, there were new engine castings and beefed-up internals. *(Roy Kidney)*

2.50 x 18-inch) wheel rims. The gas tank transfers were also the new eagle-type, rather than the large D of the 200. Although the 250 was really little changed from the 200 and 175, the Diana heralded a new era for Ducati. This was the first performance Ducati that was affordable and widely available. With an optional tuning kit, it could be transformed into an effective club racer. This kit, comprised of a 9:1 piston, Dell'Orto SS1 27A carburetor, and megaphone exhaust, was said to increase the power to 23.5 horsepower at 7,550 rpm. The top speed was claimed to be 100 mph—outstanding for a 250 at that time.

There were small differences in specification between the U.S. and European Diana (and British Daytona), mainly the carburetor jetting, and small updates every year.

The 250 Monza received a new seat in 1963, with curved aluminum beading, continuing through 1964 before it received the five-speed gearbox.

Ducati Motor

The 250 Monza of 1962 was the touring version of the Diana.

250 Scrambler (Motocross), 250 Diana Mark 3 (Four-Speed)

Roy Kidney

The 1963 250 Mark 3 was one of the most competitive club racers available in the early 1960s, but was still hampered by a four-speed transmission.

At the request of Berliner, a third 250 emerged during 1962: the 250 Scrambler. This replaced the 200 Motocross, and also spawned the more sporting 250 Diana Mark 3—a superb production racer also specific to America. Setting both these models apart from the Diana and Monza was a higher-performance engine, with higher compression, hotter cam, and larger carburetor. The ignition and electrical system was also different, with a lower output flywheel magneto, no battery, and extremely basic lighting.

Other developments included solid valve rockers with shim adjustment rather than screw and locknut.

Both the 250 Mark 3 and Scrambler expanded Ducati's change of direction with the overhead camshaft single. There was even more emphasis on off-road and racing performance than the Diana. The Diana Mark 3 came without an air filter or side covers with toolbox, and included new shock absorbers with exposed springs

With the 250 Scrambler of 1962, Ducati was more successful in creating a dual-purpose motorcycle.

(on most examples). There were clip-on handlebars, but normal footpegs and the usual rocking gearshift pedal. The tiny detachable headlight, taillight, and abbreviated front fender were shared with the Scrambler, and the only instrumentation was a white-faced Veglia tachometer, mounted centrally on a bracket on the top triple clamp. The Diana Mark 3 also came with a small front racing number plate, and each machine was supplied with a standard muffler and reverse-cone megaphone. The 18x2.25-inch wheel rims were steel.

The 250 Scrambler was also a much more serious motorcycle than its somewhat lame 200cc predecessor, and designed as a "four-in-one" model that could be a road racer, enduro, flat tracker, or street bike. Although the basic style was similar to its predecessor, there were 19-inch chrome plated steel wheels with Pirelli Motocross tires, standard 250 Diana suspension, and an open exhaust without a muffler. The engine had a slightly lower compression ratio and different camshaft, and the carburetor included an air filter. With its large 250 Diana brakes, the Scrambler was still more street than off-road oriented, but was an excellent back road machine. It also

The 250 Scrambler engine was almost as highly tuned as that of the 250 Diana Mark 3. *(Roy Kidney)*

came with a variety of extras, including valve adjustment caps, control cables, rigid struts for flat track racing, and a range of alternative front and rear sprockets. While the 250 Diana Mark 3 remained virtually unchanged until it was replaced by the five-speed version in 1964, the 250 Scrambler was restyled for 1964. A special Giuliari scrambler saddle was accompanied by a longer and lower gas tank, and ball end brake and clutch levers.

250 Diana Mark 3 1962-63, 250 Scrambler 1962-64

Engine	Single cylinder four-stroke, air-cooled	**Clutch**	Wet multiplate	**Seat height**	750mm (30 inches)
Bore	74mm	**Gear ratios**	0.97, 1.18, 1.65, 2.75	**Dry weight**	Diana: 110 kg (242 lbs.) Scrambler 109 kg (239.8 lbs.)
Stroke	57.8mm	**Final drive**	Diana: 2.647:1 Scrambler: 3.929:1		
Displacement	248.589cc	**Front suspension**	Ducati 31.5mm telescopic fork	**Top speed**	Diana: 177 km/h (109.7 mph) Scrambler: 135 km/h (83.7 mph)
Compression ratio	10:1 (9.2:1)	**Rear suspension**	Three-way adjustable twin-shock swingarm		
Valve actuation	Bevel gear-driven overhead camshaft	**Brakes**	Drum 180mm front, 160mm rear	**Colors (Mk 3 and SCR)**	Blue frame, blue and silver
Valve timing (degrees)	Diana: 62, 68, 75, 55 Scrambler: 32, 71, 50, 44	**Tires**	Diana: 2.50 x 18, 2.75 x 18 Scrambler: 3.00 x 19, 3.50 x 19	**Engine numbers (on left crankcase)**	From DM250 80001-90000 approx
Carburetion	Dell'Orto SS1 27A				
Power	30 horsepower at 8,300 rpm	**Wheelbase**	Diana: 1,320mm (52.8 inches) Scrambler: 1,350mm (54 inches)	**Frame numbers**	U.S. bikes didn't have a frame number as Berliner attached a foil tag to the frame with the same number as the engine.
Spark plug	Marelli CW260N				
Generator	6v/40W	**Length**	Diana: 2,000mm (80 inches) Scrambler: 2,020mm (80.8 inches)		
Ignition (degrees)	Magneto, fixed advance 38-41				
Primary drive	2.500:1 (24:60)	**Height**	1,090mm (43.6 inches)		

160 Monza Junior

Ducati Motor

The combination of a 160cc engine in a 250 chassis was not successful, and the 160 Monza was one of the more unpopular models of the mid-1960s. This is the 1965 example.

Berliner's influence during 1964 extended to persuading Ducati to create a smaller Monza: the 160 Monza Junior. This was very much a parts bin special, with a 160cc engine in a 250 chassis, with smaller-diameter wheels and budget suspension. It wasn't a very successful recipe and although the 160 Monza Junior ran for 4 years it didn't earn itself a strong following.

The 160 Monza Junior engine was based on the 125, rather than the 250 (or 175), and was externally identified by a lack of finning on the sump or rocker covers. Like the 250 there was a four-ring piston (with two oil scraper rings), but the wrist-pin diameter was 16mm, the big-end eye 34mm, with the 28mm crankpin running on smaller (3mm) rollers. The con-rod was also slightly narrower (19mm) than the 250 rod, and the 160 included a lower primary drive ratio. Other variations from the 250 included 8mm rocker pins, 11mm rocker bushes, lighter, 35.3-pound valve springs, and thinner-stemmed valves (7mm). Valve adjustment was by screw and locknut. The electrical system featured a flywheel magneto for the ignition, and SAFA 6v-7Ah battery to power the lights. Along with the smaller wheels, were smaller-diameter brakes (from the 125), and a lighter and cheaper front fork (very similar to the 125 Bronco).

The cycle parts were very similar to the 250 Monza, with the same 13-liter gas tank, and side covers that included a bellows to the air filter. The front fender was also the same, and looked out of place with the 16-inch wheel. There was a small rear rack, and some 160 Monza Juniors came with the large chrome-plated crash bar. Changes were mostly cosmetic for 1965, and shared with the 250 Monza. These included a reshaped, more angular, gas tank (still 13 liters), properly fitting angular front fender, new seat, and elongated side cover toolboxes. The weight also went up slightly. There were more stylistic changes for 1966, shared with the 250 Monza, and also the 350 Sebring. The angular look extended to the front headlight, and somehow the claimed maximum speed increased, but this was a dubious claim. There were no changes for 1967, and Berliner advertised the Monza Junior through 1968. With the Monza Junior, Berliner completely misread the market, and in 1967 was unable to accept a shipment of 1,800 160 Monza Juniors as they already had plenty of

For 1966, the 160 Monza Junior received an angular headlight and looked almost identical to the 250 Monza of that year.

stock. These ended up in England, but they were unloved there, too. Many remained unsold through 1971. There were still 160 Monzas left at the factory in 1969 as 32 were shipped to Australia that year.

160 MONZA JUNIOR 1964-67

Engine	Single cylinder four-stroke, air-cooled	Generator	6v/28W	Wheelbase	1,330mm (53.2 inches)
Bore	61mm	Ignition (degrees)	Magneto 21-23 static, 39-41 total	Length	1,980mm (79.2 inches)
Stroke	52mm	Primary drive	3.000:1	Height	930mm (37.2 inches)
Displacement	156cc	Clutch	Wet multiplate	Seat height	760mm (30.4 inches)
Compression ratio	8.2:1	Gear ratios	0.97, 1.18, 1.65, 2.75	Dry weight	1964: 106 kg (233.2 lbs.) 1965-67: 108 kg (237.6 lbs.)
Valve actuation	Bevel gear-driven overhead camshaft	Final drive	2.875:1		
Valve timing (degrees)	24, 40, 51,30	Front suspension	Marzocchi telescopic fork	Speed	1964-65: 102 km/h (63.24 mph) 1966-67: 113 km/h (70.6 mph)
Carburetion	Dell'Orto UB22BS	Rear suspension	Three-way adjustable twin shock swingarm		
Power	16 horsepower at 8,000 rpm	Brakes	Drum 158mm front, 136mm rear	Colors	Black/silver, cherry red
Spark plug	Marelli CW260N, Beru 260, KLG F-100	Tires	2.75 x 16, 3.25 x 16	Engine numbers	From DM160 20001

Apollo

Although not exactly a production model, the Apollo deserves to be catalogued as a few examples were produced, and it was intended for regular production. Apollo, the Greek god of the arts, represents order, harmony, civilization, and prophesy. And there was no more prophetic a motorcycle than the extraordinary 100-horsepower 1260cc V-four Ducati Apollo of 1963. That this motorcycle was designed and built in Italy, to American requirements, by a company with little experience of motorcycles over 250cc was even more amazing. At that time the Apollo reeked of extreme excess, yet for nearly 40 years its size and specification

can be considered mainstream. The Apollo was truly a motorcycle ahead of its time.

Berliner wanted to break Harley-Davidson's stranglehold on the police motorcycle market in the U.S. Official police department "specifications" required motorcycles to have engines 1200cc or larger, a wheelbase of at least 60 inches, and tires of a 5.00 x 16-inch section. He convinced Montano and Taglioni to consider such a project, but Ducati was only surviving because the government was underwriting heavy annual losses. During 1961, it was

Decades ahead of its time, the Apollo was too large and powerful for the tires of 1964.

APOLLO

Engine	90-degree vee-four four-stroke, air-cooled	**Carburetion**	Dell'Orto SS1 32 (SS1 24)	**Final drive**	Duplex chain
Bore	84.5mm	**Power**	100 horsepower (later 67)	**Front suspension**	38mm Ceriani fork
Stroke	56mm	**Maximum revs**	7,000 rpm	**Rear suspension**	Twin-shock absorber swingarm
Displacement	1,257cc	**Generator**	12v/200w, 32Ah battery	**Tires**	5.00 x 16-inch Pirelli
Compression ratio	10:1 (8:1)	**Primary drive**	Gear	**Wheelbase**	1,550mm (62 inches)
Valve actuation	Pushrod-operated overhead valves	**Gears**	Five-speed	**Dry weight**	240 kg (480 lbs.)

agreed a prototype and two engines would be built, after Berliner agreed to finance the cost of the prototype and assist in the cost of tooling for production. The project would be a joint venture between Berliner and Ducati and known as the D/B-V/4. As to the specifications Joe Berliner was quite specific. He wanted a lightweight, 1200cc V-four shaft-drive police-duty motorcycle that would outperform the Harley in every respect. Ease of maintenance was also a priority, and this called for pushrod and rocker overhead valves, with the gear-driven single camshaft positioned

between the vee, just like an American V8. The initial Apollo produced a then-shattering 100 horsepower, but a detuned version was envisaged as an option. The engine was incorporated as a stressed member in a massive frame but the Apollo's downfall was the tires. Although the Apollo was a wonderfully stable and comfortable highway machine there just weren't tires available in 1964 that could cope with sustained 120-mph speeds. The solution was to reduce the power, restricting the top speed to around 100 mph. As the largest-capacity motorcycle to emanate from a European manufacturer since World War II, the Apollo suffered from being too far ahead of its time. Fortunately, Taglioni wasn't discouraged by its failure and was able to use many of its features as an inspiration for the 750 V-twin 7 years later.

Looking at the Apollo engine, it is easy to see where the inspiration for the later V-twins came from.

FIVE-SPEED NARROW CASE OVERHEAD-CAMSHAFT SINGLES

The early 1960s were a troubled time for Ducati. Official racing was virtually nonexistent, and the company was dubiously involved developing a range of unrealistic and undesirable motorcycles. This included the Apollo and parallel twin, while an entire range of two-strokes and scooters was produced without any regard to their marketability or desirability. These were dark days indeed at Ducati, and it was a difficult time for Fabio Taglioni, who had built his reputation through racing. Saving the company during this period was the overhead-camshaft single, and further development in 1964 saw a five-speed gearbox. After 1964 the only four-speed overhead-camshaft model was the 160 Monza Junior, and the range expanded to include the 350 Sebring.

250 GT, 250 Monza

The first models to receive the five-speed gearbox were the 250 GT (Daytona in the U.K.), and 250 Mark 3 of 1964. While the Mark 3 was similar in general specification to the 1963 Diana Mark 3, the 250 GT was a hybrid model, sharing a lower specification engine and Monza chassis, but with the Diana 17-liter gas tank, saddle, and side cover toolboxes. The 250 GT also came with the large chrome crash bar as fitted to the earlier Americano, and U.S. versions generally had high cowboy-style handlebars.

Apart from the five-speed gearbox, the 250 engine in the GT and Monza was similar to that of the 1963 250 Monza. It retained the valve adjustment by screw and locknut, and because of the lower compression ratio, the cylinder was also slightly longer, at 96.1mm. Initially the GT received a different camshaft (coded black), but after engine number 87422 the camshaft was shared between the GT and Monza (coded violet). Early 250 GTs had identical inlet and exhaust valves, and the same lighter inlet and exhaust valve springs (48.5 pound). After engine 87422 the 250 GT received the larger Monza intake valve, with corresponding 59.5-pound inlet valve spring. The rocker pins on all models were 10mm, in 13mm bushes, and the four-ring pistons included two oil scraper rings. The alternator was uprated for the five-speed 250, with an

Ducati Motor

The 250 GT for 1965 had more sporting fenders and a deeper saddle.

alloy rotor and an output of 60 watts. With the five-speed engine also came an uprated oil pump, with wider gears

There were a number of small differences between the 1964 250 GTs and later examples. Early 250 GT fenders were deeper and the forks included different triple clamps, the top without a handlebar attachment. The wheels on both the 250 GT and Monza were 18x2.50-inch. The 250 GT and Monza shared the 25 watt Aprilia headlamp, incorporating a Veglia 100 mph speedometer. The best that could be said about this headlamp was that it provided bare illumination.

The five-speed 250 Monza appeared for 1965, along with a slightly revised 250 GT. Updates included a new kickstart shaft with higher gearing (18/19) instead of 20/22, and new lower bevel gears. The earlier 250 GT Silentium muffler (IGM 1984S), was standardized with the Monza (and Mach 1) in 1965. There was a deeper saddle on the 250 GT, and the handlebar and front fork standardized with the Monza, with the handlebar mounting on the top triple clamp. This year also saw levers with ball ends. The 1965 250 GT front fender was the same as that of the Monza, and both the 250 Monza and 250 GT received styling revisions for 1966. Apart from decals they were now identical. The 13-liter gas tank on both was styled along the lines of the 1965 Monza Junior, and there was a new saddle, angular headlamp, and elongated side cover toolboxes. Along with other 250s this year the front brake received an additional air-scoop, on the right.

Ducati Motor

For 1965, the 250 Monza continued much as before, but for the five-speed engine.

250 GT 1964-66, 250 Monza 1965-67

Engine	Single cylinder four-stroke, air-cooled	**Spark plug**	Marelli CW260N, Beru 260, KLG F-100	**Tires**	2.75 x 18, 3.00 x 18
Bore	74mm	**Generator**	6v/60W	**Wheelbase**	1320mm (52.8 inches)
Stroke	57.8mm	**Ignition advance (degrees)**	Static 5-8, Total 33-36	**Length**	2000mm (80 inches)
Displacement	248.589cc			**Height**	1070mm (42.8 inches)
Compression ratio	8:1	**Primary drive**	2.500:1 (24/60)	**Seat height**	800mm
Valve actuation	Bevel gear-driven overhead camshaft	**Clutch**	Wet multiplate	**Dry weight**	125 kg (275 lbs.)
Valve timing (degrees)	20, 70, 50, 30 (52,52,75,27 GT until 87421)	**Gear ratios**	0.97, 1.10, 1.35, 1.73 2.53	**Speed**	128 km/h (79.36 mph)
		Final drive	1964 (GT): 18/45 1965-66: 17/45	**Colors**	250 Monza (1966): Red and silver, silver
Carburetion	Dell'Orto UBF24BS	**Front suspension**	Ducati 31.5mm telescopic fork	**Engine numbers (on right crankcase)**	From DM250 90000 approx
Power	Monza: 22 horsepower at 7,200 rpm GT (1964): 18.4 horsepower at 7,200 rpm	**Rear suspension**	Three-way adjustable Marzocchi 295mm twin shock swingarm		
		Brakes	Drum 180 x 35 front, 160 x 30 rear		

250 Mark 3

Replacing the 250 Diana Mark 3 during 1964 for the U.S. was the 250 Mark 3. Apart from the five-speed gearbox, the general engine specifications were as for the previous model, with the same valve sizes as the 250 Monza but shim adjustment, 27mm carburetor without air cleaner, and magneto ignition. The valve springs were also the same as the Monza, 59.5 pound on the inlet and 48.5 pound on the exhaust. After engine number 87922 there was a new stator, requiring a different flywheel position for the correct ignition timing, with yet another stator after engine number 88296. All 1964 Mark 3

engines featured a fixed ignition advance. Because of the higher compression ratio the cylinder was shorter than the Monza (94.5mm), and as before each Mark 3 came with a 685mm black painted racing megaphone in addition to the Silentium muffler.

The white faced 10,000 rpm (redlined at 8,500 rpm) Veglia tachometer, was now mounted on a special bracket attached to the right headlight mount. Unlike the previous model, the 25 watt Aprilia headlight differed to the Scrambler, with a Veglia 150-mph speedometer included in the shell. The round taillight was also mounted on a larger bracket, and most 1964 Mark 3's came with high touring style handlebars rather than clip-ons. The 1964 Mark 3 had Monza and 250 GT pedals, with rubber pegs, and like the earlier examples retained the narrower 18 x 2.25-inch steel wheel rims. The 1963 and 1964 Mark 3s were visually similar, with no side cover toolboxes, an abbreviated front fender, shock absorbers with exposed springs, and a small number plate screen over the headlight.

There were a number of developments to the Mark 3 for 1965. Five-speed Mark 3's were either stamped with DM250M1 or DM250M3 engine numbers, and U.S. examples didn't have a frame number as Berliner provided foil tags with the engine number as identification. The Mark 3 engine specification was now shared with the Mach 1, with larger valves (40 and 36mm), stronger exhaust valve springs (59.5 pound), and the same camshaft and 29mm carburetor without air cleaner. Where the Mark 3 still departed from the Mach 1 was in the ignition system, with the Mark 3 retaining the 40-watt flywheel magneto. This was now similar to that on the 160 Monza Junior, and starting was easier as there was no longer a fixed maximum advance. Along with the new ignition was a rectangular CEV taillight and steel license plate bracket, similar in style to that of the 250 GT and Monza. If the taillight burned out a small switch on the rear fender had to be switched off to allow the ignition system to operate. Some 1965 Mark 3's also came with the earlier Aprilia taillight.

Ducati Motor

The five-speed 250 Mark 3 replaced the four-speed for 1964. There was a new taillight, but the magneto ignition was retained.

For 1965, there were new fenders (the same as the Mach 1), and small triangular side cover toolboxes with "Mark 3" decals. As the 1965 Mark 3 had Mach 1 foot controls that included rearset solid steel footpegs and an ineffective curved kickstart lever. Unlike the Mach 1 though the handlebars were not clip-ons, and could be specified as high or low. This year also saw ball end brake and clutch levers. There was a slightly longer wheelbase, and the saddle height (with a new seat) and weight was up slightly. A Mach 1 sporting saddle was optional. Although some early five-speed Mark 3's came with the earlier gas tank, most received the narrower Mach 1 tank with an

250 MARK 3 1964-67

Engine	Single cylinder four-stroke, air-cooled	**Ignition (degrees)**	1964: Magneto, fixed advance 38-41 1965-66: Magneto 21-23 static, 39-41 1967: Battery and coil 5-8 static, 33-36	**Wheelbase**	1964: 1320mm (52.8 inches) 1965-67: 1350mm (54 inches)
Bore	74mm			**Length**	2000mm (80 inches)
Stroke	57.8mm				
Displacement	248.589cc	**Primary drive**	2.500:1 (24/60)	**Height**	1964: 1090mm (43.6 inches) 1965-67: 1070mm (42.8 inches)
Compression ratio	10:1	**Clutch**	Wet multiplate		
Valve actuation	Bevel gear-driven overhead camshaft	**Gear ratios**	0.97, 1.10, 1.35, 1.73 2.53	**Seat height**	750mm (30 inches)
Valve timing (degrees)	1964: 62, 68, 75, 55 1965-67: 62, 76, 70, 48	**Final drive**	1964: 18/43 1965-67: 18/40	**Dry weight**	1964: 110 kg (242 lbs.) 1965-67: 112 kg (246.4 lbs.)
Carburetion	1964: Dell'Orto SS1 27A 1965-67: Dell'Orto SS1 29A	**Front suspension**	31.5mm telescopic fork		
		Rear suspension	Three-way adjustable Marzocchi 295mm twin shock swingarm	**Speed**	177 km/h (109.7 mph)
Power	30 horsepower at 8,000 rpm			**Colors**	Black frame, red and silver, black and silver
Spark plug	Marelli CW260N	**Brakes**	Drum 180 x 35 front, 160 x 30 rear	**Engine numbers**	DM250M1 prefix until 01461 From DM250M3 92000-100000 approx
Generator	1964-66: 6v/40W 1967: 6v/60W	**Tires**	2.50 x 18, 2.75 x 18		

Ducati Motor

1965 250 Mark 3's were thinly disguised Mach 1's with magneto ignition. The high handlebars were an incongruity with rearset footpegs.

Ducati Motor

The final 250 Mark 3 of 1967 was arguably the finest. This was virtually a Mach 1, but with the Veglia tachometer.

indent underneath to provide clearance for the larger carburetor. The capacity was also reduced to 16 liters.

There were only minor developments to the Mark 3 for 1966. In response to criticism over the kickstart, the footpegs and foot controls were no longer rearset, and a rear brake light switch was incorporated at the pedal. The front brake also incorporated an air-scoop on the right.

The Mark 3 was offered in the U.S. unchanged through until 1969, and in Europe it replaced the Mach 1 in 1967. This final example was identical to the Mach 1, with clip-on handlebars, rearset footpegs and controls, sporting saddle, and battery and coil ignition. High handlebars were still an option, and apart from the decals and colors, the only feature separating the Mach 1 and 1967 Mark 3 was the Veglia tachometer on the right headlight bracket.

250 Mach 1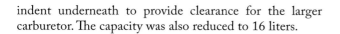

The 250 Mach 1 was another of the classic Ducatis of the 1960s. It was very similar in specification to the 250 Mark 3, but has become a more sought-after model.

Not widely sold in the U.S., the Mach 1 was one of the most outstanding sporting machines available in Europe during the 1960s.

250 Mark 3, which shared a similar engine specification, but was lighter, and had a claimed higher top speed. The claimed performance for both was very optimistic and unattainable in most circumstances. Unlike the U.S. Mark 3 the red-framed Mach 1 had a frame number. Only a few Mach 1s were imported into the U.S.

The Mach 1 was very similar to the 1965 250 Mark 3, with an identical engine specification apart from battery and coil ignition, and sharing the curved kickstart lever, and rearset footpegs and controls. Unlike the Mark 3, the Mach 1 had clip-on handlebars with softer rubber handgrips, and there was a choice of two seats, one a dual and the other a solo racing type. Also shared with the Mark 3 was the 150 mph speedometer in the headlight sheel, narrow steel wheel rims, and shock absorbers with exposed springs. The white faced Veglia tachometer was never specified for the Mach 1, although many restored examples feature it. Mach 1s had the small triangular toolbox side covers, but the SAFA 13.5 Ah battery underneath the carburetor was visible.

There were only a few changes to the Mach 1 during its relatively short production span. During 1965 there was a new frame with a rear brake light switch connector, and from 1966, an air-scoop on the front brake, and an option of high handlebars. Some Mach 1s also included larger side cover toolboxes, with the right side incorporating an air filter and bellows to the carburetor, but by 1967 the new wide-case singles were imminent. Although these had an improved kickstart and would ultimately prove more reliable, the lighter Mach 1 and Mark 3 were favored by racers for several more years.

As the 250 Mark 3 was really created to provide American riders with a competitive club racer, it wasn't widely available in Europe until 1967. The Mark 3 was also limited in its role as a useable street motorcycle as it didn't have a battery and the starting was difficult, especially on early models with a fixed ignition advance. In response to European demand for a high performance five-speed 250 roadster, Ducati created the Mach 1, or Mach/1 as it was described in many brochures. Available from the end of 1964 and into 1966, the Mach 1 has become one of the most desirable production Ducatis of any era. This status of the Mach 1 though has been at the expense of the

250 MACH 1 1964-66

Engine	Single cylinder four-stroke, air-cooled	Generator	6v/60W	Tires	2.50 x 18, 2.75 x 18 CEAT
Bore	74mm	Ignition (degrees)	Battery and coil 5-8 static, 33-36 total	Wheelbase	1,350mm (54 inches)
Stroke	57.8mm	Primary drive	2.500:1 (24/60)	Length	2,000mm (80 inches)
Displacement	248.589cc	Clutch	Wet multiplate	Height	920mm (36.8 inches)
Compression ratio	10:1	Gear ratios	0.97, 1.10, 1.35, 1.73 2.53	Seat height	760mm (30.4 inches)
Valve actuation	Bevel-gear driven overhead camshaft	Final drive	18/40	Dry weight	116 kg (255.2 lbs.)
Valve timing (degrees)	62, 76, 70, 48	Front suspension	31.5mm telescopic fork	Speed	170 km/h (105.4 mph)
Carburetion	Dell'Orto SS1 29A	Rear suspension	Three-way adjustable Marzocchi 295mm twin shock swingarm	Colors	Red frame, red and silver
Power	28 horsepower at 8,500 rpm	Brakes (mm)	Drum 180x35 front, 160x30 rear	Engine numbers (five digits)	From DM250M1 00001-01900 approx
Spark plug	Marelli CW260N			Frame numbers	DM250 00001-02700 approx

250 Motocross (Scrambler)

Later in 1964 a five-speed 250 Motocross, or Scrambler in the U.S., was produced alongside the 250 Mark 3. Initially this looked identical to the four-speed, with the same blue frame and blue and silver paint. The five-speed engine was a hybrid between the 250 Monza and 250 Mark 3, with the same valves as the Monza, but with shim adjustment, and an in-between length 95.6mm cylinder. The 250 Scrambler also shared valve springs with the 250 Monza (59.5-lb. inlet and 48.5-lb. exhaust), but had its own camshaft. The Scrambler retained the 27mm carburetor of the earlier four-speed version, and incorporated an F20 air cleaner. The late 1964 and 1965 250 Scrambler featured the 40-watt flywheel magneto of the 250 Mark 3, and early examples incorporated ignition with a fixed advance. While there was a revised flywheel from engine number 87422-87902, it wasn't until after 87903 that an automatic advance was provided. The first five-speed Scramblers retained the 36mm exhaust pipe without a muffler, small detachable 25 watt Aprilia headlamp, abbreviated chainguard, braced handlebar, and 2.50 x 19-inch wheels with knobby tires. The 1965 250 Scrambler was very similar to the 1964 five-speed version. The same 11-liter gas tank was retained, but the small Aprilia taillight attached to the top of the rear fender, behind the saddle. The folding rubber footpegs were similar to the pillion type on the 250 GT and Monza, and mounted on steel supports bolted to the frame.

Ducati Motor

The first five-speed 250 Scrambler of 1964 still featured detachable lights and 19-inch wheels.

The orientation of the 250 Scrambler moved away from off-road use for 1966, although range of optional sprockets, cables and struts was still included. The electrical system shared with the 160 Monza Junior, including a 28-watt flywheel magneto and 7 Ah battery, and different headlight and taillight. From number 92172, the taillight bracket incorporated a switch (as on the Mark 3). Options extended to a Veglia speedometer in the Aprilia headlight, muffler, while the folding steel footpegs were now purpose built for the Scrambler. The gear lever was also now a regular type, and not Ducati's traditional heel and toe

250 Motocross (Scrambler) 1965-67

Engine	Single cylinder four-stroke, air-cooled	**Ignition (degrees)**	Magneto, fixed advance 38-41 (until engine 87902) Static 21-23, total 39-41 (after 87903)	**Tires**	1964-65: 3.00 x 19, 3.50 x 19 1966: 3.50 x 19, 4.00 x 18
Bore	74mm				
Stroke	57.8mm	**Primary drive**	2.500:1 (24:60)	**Wheelbase**	1,350mm (54 inches)
Displacement	248.589cc	**Clutch**	Wet multiplate	**Length**	2,020mm (80.8 inches)
Compression ratio	9.2:1	**Gear ratios**	0.97, 1.10, 1.35, 1.73 2.53	**Height**	1,050mm (42 inches)
Valve actuation	Bevel gear-driven overhead camshaft	**Final drive**	14/55 (optional 45, 50, or 60)	**Seat height**	750mm (30 inches)
Valve timing (degrees)	32, 75, 55, 44 (coded white)	**Front suspension**	31.5mm telescopic fork	**Dry weight**	1964-65: 109 kg (239.8 lbs.) 1966: 120 kg (264 lbs.)
Carburetion	Dell'Orto SS1 27A	**Rear suspension**	Three-way adjustable Marzocchi 295mm twin-shock swingarm	**Colors**	Blue frame, blue and silver (1964) Black frame, black and silver, some red and silver
Power	28 horsepower at 8,000 rpm				
Spark plug	Marelli CW260N, Beru 260, KLG F-100	**Brakes**	Drum 180 x 35 front, 160 x 30 rear		
Generator	6v/40W (until engine 92171) 6v/28W (after 92172)			**Engine numbers**	DM250SCR 92000-104500 approx

shift. Other developments included softer rear shock absorbers, a stronger front fork with a welded (rather than pinned) fork stem, and the frame incorporated fittings for passenger footpegs. The front brake featured the additional airscoop on the right, and there were new wheels and universal tires. The rear wheel was now an 18 x 3-inch, and the weight was up slightly. The narrow-case 250 Scrambler was offered into 1967, but replaced in 1968.

Ducati Motor

By 1966, the 250 Scrambler had evolved into more of a dual-purpose motorcycle. This publicity photo shows a rocking gearshift pedal, but most 1966 Scramblers had new footpegs and levers.

350 Sebring

U.S. demand for a larger capacity model led to the 350 Sebring in 1965, a bored and stroked 250 that incorporated many components from existing models. Although it was named after the Sebring racing circuit where Franco Farnè won the debut race for the 350 SC in March 1965, the production Sebring shared more with the 250 Monza than the sporting Mark 3. Apart from a different camshaft and higher primary gears, the engine was very similar to the 250 Monza. It had the same electrical and ignition system, con-rod and crank pin, and carburetor.

The first 350 Sebring of 1965 was produced in two versions, one replicating the 250 Monza (with the same

Ducati Motor

There was very little to distinguish the 1966 350 Sebring from the 250 Monza and 250 GT of the same year.

350 Sebring 1965-67

Engine	Single cylinder four-stroke, air-cooled	**Generator**	6v/60W	**Wheelbase**	1330mm (53.2 inches)
Bore	76mm	**Ignition (degrees)**	Battery and Coil, 5-8 static, 33-36 total	**Length**	2000mm (80 inches)
Stroke	75mm	**Primary drive**	2.111:1 (27/57)	**Height**	1070mm (42.8 inches)
Displacement	340.237cc	**Clutch**	Wet multiplate	**Seat height**	800mm (32 inches)
Compression ratio	8.5:1	**Gear ratios**	0.97, 1.10, 1.35, 1.73 2.53	**Dry weight**	123 kg (270.6 lbs.)
Valve actuation	Bevel gear-driven overhead camshaft	**Final drive**	2.500:1 (18/45)	**Top speed**	125 km/h (77.5 mph) 1964-65: 142 km/h (88.04 mph)
Valve timing (degrees)	20, 70, 50, 30	**Front suspension**	31.5mm telescopic fork	**Colors**	Black frame, black and silver, red and silver
Carburetion	Dell'Orto UB24BS	**Rear suspension**	Three-way adjustable Marzocchi 295mm twin-shock swingarm	**Engine numbers**	From DM350 01000
Power	20 horsepower at 6,250 rpm	**Brakes**	Drum 180 x 35 front, 160 x 30 rear		
Spark plug	Marelli CW260N, Beru 260, KLG F-100	**Tires**	2.75 x 18, 3.00 x 18		

Ducati Motor

The 1965 350 Sebring for the U.S. was styled like the 250 Monza of the same year, with a peanut-style gas tank and high handlebars.

13-liter gas tank) for the U.S., and the other styled like the 250 GT (with 17-liter tank.). Both models had high handlebars. For 1966 the Sebring was restyled along the lines of the 1965 160 Monza Junior, and looked virtually identical to the 250 Monza of that year. Along with angular fenders and elongated side cover toolboxes, was a reshaped 13-liter gas tank, and angular headlight shell. This year there was also an airscoop on right side of the front brake. This angular style didn't prove particularly popular, but the Sebring lived for one more year with the wide-case ohc engine.

Mach 1/S, 250 and 350 SC

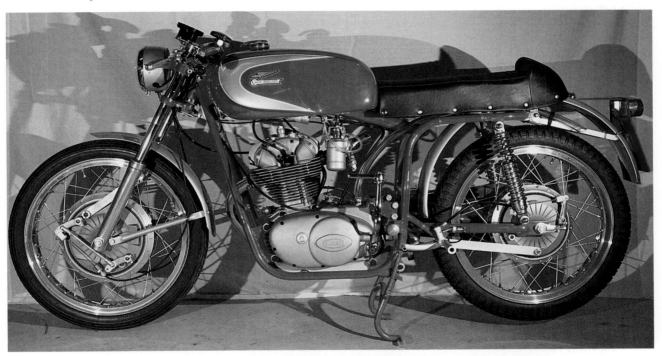

Although not functionally superior, one of the most beautiful Ducatis of any era was the 250 SC with a double-downtube frame. The 1965 version shown here had a Grimeca front brake.

Racing versions of the Mach 1 appeared during 1965, and there were two types, the Mach 1/S, and the more exotic 250 and 350 SC (Sport Corsa). Because of the rarity of both types, they have often erroneously been referred to as the Mach 1/S, but they were quite different machines. The Mach 1/S was ostensibly a Mach 1 with a stronger 250 F3 dual-rib con-rod, magneto ignition, and a 200mm Oldani front brake. Only as few were produced and they looked virtually identical to the production Mach 1 as they shared the single-downtube frame.

The SC was a different machine altogether, and like the earlier F3 was a hand-built racing machine that shared little with the production 250. The engine included sand-cast crankcases (with either 250 or 350 SC and an engine number stamped on left crankcase near the cylinder) designed to accommodate the double cradle frame. The cylinder head was the sand-cast 250 F3 type, with shorter camshafts (giving 10mm of inlet valve lift) than the Mach 1. Valve sizes were 40 and 36mm. There was also a close-ratio five-speed gearbox that was unique to the SC,

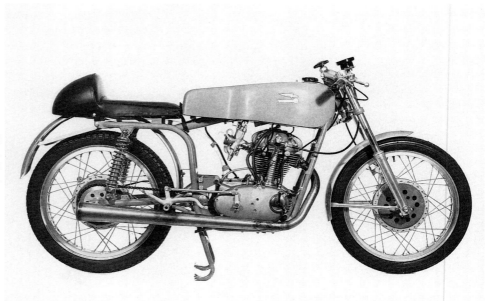

The SC for 1966 had an Oldani brake and fiberglass gas tank. The carburetor was an Amal on the 250 and Dell'Orto on the 350.

with wider gears and longer shafts. Each SC came with its individual wiring diagram and magneto ignition was optional. The carburetion for 1965 was by Dell'Orto, an SS1 30 on the 250 and an SS1 32B on the 350.

Apart from the double cradle frame with wider engine mounts that was specific to the SC, there were also special alloy Marzocchi forks with stepped fork tubes (33mm in the lower triple clamp and 31.7mm at the top). The wheels were 19-inch front and rear, and for 1965 the brakes were Grimeca. The steel fuel tank was patterned after the Mach 1, and as with the F3 there was full street equipment, including a horn. Only around 20 250 SCs

and half a dozen 350 SCs were built during 1965 and for 1966 there were some developments. The 250 SC now received an Amal carburetor (the 350 retained the Dell'Orto) and both came with Oldani brakes front and rear. There was a fiberglass tank and humpback solo seat but the frame and running gear was unchanged. The 250 and 350 SC were extremely purposeful machines but they didn't realize their potential. As racers they didn't offer any real advantage over the Mark 3 and Mach 1 which were cheaper and lighter. Although not well documented, today they stand out as some of the most desirable Ducatis of the 1960s.

250 AND 350 SC 1965-66

Engine	Single cylinder four-stroke, air-cooled	**Carburetion**	SS1 32B; 350: Dell'Orto SS1 30	**Rear suspension**	Swingarm with twin shock absorbers
Bore	250: 74mm		250 (1966): Amal 1 3/16-inch 389 monoblock	**Brakes**	1964-65: 230mm Grimeca
	350: 76mm				1966: 200mm Oldani
Stroke	250: 57.8mm	**Generator**	30 watt		
	350: 75mm	**Ignition**	Battery and coil, twin plugs (14 and 10mm Lodge RL50)	**Wheels**	19-inch
Displacement	250: 248.6cc			**Wheelbase**	1,320mm (52.8 inches)
	350: 350cc	**Clutch**	Wet multiplate	**Weight**	250: 115 kg (253 lbs.)
Compression ratio	250: 10.2:1	**Primary Drive**	Straight cut gear 2.1:1 (30/63)		350: 117 kg (257.4 lbs.)
	350: 10:1	**Gears**	Five-speed	**Top speed**	250: 190 km/h (117.8 mph)
Valve actuation	Single overhead camshaft driven by a shaft and bevel gears	**Front suspension**	Marzocchi 32mm telescopic fork		350: 200 km/h (124 mph)

125 Scrambler

While production of the narrow-case overhead-camshaft engine finished in Bologna by 1968, this engine was produced by Mototrans in Spain for several more years. During 1971 and 1972, 125cc motors were shipped to Bologna for the 125 Scrambler. Specifications included a Spanish Amal Monobloc carburetor, and Spanish silencer and, unlike other overhead camshaft singles, the frame was a duplex full-cradle type. All the other components were Italian, including Marzocchi suspension and CEV instruments. The 125 Scrambler wasn't especially popular and, although production ended during 1972, it was still listed in some catalogues for 1973 and 1974.

Although the motor of the 125 Scrambler was produced by Mototrans in Spain, the motorcycle was assembled in Bologna with Italian proprietary components.

125 SCRAMBLER 1971-72

Engine	Single cylinder four-stroke, air-cooled	**Power**	10 horsepower at 8,000 rpm	**Brakes**	Drum 158mm and 136mm
Bore	55.2mm	**Ignition and battery**	Coil, 6v 11Ah	**Tires**	2.50 x 19, 3.50 x 18
Stroke	52mm	**Primary Drive**	3.000:1	**Wheelbase**	1,340mm (53.6 inches)
Displacement	124.443cc	**Clutch**	Wet multiplate	**Length**	2,040mm (83.6 inches)
Compression ratio	8.5:1	**Gears**	Five speed	**Seat height**	850mm (34 inches)
Valve actuation	Bevel gear-driven overhead camshaft	**Final drive**	3.714:1	**Dry weight**	105 kg (231 lbs.)
Valve timing (degrees)	24, 40, 56, 22	**Front suspension**	Marzocchi fork	**Colors**	Black frame, red or orange
Carburetion	Amal 375/20	**Rear suspension**	Three-way adjustable twin-shock swingarm	**Engine numbers (five digits)**	From DM 20001-21000 approx

CHAPTER 3

TWO STROKES

One of the more dubious enterprises Ducati undertook was to produce a range of moped and lightweight two-stroke motorcycles. Designed to encourage brand loyalty and to expand the sales volume, two-stroke models outnumbered four-strokes for a while during the 1960s. Although the two-strokes proved popular in Italy, they never succeeded in the U.S. and elsewhere where the success of the new wide-case singles led to Ducati concentrating on larger machines. By 1970 the Ducati two-stroke was virtually dead, although it did make a brief return in 1975, lasting until 1979.

48/1 Brisk, 50/1 Brisk

By 1967, the Brisk has evolved into the 50/1, with angular gas tank and headlight.

Designed to appeal to students, the single-speed 48/1 Brisk was an unexciting machine. This is the 1965 version with pressed-steel frame.

The first Ducati two-stroke was the 48 Sport of 1958, the three-speed single-cylinder two-stroke engine hanging from an open tubular steel frame. The cylinder was inclined 25 degrees. Starting was by pedal, and this early 48 Sport was styled similarly to the ohv 98 TL of the same era. After only one year the 48 Sport disappeared, but the same engine made a return in 1961, in the Brisk and Piuma. The Brisk (a misnomer if there ever was one) was the basic model, in a low state of tune with only a single speed transmission. It was produced primarily for the Italian market, with its small rack designed to appeal to students.

The 48/1 Brisk used the 48cc two-stroke engine solo seat, pedal starting, and a quite sophisticated chassis for this type of machine that included a telescopic front fork and twin shock absorber rear swingarm. The first Brisk had a bulbous fuel tank, a tubular steel frame, and the taillight mounted directly on the rear fender, but by 1962

48/1 BRISK 1961-66, 50/1 BRISK 1967

Engine	Single cylinder piston-port two-stroke, air-cooled	**Power**	1.34 (1.5 from 1963) horsepower	**Rear suspension**	Twin-shock swingarm
Bore	38mm	**Maximum revs**	4,200 (5,200) rpm	**Brakes**	Drum 90 mm (3.5 in.)
Stroke	42mm	**Spark plug**	Marelli CW 225N	**Tires**	2.00 x 18
Displacement	47.633cc	**Generator**	6v-18w flywheel magneto	**Dry weight**	45 kg (99.1 lbs.) 50 kg (110.1 lbs.)
Compression ratio	6.3:1 (7:1 from 1963)	**Clutch**	Wet multiplate	**Speed**	40 km/h (24.9 mph)
Carburetion	Dell'Orto T4 12D1	**Gears**	Single speed	**Colors**	Red
		Front suspension	Telescopic fork		

the frame was pressed steel, incorporating the rear fender, and the shape of the tank was new. A single ignition coil was mounted externally, just below the steering head, and there was an automatic centrifugal clutch on the crankshaft. The engine specification changed for 1963, with a slightly higher compression ratio and more power. The 48/1 then lasted until 1965 with few developments apart from colors, decals, a new ignition coil and dual seat option.

The 48/1 was replaced by the equally unremarkable 50/1 Brisk in 1967. This was identical to the 48/1, except for styling revisions that included a square gas tank, angular front fender, and a smaller version of the 160 Monza square-bodied headlight. Again, there was an option of a solo or dual seat.

48 Piuma, 48 Piuma Export, 48 Piuma Sport, 50 Piuma Sport, 50 Piuma

Ducati Motor

Late 1960s styling was taken to excess with the 1967 50 Piuma. All show and no go!

Ducati Motor

The 48 Piuma Sport was a higher-performance version, still with the pressed-steel frame.

Alongside the Brisk was the similar Piuma (or Puma for the U.K.) with a three-speed unit gearbox, and a hand gear change incorporated in the throttle grip. Starting was still by pedal. Apart from the transmission, the Brisk and Piuma had the same engine spec's and were virtually identical, although the Piuma had larger section tires. For 1962 there was also a 48 Piuma Sport, some with a higher-output engine (with a larger carburetor) in the

same pressed-steel frame. In Italy, the 48 Piuma Sport engine was only 1.5 hp, due to Italian laws prohibiting 50cc motorcycles to exceed 40 km/h. The sporting gas tank attached to a crude plate above the frame, and there was a longer muffler. In 1966, the 48 Piuma Sport became the 50 Piuma Sport, but was otherwise unchanged. It wasn't until 1967 that the 48 Piuma became the 50 Piuma with

48 PIUMA, 48 PIUMA EXPORT, 48 PIUMA SPORT, 50 PIUMA SPORT, 50 PIUMA (1961-68)

Engine	Single cylinder piston-port two-stroke, air-cooled	**Spark plug**	Marelli CW225N (CW260N Sport and Export)	**Tires**	2.25 x 18
Bore	38mm	**Ignition (degrees)**	6v-18w flywheel magneto, 15-18	**Wheelbase**	1,160mm (45.7 in.)
Stroke	42mm	**Clutch**	Wet multiplate	**Length**	1,770mm (69.7 in.)
Displacement	47.633cc	**Gears**	Three speed	**Height (mm)**	930mm (36.6 in.)
Compression ratio	6.3:1 (9.5:1; Piuma Export)	**Final drive ratio**	2.786:1	**Seat height**	760mm (29.9 in.)
Carburetion	Dell'Orto T4 12 D1 (UA 15S Piuma Sport, Export)	**Front suspension**	Telescopic fork	**Dry weight**	Piuma: 47 kg, (103.5 lbs.) Sport: 49 kg (107.9 lbs.) Export: 50 kg (110.1 lbs.)
Power	Piuma: 1.5 horsepower Sport, Export: 4.2 horsepower	**Rear suspension**	Twin-shock swingarm	**Top speed**	Piuma: 50 km/h (31.1 mph) Sport, Export: 80 km/h (49.7 mph)
Maximum revs	Piuma: 5,200 rpm Sport: 8,600 rpm	**Brakes**	Drum 90 mm (3.5 in.) Export: 105mm (4.1 in.)		

the angular gas tank and headlight of the similar Brisk that year. Styling touches extended to white-walled tires.

There was also a Piuma Export from 1962, initially with the lower-output Piuma engine, but in a chassis with an integrated headlight, dual seat, larger brakes, and fully enclosed drive chain. U.S. examples included the higher-specification 48 Sport engine. For England, the Piuma Export was known as the Puma De-Luxe, and came with 19-inch wheels.

Apart from the three-speed transmission operated by the handlebar grip, and deeper fenders, the 48 Piuma was identical to the 48 Brisk.

48 Sport (Falcon 50)

For 1962, three more 48cc models were available alongside the Brisk and Piuma. These were the 48 Sport, and similar 48 Sport Export and 48 Sport USA. Compared to the Brisk and Piuma, the 48 Sport was a mini motorcycle, with a tubular steel duplex cradle frame, and clip-on handlebars. The 48 Export 9.6-liter gas tank mirrored the 200 Élite, while the domestic 48 Sport included a 12-liter 250 Diana-style tank and different side covers. Both versions had twin rear shock absorbers that featured exposed springs, and 19-inch wheels. Starting was by a kickstart or pedals, but setting the 48 Sport apart from the mopeds was the higher-compression engine with downdraft Dell'Orto carburetor and polished alloy bell mouth. There was a speedometer incorporated in the headlight, and the three-speed gearshift was still hand operated. For the U.S. the 48 Sport was titled the Falcon 50, and included the 12-liter gas tank, a solo saddle, 18-inch wheels, and a kickstart. For 1963, it also featured the

The 48 Sport Export of 1962 stood out among a myriad of small two-stroke models. From the downdraft carburetor to double-cradle frame and Élite-style gas tank, the 48 Sport looked like it meant business.

single-downtube frame of the 80 Setter, using the engine as a stressed member, much like the ohc singles. This frame was also used on the Italian market 48 Sport, while the Export model continued with the duplex frame and

48 Sport (Falcon 50) 1962-65

Engine	Single cylinder piston-port two-stroke, air-cooled (fan-cooled from 1964)	Power	4.2 horsepower	Rear suspension	Twin shock swingarm
		Maximum revs	8,600 rpm	Brakes (mm)	Drum 105 mm (4.1 in.)
Bore	38mm	Spark plug	Marelli CW260N	Tires	2.25 x 19 (2.25 x 18; U.S.)
Stroke	42mm	Ignition (degrees)	6v-18w flywheel magneto, 15-18	Dry weight	49 kg (107.9 lbs.) U.S.: 50 kg (110.1 lbs.) Export: 54 kg (118.9 lbs.)
Displacement	47.633cc	Clutch	Wet multiplate		
Compression ratio	9.5:1	Gears	Three speed	Top speed	80 km/h (49.7 mph)
Carburetion	Dell'Orto UA 15S	Front suspension	Telescopic fork	Colors	Red and bronze

sculpted gas tank. To further confuse identification, some 48 Sports featured cylinder heads without the downdraft carburetor.

There were a number of changes to the 48 Sport and 50 Falcon for 1964. The engine received fan cooling, with the fan driven by an alloy plate bolted to the flywheel magneto, and a metal shroud around the cylinder and cylinder head. The carburetor was no longer a downdraft design, and the frame was again the dual-cradle type. The Falcon retained the 12-litre gas tank, but included the sporting saddle of the 48 SL. In 1966, the fan-cooled 48s were discontinued and the Sport and Falcon didn't survive the transition to the new air-cooled 50 model.

The 1963 Falcon 50 for the U.S. included a solo seat, single downtube frame, and kickstart.

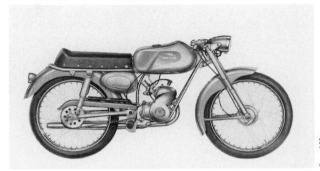

For 1964, the 48 Sport received fan cooling, but was otherwise unchanged.

80 Setter, 80 Sport

At the same time as the 48 Sport hit the showrooms, Ducati released the 80 Setter (Super Falcon 80 in the US). Styled similarly to the domestic market 48 Sport (with a 12-liter gas tank), the 80 Setter included a single downtube frame (using the engine as a stressed member), and deeper fenders. While the 48 Sport was nicely executed little sporting machine, the 80 Setter failed to find a market. The power was similar to the 48 Sport, but with more weigh the performance was inferior. There was a higher-performance 80 Sport version available for 1963, with clip-on handlebars and a more sporting gas tank (similar to the later Cadet). Even this didn't entice buyers in America and England, where it wasn't offered after 1963. In Italy, the 80 Setter and Sport were available until 1966, along with a similar 80 Mountaineer.

The largest two-stroke of the early 1960s was the 80 Setter or Super Falcon 80, but it proved less popular than the 50s.

80 Setter, 80 Sport 1962-66

Engine	Single cylinder piston-port two-stroke, air-cooled	Power	4.25 horsepower (5.5 HP)	Rear suspension	Twin-shock swingarm
Bore	47mm	Maximum revs	7,200 rpm (7,800 rpm)	Brakes	Drum 118mm (4.6 in.)
Stroke	46mm	Spark plug	Marelli CW225N	Tires	2.25 x 18, 2.50 x 17
Displacement	79.807cc	Ignition	6v-30w flywheel magneto	Dry weight	62 kg (136.6 lbs.)
Compression ratio	7.1:1	Clutch	Wet multiplate	Speed	75 km/h (46.6 mph)
Carburetion	Dell'Orto ME 15BS	Gears	Three speed	Colors	Blue and silver
		Front suspension	Telescopic fork		

48 SL 1964-68, 48 Cacciatore

Created specifically for the Italian market in 1964, the 48 SL combined components from the 48 Sport and 80 Setter. The 48 Sport fan-cooled engine was detuned to pass the 1.5-horsepower limit, and placed in a duplex frame with 80 Setter wheels and brakes. There was a new 11.6-liter tank, and sporting saddle and side covers. The gas tank was shared with the 90 Cacciatore and 90 Cadet. The 48 SL continued with the fan-cooled engine (and pedal starting) into 1967, styled like the 50 SL/1, with a higher exhaust (on the left) and exposed fork springs. Another version shared the styling of the 50 SL/2A, with higher handlebars and a new saddle. The Cacciatore (also a Falcon in the U.S. to confuse everybody) was a dual-purpose model, based on the 48 SL, with universal tires, higher braced handlebar, higher exhaust on the left, solo saddle, rear rack, and dual rear sprockets. None of these 48cc examples received the upgraded 50cc engine of the 50 SL from 1966.

One of the more interesting two-strokes of the era was the 1967 48 SL. While the SL still retained the earlier fan-cooled engine, the gas tank and exposed fork springs lent it an air of purpose.

Another dual-purpose model was the 48 Cacciatore, based on the 48 SL of 1964-66. It was called the Falcon in the U.S.

The 1968 48 SL still featured the fan-cooled engine, but with styling similar to the 50/SL2A.

48 SL 1964-68, 48 Cacciatore 1964-68

Engine	Single cylinder piston-port two-stroke, fan-cooled	Power	1.3 horsepower	Front suspension	Telescopic fork
Bore	38mm	Maximum revs	4,300 rpm	Rear suspension	Twin-shock swingarm
Stroke	42mm	Spark plug	Marelli CW260N	Brakes	Drum 118 mm (4.6 in.)
Displacement	47.633cc	Ignition	6v-18w flywheel magneto	Tires	SL: 2.25 x 18, 2.50 x 17 Cacciatore: 2.50 x 18, 3.25/3.50 x 16
Compression ratio	9.5:1	Clutch	Wet multiplate		
Carburetion	Dell'Orto UA 15S	Gears	Three speed	Dry weight	SL: 58 kg (127.8 lbs.) Cacciatore: 63 kg (138.8 lbs.)

90 Cacciatore (Mountaineer), 90 Cadet (Falcon)

American demand for larger capacity models led to the 90 Cacciatore (Mountaineer in the U.S.) and 90 Cadet (yet another Falcon for the U.S.) late in 1963, as 1964 models. The 87cc fan-cooled engine was ostensibly identical to the 48cc unit, but with a higher output alternator and larger carburetor. The left engine cover incorporated a large orifice to allow hot air to escape. Because of this, the exhaust exited on the right rather than the left. Both the 90 Cadet and Mountaineer were based on the 48 Cacciatore, with hand gear change, the same gas tank, dual-cradle frame and solo seat with rack. Setting the larger versions apart were different wheel sizes.

Ducati Motor

For 1964, there was the fan-cooled 90 Mountaineer. It was very similar to the 48 Cacciatore.

90 Cadet 1964, 90 Cacciatore (Mountaineer) 1964

Engine	Single cylinder piston-port two-stroke, fan-cooled	Ignition (degrees)	6v-30w flywheel magneto, 16-18	Length	1,810mm (71.3 in.)	
Bore)	49mm	Clutch	Wet multiplate	Height	1,000mm (39.4 in.)	
Stroke	46mm	Gears	Three speed	Width	660mm (26 in.)	
Displacement	86.744cc	Front suspension	Telescopic fork	Seat height	750mm (29.6 in.)	
Compression ratio	8.5-9:1	Rear suspension	Twin-shock swingarm	Dry weight	Cadet: 66 kg (145.4 lbs.) Cacciatore: 68 kg (149.8 lbs.)	
Carburetion	Dell'Orto UA 18S	Brakes	Drum 118 mm (4.6 in.)	Top speed	90 km/h (56 mph)	
Power	6 horsepower	Tires	Cadet: 2.25 x 18, 2.50 x 18 Cacciatore: 2.50 x 16, 3.25/3.50 x 16;			
Maximum revs	7,000 rpm					
Spark plug	Marelli CW260N, Beru 260-14, KLG F-100	Wheelbase	1,160mm (45.7 in.)			

100 Mountaineer, 100 Cadet (Falcon)

After only one year the 90 Cadet and Mountaineer were replaced by the similar 100 Cadet and Mountaineer. The engine was bored to 94cc, but the power was unchanged. The 100 Cadet now featured a dual seat. More developments were in store for 1966, with the 100 Cadet and Mountaineer receiving a four-speed transmission, and finally a foot change on the right (by the traditional rocking pedal). Fan cooling remained this year.

Ducati Motor

The 90 Cadet grew to 100cc with the 100 Falcon of 1965, shown here in a period publicity photo.

100 CADET 1965-66, 100 MOUNTAINEER 1965-66

Engine	Single cylinder piston-port two-stroke, fan-cooled	Ignition	6v-30w flywheel magneto	Wheelbase	Cadet: 1,160mm (45.7 in.)
Bore	51mm	Clutch	Wet multiplate		Mountaineer: 1,170mm (46.1 in.)
Stroke	46mm	Gears	Three -speed (four-speed from 1966)	Length	Cadet: 1,810mm (46.5 in.)
Displacement	94cc	Front suspension	Telescopic fork		Mountaineer: 1,830mm (72 in.)
Compression ratio	10:1	Rear suspension	Twin-shock swingarm	Height	1,000mm (39.4 in.)
Carburetion	Dell'Orto UA 18S	Brakes	Drum 118mm (4.6 in.)	Width	Cadet: 660mm (26 in.)
Power	6 horsepower	Tires	Cadet: 2.25 x 18, 2.50 x 18		Mountaineer: 700mm (27.6 in.)
Maximum revs	7,000 rpm		Mountaineer: 2.50 x 16, 3.25/3.50 x 16;	Seat height	Cadet: 750mm (29.5 in.)
Spark plug	Marelli CW260N, Beru 260-14, KLG F-100				Mountaineer: 760mm (30 in.)

Brio and 3R Fattorino

Apparently undeterred by the disastrous Cruiser experience, Ducati released another scooter, the Brio, in 1963. This is the 48 Brio, with a shorter seat.

Ducati Motor

Intent on creating as many two-stroke variants as possible, the 48cc fan-cooled engine was drafted into the Brio scooter and 3R Fattorino (errand boy) Carrier during 1963. Harking back to the ill-fated Cruiser of 1952, the Brio was a genuine scooter in the Vespa and Lambretta mould, while the Carrier was a commercial three-wheeler available in several guises. These uninspiring machines were created primarily for the Italian market, but small numbers were exported and the 100 and 100/25 Brio were available in the U.S. between 1965 and 1967. Unfortunately for Ducati, by the time the Brio was released, the scooter boom had passed, and Brios weren't even particularly popular in Italy.

48/50 BRIO 1963-67, 100 BRIO (1964-65), 100/25 BRIO (1966-68)

Engine	Single cylinder piston-port two-stroke, fan-cooled	Carburetion	48/50: Dell'Orto SHA 14/12	Front suspension	Swinging shackle fork
Bore	48/50: 38mm		100, 100/25: (SHB 18/16)	Rear suspension	Swingarm with rubber shock absorbers
	100, 100/25: 51mm	Power	48/50: 1.5 horsepower	Brakes	Drum 105mm (4.1 in.)
Stroke	48/50: 42mm		100, 100/25: 7 horsepower	Tires	48/50: 2.75 x 9
	100, 100/25: 46mm	Maximum revs	5,200 rpm		2.45 x 8, 3.50 x 8
Displacement	48/50: 47.633cc	Ignition	48/50: 6v-18w flywheel magneto 100: (30w; 100 Brio)	Dry weight	48/50: 63.5 kg (139.9 lbs.)
	100, 100/25: 94cc				100: 80 kg (176.2 lbs.)
Compression ratio	48/50: 7:1	Clutch	Wet multiplate	Top speed	48/50: 50 km/h (31 mph)
	100, 100/25: (8.5:1, 10:1; 100/25)	Gears	Three speed		100, 100/25: 76 km/h (47.2 mph)

The 48 Brio was released in 1963, and joined by the 100 in 1964. The 48 had a shorter rear engine cover and seat, and larger-diameter steel disc wheels, but was similar to the 100. For 1966 the 100 brio became the 100/25 (with a higher compression ratio), lasting until 1968, while the 48 Brio became the 50 Brio for 1967 (with a slightly larger 49.6cc engine). Although the 100 Cadet and Mountaineer received a four-speed gearbox, all Brios remained three-speed throughout their life.

50 SL, 50 SL/1, 50 SL/2, 50 SL/1A, 50 SL/2A

It may have only displaced 50cc, but the 50 SL/1 of 1967 was a beautiful, and extremely purposeful, machine.

While the two-stroke era was characterized by a range of unspectacular machines that were unable to counter the Japanese onslaught during the 1960s, Ducati did manage to produce some interesting small capacity two-strokes. Some of these were variations on the new 50 SL of 1966. The 50 SL itself was another bland rendition of the 48 SL, but with a new air-cooled engine, and the angular styling (fenders and headlight) that was prevalent that year. The 1966 version had a lower exhaust, and the 1967 a higher pipe, both on the right.

The most important developments were to the engine, without fan-cooling, and incorporating a foot-operated four-speed gearbox. The 50 SL was joined by a sporting 50 SL/1 at the end of 1966, with a long gas tank and abbreviated saddle. The tank featured twin filler caps, and the front fork had exposed springs. The cylinder head was new, the barrel included cross ports, and there was a higher compression ratio. The carburetor breathed through an alloy bellmouth, there was a low sporting handlebar, and the option of a low or high exhaust pipe with heat shield. It may have only been 50cc, but the 50 SL/1 was one of the most purposeful-looking Ducatis of the era. For 1968, the 50 SL1/A received a revised front fender, but was otherwise unchanged.

Other variations of the 50 SL followed—all with the higher-compression engine and carburetor without an air filter. The 50 SL/2 had its own distinctive sculptured gas tank, but was a touring model with high handlebars and a high exhaust pipe. A sporting 50 SL/1A, with a racing style saddle and single filler fuel tank, emanated from the 50 SL/1, while the 50 SL/2A was the same 50 cc engine sharing the chassis and styling of the 1968 48 SL. Most of these models were intended for the domestic market and few appeared outside Italy.

The long gas tank and twin filler caps accentuated the sporting nature of the 50 SL/1.

50 SL, SL/1, SL/2, SL/1A, SL/2A 1966-68

Engine	Single cylinder piston-port two-stroke, air-cooled	Carburetion	Dell'Orto SHA 14/12 SL/1, SL/2: (UA 18S, UAO 18S; SL/1 and SL/2)	Front suspension	Telescopic fork
Bore	38.8mm	Power	4.2 horsepower (6 hp)	Rear suspension	Twin-shock swingarm
Stroke	42mm	Maximum revs	8,600 rpm	Tires	2.25 x 19
Displacement	49.660cc	Clutch	Wet multiplate	Dry weight	58 kg (127.8 lbs.) 1A and 2A: (61 kg; 1A and 2A) (134.4 lbs.)
Compression ratio	9.5:1 (11:1)	Gears	Four speed	Top speed	80 km/h (49.7 mph)

The final variant of the 50 SL lineage was the touring 50 SL/2A of 1968.

The 50 SL, a development of the 48 SL, had a foot-operated four-speed gearbox and was air-cooled.

Ducati Motor

The 50 SL/2 was a more touring-oriented version of the 50 SL, with a high exhaust and handlebar.

Ducati Motor

The 50 SL/1A replaced the 50 SL/1 for 1968. It still had clip-on handlebars and exposed fork springs, but with a more conventional gas tank.

100 CADET AND 100 MOUNTAINEER (1967-69)

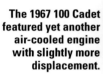

The 1967 100 Cadet featured yet another air-cooled engine with slightly more displacement.

Phil Aynsley; Two Wheels

100 CADET 1967-9, 100 MOUNTAINEER 1967-69

Engine	Single cylinder piston-port two-stroke, air-cooled	**Gears**	Four-speed, 3.27:1, 1.94:1, 1.34:1, 1.04:1	**Height**	1,000mm (39.4 in.)	
Bore	52mm	**Front suspension**	Telescopic fork	**Width**	Cadet: 660mm (26 in.) Mountaineer: 700mm (27.6 in.)	
Stroke	46mm	**Rear suspension**	Twin-shock swingarm			
Displacement	97.69cc	**Brakes**	Drum 118mm (4.6 in.)	**Seat height**	Cadet: 750mm (29.5 in.) Mountaineer: 760mm (29.9 in.)	
Compression ratio	11.2:1	**Tires**	Cadet: 2.25 x 18, 2.50 x 18 Mountaineer: 2.50 x 16, 3.25/3.50 x 16			
Carburetion	Dell'Orto UBF 24 BS			**Dry weight**	Cadet: 66 kg (145.4 lbs.) Mountaineer: 68 kg (149.8 lbs.)	
Power	7.2 horsepower at 6,250 rpm	**Wheelbase**	1,160 mm (45.7 in.) (1,170) mm (46 in.)	**Top speed**	90 km/h (55.9 mph)	
Ignition	Flywheel magneto 6v/25w	**Length**	Cadet: 1,810mm (71.3 in.) Mountaineer: 1,830mm (72 in.)	**Colors**	Red frame, red and silver (Mountaineer)	
Clutch	Wet multiplate					

Phil Aynsley, Two Wheels

Sharing the new engine was the 100 Mountaineer, but otherwise this was very similar to the previous model.

For 1967 the two-stroke Cadet and Mountaineer received their fourth engine development in as many years, although the earlier fan-cooled versions were sold in the U.S. through 1967. The revised engine had a new cylinder head and chrome-plated cylinder, and was no longer fan-cooled. Another bore increase saw more displacement, and there was a larger carburetor. Apart from the new engine both the 100 Cadet and Mountaineer were unchanged.

ROLLY

With its single-speed 50cc two-stroke engine, the Rolly moped was another machine that failed to hit the target.

Joining the single speed 48 Brisk for 1968 was the Rolly, with the same single-speed engine in a steel chassis with no rear suspension. The front fork was a rudimentary hydraulic telescopic and the headlight the later Piuma angular type. The Rolly continued after the demise of the Brisk, but by this time there was no market for mopeds.

ROLLY 1968

Engine	Single cylinder piston-port two-stroke, air-cooled		Power	4.5 horsepower		Front suspension	Telescopic fork
Bore	38mm		Maximum revs	5,200 rpm		Rear suspension	Rigid
Stroke	42mm		Spark plug	Marelli CW 225N		Brakes	Drum 90mm (3.5 in.)
Displacement	47.633cc		Generator	6v-18w flywheel magneto		Tires	2.00 x 18
Carburetion	Dell'Orto UA 18S (UFB 24BS)		Clutch	Wet multiplate		Dry weight	42 kg (92.5 lbs.)
			Gears	Single speed		Top speed	50 km/h (31 mph)

50 and 100 Scrambler

The final small-capacity two-strokes of the 1960s were the 50 and 100 Scrambler. This is the 100 of 1969.

Ducati Motor

Although the production of most two-stroke models ended at the end of 1968, the 50 SL and 100 Mountaineer engines continued in two Scramblers, the 50 Scrambler and 100 Scrambler. Produced in response to the then current fashion for dual-purpose motorcycles in Italy, like the earlier Brio, producing the Scrambler was a misguided idea. The 50 Scrambler was styled similarly to the four-stroke 125 Cadet Scrambler, while the 100 had a different gas tank and racing number side panels. While the frame was the same dual cradle type of the Cadet and SL, the front fork was a more modern Ceriani type with exposed fork tubes. Both Scramblers included a high-rise exhaust and a high front fender, and although the 50 included a metal grill over the headlight, these were not really serious off-road motorcycles. The 50 and 100 Scramblers weren't particularly popular and by 1970, Ducati's new management decided the future lay in more-profitable, larger-displacement motorcycles. The two-strokes eventually died, for a short while at least, although the 50 Scrambler lasted through until 1973.

PRODUCTION	1973
50 Scrambler	179

50 SCRAMBLER, 100 SCRAMBLER 1969-73

Engine	Single cylinder piston-port two-stroke, air-cooled	**Power**	3.27 horsepower (6.27 hp)	**Brakes mm**	Drum 118mm (4.6 in.)
Bore	50: 38.8mm 100: 52mm	**Maximum revs**	50: 6,500 rpm 100: 6,000 rpm	**Tires**	50: 2.50 x 18, 2.50 x 17 100: 2.75 x 18, 3.75 x 16
Stroke	50: 42 100: 46mm	**Ignition**	6v/18w (30w) flywheel magneto	**Wheelbase**	50: 1,150mm (45.3 in.) 100: 1,180mm (46.5 in.)
Displacement	50: 49.66cc 100: 97.69cc	**Clutch**	Wet multiplate	**Length**	50: 1,770mm (69.7 in.) 100: 1,840mm (72.4 in.)
Compression ratio	50: 10.5:1 100: 11.2:1	**Gears**	Four-speed	**Width**	800mm (31.5 in.)
Carburetion	Dell'Orto UBF 24 BS	**Front suspension**	Telescopic fork	**Seat height**	730mm (28.7 in.)
		Rear suspension	Twin-shock swingarm	**Dry weight**	50: 70 kg (154.2 lbs.) 100: (71) kg (156.4 lbs.)

125 Regolarità

The 1960 and 1970s were characterized by a number of dubious production and marketing decisions, and 1975 was a particularly low point. That year saw the entire range of overhead-camshaft singles disappear, and the 125 Regolarità left as the only Ducati single. Although two 125cc two-strokes were initially envisaged—the 125 Sperimentale street bike and the 125 Regolarità Six Days—only the Regolarità made it into production. For a company with little experience in off-road competition the Regolarità was an ambitious undertaking and suffered because it wasn't a serious off-road competition machine.

Powering the 125 Regolarità was an all-new two-stroke engine, with a chrome bore and the usual built-up crankshaft running in needle roller and ball bearings. There was also a needle roller bearing on the wrist-pin.

The 125 Regolarità of 1975 looked impressive, but was only a half-hearted attempt to produce a real off-road machine.

125 REGOLARITÀ SIX DAYS 1975-79

Engine	Single cylinder piston-port two-stroke, air-cooled	**Electrical system**	6v/75w flywheel magneto, 6v 7Ah battery	**Tires**	3.00 x 21, 3.75 x 18 Metzeler Six Days
Bore	54mm	**Clutch**	Wet multiplate	**Wheelbase**	1,420mm (56 in.)
Stroke	54mm	**Gears**	Six-speed	**Length**	2,160mm (85 in.)
Displacement	123.7cc	**Front suspension**	Telescopic fork	**Width**	920mm (36.2 in.)
Compression ratio	10.5:1	**Rear suspension**	Twin-shock swingarm	**Dry weight**	108 kg (237.9 lbs.)
Carburetion	Dell'Orto PHB 30	**Brakes**	Drum 125 mm (front) (4.9 in.) 140 mm (rear) (5.5 in.)	**Top speed**	120 km/h (74.6 mph)

The rear suspension included twin oleo pneumatic remote reservoir Marzocchi shock absorbers. The frame was a double-cradle type, with a large-diameter backbone tube, but although there was a protective plate for the exhaust pipe, the low exhaust limited the usefulness of the Regolarità off-road. And while other manufacturers were including automatic oiling, the Regolarità still required 5 percent premix in the tiny 6-liter gas tank. The 6-volt electrical system was also marginal.

The 125 Regolarità was produced primarily for Italy and France, and only small numbers were produced through until 1979.

PRODUCTION	1975	1976	1977	1978	1979
125 Italy	1,149	694			
125 France	460	483	300	300	100
Total	1,609	1,177	300	300	100

125 SIX DAYS

Although an improved model, the 125 Six Days of 1977 was even less successful than the Regolarità. New for the Six Days was an 8-liter aluminum gas tank, with vented filler cap, and a proper enduro high exhaust exiting on the left. The twin Marzocchi shock absorbers were mounted with the reservoirs at the top, with a choice of four mounting positions on the frame and swingarm. While the redesigned frame was stronger, the suspension was still obsolete, and despite more power and less weight, the 125 Six Days was a failure.

This bike was not one of the more memorable Ducatis, and with the death of the Six Days, so ended the era of the Ducati two-stroke.

PRODUCTION	1977	1978	1979
125 6 Days Italy	998		150
125 6 Days France		300	
Total	998	300	150

Although an improvement on the Regolarità, the 125 Six Days didn't convince detractors that Ducati could build a competitive enduro motorcycle.

125 SIX DAYS 1977-79

Engine	Single cylinder piston-port two-stroke, air-cooled	**Electrical system**	6v/75w flywheel magneto, 6v 4Ah battery	**Tires**	3.00 x 21, 4.00 x 18 Cross-Enduro
Bore	54mm	**Clutch**	Wet multiplate	**Wheelbase (mm)**	1,430mm (56.3 in.)
Stroke	54mm	**Gears**	Six-speed	**Length**	2,120mm (83.5 in.)
Displacement	123.7cc	**Front suspension**	Telescopic fork	**Width**	950mm (37.4 in.)
Compression ratio	14.5:1	**Rear suspension**	Twin shock swingarm	**Dry weight**	97 kg (213.7 lbs.)
Carburetion	Bing 32	**Brakes**	Drum 125mm (front (4.9 in.) 140 mm (rear) (5.5 in.)	**Maximum speed**	110 km/h (68.4 mph)

CHAPTER 4

OVERHEAD-CAMSHAFT SINGLES (WIDE-CASE) AND PARALLEL TWINS

Although Ducati struggled through the 1960s, and concentrated on producing two-strokes, the overhead camshaft single was further developed during 1967. The result was the "wide-case" single, and the new engine made its first appearance in the 350 Scrambler. Soon there was a 250 Scrambler, 350 Sebring, and 250 Monza, 250 and 350 Mark 3's, and Desmos. Although the same basic overhead camshaft engine architecture was retained, the revised crankcases were much wider at the rear where it mounted the frame. The sump capacity was increased to 2.5 liters, and the kickstart was much stronger, as was the new rear frame section. While strength and reliability was improved, the new singles were also heavier than their predecessors. As with many Ducati designs, the wide-case singles emanated from racing designs, in this case the SCD.

250 and 350 SCD (Sport Corsa Desmo)

Unlike the 250 and 350 SC, the 350 SCD (Desmo) featured a single-downtube frame.

At Daytona in March 1967, Ducati entered seven SCDs, six 250s and one 350, but the desmodromic Ducatis failed the AMA technical inspection as the valve system was considered "a change in basic design." The Desmos didn't race but Ducati received a lot of publicity. These SCDs were quite different to the earlier SC, and were a precursor to the new production wide crankcase singles. Rather than special sand-cast crankcases, to save weight and cost, the SCD featured regular diecast crankcases with a standard ratio five-speed gearbox. This had six selector dogs rather than five, and there were the usual straight-cut primary drive gears and wet multi-plate clutch. Both the 250 and 350 SCD were virtually identical, sharing the 135mm con-rod and larger diameter stepped crankpin (30/32mm). The cylinder head was from the 250 F3 and 250 SC (already set up for desmodromic valve gear), with the exhaust retained by studs and with twin spark plug ignition. There was also an external oil delivery from the cylinder head to the crankcase, just inboard of the timing case.

Like the production overhead camshaft singles the SCD also had a single downtube frame, but it was constructed of chrome-molybdenum without a loop over the swingarm pivot. There were special shorter 35mm Marzocchi forks with alloy fork legs and a steel lower triple clamp, the fork tubes no longer stepped, and similar to those on the Scrambler. Only a few SCDs were produced, and some were developed into successful racers, particularly by Reno Leoni in the U.S.

250 AND 350 SCD 1967-8

Engine	Single cylinder four-stroke, air-cooled	Power	250: 35 horsepower at 11,500 rpm 350: 41 horsepower at 10,500 rpm	Gears	Five-speed
Bore (mm)	250: 74mm 350: 76mm			Front suspension	Marzocchi 35mm telescopic fork
Stroke (mm)	250: 57.8 350: 75	Generator	30 watt	Rear suspension	Swingarm with twin shock absorbers
Displacement (cc)	340: 248.6	Ignition	Battery and coil, twin plugs	Brakes	Oldani
Valve actuation	Single desmodromic overhead camshaft driven by a shaft and bevel gears	Clutch	Wet multiplate	Wheels	18-in.
		Primary Drive	Straight cut gear		

250 and 350 Scrambler (1967-75)

Ducati Motor

The 1968 250 Scrambler for the U.S. had a different gas tank and seat.

Less than a year after the SCD made its first appearance, so did the new-generation wide crankcase production overhead-camshaft single. As with the narrow-case singles, there were several similar wide-case versions in varying capacities. The 350 Scrambler was the first wide-case model available, with production beginning before the end of 1967. In the U.S. for 1968, the Scrambler was sold alongside the narrow-case 250 Monza, Mark 3, and 350 Sebring. The 1968 250 and 350 Scramblers were more road-oriented than before, with a 19-inch front wheel and

Silentium muffler. Early U.S. examples were also fitted with a less restrictive silencer on a longer exhaust header pipe.

The basic engine specifications were unchanged for the 250 Scrambler, but the first examples had a smaller-diameter (27/31mm) stepped crankpin. At the end of 1969 this was changed to the straight 30mm crankpin of the 350, but the 250 retained the full circle flywheels. The 350 crank flywheels were full circle on the right, and flattened on the drive side. Both used a 136mm con-rod. The Scrambler still featured shim valve adjustment,

and the 250 included 36 and 33mm valves, while the 350 Scrambler had 40 and 36mm valves, and a three-ring Borgo piston. The earliest 1968 Scramblers also had flywheel magneto ignition and a small 7Ah battery to power the lights, but after engine 105001 (250) and 05106 (350) there was a 70-watt alternator and battery and coil ignition with an electronic regulator. With the wide-case engine came a larger drive-side main bearing (30 x 72 x 19mm), although until engine number 108620 (250) and 11051 (350) the right-side main bearing was still the smaller 30 x 62 x 16mm as used on both sides of the narrow-case singles. Towards the end of 1970, after

Ducati Motor

By 1973 the 250 Scrambler included alloy wheel rims and a Spanish Amal carburetor.

108621 (250) and 11052 (350), both main bearings were standardized to the larger size. The 350 Scrambler had stronger (59.5-lb.) exhaust valve springs, and a valve lifter to aid starting. The five-speed gearbox was similar to the narrow-case, but with a slightly higher-ratio first gear.

By 1970, the Silentium muffler was reshaped, with a sharp cut-off at the end rather than the earlier cigar shape. All the 1968 Scramblers also came with Dell'Orto SS remote float bowl carburetors, and small (100mm) round air filters. The engine number sequence continued where the narrow-case ended, but with the numbers stamped on the right crankcase.

The steering head bearings on early Scramblers were 14mm ball races, but soon these were changed to 16mm. The front fork was a newer Marzocchi design, with the fork springs inside the tubes. Initially they came with 315mm Marzocchi shock absorbers, later replaced by 310mm items, with the option of a rigid strut as before. Both the front fork and rear shock absorbers had protective rubber gaiters. U.S. scramblers had a round CEV taillight, while European versions featured the rectangular style, and until

350 SCR number 5105 there was an off switch fitted to the taillight bracket. After number 5106 there was also a new taillight bracket, with a single mounting point to the frame for European models. Until 350 SCR number 05495, the 100-mph (or 160 km/h) Veglia speedometer was incorporated in an Aprilia headlight shell, but from 05496 on the speedometer was mounted on the top triple clamp.

When it came to styling, there were a few variations of the early wide-case 250 and 350 Scrambler. Early 1968 examples had a similar gas tank to the last narrow-case Scrambler, with a Giuliari saddle. Soon after they were released they were restyled, with a new 11-liter gas tank with silver painted panels and screwed-on badges. The 350 also became the 350SSS (Street Scrambler Sport) for the U.S. market in 1969.

The next year saw the introduction of the 450 Scrambler and few changes to the 250 and 350. During 1970, a Dell'Orto VHB square-slide carburetor replaced the SS-type. The 350 received a 29mm VHB carburetor, while the 250 was downsized to 26mm, but, unlike the

Ducati Motor

The first wide-case single was the Scrambler of 1968, in 250 (shown here) or 350. The style of the as tank was similar to the narrow-case, and there was no muffler on this example.

250, 350 SCRAMBLER 1967-75

Engine	Single cylinder four-stroke, air-cooled	**Power**	19 horsepower at 7,000 rpm (7,500)	**Brakes**	Drum 180 x 35mm front (7.1 x 1.4 in.) 160 x 30mm rear (6.3 x 1.2 in.)
Bore	250: 74mm 350: 76mm	**Spark plug**	Marelli CW260N, Lodge 2HN	**Tires**	3.50 x 19, 4.00 x 18 Pirelli
Stroke	250: 57.8mm 350: 75mm	**Generator**	6v/30W (6v/70W after # 05106)	**Wheelbase**	1,380mm (54.3 in.)
Displacement	250: 248.6cc 350: 340.2cc	**Ignition (degrees)**	Points and coil; 5-8 static, 33-36 total Electronic from 1973 (350)	**Length**	2,120mm (83.5 in.)
Compression ratio	250: 9.2:1 350: 10:1			**Height**	1,150mm (45.3 in.)
Valve actuation	Bevel gear-driven overhead camshaft	**Battery**	SAFA 3L3 13.5 Ah (Yuasa B38, Varta 01490)	**Width**	940mm (37 in.)
Valve timing (degrees)	250: 27, 75, 60, 32 (coded white) 350: 65, 76, 80, 50 (1968) 70, 84, 80, 64 (coded white and green from 1969)	**Primary drive**	250: 2.500:1 (24:60) 350: 2.111:1 (27/57)	**Seat height**	770mm (30.3 in.)
		Clutch	Wet multiplate	**Dry weight**	250: 132kg (290.7 lbs.) 350: 133kg (293 lbs.)
		Gear ratios	0.97, 1.10, 1.35, 1.73, 2.46	**Colors**	1968: red and silver, black frame 1969-after: Black, white, yellow, orange.
Carburetion	Dell'Orto SS1 27D (SS1 29D; 350) Dell'Orto VHB 26 BD (VHB 29 AD; 350) from 1970 Amal 27mm (250 from 1973)	**Final drive**	250: 3.000:1 350: 3.214:1		
		Front suspension	35mm Marzocchi fork (515mm, later 540mm)	**Engine numbers**	From DM250 104501 From DM350 05001 approx.
		Rear suspension	Three-way adjustable Marzocchi 315 (310)mm twin-shock swingarm		

PRODUCTION	1973	1974	1975	TOTAL
250 Scrambler	200	200	112	512
350 Scrambler	1,156	331	248	1,735

450, the 250 and 350 Scramblers retained the smaller air filter. The silver gas tank panels were reshaped and a CEV tachometer joined the CEV speedometer on the top triple clamp. On yellow-painted examples the tank panels were chrome plated. There was also a new muffler from 1969The cigar shape returned on some examples, while others had a choice of a short or long Silentium with the cut-off end. One theme characterized Ducatis of this period: inconsistency in exact specification.

From 1971, some Scramblers included removable plastic toolboxes on each side. This year there was a new round CEV taillight with the bracket attaching to the steel fender. The front fork was also slightly longer this year. Small developments continued from May 1973. The wheel rims became alloy Borrani, and the 250 received a larger (27mm) Spanish Amal carburetor with the larger round air filter of the 450. There was no change to the 250 chassis, and it retained the same headlight, brakes and suspension as the earlier model (for a while at least, until stocks ran out).

Also, from May 1973, the 350 Scrambler was updated with many components from the Mark 3 of the same year. The 35mm Marzocchi front fork had exposed fork tubes and black-painted legs, there was a new cut down front fender, and the front brake was a four leading shoe. There were no longer protective covers for the rear shock absorbers, and the throttle, handgrips, and CEV headlight were new. Also setting these final 350 Scramblers apart were the larger air cleaner, and fiberglass side covers. From the end of 1972 they received Motoplat or Ducati Energia electronic ignition, and from 1973 the tachometer drive on the bevel gear cover was a one-piece casting. This year also saw the 250 Scrambler receive side covers and Spanish Telesco forks without gaiters. The engines for the final 250 Scramblers were built by Mototrans in Spain, and continued with the battery and points ignition. After 1974, the 350 Scrambler engines were also supplied by Mototrans, with only the 450s built at Borgo Panigale.

250 Monza, 350 Sebring 1968

There was very little to distinguish the wide-case 350 Sebring and 250 Monza. Both these models appeared only in 1968.

250 MONZA, 350 SEBRING 1968

Engine	Single cylinder four-stroke, air-cooled	**Spark plug**	Marelli CW260N, Lodge 2HN	**Rear suspension**	Three-way adjustable Marzocchi twin-shock swingarm
Bore	250: 74mm 350: 76mm	**Generator**	6v/70W	**Brakes**	Front: Drum 180 x 35mm (7.1 x 1.4 in.) Rear: Drum 160 x 30mm (6.3 x 1.2 in.)
Stroke	250: 57.8 350: 75	**Ignition (degrees)**	0 static, 28 total		
		Battery	SAFA 3L3		
Displacement	250: 248.6cc 350: 340.2cc	**Primary drive**	250: 2.500:1 (24:60) 350: 2.111:1 (27/57)	**Tires**	2.75 x 18, 3.00 x 18
Compression ratio	250: 9.2:1 350:9.5:1	**Clutch**	Wet multiplate	**Wheelbase**	1,365mm (53.5 in.)
Valve actuation	Bevel gear-driven overhead camshaft	**Gear ratios**	0.97, 1.10, 1.35, 1.73, 2.46	**Length**	2,000mm (78.7 in.)
				Width	850mm (33.5 in.)
Valve timing (degrees)	20, 70, 50, 30 (coded violet)	**Final drive**	3.008:1 (3.214:1)	**Seat height**	800mm (31.5 in.)
Carburetion	250: Dell'Orto SS1 27D 350: SS1 29D	**Front suspension**	31.5mm Ducati telescopic fork	**Dry weight**	127 kg (279.7 lbs.)
				Colors	Black, red, or green

The early wide-case Scramblers may have looked similar to their immediate predecessors, but the wide-case 250 Monza and 350 Sebring looked virtually identical. It took a sharp eye to notice the new side cover toolboxes and rear frame section. The Monza and Sebring retained the earlier fork and shock absorbers, painted to match the other cycle parts, and angular Aprilia headlight with speedometer incorporated in the shell. U.S. versions featured a sealed beam headlight. The fenders were also the earlier angular type. The engine specifications were also similar to the previous models, retaining screw and locknut valve adjustment. The 250 Monza initially had a 27mm crankpin, but this was later 30mm, and smaller diameter valves. Carburetion was by Dell'Orto SS, with a round 114mm air filter, and the electrical system was the same as the second series Scrambler, with an electronic regulator. These two models seemed to have been created to use up a supply of spare parts, and they only lasted for one year. Towards the end of the production run some

Monzas were also fitted with Mark 3 saddle, stainless-steel fenders and single filler cap gas tank, possibly because earlier stock was depleted.

After the introduction of the wide-case single the 250 Monza continued, visually similar except for the rear engine supports and side covers.

239, 250, 350 Mark 3 (1968-75)

A gradual evolution of the Mark 3 saw a new gas tank and seat on the 350 Mark 3 for 1972.

The 250 Diana Mark 3 narrow-case was available in the U.S. during 1968, while the wide-case 250 and 350 Mark 3 were produced for Europe. The engine specifications for the 250 were similar to the narrow-case Mark 3, and the 350 Mark 3 engine was shared with the 350 Scrambler. Specifications included shim valve adjustment, and both models featured 40 and 36mm valves. Unlike the 250 Scrambler, the 250 Mark 3 also included a 29mm SS1 carburetor without an air filter. The muffler was the cigar

type in 1968. The power was similar to the narrow-case, and the weight was up, the 250 was an unremarkable performer. The 350 assumed the role of high-performance single previously reserved for the 250 Mark 3, but both were really overshadowed by the Desmo versions.

1968 Mark 3's featured the same 31.5mm Ducati fork, steel 18-inch wheels, and Veglia tachometer of the earlier Mark 3. The speedometer was also in the headlight shell.

250, 350 MARK 3 1968-75, 239 MARK 3 1974-5

Engine	Single cylinder four-stroke, air-cooled	**Spark plug**	Marelli CW260N, Lodge 2HN	**Tires**	2.75 x 18, 3.00 x 18
Bore	250: 74mm 350: 76mm 239: 72.5mm	**Generator**	6v/30W (6v/70W after # 05106)	**Wheelbase**	1,360mm (53.6 in.)
Stroke	250: 57.8 350: 75	**Ignition (degrees)**	Points and coil; 5-8 static, 33-36 total Electronic from 1973	**Length**	2,000mm (78.7 in.)
				Height	940mm (37 in.)
Displacement	250: 248.6 350: 340.2	**Battery**	250: SAFA 3L3 13.5 Ah 350: Yuasa B38 12 Ah	**Width**	600mm (23.6 in.)
Compression ratio	250: 10:1 (9.7:1 from 1972) 350: 9.5:1 (10:1 from 1972)	**Primary drive**	250: 2.500:1 (24:60) 350: 2.111:1 (27:57)	**Seat height**	735mm (29 in.)
				Dry weight	127 kg (279.7 lbs.) 128 kg (282 lbs.)
Valve actuation	Bevel gear-driven overhead camshaft	**Clutch**	Wet multiplate	**Top speed**	143 km/h (88.9 mph) 170 km/h (105.6 mph)
		Gear ratios	0.97, 1.10, 1.35, 1.73, 2.46		
Valve timing (degrees)	250: 62, 76, 70, 48 (coded grey) 350: 70, 84, 80, 64 (coded white and green)	**Final drive**	250: 2.812:1 350: 3.214:1	**Colors**	1968; Red frame, red and chrome tank Silver fenders and headlight 1969-70 Black frame, red or yellow and chrome tank 1973-75 Black frame, blue and gold
		Front suspension	31.5mm Ducati fork (35mm Marzocchi fork from 1973)		
Carburetion	Dell'Orto SS1 29D Dell'Orto VHB 29 AD from 1970	**Rear suspension**	Three-way adjustable Marzocchi twin-shock swingarm		
				Engine numbers	From DM250M3 104501 From DM350M3 05001 approx
Power	20 horsepower at 8,000 rpm (22 hp at 7,500)	**Brakes**	Front: Drum 180 x 35mm (7.1 x 1.4 in.) Rear: Drum 160 x 30mm (6.3 x 1.2 in.)		

PRODUCTION	1973	1974	1975	TOTAL
250 Mark 3	353	183	150	686
350 Mark 3	476	324		800
239 Mark 3		150	100	250
Total	829	657	250	1,736

The 350 also included a valve lifter like the 350 Scrambler. Handlebars were clip-ons, although high bars were available. Apart from the painted steel fenders, the Mark 3 was visually similar to the Desmo also released that year. A unique feature of the 1968 250 and 350 1968 Mark 3's was the twin filler cap gas tank. Similar in style to that on the 50 SL/1 of 1967, this tank was also fitted to the 1968 Desmo and early 1969 examples. Most 1969 Mark 3's had the single filler gas tank, shared with the 450, and Mark 3's for the U.S. from 1970 had the Scrambler gas tank, along with high handlebars. While the 450 Mark 3 received a speedometer and tachometer mounted on the top triple clamp from 1969, the 250 and 350 Mark 3 retained the earlier white-faced Veglia tachometer and speedometer in the headlight shell. At some stage during 1970, the 250 and 350 Mark 3 incorporated the 450 instrument layout, but with shallower instrument housings.

The 1971 and 1972 Mark 3 received a reshaped larger (15-liter) gas tank, round CEV taillight, and smaller black plastic housings for the CEV instruments. Most developments appeared for 1973. Styling revisions saw a new gas tank, seat, and side covers, while the wheels were now alloy Borrani. There was a 35mm Marzocchi fork, a painted steel front fender with chrome stays, and a four leading shoe front brake (as fitted to the 1971 Desmo).

The headlight, taillight and instrument layout were new, there were detail changes to the frame and the ignition was electronic. Instruments were now either CEV or Smiths. For 1974, there was a smaller 239cc version of the 250 Mark 3 produced for the French market to circumvent taxes on motorcycles over 240cc. These 239s also used a Dell'Orto PHF 30mm carburetor, and had regular coil valve springs instead of hairpin versions. The electrical system was also 12-volt like that of the 450 TS. The 239 also received the stronger 450 frame, and while it was the most-developed of the overhead-camshaft singles, only a few were produced.

After 1971, the range of street singles was discontinued in the U.S. Berliner deciding to concentrate on the 450 R/T. For 1972 the street single made a return in the 250

"Road," which essentially identical to the Scrambler, but with a Mark 3 dual seat and frame. For 1973, the 250 was joined by a similar 350. The 250 and 350 "Road" were rather unusual models and incorporated a number of unique features. While the instruments and headlight were the usual CEV and Aprilia of the Mark 3, the headlight brackets were the wire type of the 750 GT. Both the U.S. 250 and 350 retained the single leading shoe front brake, 250 Scrambler-style front fender, Amal

carburetor, and a Conti exhaust like the 750 twin. The 350 also received electronic ignition. These U.S. singles also had a unique taillight, Telesco forks with exposed fork tubes and polished legs, and Spanish Akront alloy wheel rims. While the frame was that of the Scrambler, the swingarm incorporated the snail cam chain adjusters of the 450 R/T. Also, like the Scrambler and R/T, they had a steel sump guard. They didn't prove very popular and weren't offered in 1974.

250, 350 Mark 3 Desmo (1968-70)

The first production Desmo was the Mark 3 D of 1968. Only the 1968 Desmos had the red frame.

Richard Kennedy

During 1968, Fabio Taglioni realized his dream of producing the first production motorcycle with desmodromic valve gear. Previously reserved for racing machines, the desmodromic system was the same as used on the SCD of 1967, with a single four-lobe camshaft and four rockers. Hairpin valve springs were retained to assist starting, but these were the lighter 35.3-lb. type.

The Desmo used different camshaft timing, but in all other respects the engine was identical to the Mark 3. The chassis was also identical to the Mark 3, and it was only the chrome fenders and small "D" decal on the side covers that set the two apart. U.S. examples also featured a small CEV taillight rather than the rectangular style. Several options were available for the Desmo, including a

250, 350 MARK 3 DESMO 1968-70

Engine	Single cylinder four-stroke, air-cooled	**Ignition (degrees)**	Points and coil; 5-8 static, 33-36 total	**Length**	2,000mm (78.7 in.)
Bore	250: 74mm 350: 76mm	**Battery**	SAFA 3L3 13.5 Ah	**Height**	940mm (37 in.)
Stroke	250: 57.8 350: 75	**Primary drive**	250: 2.500:1 (24:60); 350: 2.111:1 (27:57)	**Width**	600mm (23.6 in.)
Displacement	250: 248.6 350: 340.2	**Clutch**	Wet multiplate	**Seat height**	735mm (29 in.)
Compression ratio	10:1	**Gear ratios**	0.97, 1.10, 1.35, 1.73, 2.46	**Dry weight**	250: 127kg (279.7 lbs.) 350: 128kg (282 lbs.)
Valve actuation	Bevel gear driven overhead desmodromic camshaft	**Final drive**	250: 2.812:1 350: 3.214:1	**Top speed**	250: 150 km/h (93.2 mph) 350: 165 km/h 180 with megaphone (102.5 mph)
Valve timing (degrees)	70, 82, 80, 65 (coded white and blue)	**Front suspension**	31.5mm Ducati fork	**Colors**	1968: Red frame, red and chrome tank 1969-70: Black frame, red and chrome tank
Carburetion	Dell'Orto SS1 29D (VHB 29A)	**Rear suspension**	Three-way adjustable Marzocchi twin-shock swingarm		
Power	20 horsepower at 8,000 rpm (22 hp at 7,500)	**Brakes**	Front: Drum 180 x 35mm (7.1 x 1.4 in.) Rear: Drum160 x 30mm (6.3 x 1.2 in.)	**Engine numbers**	250: From DM250M3 104501 350: From DM350M3 05001 approx
Spark plug	Marelli CW260N, Lodge 2HN	**Tires**	2.75 x 18, 3.00 x 18		
Generator	6v/30W (6v/70W after # 05106)	**Wheelbase**	1,360mm (53.5 in.)		

Richard Kennedy

The chrome tank panels may have been garish, but the 1968 350 Mark 3 Desmo was another classic sporting Ducati in the mold of the Mach 1.

Richard Kennedy

The 1968 Mark 3 was distinguished by the unique twin-filler gas tank.

as standard equipment. Each Mark 3 Desmo was also provided with a factory test certificate.

1968 Mark 3 Desmos featured the twin filler gas tank, which was also fitted on many 1969 models. With the release of the 450 Desmo during 1969, the tank was standardized to the single-filler type, although the shape was similar and it retained the chrome side panels. The 1968 Mark 3 and Desmo also retained an air pump on the front frame downtube. While the 450 Desmo featured a new twin instrument layout, the smaller Desmos still featured the earlier headlight and separate Veglia tachometer through 1970. From 1970 there was also the option of a Scrambler tank for the Mark 3 Desmo in the U.S. While the 450 received the Dell'Orto VHB carburetor from 1969, it wasn't until some time during 1970 that this carburetor made it to the 250 Mark 3 Desmo. Some versions had an air filter, while others a velocity tube. Most 350 Mark 3 Desmos continued with the SS1 carburetor throughout 1970.

high, touring-style handlebar, and a racing kit containing a camshaft, a range of main jets, a megaphone and a full fairing. U.S. models included high and low handlebars, racing shield for the headlight, air cleaner and velocity tube, a range of carburetor jets and valve adjusting caps

450 Scrambler (Jupiter)

The Scrambler received a 450 motor for 1969, and a stronger frame. This model lasted with few changes until 1978 and was one of the most popular wide-case singles. This is one of the earliest 450 Scramblers of 1969.

During 1969, the overhead-camshaft single-cylinder engine grew to 436cc, with new crankcases and cylinder head casting to accommodate the increase in capacity. Although the stroke was the same as the 350, there was a longer forged con-rod (140mm), and a machined right-side crank flywheel to complement the 350-style flywheel on the drive side. The wrist pin was 22mm, with a 32mm crankpin. A full 500 wasn't created because the 75mm stroke was the largest that could be used with the crankshaft throw still missing the gearbox. The main bearings on the 450 were the same size as those on the 350, but after engine number 453509 (towards the end of 1970) the right side bearing was increased to match the left-side bearing.

Inside the cylinder head were the same 40 and 36mm valves as on the Mark 3, with shim valve adjustment. The hairpin valve springs were the stronger 59.5-lb. type, and there was a valve lifter as fitted to the 350. The rocker pins were a smaller diameter (8mm) than on the 250 and 350 Scrambler, and the cylinder was longer (114.5mm). The clutch also included stronger 27.5mm springs. All 450's had the Dell'Orto VHB 29 AD carburetor, and the Scrambler had a large round air filter on the right. The air filter case was smooth on U.S. examples, rather than slotted, and the earliest models had a short cut-off Silentium muffler. The U.S. model was also called the Jupiter for 1969.

While the basic running gear was shared with the 250 and 350 Scrambler, the 450 frame featured additional gusseting along the top frame tube. The final drive chain and sprockets were also larger (5/8 x 3/8-inch). Early 450 Scramblers used the same 515mm Marzocchi fork of the 250 and 350, but this was lengthened to 540mm during 1971. The 11-liter gas tank was shared with the 250 and 350 Scrambler, and the 120 mph CEV speedometer mounted on the top triple clamp, with an optional tachometer. U.S. examples featured a small round CEV taillight, with European models the rectangular type. There were few developments over the next few years. By 1971 a tachometer was standard, and there was a cigar-shaped muffler. 1972 saw a Mark 3-type CEV taillight and smaller instrument housings, while 1973 saw more components shared with the 450 Mark 3, including the Marzocchi fork, Borrani alloy wheel rims and CEV headlight. There were fiberglass side covers and electronic ignition this year. Only a few 450 Scramblers were produced after 1973, most for the Italian market, but the Scrambler had a long production run and was the most popular of all the wide-case singles.

Production	1973	1974	1975	1978	Total
450 Scrambler	1,336	73	400	23	1,832

Apart from new instruments and taillight, the 1972 450 Scrambler looked very similar to the first model. Only the 450 had the large air filter canister this year.

450 Scrambler 1969-78

Engine	Single cylinder four-stroke, air-cooled	**Ignition (degrees)**	Points and coil; 0 static, 28 total	**Tires**	3.50 x 19, 4.00 x 18 Pirelli	
Bore	86mm		Electronic from 1973	**Wheelbase**	1,380mm (54.3 in.)	
Stroke	75mm	**Battery**	SAFA 3L3 13.5 Ah (Yuasa B38 12 Ah)	**Length**	2,120mm (83.5 in.)	
Displacement	435.7cc	**Primary drive**	2.111:1 (27/57)	**Height**	1,150mm (45.3 in.)	
Compression ratio	9.3:1	**Clutch**	Wet multiplate	**Width**	940mm (37 in.)	
Valve actuation	Bevel gear-driven overhead camshaft	**Gear ratios**	0.97, 1.10, 1.35, 1.73, 2.46	**Seat height**	770mm (30.3 in.)	
Valve timing (degrees)	27, 75, 60, 32 (coded white)	**Final drive**	2.917:1	**Dry weight**	133 kg (293 lbs.)	
Carburetion	Dell'Orto VHB 29 AD	**Front suspension**	35mm Marzocchi fork (515, later 540mm)	**Colors**	Yellow, orange, black, gold	
Power	23 horsepower at 6,500 rpm	**Rear suspension**	Three-way adjustable Marzocchi 315 (310)mm twin-shock swingarm	**Engine numbers**	DM450 450001-470000 approx	
Spark plug	Marelli CW260N, Lodge 2HN	**Brakes**	Drum 180 x 35mm front (7.1 x 1.4 in.)	**Frame numbers**	DM450S 450001-470000 approx	
Generator	6v/70W		160 x 30mm rear (6.3 x 1.2 in.)			

Because it was more street- than off-road oriented, the 450 Scrambler was arguably the best road single in the range. The second left side handlebar lever is for decompression.

All three 1973 Mark 3's (250, 350, and 450) were similar, with Borrani alloy wheel rims and a four-leading shoe front brake. The blue and gold colors were particularly attractive.

Along with the 450 Scrambler, there was also a 450 Mark 3 and 450 Mark 3 Desmo for 1969 (although they didn't reach America until 1970). The 450 Mark 3 was ostensibly identical to the 1969 250 and 350 Mark 3, but with the 450 Scrambler engine. As with the other Mark 3 Desmos, the 450 Mark 3 Desmo was basically the same as the 450 Mark 3, except for the desmodromic cylinder head. Some of the earliest 450 Desmos had a valve decompression lever, but most didn't. The carburetor on all 450s was a square-slide Dell'Orto VHB 29. There was a new single filler cap 13-liter gas tank (with chrome panels) for the 450, but some U.S. versions received the smaller Scrambler tank. The 450 Mark 3 and Desmo also had an individual CEV speedometer and tachometer with the instruments in alloy housings. The front fork top triple clamp was also polished, and the 450 Mark 3 Desmo fenders were chrome. For 1971, the instrument housings were smaller, and the Mark 3 was restyled with a larger (15-liter) and rounder gas tank. This year saw a new Desmo catalogued separately.

The 1971-72 450 Mark 3 was mechanically identical to the 1970 model. Joining it was the 450 T and TS.

Both these had a low-compression piston, with a large cutout in the crown, and a 12-volt electrical system. The T had a milder camshaft. Equipment included a touring

With its square-slide Dell'Orto VHB 29 carburetor, the 450 engine changed little between 1969 and 1975.

450 MARK 3 (1969-75), 450 MARK 3 DESMO (1969-70), 450 T/TS (1971-72)

Engine	Single cylinder four-stroke, air-cooled	Ignition (degrees)	Points and coil: 0 static, 28 total (450 TS: 5.8 static, 33.8 total) Electronic from 1973	Tires	2.75 x 18, 3.00 x 18 (T/TS: 3.50 x 18, 3.50 x 28)
Bore	86mm			Wheelbase	1,360mm (53.5 in.)
Stroke	75mm	Battery	SAFA 3L3 13.5 Ah (Yuasa B38) (450 T/TS: 12v/20Ah Yuasa)	Length	2,000mm (78.7 in.)
Displacement	435.7cc			Height	940mm (37 in.)
Compression ratio	Mark 3: 9.3:1 T and TS: 8.4:1			Width	600mm (23.6 in.)
Valve actuation	Bevel gear-driven overhead camshaft	Primary drive	2.111:1 (27/57)	Seat height	735mm (29 in.)
Valve timing (degrees)	Mark 3: 27, 75, 60, 32 (coded white) Desmo: 70, 82, 80, 65 (coded white and blue) 450 T: 52, 52, 75, 27	Clutch	Wet multiplate	Dry weight	130 kg (286.3 lbs.)
		Gear ratios	0.97, 1.10, 1.35, 1.73, 2.46	Colors	T/TS white or lemon 1973-4 Black frame, blue and gold
		Final drive	2.666:1		
Carburetion	Dell'Orto VHB 29 AD	Front suspension	35mm Marzocchi fork		
Power	Mark 3: 25 horsepower at 6,500 rpm	Rear suspension	Three-way adjustable Marzocchi twin shock swingarm	Engine numbers (six digits)	DM450 450001-
Spark plug	Marelli CW260N, Lodge 2HN	Brakes	Front: Drum 180mm (7.1 in.) Rear: 160mm (6.3 in.)	Frame numbers (six digits)	DM450M3 450001-460000 approx DM450M3 700001- (from 1973)
Generator	Mark 3 and Desmo: 6v/70W 450 T/TS: 12v/70W				

PRODUCTION	1973	1974	TOTAL
450 Mark 3	350	263	613

handlebar, valanced fenders, hard rear side panniers, crash bar, and a headlight mounted in the black headlight shell like earlier singles. The rear shock absorbers had enclosed springs and were also like those of the earlier Monza. The 450 T and TS were generally only available in Italy and were not produced after 1972.

The final development of the 450 Mark 3 appeared in 1973, continuing into 1974. This was visually identical to the 250 and 350 Mark 3 of the same year. The final 1974 models had steel wheel rims, and badges instead of decals on the gas tank.

Ducati Motor

The first 450 Mark 3 Desmo of 1969 looked virtually identical to the 450 Mark 3, but for the "D" decal on the side covers. There was a single filler cap on the gas tank.

The small CEV or Smiths instruments were a feature of all wide-case singles of 1973 and 1974.

One of the most interesting of all the wide-case singles was the 450 R/T—a more serious attempt to produce an off-road motorcycle. This was the only desmo with the decompression valve.

While the 450 Scrambler was a successful attempt at creating a dual-purpose motorcycle with street orientation, Berliner wanted a more effective dirt motorcycle to take on the BSA 441 Victor in America. In 1970, Berliner persuaded Ducati to develop the 450 R/T, and the resulting machine was quite different than the Scrambler or other overhead-camshaft singles. Ducati enlisted 1966 Italian scrambles champion Walter Reggioli to assist in the development, and the 450 R/T appeared by the end of 1970. It was sold in the U.S. as an off-road machine, with a kit providing street equipment, while elsewhere it was more street oriented. Either way, the 450 R/T was a much

450 R/T (1971-74), 350 R/T (1974)

Engine	Single cylinder four-stroke, air-cooled	**Spark plug**	Marelli CW260N	**Brakes**	Front and rear: Drum 160mm (6.3 in.)
Bore	450: 86mm 350: 76mm	**Generator**	6v/35 W (70W)	**Tires**	3.00 x 21, 4.00 x 18 Pirelli Cross
Stroke	75	**Ignition (degrees)**	Flywheel magneto, or battery, and coil: 0 static, 28 total	**Wheelbase**	1,450mm (57.1 in.)
Displacement	450: 435.7cc 350: 340.2cc	**Battery**	SAFA 3L3 13.5 Ah	**Length**	2,181mm (85.9 in.)
Compression ratio	450: 9.3:1 350: 10:1	**Primary drive**	2.111:1 (27/57)	**Height**	1,200mm (47.2 in.)
Valve actuation	Bevel gear-driven overhead desmodromic camshaft	**Clutch**	Wet multiplate	**Width**	940mm (37 in.)
Valve timing (degrees)	70, 82, 80, 65 (coded white and blue)	**Gear ratios**	0.97, 1.10, 1.35, 1.73, 2.46	**Seat height**	820mm (32.3 in.)
Carburetion	Dell'Orto VHB 29 AD	**Final drive**	2.917:1 (12/35) or 4.166:1 (12/50)	**Dry weight**	128 kg (282 lbs.)
Power	36 horsepower at 6,500 rpm	**Front suspension**	35mm Marzocchi fork	**Colors**	Black or silver frame, yellow
		Rear suspension	Three-way adjustable Marzocchi 320mm twin shock swingarm	**Engine numbers (450 R/T)**	From DM450 453000 approx

more successful off-road motorcycle than the Scrambler, and was supplied to the Italian ISDT team for the 1971 ISDT at the Isle of Man. Unfortunately, the R/T was also a flawed machine, with the soft wheels (without rim locks) and fiberglass bodywork unsuited to the rigors of off-road use.

The 450 R/T engine was the same desmodromic unit fitted to the 450 Desmo, with all the associated quality components, such as polished valve rockers. Setting the R/T engine apart from other Desmos, though, was a compression release on the right side, behind the bevel gear camshaft drive. The rear oil return line was kinked around the release, which was vulnerably exposed in the event of a fall. The carburetor included a round Scrambler air cleaner under the side number plate. A variety of exhaust systems were also available for the 450 R/T, with U.S. versions receiving a high-rise straight exhaust pipe, and European examples a 450 Scrambler low exhaust with long Silentium muffler. On the U.S. (and Australian) version there was no ignition switch, and stopping was rather crude as it required the rider to pull the compression release. The ignition used a flywheel magneto and there was no battery. Some 450 R/Ts for other markets were supplied with a CEV headlight, ignition key, CEV taillight on a rubber bracket and twin CEV instruments from the Mark 3. There was the usual 6-volt alternator and battery of the other singles.

A completely new frame was designed for the R/T, sharing several features with the 750 GT frame developed at the same time. Although retaining a single downtube like the other singles, the backbone and steering head were reinforced by horizontal tubes from the subframe, with a bolted-on rear section. The steering head bearings

Production	1974
350 R/T	35
450 R/T	65

were also tapered roller design like the 750 (26x 52 x 15mm), but the swingarm with, its cam washer rear wheel adjuster, was unique to the R/T. The suspension included a Marzocchi fork with polished aluminum legs and exposed tubes providing 7 inches of travel. The rear Marzocchi shock absorbers were provided with four mounting positions on the frame for different leverage. Also specific to the R/T were spring-loaded folding steel footpegs. On early examples these were round; on later versions flat.

Separating the R/T from the Scrambler was the 21-inch front wheel with Borrani alloy rim, and smaller front brake. The more off-road-oriented versions also included a larger rear sprocket and chain guide with no chainguard. Some examples included a chain oiler, consisting of a plastic bottle with a valve, mounted to the frame tube above the chain. New for the R/T were the 10-liter fiberglass gas tank (with screw filler cap), rubber-mounted fiberglass fenders, and fiberglass side number plates. There was only a solo seat, a wide, braced, motocross handlebar, and a quick-action Tomaselli throttle. Early examples featured fine steel cable adjusters. On later versions the larger adjuster was also shared with the 750 GT.

The 450 R/T was available in the U.S. during 1971 and into 1973, although none were produced that year. A few more were built during 1974, along with the 350 R/T for Italy only. The 350 was powered by a normal valve spring engine, with the valve lifter on the exhaust valve.

239, 250, 350, 450 Desmo 1971-78

For 1971, Ducati transformed the Mark 3 Desmo into one of the definitive sporting Ducati singles, the Desmo 250, 350, and 450. Not only was the Desmo restyled, its focus was now that of a true café racer, with clip-on handlebars, rear-set footpegs, and the absolute minimum of street equipment.

Although the engine specifications were unchanged, there was a new 12-liter fiberglass tank, with flip-up filler cap, and steel rear-set footpegs, folding on the left to provide clearance for the kickstart. There were also new fiberglass side covers to cover the air filter and toolbox, although most of these Desmos weren't fitted with an air filter. The carburetor on the 1971 350 Desmo was still an SS1 29, although the 450 retained the VHB 29. The

The final desmo single of 1974 featured a Ceriani front fork and Brembo front disc brake.

The Desmo single was restyled for 1973. The color scheme was shared with the 750 Sport, and there was a new seat and instrument layout.

239, 250, 350, 450 Desmo 1971-78

Engine	Single cylinder four-stroke, air-cooled	**Spark plug**	Marelli CW260N, Lodge 2HN	**Tires**	2.75 x 18, 3.00 or 3.25 x 18
Bore	250: 74mm 350: 76mm 450: 86mm 239: 72.5mm	**Generator**	6v/70W	**Wheelbase**	1,360mm (53.5 in.)
		Ignition (degrees)	Points and coil; 5-8 static, 33-36 total Electronic after 1973	**Length**	2,000mm (78.7 in.)
Stroke	239 and 250: 57.8mm 350 and 450: 75mm			**Height**	940mm (37 in.)
Displacement	250: 248.6cc 350: 340.2cc 450: 435.7cc	**Battery**	SAFA 3L3 13.5 Ah (Yuasa B38)	**Width**	600mm (23.6 in.)
		Primary drive	250: 2.500:1 (24:60) 350 and 450: 2.111:1 (27:57)	**Seat height**	735mm (29 in.)
Compression ratio	250: 9.7:1 350: 10:1 450: 9.5:1	**Clutch**	Wet multiplate	**Dry weight**	127 kg 250 (279.7 lbs.) 128 kg 350 (282 lbs.) 130 kg 450 (286.3 lbs.)
Valve actuation	Bevel gear-driven overhead desmodromic camshaft	**Gear ratios**	0.97, 1.10, 1.35, 1.73, 2.46	**Colors**	Black frame, silver (1971-72) Black frame, yellow (1973-74)
Valve timing (degrees)	70, 82, 80, 65 (coded white and blue)	**Final drive**	350: 2.6:1 (16/42)		
Carburetion	Dell'Orto VHB 29A SS1 29 D (1971 350)	**Front suspension**	35mm Marzocchi fork 35mm Ceriani (1974)	**Engine numbers**	From DM450D 462000 approx (450)
		Rear suspension	Three-way adjustable Marzocchi twin shock swingarm	**Frame numbers**	From DM450M3 701500 approx (450)
Power	250: 22 horsepower at 8,500 rpm 350: 24 horsepower at 8,000 rpm 450: 27 horsepower at 6,700 rpm	**Brakes**	Front: Drum 180 x3 5mm (7.1x1.4 in.) Rear: Drum 160 x 30mm (6.3x1.2 in.) 1974: 280mm front disc (11 in.)		

Production	1973	1974	1978	Total
239 Desmo		150		150
250 Desmo	300	277		577
350 Desmo	389	595		984
450 Desmo	330	454	15	799
Total	1,019	1,476	15	2,510

Only small decals on the rear seat unit distinguished the three Desmos. The gas tank was steel for 1973, with the front fender crudely clamped to the fork legs.

rather garish metalflake silver color scheme extended to a solo racing style seat, and a sporting front fender, retained by hose clamps to the polished alloy Marzocchi fork leg. The wheel rims were alloy Borrani, and the front brake a Grimeca four-leading shoe. The rear fender was stainless steel, with the small round CEV taillight and steel bracket of the Mark 3 that year. 1972 Desmo singles were identical to the 1971 versions, except the VHB square-slide carburetor was universal.

Leopoldo Tartarini of Italjet was engaged to style the sporting Ducatis for 1973 and created the 750 Sport and updated Desmo single. Although the two bikes looked similar, in distinctive yellow and black, the Desmos received a steel gas tank, abbreviated side covers, and an angular tailpiece that included the seat and rectangular taillight. Other developments included a new CEV headlight and instrument layout, electronic ignition, and black painted fork legs. The Desmos for 1973 retained the drum front brake, and the fiberglass fender was still rather crudely clamped to the fork leg. Most Desmos also

had an air filter. While they were still pretty machines, the 1973 styling was a curious blend of round and angular and wasn't totally successful.

The final regular production year for the Desmo single was 1974. The bikes from this year were very similar to the 1973 examples, except most were fitted with a 35mm Ceriani fork and front disc brake with Brembo 08 twin-piston caliper. Because of the 750-style front hub, the 18-inch WM2 Borrani had 40 spokes, rather than the 36 of the drum-braked versions. One improvement was the bolting of the fiberglass front fender to the fork legs. This year there were also a few 239 Desmos produced, primarily for France, but some were exported to England. Like the 239 Mark 3, the few 239 Desmos were also fitted with a Dell'Orto 30mm concentric carburetor. A handful of 450 Desmos were also manufactured in 1978.

The last Desmo singles were a contradiction. On one hand they were relics of the past, and on the other they were thoroughly modern. Although the electronic ignition cured starting difficulties, the 6-volt lighting system was marginal. The bevel-drive engine was almost as expensive to manufacture as a twin and, in the end, it was economic reality that killed the overhead-camshaft single.

Although never officially catalogued as a Ducati, the 350 Condor was produced by Ducati in 1973 for the Swiss Army. It was based on the earlier 350 Militaire made for the Italian Army.

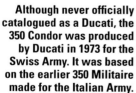

For 1971, the Desmo single became a real café racer, with rearset footpegs and a solo seat. The 250 and 350 were visually similar to the 450 shown here.

Above: **With their small racing saddles and minimal instrumentation, the silver Desmos were extremely purposeful machines.**

Right: **Alloy wheel rims, a Marzocchi fork, and racing brake were new for the Desmo single from 1971, as were the metalflake silver colors.**

PARALLEL TWINS

Ducati headed down a new path following the end of the singles. By 1973, Ducati's new management believed the future for middleweights was in parallel twins. There were already a few parallel twins in Ducati's history, but none were successful, so this was a surprising move. In hindsight, it was a mistake but, although much maligned, the parallel twins were reasonable, if not exceptional, motorcycles. Their cause wasn't helped when Fabio Taglioni refused to become involved, although he did design the desmodromic cylinder head for the Sport. The basis of the design did come from Taglioni's 1965 360-degree overhead valve parallel twin, produced as a prototype at Berliner's request.

350 and 500 GTL

Ducati Motor

Although the 500 GTL was fitted with quality components, it was ugly, slow, and unreliable.

The parallel twin was Ducati's first completely new production engine design for more than 15 years. In the past, Ducati adhered to the Taglioni philosophy of gradual evolution, but without this luxury Ing. Tumidei had to start virtually from scratch. As manufacturing costs needed to be reduced, unlike the singles (and 750 Vee-twin) the design of the parallel twin began life as a compromise, and suffered as a result.

Some traditional Ducati features were retained, like the vertically split aluminum crankcases, with the cylinders canted forward 10 degrees. The forged one-piece

Production	1975	1976	1977	Total
350 GTL	530	400		930
500 GTL	447	198	100	745
500 GTL USA		87	273	360
Total	977	685	373	2,035

500 AND 350 GTL 1975-77

Engine	Twin cylinder four-stroke, air-cooled	**Spark plug**	Champion L81	**Front brake**	Brembo 260mm dual disc (single disc on 350)
Bore	500: 78mm 350: 71.8mm	**Generator**	12v 150w	**Rear brake**	160mm single leading shoe drum
Stroke	500: 52mm 350: 43.2mm	**Ignition (degrees)**	Points and coil; 20-22 static, 40-42 total	**Tires**	3.25 x 18, 3.50 x 18
Displacement	500: 496.9cc 350: 349.6cc	**Battery**	12v 18 Ah Yuasa Y50-N18L-A1	**Wheelbase**	1,400mm (55.1 in.)
Compression ratio	9.6:1	**Primary drive**	2.125:1 (32/68)	**Length**	2,080mm (81.9 in.)
Valve actuation	Chain-driven overhead camshaft	**Clutch**	Wet multiplate	**Height**	1,100mm (43.3 in.)
Valve timing (degrees)	500: 32, 70, 68, 39 350: 44, 85, 80, 50	**Gear ratios**	1.900, 1.074, 1.333, 1.714, 2.50	**Width**	840mm (33 in.)
Carburetion	500; Dell'Orto PHF 30 BS/BD 350; Dell'Orto VHB 26 FS/FD	**Final drive**	2.923:1 (13/38)	**Seat height**	760mm (30 in.)
		Front suspension	35mm Marzocchi fork	**Dry weight**	170 kg (374.4 lbs.) 163 kg (359 lbs.)
Power	500: 35 horsepower at 6,500 rpm	**Rear suspension**	Three-way adjustable Marzocchi 320mm twin-shock swingarm	**Top speed**	170 km/h (105.6 mph) 147 km/h 350 (91.3 mph)
				Colors	Black frame, blue, green, red

crankshaft, with the crankpins spaced at 180 degrees, was new. Originally, the design had a 360-degree crankshaft with balance shafts like the disastrous Yamaha TX750, and cases were cast with balance shaft mounting bosses. The crankshaft was supported by two generous plain main bearings (50 x 25mm). The con-rod big-ends also ran in plain bearings (45 x 22mm). There was a large central flywheel and no center bearing. To minimize engine width, the camshaft drive was taken from the rear of the clutch hub to a countershaft behind the cylinders with a single row chain running up a narrow sleeve between the cylinders. The camshaft itself was in two pieces, coupled to the central sprocket.

The cylinder layout of the parallel twin was more modern than the singles and vee-twins. The 500 had two 37mm and 33mm valves set at the shallower included angle of 60 degrees, as used on the 1973 Imola F750 racing bikes. The 350 had smaller, 35mm and 31mm valves. Valve adjustment was by screw and locknut, and primary drive by helical gear—on the right rather than the left because the parallel twin was designed with a left-side gearshift to meet impending U.S. regulations. While the GTL retained a kickstart, there was also a small electric starter motor fitted in front of the engine. Ignition was by battery, coil and contact breakers.

The GTL chassis followed the usual Ducati practice of using the engine as a stressed member, and the frame was a single downtube type. The styling of the 19-liter gas tank and side covers mimicked Giugiaro's 860, and many components were similar, including the Smiths or Veglia instruments, controls and ugly Lafranconi mufflers. Along with Marzocchi suspension, Brembo front disc brakes with small 05 calipers, Borrani alloy wheel rims, and the eccentric adjuster at the swingarm pivot for chain adjustment, the GTL was almost a mini-860. 1975 examples had painted steel fenders. The rear Marzocchi shock absorbers had a black spring cover like the 860 GT. For 1976 and 1977 there were stainless-steel fenders and shock absorbers with exposed springs. After 1977, the GTL was replaced by the GTV, but crankshaft failure and short-lived valve gear masked any positive attributes. The GTL handled and braked well enough, but the engine lacked character, the performance was lackluster, and the styling was ugly.

500 and 350 Sport Desmo (1976-83)

The 500 Sport Desmo of 1977 was an improvement over the GTL, but was still poorly finished and unreliable.

Soon after the release of the GTL, the parallel twin was sent off to Leopoldo Tartarini of Italjet to create a sporting version. Fabio Taglioni developed a desmodromic cylinder head, and the result was the Sport Desmo.

Except for the cylinder head, the engine was almost identical to the GTL. Because of the rearset footpegs and foot controls there was no kickstart, and the right side engine cover was plugged. Later versions featured a specific cast cover without a plug. The chassis and styling were also new for the Sport Desmo. The frame featured a double front downtube, but was otherwise similar, and still retained the eccentric chain adjuster. The 14-liter gas tank was shaped to blend in with the racing-style saddle and ducktail, l—later replicated on the 900 Darmah (also a Tartarini styling effort). The cast-alloy wheels (magnesium was optional) were by FPS, and there was a rear Brembo disc brake to complement the dual front discs. The front fork was now a Paioli, and the exhaust system and Lafranconi mufflers were black. The Veglia instruments and Aprilia switchgear was the same as the 860, changing to CEV during 1978. Although extremely rare in the U.S., a reasonable number of 500 Sport Desmos were produced. The final batch came out in 1983 with Oscam wheels, Marzocchi front fork, and 500 GTV instruments. The 350 Sport Desmo was produced primarily for the Italian market to entice younger riders limited to 350cc, and was arguably more attractive than the 500, in yellow, or blue, and black. Interest in the sporting parallel twins declined after 1979 following the release of the Pantah, which was faster, smoother, and more reliable.

Production	1976	1977	1978	1979	1980	1981	1982	1983
350 Sport Desmo		456	276	200	234			1,166
500 Sport Desmo	441	1,159	110	130	93	172	67	2,172
500 Sport USA		25						25
Total	441	1,640	386	330	327	172	67	3,363

350 AND 500 SPORT DESMO 1976-83

Engine	Twin cylinder four-stroke, air-cooled	Spark plug	Champion L81	Rear brake	Brembo 260mm disc
Bore	500: 78mm / 350: 71.8mm	Generator	12v 150w	Tires	3.25 x 18, 3.50 x 18
Stroke	500: 52mm / 350: 43.2mm)	Ignition (degrees)	Points and coil; 20-22 static, 40-42 total	Wheelbase	1,400mm (55.1 in.)
Displacement	500: 496.9cc / 350: 349.6cc	Battery	12v 18 Ah Yuasa Y50-N18L-A1	Length	2,050mm (80.7 in.)
Compression ratio	9.6:1	Primary drive	2.125:1 (32/68)	Height	1,060mm (41.7 in.)
Valve actuation	Desmo chain driven overhead camshaft	Clutch	Wet multiplate	Width	710mm (28 in.)
Valve timing (degrees)	32, 75, 60, 45	Gear ratios	1.900, 1.074, 1.333, 1.714, 2.50	Seat height	760mm (30 in.)
Carburetion	500: Dell'Orto PHF 30 BS/BD / 350: Dell'Orto VHB 26 FS/FD	Final drive	2.923:1 (13/38)	Dry weight	500: 185 kg (407.5 lbs.) / 350: 181 kg 350 (398.7 lbs.)
		Front suspension	35mm Paioli fork	Top speed	350: 185 km/h (115 mph)
Power	500: 50 horsepower at 8,500 rpm	Rear suspension	Three-way adjustable Marzocchi 330mm twin shock swingarm	Colors	Black frame, red or blue with white stripes (500); yellow with black stripes, blue with black stripes (350)
		Front brake	Brembo 260mm dual disc		

500 and 350 GTV (1977-81)

In response to the poor reception of the GTL's 860-like styling, the 350 and 500 GTL were replaced by the 350 and 500 GTV during 1977. These were essentially 350 and 500 Sport Desmos with valve spring engines. They featured the Sport double-downtube frame, Paioli fork, FPS wheels, rear disc brake, but with stainless-steel fenders and a touring handlebar. The exhaust system was chrome plated, and the engine covers on either side were black. The GTV also included a kickstart and a revised rear brake linkage setup. The seat was a dual rather than single as on the Sport Desmo. Many components, such as the Bosch headlight, were shared with the 500 SL Pantah, and some 1978 models had gold Speedline magnesium wheels. Although the GTV was an improvement on the GTL, the damage was done. No one wanted a touring parallel twin. This was another model that was sold mainly in Italy.

Production	1977	1978	1979	1980	1981	Total
350 GTV	360	138	100	190	170	958
500 GTV	453	23		100	124	700
Total	813	161	100	290	294	1,658

Ducati Motor

Produced primarily for the Italian market, the 350 Sport Desmo and 350 GTV of 1978 were similar.

500 AND 350 GTV 1977-81

Engine	Twin cylinder four-stroke, air-cooled	**Spark plug**	Champion L81	**Rear brake**	Brembo 260mm disc
Bore	500: 78mm 350: 71.8mm	**Generator**	12v 150w	**Tires**	3.25 x 18, 3.50 x 18
Stroke	500: 52mm 350: 43.2mm	**Ignition (degrees)**	Points and coil; 20-22 static, 40-42 total	**Wheelbase**	1,400mm (55.1 in.)
Displacement	500: 496.9mm 350: 349.6mm	**Battery**	12v 18 Ah Yuasa Y50-N18L-A1	**Length**	2,050mm (80.7 in.)
Compression ratio	9.6:1	**Primary drive**	2.125:1 (32/68)	**Height**	1,060mm (41.7 in.)
Valve actuation	Chain-driven overhead camshaft	**Clutch**	Wet multiplate	**Width**	760mm (30 in.)
Valve timing (degrees)	500: 32, 70, 68, 39 350: 44, 85, 80, 50	**Gear ratios**	1.900, 1.074, 1.333, 1.714, 2.50	**Seat height**	760mm (30 in.)
Carburetion	500: Dell'Orto PHF 30 BS/BD 350: Dell'Orto VHB 26 FS/FD	**Final drive**	2.923:1 (13/38)	**Dry weight**	500: 183 kg (403.1 lbs.) 350: 181 kg (398.7 lbs.)
		Front suspension	35mm Paioli fork	**Top speed**	500: 175 km/h (108.7 mph) 350: 145 km/h (90.1 mph)
Power	500: 35 horsepower at 6,500 rpm	**Rear suspension**	Three-way adjustable Marzocchi 320mm twin-shock swingarm	**Colors**	500: Blue 350: Green or black and gold
		Front brake	Brembo 260mm dual disc		

CHAPTER 5

BEVEL-DRIVE TWINS

During the 1960s Ducati gained an enviable reputation for producing quality sporting singles, but it was the transition to the manufacture of larger capacity machines that set the company on the path of glory that continues today. The impetus to develop the 750 was undoubtedly another Berliner initiative, and during 1970 Fabio Taglioni created the 90-degree 750 V-twin. After a year of development, the 750 went into production during July 1971, and formed the basis of the Imola 750-winning racers of 1972. This victory at Imola was a pivotal event in the history of Ducati, giving the fledgling 750 credibility in a market then saturated with new Superbikes from Japan and Europe. Imola led to the 750 Sport and 750 Super Sport, and soon a whole range of bevel-drive twins, before they died in 1986. This family of bevel-drive twins is now considered one of the classic, and most collectible, of the entire production series.

750 GT (1971-78))

Where the Ducati 90-degree V-twin began—the first 750 of 1971. The tradition continues today.

Although it was continually developed over its 15-year lifespan, the basic 750 GT engine design lasted until the final Mille of 1986. Many design characteristics were inherited from the wide-case overhead camshaft single, but there were some significant differences. The aluminum crankcases were still vertically split, but with the front cylinder inclined upwards 15-degrees. The crankcases on the very earliest engines were sand-cast, and until engine number 750404 featured recesses in both crankcase halves. The steel crankshaft was a three-piece pressed-up assembly with two forged one-piece 150mm connecting rods on a 36mm crankpin, with a 22mm wrist-pin. The main bearings were considerably uprated from the overhead camshaft single, which was now a fiber-caged axial thrust

The very earliest 750 GTs, like this example with frame #2, featured a number of unique components. These were hand-built pre-production models.

35 x 80 x 21mm. Pistons were forged aluminum Borgo, and a relatively heavy three-ring full skirt design.

With a wide included-valve angle of 80 degrees, the cylinder head design originated from the singles, and the valve sizes were the same as the 350 and 450 (40 and 36mm), with shim valve adjustment. To keep the rocker box as narrow as possible, single coil valve springs replaced the hairpin valve springs of the single. Distinguishing the 750 engine was the combination of bevel gears to drive the two camshafts. Extremely time consuming to assemble with the correct backlash on all gears, the camshaft drive began at the crankshaft, and consisted of five lower bevel gears. Lubrication for the 750 engine was by wet sump, with a single gear-driven oil pump, and the only oil filtration was a gauze filter in the sump. While the electrical system was upgraded to 12 volts, the alternator was barely adequate. Ignition was by battery, coil and points, with the points located in a housing, with the condensers, between the two vertical bevel shafts.

To minimize engine length, the constant-mesh direct-type five-speed gearbox had the layshaft above the mainshaft. The engine rotated backwards, and while the general design of the gearbox and selector mechanism followed that of the overhead camshaft single, all the bearing sizes were increased. The sliding gears featured six engagement dogs, but suffered from poor hardening, with fifth gear particularly prone to wear. The gear selector mechanism incorporated in the right rear outer engine cover was carried over from the singles.

Although the crankcases included a deep recess for a future electric start motor, only a kickstart was fitted on

By 1972, the 750 GT was in regular production. U.S. models like this had high handlebars, but the Lockheed disc, stainless-steel fenders, and fiberglass tank remained.

the early 750, on a 300mm shaft. Early 750s had Amal concentric carburetors, and air filtration consisted of two separate black plastic air boxes, each with a dry paper element, fed via a restrictive pleated plastic tube. The exhaust system included twin Conti mufflers.

The 750cc Vee-twin was housed in a tubular steel frame that used the engine as a stressed member in the usual Ducati fashion. Like the 450 R/T, the steering head bearings were a tapered roller design. While not particularly light, the frame was strong enough to see the 750 GT soon earn a reputation as the best-handling large-capacity motorcycle available. The Marzocchi front fork was a leading axle type, with mounts for a Lockheed twin-piston brake caliper. Only a single front disc was fitted to the 750 GT, while the rear brake was a twin-leading shoe drum on the very earliest models, but soon changed to a single leading shoe design. The rear shock absorbers were Marzocchi, with alloy spring covers. The wheels included Borrani alloy rims wheels with straight-pull spokes on the front. Early 750 GTs came with a metalflake fiberglass

By 1973, Dell'Orto carburetors replaced the Amals, and the tachometer drive was a one-piece casting.

Only a few 750 GTs were produced with electric start. This is typical of a late 1973 or early 1974 750 GT. Steel gas tank, painted fenders, leading axle fork and Scarab front brake. GTs of this period were either orange or deep red.

During 1974 centre-axle forks replaced the leading axle Marzocchi. These are centre-axle Marzocchi with a Scarab brake, although some GTs had Ceriani with a Brembo disc. U.S. examples had polished alloy fork legs.

17-liter fuel tank, stainless-steel fenders, and a number of subtle differences that set them apart from later examples. These included footpegs positioned further forward, specific Smiths instruments and thicker saddle.

By 1972 the 750 GT had entered regular production, and there were a few changes from the earliest examples. From engine number 750405 on the engine crankcases were standardized without the additional bolt through the sump. After engine number 751501, the kickstart shaft

was lengthened to 315mm like the 750 Sport, requiring a new lever and outer engine cover. An electric start version also became available, with a different clutch cover and toothed flywheel gear. A 2-horsepower Marelli electric motor sat between the two cylinders and drove the engine through a large solenoid switch. As the 750 GT was created primarily for the U.S. market, soon after the earliest series a specific U.S. specification model with a higher handlebar was produced. Towards the end of 1972 (around engine number 752000) a Scarab front brake caliper and master cylinder replaced the Lockheed. While essentially copies, these Italian units were inferior to the original and were prone to leaking. Smiths instruments continued to be fitted for 1972, but most 1973 750 GTs came with Veglia instruments with an electronic tachometer. In 1973 (after around engine number 753500), the Amal carburetors were replaced by twin Dell'Orto. Most changes occurred to the frame and bodywork. The gas tank was now steel,

Production	1971	1972	1973	1974	1978	Total
750 GT	82	519	943	551	40	2,135
750 GT US			545	868		1,413
750 GT Elec			329	201		530
750 Bologna Police				55		55
Total	82	519	1,817	1,675	40	4,133

750 GT 1971-78

Engine	Twin cylinder four-stroke, air-cooled	Battery	Yuasa 12N-12A-4A-12V (B68 32Ah; electric start)	Length	2,250mm (88.6 in.)
Bore	80mm			Height	1,070mm (42.1 in.)
Stroke	74.4mm	Primary drive	2.448:1 (29/71) 1974: 2.187:1 (32/70)	Width	710mm (28 in.)
Displacement	748cc	Clutch	Wet multiplate	Seat height	780mm (30.7 in.)
Compression ratio	8.5:1	Gear ratios	0.887, 1.000, 1,203, 1.562, 2.237	Dry weight	185 kg (407.5 lbs.)
Valve actuation	Bevel gear-driven overhead camshaft	Final drive	2.250:1 (16/36)	Top speed	200 km/h (124.3 mph)
Valve timing (degrees)	65, 84, 74, 58	Front suspension	38mm Marzocchi fork Ceriani from 1974)	Colors	Black frame (silver on some early examples) Metalflake blue, orange, green (1971-72) Red or black (1972-73) Deep red or orange (from 1973)
Carburetion	30mm Amal R 930/76 and /77 (Dell'Orto PHF 30 A)	Rear suspension	Three-way adjustable Marzocchi 305mm twin shock swingarm		
Power	57 horsepower at 7,700 rpm	Front brake	275mm (10.8 in.) 280mm single disc (11 in.)	Engine numbers	DM750 750001-757500 approx.
Spark plugs	Marelli CW 260 T, Lodge 3HN	Rear brake	200mm drum (7.9 in.)	Frame numbers	DM750S 750001-757500 approx.
Generator	12v/150W	Tires	3.25 x 19, 3.50 x 18		
Ignition (degrees)	Points and coil; 10 static, 38 total	Wheelbase	1,530mm (60.2 in.)		

there were new fiberglass side covers and the stainless-steel fenders were replaced by painted steel.

1974 750 GTs were more inconsistent in specification than earlier examples. Inside the cylinder head were new camshafts, with the same timing, but more valve lift and steeper ramps to improve top-end power and to compensate for the quieter Lafranconi mufflers. Along with the camshafts came new valves and rockers with screw-type valve adjusters, and there was a higher primary drive ratio. There were significant changes to the front suspension and brakes. A Ceriani front fork with Brembo disc was fitted to many examples after approximately engine number 754000. A center-axle Marzocchi was also fitted to some 750 GTs during 1974, with either a Scarab or Brembo front disc. At this time the wheel rims were also chrome-plated steel Radaelli.

Coinciding with the production of the 860 GT, the 750 GT also started to share much of its ancillary equipment with the larger model. This included the wiring loom and CEV handlebar switches, with the ignition switch located on a bracket on the left side, underneath the fuel tank.

Here is an example of one of the final 750 GTs. This U.S. spec version has a black-painted Marzocchi fork and Brembo front disc brake. These GTs featured many 860 components, including the wiring loom and relocated ignition switch.

By the end of 1974, not only was the round-case engine costly to produce, noise regulations were hurting the 750s performance. In addition, U.S. DOT regulations required mandatory left-side shifting. The 750 GT died, and with it one of Ducati's finest and most unappreciated models.

750 SPORT (1972-78)

The 750 Sport was created in 1972 out of the GT. It still had the wide rear subframe, but featured a higher-performance motor.

Thorsten Schulze

Soon after the 750 GT went into production, development began on a sporting version: the 750 Sport. The first examples appeared in 1972 and were very similar to the 750 GT. The engine had a lighter crankshaft assembly, higher-compression Mondial slipper pistons, and larger Dell'Orto carburetors (without air filters), but was other wise unchanged. Despite these few developments, the engine performance was considerably stronger. The combination of radical valve timing, higher compression and bigger carbs contributed to one of Ducati's finest

The 750 Sport evolved into one the finest sporting Ducatis for 1973. Still with black engine cases, this narrow, long and low machine was spectacular.

power units. Also setting the Sport engine apart from the GT were the black painted engine covers.

The frame on the 1972 Sport was also based on the 750 GT, with a wide rear subframe. The suspension was similar, although the leading axle Marzocchi fork was painted black and the rear shock absorbers had exposed springs. The front brake on the early examples was a Lockheed, but this was changed to a Scarab late in 1972. Along with clip-on handlebars and rearset footpegs, there were separate Veglia instruments and the tachometer was electronic. The 19-liter gas tank was fiberglass and a lot slimmer than the GT tank. This early Sport also had distinctive Z-stripe decals and a wide solo seat. The fenders were fiberglass. A frame-mounted half fairing was optional. Only a few 1972 750 Sports were produced, but without factory

records this is difficult to authenticate. Matters are further complicated by the fact that the Sport and GT shared their engine and frame number sequences.

While the basic layout of the 750 Sport was unchanged for 1973, there were some updates to further emphasize its sporting nature. These centered on the frame and bodywork, with the engine (still with black-painted outer engine covers) remaining essentially unchanged. The frame now featured a narrower rear subframe with the top shock absorber mount outboard instead of underneath.

Production	1973	1974	1978	Total
750 Sport	746	656	23	1,425
750 Sport US		200		200
Total	746	856	12	1,625

750 Sport 1972-78

Engine	Twin cylinder four-stroke, air-cooled	**Ignition (degrees)**	Points and coil; 10 static, 38 total	**Tires**	3.25 x 19, 3.50 x 18 (4.10 x 18)
Bore	80mm	**Battery**	Yuasa 12N-12A-4A-12V	**Wheelbase**	1,530mm (60.2 in.)
Stroke	74.4mm	**Primary drive**	2.448:1 (29/71) 2.187:1 (32/70) from 1974	**Length**	2,200mm (86.6 in.)
Displacement	748cc	**Clutch**	Wet multiplate	**Height**	1,070mm (42.1 in.)
Compression ratio	9.3:1	**Gear ratios**	0.887, 1.000, 1,203, 1.562, 2.237	**Width**	710mm (28 in.)
Valve actuation	Bevel gear-driven overhead camshaft	**Final drive**	2.250:1 (16/36)	**Seat height**	780mm (30.7 in.)
Valve timing (degrees)	65, 84, 74, 58	**Front suspension**	38mm Marzocchi fork Ceriani (from 1974)	**Dry weight**	182 kg (400.9 lbs.)
Carburetion	Dell'Orto PHF 32 A	**Rear suspension**	Three-way adjustable Marzocchi 305mm twin-shock swingarm	**Top speed**	210 km/h (130.5 mph)
Power	62 horsepower at 8,200 rpm	**Front brake**	275mm (10.8 in.) 280mm single disc (11 in.)	**Colors**	Black frame, yellow and black
Spark plugs	Marelli CW 260 T, Lodge 3HN	**Rear brake**	200mm drum (7.9 in.)	**Engine numbers**	From DM750 751200-757500 approx.
Generator	12v/150W			**Frame numbers**	From DM750S 751000-757500 approx.

The revised frame required a new fiberglass (or sometimes steel) fuel tank, seat and rear fender. All 1973 750 Sports had a Scarab front disc brake, and at some stage (around engine number 753500) the electronic tachometer was replaced by a mechanical Veglia.

With the release of the 750 Super Sport for 1974, the 750 Sport was softened slightly. There were new camshafts, and the outer engine covers were now polished aluminum. Other updates included a higher primary gear ratio, but most changes were to the cycle parts. The steel gas tank was standardized, and a dual seat was offered. The front suspension was either a center axle Ceriani or Marzocchi fork, with a Brembo front brake on the Ceriani and Scarab on the Marzocchi. Along with the 860 wiring loom, there were new off-set clip-on handlebars and CEV switches. Turn signal indicators were also fitted this year and, like the 860 and 750 GT, there was a town and country dual-level horn switch between the speedometer and tachometer. Apart from a few manufactured in 1978 for Australia,

production of the 750 Sport finished at the end of 1974. The 750 Sports, in particular the 1973 version, were among the most focused of all sporting Ducatis. Light, narrow, and handsome, they were spectacular machines.

By 1974, the 750 Sport had a steel gas tank, and some had a Ceriani fork with Brembo disc. The engine covers were polished alloy.

750 Super Sport (1973-74)

The 1974 desmodromic 750 Super Sport was a replica of the machines that won at Imola in 1972.

The 750 Super Sport cockpit was quite basic, and included Smiths instruments.

The sculptured fiberglass Super Sport gas tank had a clear strip that was an instant fuel gauge. *(Roy Kidney)*

When Paul Smart and Bruno Spaggiari headed a spectacular 1-2

victory at the first Imola 200 race in April 1972 on a pair of desmodromic 750s, the face of Ducati changed forever. Fabio Taglioni had again shown to the world the virtues of desmodromic valve gear, and this would eventually become a Ducati trademark. Immediately after, the Imola 200 production desmodromic twins were promised, but these took a while to appear. Although a handful of Super Sports were produced out of 750 Sports during 1973, the 750 Super Sport wasn't generally available until 1974. At the time it was one of the most exotic production motorcycles available, a true race replica boasting triple disc brakes, racing fairing, and a race-shop prepared engine.

Unlike the 750 Sport, the Super Sport engine was substantially developed from the 750 GT. While the crankcase castings were the same, most 750 Super Sport crankcases featured a plugged oil cooler outlet on the right below the ignition housing. The crankshaft included milled and machined con-rods, patterned on those from the Imola racer, and featured dual strengthening ribs around the big-end eye. Although the pistons were the same as the 750 Sport, there were Dell'Orto 40mm carburetors, and desmodromic cylinder heads. The valve sizes were unchanged at 40 and 36mm, but all the valve rockers were highly polished. While the 1973 Super Sport featured the black engine cases of the 750 Sport, all 1974 750 Super Sports had polished engine cases.

The chassis was based on that of the 750 Sport, with a narrow rear subframe, but with a center axle Marzocchi fork and 18-inch front wheel. There were twin Scarab front disc brakes, and a single Lockheed disc at the rear. The sculptured 20-liter fiberglass gas tank with clear "fuel gauge" stripe, and solo racing saddle with zipper compartment, were inspired by the 1972 Imola racers. As a frame-mounted half fairing was standard, this mounted

to a support on the steering head and incorporated the instrument layout with Smiths instruments.

Only one series of the round-case 750 Super Sport was produced in 1974, and while they were flawed, with substandard brakes and fiberglass, the Super Sport was the closest production Ducati in specification to any factory racer. They were also the only round-case with desmodromic valve gear, and only a minimal concession was made to adapt it to the street. Rare, beautiful, exotic, and functionally superior, the round-case 750 Super Sport has justifiably earned a place as the most-desirable production Ducati.

Production	1974
750 Super Sport	401

The 750 Super Sport was the only round case model with desmodromic valve gear.

750 SUPER SPORT 1973-74

Engine	Twin-cylinder four-stroke, air-cooled	**Generator**	12v/150W	**Tires**	3.50 x 18, 3.50 x 18 C7 Metzeler Racing
Bore	80mm	**Ignition (degrees)**	Points and coil; 8 static, 36 total	**Wheelbase**	1,500mm (59.1 in.)
Stroke	74.4mm	**Battery**	Yuasa 12N-12A-4A-12V	**Length**	2,200mm (86.6 in.)
Displacement	748cc	**Primary drive**	2.187:1 (32/70)	**Height**	1,050mm (41.3 in.)
Compression ratio	9.5:1	**Clutch**	Wet multiplate	**Width**	660mm (26 in.)
Valve actuation	Bevel gear-driven desmodromic overhead camshaft	**Gear ratios**	0.887, 1.000, 1,203, 1.562, 2.237	**Seat height**	760mm (30 in.)
Valve timing (degrees)	63, 83, 80, 58	**Final drive**	2.500:1 (16/40)	**Dry weight**	180 kg (396.5 lbs.)
Carburetion	Dell'Orto PHM 40 A	**Front suspension**	38mm Marzocchi fork	**Top speed**	230 km/h (143 mph)
Power	70 horsepower at 9,000 rpm	**Rear suspension**	Three-way adjustable Marzocchi 305mm twin shock swingarm	**Colors**	Blue/green frame, silver
Spark plugs	Lodge RL 51, Champion L82Y	**Front brake**	275mm dual disc (10.8 in.)	**Engine numbers**	DM750.1 075001-075411
		Rear brake	230mm disc (9.1 in.)	**Frame numbers**	DM750SS 075001-075411

860 GT, 860 GTE, 860 GTS; 900 GTS (1974-79)

To maintain performance with more stringent mufflers than the barking Contis of the 750, the easiest solution for Ducati was to increase displacement. As with the earlier singles, the design of the 750 allowed an easy displacement increase, and it was a relatively simple process to install 450 single pistons in the 750 to give 860cc. While an 860 was anticipated from 1971, the eventual form took many by surprise. Rather than continue the sporting emphasis of the 750, the 860 placed styling first, along with a revamp of the engine and chassis. This wasn't a successful formula, and in almost every respect the 860 was inferior to the 750 it replaced. The 860 hasn't become one of Ducati's cherished models, but some amends were made when the engine gained desmodromic heads and it became the 900 Super Sport, and the later Darmah.

860 GT and 860 GTE

Ducati Motor

The 860 GT replaced the 750 GT after 1974, but it was ugly, unreliable and not a success.

To make the 90-degree twin more attractive for the U.S. market, the 750 GT was redesigned and restyled. The engine underwent considerable modification, firstly to simplify manufacture, and secondly to improve reliability and minimize maintenance. Taglioni was instructed to redesign the 750 engine so that it was much less labor intensive to assemble and cheaper to manufacture. At the same time, Giorgetto Giugiaro at Studio Italdesign in Turin was given the styling assignment, and the engine cases were redesigned to match the angular 860 look.

There was a lot more to the engine redesign, though, than merely the shape of the outer engine covers. Apart from the gearbox, most of the internal parts were not interchangeable with the 750. The bevel-gear layout to drive the two vertical shafts included spur gears mounted onto an outrigger plate. It was a far easier system to assemble because the two vertical shafts could be set up individually. Other improvements included an oil filter between the cylinders and an uprated oil pump.

In an effort to shorten the engine slightly, the con-rod length was reduced to 145mm, and the wrist-pin shortened to 20mm. The crankpin and big-end bearings were unchanged from the 750, but the Borgo pistons were a slipper type like the 750 Sport. Along with new camshaft timing, the primary gears were new due to the fact that the crankshaft primary gear was bolted onto a new flywheel that incorporated the Ducati Electtrotecnica electronic ignition magnets. The ignition stator bolted to the crankcase inside the flywheel as had been provided for on the 750 engine. While the valve sizes were unchanged for the 860, the carburetors were larger. Valve adjustment was by screw and locknut, and the exhaust system included Lafranconi mufflers, styled to blend with the 860 tank, and seat. In view of forthcoming U.S. legislation, the gearshift was crudely moved to the left side of the engine via a rod running behind the engine. Much of the precision of the 750 gear change was lost in the process. Unlike the 750 GT, an electric starter was integral to the concept of the 860, although a kickstart was still fitted.

The 860 GT/GTE cycle parts were quite different from the 750 GT components, and included a different frame and running gear. The frame was shorter, the swingarm used eccentric pivot chain adjusters, and the kinked front downtubes were braced. The bolt tabs on the front downtubes were flattened and the steering head angle was also increased to 31 degrees. The front fork was Ceriani, with a single Brembo front disc brake, while the longer shock absorbers were Marzocchi. Like the 750 SS, the 860 also had an 18-inch front wheel, although the wheel rims were chrome steel Radaelli. A big effort was made with the 860 to improve many components that had come under criticism on the 750 and to meet new U.S. standards. The CEV switches and electrical system were completely new, but it is questionable whether they were an improvement, and there were many updates during the first year of production.

860 GTS and 900 GTS

The 860 GTS was produced in response to the poor reception of the 860 GT. It had a new gas tank and seat, dual front disc brakes, and lower handlebars.

Responding to poor sales, Ducati hurriedly restyled the 860 GT during 1975 to create the 860 GTS. There were very few changes to the engine, and all 860 GTS bikes came with an electric starter. 860 GTS engine numbers began at around 853000. Along with a new 18-liter gas tank and seat, dual front disc brakes were standard and the handlebar was lower. There was also a new instrument panel, with the Smiths instruments mounted in the plastic pods of the 750 Sport. During 1976, a Marzocchi front fork replaced the Ceriani, and there were stainless-steel mudguards instead of the painted steel type. The 860 GTS was called the 900 GTS for 1978, but there were no other changes except to the electrical system and switches. Just as it was about to finish, the 900 GTS for 1979 incorporated many of the engine updates of the 900 SD Darmah. These included the Bosch electronic ignition, improved crankshaft, and proper left side gearshift.

Ducati Motor

The 900 GTS of 1978 was virtually unchanged, except for a Marzocchi front fork and stainless-steel fenders.

Production	1974	1975	1976	1977	1978	1979	Total
860 GT	568	477					1,045
860 GT USA	776						776
860 GTE	244	601					845
860 GTE USA	83	238					321
860 GTS		570	510	458	220	110	1,868
860 GTS USA				242	30	40	312
Total	1,671	1,886	510	700	250	150	5,167

860 GT, 860 GTE, 860 GTS, 900 GTS 1974-79

Engine	Twin cylinder four-stroke, air-cooled	**Ignition (degrees)**	Electronic; 10 static, 35-38 total	**Rear brake**	200mm drum (7.9 in.)
Bore	86mm	**Battery**	GT: Yuasa 12N-12A-4A-12V GTE, GTS:B68-12 36Ah	**Tires**	3.50 x 18, 3.50 x 18 (120/90 x 18)
Stroke	74.4mm			**Wheelbase**	1,550mm (61 in.)
Displacement	863.9cc	**Primary drive**	2.187:1 (32/70)	**Length**	2,200mm (86.6 in.)
Compression ratio	9:1	**Clutch**	Wet multiplate	**Height**	1,170mm (46 in.)
Valve actuation	Bevel gear-driven overhead camshaft	**Gear ratios**	0.887, 1.000, 1,203, 1.562, 2.237	**Width**	900mm (35.4 in.) 750mm (29.5 in.)
Valve timing (degrees)	48, 83, 83, 48 (51, 75, 74, 46 from 853788)	**Final drive**	GT: 2.500:1 (16/40) GTS: 2.533:1 (15/38)	**Seat height**	800mm (31.5 in.)
Carburetion	Dell'Orto PHF 32 A (C)	**Front suspension**	38mm Ceriani fork (Marzocchi after 853669)	**Dry weight**	185 kg (407.5 lbs.)
Power	57 horsepower at 7,700 rpm	**Rear suspension**	Three-way adjustable Marzocchi 320mm twin shock swingarm	**Top speed**	195 km/h (121.2 mph)
Spark plugs	Champion L88A, Bosch WM7	**Front brake**	280mm single [twin] disc (11 in.)	**Colors**	Black frame, orange, red, blue, black, yellow, green
Generator	12v/150W (until 851683) 12v/200W (from 8511684)			**Engine numbers**	DM860 850001-855500 approx
				Frame numbers	DM860S 850001-855500 approx

750/900 SUPER SPORT 1975-82

When the 860 GT was conceived in late 1973, Ducati had no intention of creating a Super Sport version. Limited edition race replicas were costly to produce, but the failure of the 860 GT brought another limited production run of Super Sports during 1975. Arguably the finest of all the Super Sports, they flew in the face of legislation by retaining a right-side gearshift, Conti mufflers, and unfiltered 40mm carburetors. Not legally saleable in the U.S., this small series was so successful that it led to the regular production of both the 750 and 900 Super Sport for 1976, adapted especially for America.

1975 750/900 Super Sport

The 1975 750 Super Sport was almost identical to the 900, but it had a sleeved-down motor and a silver fairing.

Continuing where the 1974 750 Super Sport left off, the 1975 900 Super Sport was also a race bike with lights.

The 1975 Super Sport was produced in 750 and 900cc versions, with the square-case engine for both derived from the 860 GT. The chassis was essentially that of the earlier 750 SS, continuing the 750 SS frame number sequence. The result was an intoxicating blend of the high-torque, square-case engine in the excellent 750 chassis. Like the round-case 750 SS, the 1975 examples were also hand-built limited editions, although the crankshaft and con-rods weren't as exotic. The con-rod was the usual forged 860 type, but with a dual strengthening rib around the big-end. The pistons were Borgo, rather than Mondial, and the cylinder heads were identical to the 1974 Super Sport. The 750 was identical to the 900, except for sleeved cylinders and a revised squish in the cylinder head. The 750 also retained the "750" camshaft bearing supports on the cylinder head.

Apart from the cylinder heads, carburetors, and crankshaft, the 1975 Super Sport engine was pure 860 GT. Only the larger alternator was fitted, and the Ducati Elettrotecnica ignition allowed it to be run without a battery if neccessary. There was no electric start version, and the gearshift was on the right side like the 750. Completing the performance specifications were open bell mouths on the 40mm carburetors, and Conti mufflers.

The silver-painted frame was almost identical to that of the earlier 750 SS, as was the fiberglass bodywork, although the 20-liter fiberglass fuel tank didn't feature a clear strip "fuel gauge." The front fender had four mounts rather than two, and the front Marzocchi had a Brembo brake caliper attachment. The rear Marzocchi shock absorbers were slightly longer, but the 18-inch Borrani wheels and Metzeler tires were identical to those on the 1974 version. The brake discs were now drilled. Most of the ancillary equipment was from the 750 SS, not the 860. This included the headlight, taillight, Smiths instruments and Aprilia switches. There was no provision for frame-mounted direction indicators, making the 1975 Super Sport the end of an era. Although not perfect, with a suspect ignition system and weak bottom-end, these were the last production motorcycles that barely conformed to street legality.

Still retaining a right-side gearshift and fiberglass gas tank, the 1975 Super Sport was a styling triumph.

1976-77 750/900 Super Sport

Ducati Motor

The 750 Super Sport continued as a sleeved-down 900 for 1976 and 1977. All Super Sports of this era left the factory with 32mm carburetors and Lafranconi mufflers.

It was obvious from the uncompromised specification and limited availability that the 1975 Super Sport was only intended as a one-off series. With the 860 languishing in showrooms, demand for the return of the sporting Ducati saw the Super Sport make it into regular production during 1976. Berliner wanted the model in the U.S., and this also required a left-side gearshift, and a quieter intake and exhaust system. While the desmodromic engine was the same as before, the Super Sport gained the ugly Lafranconi mufflers, and smaller carburetors with air filters. The gearshift was moved to the left via a crossover

rod, and the brake to the right, along with a revised footpeg setup. The fiberglass Imola gas tank was swapped for a smaller (18-liter) steel 750 Sport type, and turn signals were fitted along with new Aprilia (and later CEV) switches. A revised instrument layout incorporated the ignition switch. The tires were now Pirelli or Michelin.

The 1976 and 1977 Super Sport re-established Ducati as a premier manufacturer of sporting motorcycles, and maintained its reputation for outstanding handling and braking.

For 1976, the 900 Super Sport was adapted for the U.S. with a left-side gearshift, steel gas tank, and turn signals.

Only a few 750 Super Sports were produced during 1978. They retained Borrani wheels, but incorporated the engine improvements introduced with the Darmah. Dual seats were also standard this year.

Although for some purists the 1976 and 1977 Super Sport represented a backward step over the very single-purpose 1974 and 1975 versions, changes were inevitable for the Super Sport to survive. The 1976 and 1977 models were rather hastily conceived, retaining the ignition and crankshaft of the earlier model and incorporating a sloppy gearshift setup. Most criticisms were addressed with the Super Sport for 1978. The engine improvements of the 900 SD Darmah were incorporated, including an improved ignition and bottom-end, and there was a more efficient left-side gearshift.

The 1978 engine was based on that of the Darmah, rather than the earlier 860 GT, with the new crankshaft assembly incorporating a 38mm crankpin, smaller-diameter roller bearings, and a 750-style flywheel. There was a new two-wire alternator stator, and a Bosch electronic ignition with a much improved four-step ignition advance. The gearbox was unchanged, but there was a new gear selector drum and selector mechanism. This was now situated on the left, beneath the clutch. While not as accessible as the earlier system, the left-side shift was much improved, even if it didn't offer quite the precision of the right-side gearshift on pre-1976 versions. There was a new clutch cover, incorporating the ignition pick-ups and an inspection hole, along with a new right-side engine sprocket cover, which no longer incorporated the gear selector mechanism.

Both solo and dual seats were used, with most 1978 Super Sports having a dual seat. All Super Sports shared their wire-spoked Borrani wheels and Brembo brakes with the previous model. The few 1978 750 Super Sports received Brembo "Goldline" 08 calipers. 1978 models received new steel folding footpegs. Most of the electrical equipment was CEV, rather than Aprilia. Instruments were from either Smiths or Veglia. There was also a new five-light dashboard.

In many respects the 1978 Super Sport was one of the finest examples of the genre. It was the final model with Borrani wire spoked wheels, and the last wearing the classic blue and silver. During 1978, the 900 Super Sport became black and gold, with Speedline magnesium alloy wheels, although the 750 Super Sport remained in silver with wire-spoked wheels. The black and gold 900 was initially intended for the British market (and had different decals), but can be considered a 1979 model for other markets.

1979-80 900 Super Sport

1979 and 1980 900 Super Sports were black and gold, with cast-alloy wheels.

There were few developments to the 900 Super Sport engine for 1979. The unit was also shared with the Mike Hailwood Replica, so the engine and frame number sequences were now noticeably divergent. During 1979, Silentium mufflers replaced the Lafranconi, but the Contis were always an option. Fashion dictated a switch from Borrani wire-spoked to magnesium Speedline wheels, with a correspondingly larger rear disc brake. The rear rim width increased to 2.50 inches. Later in 1979, the Speedline wheels were replaced by a superior aluminum six-spoke FPS. Most of these black and gold 900 SS's came with a dual seat, although the solo saddle was always optional. The cast wheels weren't functionally superior, but the black and gold Super Sport was a particularly attractive model.

1981-82 900 Super Sport

After 8 years with little development, the Super Sport came in for a mild update for 1981. There were a number of engine updates, mainly to the cylinder heads, gearbox and Bosch ignitionbut quality control was poor. Cast-iron valve seats replaced the bronze type, and there were new valve guides. Many of the electrical components were now shared with the Pantah, including ignition transducers and alternator rotor. The most important change was to the gearbox (after engine 092920), where three-dog design replaced the problematic six-dog type.

Most of the changes for 1981 were to the bodywork. There were new colors and decals for the steel fuel tank, half fairing, dual seat and side covers. There were also new ABS fenders. The dual seat a new design with a removable (and lockable) seat pad. The seat sat low over the rear subframe with a cut-out over the top shock absorber mount (but this was revised after frame number 090695).

Later seats didn't sit so low and cleared the shock absorber without a cut-out.

There was considerable inconsistency as to the exact specification of Super Sports during this period. Some 1982 models came with modified Mike Hailwood Replica frames with a fold-out lever near the left side cover to aid putting on the centerstand. Some fairings had a cross brace, and later examples a more angular front fender. There were two types of Marzocchi fork, and either four- or six-bolt discs on the FPS wheels.

Changes to the electrical system included a Nippon Denso left handlebar switch and a Bosch horn. While most 1981-82 Super Sports had Veglia instruments, Smiths were still fitted on occasion. There were also small changes to some components, such as a Pantah-style clutch cable adjuster. There is no really definitive example of this period because often the components fitted reflected what was available in the depleted parts store at the time of manufacture.

By 1982, demand for the Super Sport was diminishing and in a fashion-conscious world there was no market for a relic of the 1970s. Times have changed, and now the qualities of the Super Sport are fully appreciated, and it is considered one of the classic Ducatis.

PRODUCTION	1975	1976	1977	1978	1979	1980	1981	1982	TOTAL
750 SS	249	120	100	30					499
900 SS	246	800	496	984	774	713	1,085	335	5,433
900 SS US		220	137	33	160	40	80		670
Total	495	1,140	733	1,047	934	753	1,165	335	6,602

The final 900 Super Sport of 1981-82 featured a new seat, although it was essentially similar to the original of 1975.

750 AND 900 SUPER SPORT 1975-82

Engine	Twin cylinder four-stroke, air-cooled	Battery	Yuasa 12N-12A-4A-12V	Width	660mm (26 in.)
					675mm (26.6 in.)
Bore	750: 80mm	Primary drive	2.187:1 (32/70)	Seat height	760mm (30 in.)
	900: 86mm	Clutch	Wet multiplate	Dry weight	180 kg (396.5 lbs.)
Stroke	74.4mm	Gear ratios	0.887, 1.000, 1,203, 1.562, 2.237		188 kg (414.1 lbs.)
Displacement	750: 748cc			Top speed	230 km/h (143 mph)
	900: 863.9cc	Final drive	750: 2.500:1 (16/40)		
Compression ratio	750: 9.65:1		900: 2.312:1 (16/37), 2.250:1 (16/36)	Colors	Silver frame, silver and blue
	900: 9.5:1	Front suspension	38mm Marzocchi fork		Black frame, black and gold (1979-80)
Valve actuation	Bevel gear-driven desmodromic overhead camshaft	Rear suspension	3-Three-way adjustable Marzocchi 310mm twin shock swingarm		Black frame, silver (1981-82)
Valve timing (degrees)	63, 83, 80, 58	Front brake	280mm dual disc (11 in.)	Engine numbers 750 SS	DM750.1 075412-076100 approx
Carburetion	Dell'Orto PHM 40 A, B or C (PHF 32A)	Rear brake	229mm disc (9 in.)	Frame numbers 750 SS	DM750SS 075412-076300 approx
Power	57 horsepower at 7,400 rpm	Tires	3.50x18, 3.50x18 (120/90x18), 100/90x18, 110/90x18 (1979 on)	Engine numbers 900 SS	DM860.1 086001-095000 approx
	(1982 32mm carbs)			Frame numbers 900 SS (1975)	DM750SS 075412-075900 approx
Spark plugs	Champion L81, L82Y, L88A, Bosch W7B	Wheelbase	1,500mm (59 in.)		
Generator	12v/200W	Length	2,200mm (86.6 in.)	Frame numbers 900 SS (1976-82)	DM860SS 086001-095000 approx
Ignition (degrees)	Electronic 10 static, 35-38 total (32-34; 1976) (1978-later: 6 static, 32 total)	Height	1,050mm (41.3 in.)		

Formula 1 900 NCR (1977-79)

Undoubtedly one of the most beautiful Ducatis of any era, the F1 900 NCR was also one of the most successful. Mike Hailwood rode one to victory at the Isle of Man in 1978.

FORMULA 1 900 NCR 1977-79

Engine	Twin cylinder four-stroke, air-cooled	**Power**	105 horsepower at 8,800 rpm.	**Front suspension**	38mm Marzocchi fork
Bore	86mm	**Spark plugs**	Champion L2G or L3G (Gold Palladium)	**Rear suspension**	320mm gas Marzocchi twin-shock swingarm
Stroke	74.4mm	**Generator**	12v/200W	**Front brake**	280mm dual disc (11 in.)
Displacement	863.91cc	**Ignition (degrees)**	Points and coil, 10 static, 38 total	**Rear brake**	280mm disc (11 in.)
Compression ratio	10:1	**Battery**	Yuasa 12N-12A-4A-12V	**Tires**	Michelin 3.50 x 18 S41 PZ2
Valve actuation	Bevel gear-driven desmodromic overhead camshaft	**Primary drive**	2.419:1 (31/75)		Michelin TV2 4.00/5.60 x 18
Valve timing (degrees)	69, 103, 98, 73	**Clutch**	Dry multiplate	**Dry weight**	160 kg (352.4 lbs.)
Carburetion	Dell'Orto PHM 40	**Gear ratios**	0.741, 0.814, 0.928, 1.120, 1.455	**Colors**	Red and silver
		Final drive	15/33 to 15/42		

While all the factory endurance racers of the 1970s were one-off specials, the creation of the TT1 World Championship saw Ducati offer the 900 NCR Formula 1 machine. This was a catalogued model for those who had good connections, and could afford it. The price in Italy was 7.425.000 lire, more than twice that of a 900 SS. Scuderia NCR (Nepoti Caracchi Racing) was located near to the factory in Bologna and they were the front for the official racing team.

The Formula 1 900 NCR was less exotic than the endurance racers, and reputedly 18 complete machines were built, along with 20 spare engines. They carried 900 SS engine numbers (in the 088-series) but featured specially cast crankcases incorporating a spin-on oil filter. The engines retained the earlier round-case 750 bevel-drive layout with points ignition and a right-side gearshift. The displacement was the same as the production 900 SS, as was the 80-degree included valve angle. There were special 44 and 38mm nimonic valves, lighter Borgo pistons, 12mm lift desmodromic camshafts, and a lightened crankshaft (7.4 kg as opposed to 8 kg). The con-rods were the same 150mm length as the round-case 750, rather than the shorter square-case rod, but with a 19mm wristpin. The F1 900 NCR also featured a closer ratio six-dog gearbox and straight-cut primary gears.

The chrome-molybdenum Daspa frame was different than the production Verlicchi. It weighed only 12 kg and featured additional bracing. The Marzocchi fork was also narrower at 180mm (as opposed to the 195mm of the street bike). Beautiful pieces adorned the NCR 900, notably the vernier adjusters for the milled foot levers, and the one-piece fiberglass 24-liter tank and seat unit. The wheels were magnesium Campagnolo (MT2.15 x 18 and MT4.00 x 18), and the brakes 08 Brembo. This was the machine that Mike Hailwood rode to victory in the 1978 Formula 1 race at the Isle of Man.

900 Sport Desmo "Darmah" 1977-82

With the failure of the 860 GT and GTS to earn a loyal following, Ducati again turned to Leopoldo Tartarini in 1976 to create a replacement. The resulting 900 SD Darmah was a more successful rendition than the Giugiaro 860 and incorporated a number of technical improvements.

900 SD 1977-78

The 900 SD Darmah was a significant model in that included a number of technical and styling innovations. The earliest versions, like this 1977 model, had a Ceriani front fork, Campagnolo wheels and Lafranconi mufflers.

Ducati Motor

By 1978, the Darmah had a Marzocchi front fork, Speedline wheels, and new colors.

Ducati Motor

One of the most important alterations was to the crankshaft. While the forged con-rods were unchanged from the 860 GTS, the big-end bearings were caged 3mm rollers that provided more bearing surface area. The crankpin diameter was increased to 38mm. The three-ring forged Borgo slipper pistons were now shared with the 900 Super Sport, as were the desmodromic camshafts and valves. While the cylinder head internals were the same as the Super Sport, the cylinder heads only had a narrow (52mm) inlet stud setup for the 32mm Dell'Orto carburetors.

The gearshift and selector mechanism was now located on the left side underneath the clutch housing. There was a new right-side engine cover, and new crankcases with the ignition wires exiting through the clutch cover. The exhaust system included Lafranconi mufflers, but Contis were always a more attractive and more functional option.

The biggest changes occurred to the electronic ignition and electric start. The unreliable Ducati Elettrotecnica ignition system was replaced by a Bosch system, with the ignition pickups mounted inside the clutch cover and the ignition rotor bolted onto the end of the crankshaft. The ignition pickups ran in the engine oil so it wasn't the perfect solution, but the system was more reliable than the earlier Ducati Elettrotecnica type. The greatest advantage the Bosch system provided over the Ducati Elettrotecnica was an improved four-stage ignition advance.

While all early 900 SDs still came with a kickstart mechanism, an electric start was standard. Along with a larger battery, the electric start was considerably improved over the 860 GTE and GTS. Still using the heavy Marelli starter motor, the switch and drive system was totally revised and simplified. The crankshaft starter gear was independently attached to the crankshaft with a freewheel bearing inside the flywheel. Generally, this worked well, but there were occasional problems with the disengagement of this bearing, which could result in the starter motor turning with the engine.

Not only were the engine modifications significant, the Darmah chassis and components represented a radical departure for Ducati. The frame was derived from the 860 GT (with eccentric chain adjustment), rather than 900 SS. Suspension also followed the 860, with a long Ceriani front fork, but with short Marzocchi shock absorbers. Soon after it was introduced, the Ceriani fork was shortened to improve the steering. Five-spoke gold Campagnolo cast-magnesium alloy wheels were fitted, with undrilled Brembo disc brakes front and rear. Also new was a rather ineffective seven-position hydraulic Paioli steering damper connecting the lower triple clamp to the front frame downtube.

All the bodywork was new for the Darmah. The steel fuel tank only held 15 liters and the fiberglass saddle incorporated Tartarini's distinctive duck tail. Both the front and rear fenders were stainless steel. The instrument panel and controls were also new, featuring Nippon Denso instruments, throttle and switches, and a seven-warning light dashboard. Another improvement was the 180mm Bosch H4 headlight. There were only a few updates for 1978, most noticeably a switch to a Marzocchi front fork and longer shock absorbers. Black and gold was also offered, and dual five-spoke magnesium Speedline wheels replaced the Campagnolos.

The Darmah received a new seat with more padding in 1979, and lost the kickstart. This was one of the final examples with Speedline wheels.

The Darmah was continually evolved, and from engine number 903026, the cylinder heads were those of the 900 Super Sport with a wider stud mount (58mm) and larger inlet tract. This enabled 40mm Dell'Orto carburetors to bolt straight on with a significant performance increase if they were used with Conti mufflers. After engine number 903762 the entire kickstart assembly was removed and the alternator cover plugged. Silentium mufflers also replaced the Lafranconis around this time. From engine number 904414 there was a shorter gear lever, with a correspondingly shorter shaft (149mm instead of 134mm), and revised clutch cover.

There were also a few changes to the running gear during the course of 1979. From frame number 902960, longer Marzocchi oleo pneumatic shock absorbers were fitted, and a new dual seat appeared during 1979 with more padding and a hinged tool compartment.

During 1980, aluminum six-spoke FPS wheels were fitted, still with solid four-bolt cast-iron discs. Between frame numbers 951261 and 951376, the FPS wheels had six bolt holes and took the drilled discs with alloy carriers

of the 900 SSD. By 1981, the Darmah specification became quite erratic. In November 1981, after engine number 906306, the six-dog gearbox was replaced by a three-dog type.

One of the most significant frame alterations came in May 1981, after frame number 952251. The 860 GT-style swingarm without axle adjusters was replaced by a swingarm that included Super Sport Seeley-style axle

Ducati Motor

The final Darmah of 1982 received a new color scheme. The mufflers were Silentium, and the swingarm had Super Sport-style chain adjusters.

adjustment, while the eccentric adjustment at the pivot was also retained. The final Darmah of 1982 featured different colors and graphics, and later specification Brembo brakes and Marzocchi suspension. Although neither rare nor exotic, the Darmah represents outstanding value for those looking to experience the world of the desmodromic bevel-drive twin. A brilliant recipe, with an electric start broadening the appeal of the desmodromic twin, the Darmah remains largely unappreciated.

Production	1977	1978	1979	1980	1981	1982	Total
900 SD	1,610	1,671	747	390	643	317	5,378
900 SD US		20	80	80	40		220
Total	1,610	1,691	827	470	683	317	5,598

900 Sport Desmo Darmah 1977-82

Engine	Twin cylinder four-stroke, air-cooled	Primary drive	2.187:1 (32/70)	Wheelbase	1,550mm (61 in.)
Bore	86mm	Clutch	Wet multiplate	Length	2,260mm (88.9 in.)
Stroke	74.4mm	Gear ratios	0.887, 1.000, 1,203, 1.562, 2.237	Height	1,090mm (42.9 in.)
Displacement	863.9cc	Final drive	2.533:1 (15/38)	Width	780mm (30.7 in.)
Compression ratio	9.3:1	Front suspension	38mm Ceriani (608, or 580mm) fork / From 901174 Marzocchi (600mm) fork	Seat height	780mm (30.7 in.) / 813mm (32 in.)
Valve actuation	Bevel gear driven desmodromic overhead camshaft			Dry weight	216 kg (475.8 lbs.)
Valve timing (degrees)	63, 83, 80, 58	Rear suspension	Three-way adjustable Marzocchi 300mm (until 900989) twin-shock swingarm / From 900990 Marzocchi 315mm / From 902960 Marzocchi 330mm	Top speed	190 km/h (118.1 mph)
Carburetion	Dell'Orto PHF 32 A, B or C			Colors	Black frame, red and white, or black and gold (1977-81) / Black frame, silver, blue, burgundy (1982)
Spark plugs	Champion L88A, Bosch W7B				
Generator	12v/200W	Front brake	280mm dual disc (11 in.)	Engine numbers	DM860 900001-907000 approx.
Ignition (degrees)	Bosch Electronic; 6 static, 32 total	Rear brake	280mm disc (11 in.)	Frame numbers	DM860SS 900001-903500 approx. / –1979-After: DM900SD 950001-953200 approx.
Battery	Yuasa B68 36 Ah	Tires	3.50 x 18, 4.25/85 x 18 (120/90 x 18)		

900 Super Sport Desmo "Darmah"

During 1978, the Sport Desmo Darmah was developed into the Super Sport Darmah. It was an attractive adaptation of the Super Sport café racer to the Darmah engine and chassis. The engine and drivetrain were shared with the regular 900 SD, without a kickstart, and all the cylinder heads had the wider studs to allow fitting of 40mm carburetors. Like the SD, two types of clutch cover were fitted to the SSD, with a shorter gearshift shaft after engine number 904415. Early examples featured Lafranconi mufflers, with Silentium during 1979, but Contis were always an option. Apart from brackets for the steering head-mounted headlight and fairing support, and the rear-set footpegs, the black-painted frame and swingarm were identical to that of the 900 SD.

Production	1978	1979	1980	1981	Total
900 SSD	200	309	345		854
900 SSD UK			100		100
900 SSD US		100			100
900 SSD Australia			260	126	386
Total	200	409	705	126	1,440

Setting the 900 SSD apart from both the 900 SD and 900 SS was the distinctive two-tone blue paintwork. The bodywork was based on the first series 900 SD, with the same fuel tank, ducktail seat, and side covers, but with a

900 SUPER SPORT DESMO DARMAH 1978-81

Engine	Twin cylinder four-stroke, air-cooled	**Ignition (degrees)**	Bosch Electronic; 6 static, 32 total	**Wheelbase**	1,550mm (61 in.)	
Bore	86mm	**Battery**	Yuasa B68 36 Ah	**Length**	2,260mm (88.9 in.)	
Stroke	74.4mm	**Primary drive**	2.187:1 (32/70)	**Height**	1,280mm (50.4 in.)	
Displacement	863.9cc	**Clutch**	Wet multiplate	**Width**	700mm (27.6 in.)	
Compression ratio	9.5:1	**Gear ratios**	0.887, 1.000, 1,203, 1.562, 2.237	**Seat height**	740mm (29.1 in.)	
Valve actuation	Bevel gear-driven desmodromic overhead camshaft	**Final drive**	2.400:1 (15/36)	**Dry weight**	216 kg (475.8 lbs.)	
Valve timing (degrees)	63, 83, 80, 58	**Front suspension**	Marzocchi (600mm) fork	**Top speed**	205 km/h (127.4 mph)	
Carburetion	Dell'Orto PHF 32C	**Rear suspension**	Marzocchi 330mm	**Colors**	Black frame, two-tone blue	
Spark plugs	Bosch W7B	**Front brake**	280mm dual disc (11 in.)	**Engine numbers**	DM860 903027-905000 approx.	
Generator	12v/200W	**Rear brake**	280mm disc (11 in.)	**Frame numbers**	DM860SS 902960-903500 approx. From 1979 DM900SD 950001-951000 approx.	
		Tires	3.50 x 18, 120/90 x 18			

Ducati Motor

The 900 SSD was a cosmetic alteration of the 900 SD. This 1978 example has high footpegs, Speedline wheels and Lafranconi mufflers.

Super Sport-style half fairing. The suspension was also identical to that on the 900 SD of the same period, with a Marzocchi fork, and Marzocchi oleo-pneumatic shock absorbers. Until frame number 950761, the folding steel footpegs screwed into lugs welded on the frame, and were mounted very high. Criticism of the riding position led to a redesign of the lever and footpeg layout for 1980 (from frame number 950762). These were now located

By 1980, the 900 SSD had FPS wheels and lower footpegs. The SSD was one of the most attractive Ducatis of the era.

on brackets bolted to the frame serrations underneath the swingarm pivot.

The first examples of the 900 SSD came with magnesium Speedline wheels, but were changed to aluminum FPS during 1979. All SSDs featured a six-bolt front disc attachment and the three drilled disc rotors had aluminum carriers. There were a number of components specific to the SSD. The clip-on handlebars were offset forwards and upwards, and instruments and warning lights were mounted on a steering head bracket, rather than the top triple clamp. While undoubtedly one of the most attractive Ducatis of the era, the 900 SSD was too heavy to be a real Super Sport, and its overall performance inferior. Management decided the 900 S2 was the future for the bevel-drive twin, leaving the short-lived SSD as one of the rarest bevel-drive twins.

900 Mike Hailwood Replica 1979-84

When the great road racer Mike Hailwood came out of semi-retirement at the age of 38 to win the 1978 Isle of Man Formula One race on an NCR Ducati, Ducati was presented with another opportunity to market a race replica. Although it was more than 12 months before a production Mike Hailwood Replica appeared, when it did so it was basically a cosmetic alteration of a 900 Super Sport. But the MHR had a certain appeal. It was very distinctive and was destined to become Ducati's most popular model in the early 1980s.

900 Replica 1979-80

Towards the end of 1979, the first series of 200 Mike Hailwood Replicas was produced, primarily for the British market, each coming with a certificate. The kickstart engine was identical to that of the 900 Super Sport and shared the same number sequence. As the MHR was to spearhead the lineup, all early examples came with 40mm carburetors and Conti mufflers. There were new exhaust header pipes that routed closer to the engine to enable the fairing to fit more closely. During 1980, some Replicas came with Silentium mufflers.

The 900 Replica shared its chassis with the 900 SS, but there were a small number of changes. Apart from various brackets and a different headlamp support, the red-painted frame was the same as that of the Super Sport. It was the bodywork that set the 900 Replica apart. There was nothing conservative about the red, white and green colors inherited from Hailwood's Sports Motorcycle machine that was sponsored by Castrol oil. The first 200 examples came with a fiberglass cover (replicating the NCR tank shape) over the regular Super Sport 18-liter steel fuel tank,

and a single seat as standard equipment. Converting to a dual seat required substituting a replacement seat pad. For the next series the there was a 24-liter steel tank specifically made for the Replica, and a more easily convertible dual seat. All early 900 Replicas came with a large fiberglass one-piece full fairing, incorporating the front turn signal indicators, and complicating basic servicing. There were no side covers on 1979-80 ReplicasThe battery, regulator, and rear carburetor were all visible. Both fenders were red fiberglass.

Different suspension set the 900 Replica apart from the Super Sport. The front fork featured polished aluminum legs while retaining the black-painted triple clamps, but during 1980 the fork legs were black. All Replicas were fitted with cast-alloy wheels, either magnesium Speedline or Campagnolo on the first series. On the second series (with a 24-liter steel tank and revised seat), the wheels were mostly aluminum FPS, or occasionally Campagnolo. The 1979-80 Replica shared its brakes with the 900 Super Sport, and featured Brembo 08 "Goldline" brake calipers.

The 1980 900 Replica had a one-piece fairing and replicated the Mike Hailwood race-winning Formula 1 machine.

The electrical system of the 900 Replica was derived from that of the 900 SSD "Darmah," with a mixture of CEV and Nippon Denso equipment. The CEV headlamp, taillight, and direction indicators were similar to that of the Super Sport, but with an SSD Nippon Denso left handlebar switch, and Nippon Denso instruments. As only a small number of 900 Replicas were produced in 1979 and 1980, and they were remarkably raw and uncompromised machines for the period, Ducati decided to adapt the model for series production. The Mike Hailwood Replica then went on to sustain the company until the Cagiva acquisition of 1985.

900 Mike Hailwood Replica 1981-84 (Kickstart)

Most of the updates to the 900 Replica for 1981 were practical or cosmetic, and while the kickstart Super Sport engine was retained with 40mm carburetors, generally it had Silentium mufflers. During 1982 and 1983 some 900 MHRs also came with air filters. The main update for 1981 was the inclusion of a two-piece fairing with a removable lower section. While the shape was similar to previous years, this was a practical development as it meant that simple maintenance (such as oil changing) was possible without removing the entire fairing. To hide the battery and rear carburetor there was a new seat unit and side covers. From frame number 901301 on the "Goldline" brake calipers were replaced by the regular black 08 caliper fitted to other 900 Ducatis. The kickstart version of the 900 MHR also continued alongside the revamped electric start 900 MHR of 1983 and into 1984, although these final kickstart models incorporated the 900 Super Sport engine in the revised S2-derived chassis. The engine included all the updates of the Super Sport, such as new valve guides and three-dog gearbox. After 096314 there was an oil level sight glass and spin-on oil filter, and an additional magnetic sump plug. The dipstick filler hole was cast over.

The 1981-82 900 MHR also included side covers to hide the battery.

While the 1981 900 MHR looked similar to the 1980 version, the fairing was in two pieces and had new decals.

900 Mike Hailwood Replica 1983-84 (Electric Start)

As a prelude to the Mille, during 1983 the 900 Mike Hailwood Replica came in for its first major revision since 1979. The kickstart engine was phased out for an updated electric start version and placed in a frame derived from the S2, rather than Super Sport. The engine included Gilnisil-coated cylinders without removable liners, with matched pistons. To reduce engine noise there were rubber plugs inserted between the fins. A spin-on oil filter was now incorporated between the cylinders. The alternator was a three-wire Saprisa. The coils were Motoplat instead of Bosch.

One of the main updates was to the clutch. It was now a dry hydraulically actuated type, and there was a much smaller (and lighter) 0.7-kilowatt Nippon Denso starter motor. To incorporate the new electric start and dry clutch the outer clutch and primary drive cover was two-piece, accompanied by a new alternator and hydraulic slave cylinder cover on the right. While it was not as attractive

as the earlier round case, there was an attempt to tidy the electric start cover and make the alternator cover more compact.

Although it looked visually similar to the previous 900 Mike Hailwood Replica, the entire running gear was now 900 S2-derived, rather than Super Sport-based. Unfortunately, this chassis was also inferior, and the new MHR, despite factory claims, was heavier, longer, and taller than its predecessor. The steering was even heavier, and handling lacked the finesse and high-speed stability of the earlier Super Sports. The frame was cheaper to produce, and providedg improved ground clearance and room for a larger battery. Much of the frame construction was derived from the 860. The two front downtubes were flattened at the ends, but the real weakness was the rear downtubes that were hollowed out to provide battery clearance. The swingarm included Seeley-style chain adjusters.

For 1983, and 1984 the 900 MHR had an electric start and a new frame and fairing.

900 MIKE HAILWOOD REPLICA 1979-84

Engine	Twin cylinder four-stroke, air-cooled
Bore	86mm
Stroke	74.4mm
Displacement	863.9cc
Compression ratio	9.5:1 (9.3:1)
Valve actuation	Bevel gear-driven desmodromic overhead camshaft
Valve timing (degrees)	63, 83, 80, 58
Carburetion	Dell'Orto PHM 40B
Power	80 horsepower at 7,000 rpm
	63 horsepower at 7,400 rpm (1981)
	72 horsepower at 7,000 rpm (1983)
Spark plugs	Bosch W7B
Generator	12v/200W

Ignition (degrees)	Bosch Electronic; 6 static, 32 total (5, 28; from 1983)
Battery	Yuasa 12N-12A-4A (19Ah from 1983)
Primary drive	2.187:1 (32/70)
Clutch	Wet multiplate (dry from 1983)
Gear ratios	0.887, 1.000, 1,203, 1.562, 2.237
Final drive	2.400:1 (15/36), 2.200:1 (15/33) 1981-84
Front suspension	Marzocchi 38mm fork (590mm)
Rear suspension	Marzocchi 330mm
Front brake	280mm dual disc (11 in.)
Rear brake	280mm disc (11 in.)
Tires	100/90 x 18, 110/90 x 18 (120/90 x 18)
Wheelbase	1,510mm (59.4 in.) 1,500mm 1983 (59.1 in.)
Length	2,200mm (86.6 in.)

Height	1,280mm (50.4 in.) 1,250mm 1983 (49.2 in.)
Width	700mm (27.6 in.)
Seat height	780mm (30.7 in.) 800mm 1983 (31.5 in.)
Dry weight	205 kg (451.5 lbs.) 212.5 kg 1983 (468 lbs.)
Top speed	220 km/h (136.7 mph) 1983: 222 km/h 1983 (138 mph)
Colors	Red frame, red, white and green
Engine numbers (kickstart)	DM860 089400-097000 approx
Engine numbers (electric start)	DM860 907800-909300 approx
Frame numbers (kickstart)	DM860SS 900001-901500 approx From 1979 DM900R 901500-904000 approx (kickstart)
Frame numbers (electric start)	DM900R1 905002-906500 approx

Production	1979	1980	1981	1982	1983	1984	Total
900 MHR kickstart	300	447	1,500	1,549	780	25	4,601
900 MHR electric start					687	770	1,457
Total	300	447	1,500	1,549	1,467	995	6,058

A narrower and taller fiberglass two-piece fairing set the 1983-84 900 MHR apart from earlier versions. While the brakes and suspension were largely unchanged (except for the positioning of the front brake calipers behind the fork leg), the aluminum Oscam wheels could now accommodate tubeless tires. Most of the frame fittings (footpegs and levers) were shared with the S2. While the instruments were still Nippon Denso, there was a new dashboard and LED warning light arrangement, and a 170mm Carello headlamp. Also new were the large, and ugly, rectangular CEV taillight and stalk turn signal indicators.

Although conceived as an interim model between the kickstart MHR and Mille, the 1983-84 electric start 900 was an excellent machine. Although the frame was flawed, the engine was exceptional. Smooth, powerful, and the most reliable, in many ways it epitomized the finest attributes of the 900 bevel-drive, and in some respects was superior to the Mille.

900 S2 1982-84

1984 900 S2s had a fairing belly-pan and Oscam wheels, but retained the earlier square-case engine.

Another dubious marketing decision was the replacement of the long-running Super Sport with the S2. While the S2 was primarily a styling exercise, it was also an attempt to introduce an electric start to the Super Sport to widen its appeal. The S2 thus combined features of both the Super Sport and Darmah, and most had electric start. Although the 900 MHR of 1983-84 was relatively easy to categorize, the same cannot be said about the 900 S2, which was another incredibly inconsistent model in specification.

The kickstart engine was shared with the 900 MHR and new crankcases with a spin-on oil filter appeared during 1983, after engine number 096314. Although no kickstart-only 900 S2s were produced in 1984, some electric start versions also featured a kickstart and were apparently leftover kickstart engines with an added electric start. Electric start S2s continued with the earlier square-case engine, rather than the new 900 MHR series, and while many of the later 900 S2s had an oil level sight glass in the right sump, along with a spin-on oil filter, all came with the earlier Marelli electric start and a wet, cable-operated clutch.

The S2 frame was similar to the final series of MHR, and was an amalgam of the Super Sport and Darmah types. With its flattened engine mounting points and bowed rear section, it was also functionally inferior. In other respects the 900 S2 was an unremarkable styling development of the 900 Super Sport. The 18-liter steel 900 SS gas tank came with a lockable black recessed fuel

filler cap. The ABS fairing was taken from the 600 SL Pantah and modified to provide clearance for the electric start motor. Some 1984 900 S2s had plastic silver tank badges rather than decals, and generally included a belly pan under the engine.

While the Marzocchi fork was similar to the later 900 MHR, there was a rear Brembo brake caliper mount. During 1984 some 900 S2s came with air caps in the top of the fork legs. Aluminum six-spoke FPS wheels were used, but during 1984 Oscam wheels were also fitted.

Ducati Motor

The 900 S2 was intended to replace the 900 Super Sport in 1982, but it wasn't a success.

Production	1982	1983	1984	Total
900 S2 kickstart	173	180		353
900 S2 electric start	476	202	205	883
Total	649	382	205	1,236

900 S2 1982-84

Engine	Twin cylinder four-stroke, air-cooled	**Primary drive**	2.187:1 (32/70)	**Seat height**	840mm (33.1 in.)	
Bore	86mm	**Clutch**	Wet multiplate	**Dry weight**	190 kg (419 lbs.)	
Stroke	74.4mm	**Gear ratios**	0.887, 1.000, 1.204, 1.562, 2.237	**Top speed**	205 km/h (127.4 mph)	
Displacement	863.9cc	**Final drive**	2.200:1 (15/33)	**Colors**	Black frame, bronze	
Compression ratio	9.3:1	**Front suspension**	Marzocchi 38mm fork		Red frame, red or black (from 1983)	
Valve actuation	Bevel gear driven desmodromic overhead camshaft	**Rear suspension**	5-way adjustable Marzocchi ET 85 (AG Strada from 1983)	**Engine numbers (kickstart)**	From DM860 095000 approx	
Valve timing (degrees)	63, 83, 80, 58	**Front brake**	280mm dual disc (11 in.)	**Engine numbers (electric start)**	From DM860 907000-907800 approx	
Carburetion	Dell'Orto PHF 30A or PHM 40B	**Rear brake**	280mm disc (11 in.)	**Frame numbers (kickstart)**	From DM860SS 092001 approx	
Spark plugs	Bosch W7B	**Tires**	100/90 x 18, 110/90 x 18 (120/90 x 18)		From DM 900 SS A92400 approx (1983)	
Generator	12v/200W	**Wheelbase**	1,500mm (59.1 in.)	**Frame numbers (electric start)**	From DM860SS 092001 approx	
Ignition (degrees)	Bosch Electronic; 6 static, 32 total (5, 28; from 1983)	**Length**	2,220mm (87.4 in.)		From DM 900S2 095001-097000 approx (1983-84)	
Battery	Yuasa 19Ah	**Height**	1,250mm (49.2 in.)			
		Width	700mm (27.6 in.)			

Generally, the 900 S2 electrical system, switches and instruments were identical to those of the 900 MHR. New for the 900 S2 were the large rectangular CEV twin-bulb taillight and matching turn signal indicators. The 1982, and some 1983, 900 S2s had flush-mounted front indicators in the fairing, but later examples featured indicators on stalks. Some of the final 900 S2s also had the later 900 MHR instrument panel. These were some of the most variable machines in specification ever to emanate from Bologna, especially those of 1984, and they were among the least satisfactory in aesthetics and performance.

Mille Mike Hailwood Replica and Mille S2 1984-86

Apart from the decals and red front fender, the Mille MHR was virtually indistinguishable from the 1984 900 MHR. This 1984 Mille also had different decals on the fairing.

The final bevel-drive twin, the Mille, emerged during 1984 and incorporated many great developments. The engine was arguably the finest rendition of the series. With its dry clutch, and similar external engine covers, the Mille engine looked externally similar to the final 900, but internally it was a different story. A bore and stroke increase provided nearly 1000cc, and the valve sizes were increased to 42 and 38mm, although the earlier 80-degree included valve angle was maintained. Apart from the capacity increase, the most significant development was a forged one-piece crankshaft with plain big-end bearings, along with an upgraded lubrication system that included a larger spin-on oil filter. As with the final 900 MHR, the cylinders were Gilnisil coated, but there was a higher

Some Mille MHRs and S2s came with a two-into-one Conti exhaust exiting on the left.

Most Mille MHRs had a red-painted front fork and "Mille" decals on the fairing.

primary drive ratio, accompanied by new transmission ratios for the lower three gears, providing wider overall spacing. The small Nippon Denso starter motor also came from the last 900, and it was always problematic on the larger engine.

The chassis and bodywork for both the Mille MHR and S2 was almost identical to the 1984 900 MHR and 900

S2. To increase ground clearance the Marzocchi front fork had longer fork tubes. On early examples the fork legs and triple clamps were painted black. Most Mille MHRs had red-painted fork legs and triple clamp, with air caps on each fork leg.

While the Mille engine was stronger than the 900, it was compromised by the wider ratio gearbox. On the road, performance wasn't really superior, except for the tremendous mid-range torque. The Mille MHR and S2 were also much larger and heavier than the earlier 750s and 900s, negating many of the benefits of the extra capacity. But as the ultimate development of the classic bevel twin, the Mille deserves a special place. It is relatively rare, and potentially the most reliable.

Still celebrating a race victory 6 years earlier, the 1984 Mille MHR looked very similar to the original production 900 Replica.

Production	1984	1985	1986	Total
Mille MHR	662	199	250	1,111
Mille S2	71	100		171
Total	733	299	250	1,282

Mille MHR, Mille S2 1984-86

Engine	Twin cylinder four-stroke, air-cooled	Ignition (degrees)	Bosch Electronic; 5 static, 28 total
Bore	88mm	Battery	Yuasa 19Ah
Stroke	78mm	Primary drive	1.769:1 (39/69)
Displacement	973cc	Clutch	Dry multiplate
Compression ratio	9.3:1	Gear ratios	0.887, 1.000, 1.250, 1.761, 2.720
Valve actuation	Bevel gear-driven desmodromic overhead camshaft	Final drive	2.733:1 (15/41)
Valve timing (degrees)	63, 83, 80, 58	Front suspension	Marzocchi 38mm fork
Carburetion	Dell'Orto PHM 40B	Rear suspension	330mm Marzocchi twin-shock swingarm
Power	76 horsepower at 6,700 rpm	Front brake	280mm dual disc (11 in.)
Spark plugs	Bosch W7B	Rear brake	280mm disc (11 in.)
Generator	12v/200W	Tires	100/90x18, 130/80x18
		Wheelbase	1,500mm (59.1 in.)

Length	2,200mm (86.6 in.)
Height	1,250mm (49.2 in.)
Width	700mm (27.6 in.)
Seat height	800mm (31.5 in.)
Dry weight	198 kg (436.1 lbs.)
Top speed	222 km/h (138 mph)
Colors	MHR: Red frame, red, white and green S2: Red frame, black
Engine numbers	MHR: ZDM1000 100001-101300 approx. S2: From ZDM1000 100700 approx.
Frame numbers	ZDM1000R 100001-101110 approx From ZDM1000S2 100001 (some early S2s had 1000R frames)

CHAPTER 6

BELT-DRIVE TWO-VALVE TWINS

In 1976, with the parallel twin struggling to find acceptance, 1976 Fabio Taglioni was allowed to develop the middleweight design he had envisaged since 1971: the Pantah. This was a 90-degree Vee-twin that was a synthesis of the 500cc bevel-drive Grand Prix motorcycle of 1970, and the belt-drive double-overhead camshaft four-valve Armaroli racer of 1973. The Pantah shared the bore and stroke of the 500cc racer, but incorporated toothed rubber belts to drive the single overhead camshafts. In 1973, belt camshaft drive was unusual for a motorcycle, but for Taglioni it seemed the ideal alternative to bevel gears because it was less expensive to manufacture and made the bikes run quieter. This was such an advanced design that it still forms the basis of all current production Ducatis.

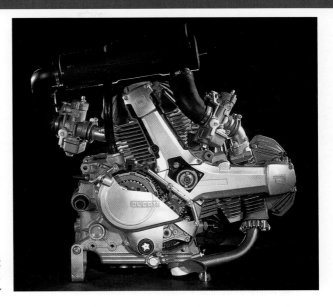

Fabio Taglioni's Pantah was so advanced that it continues to form the basis of all modern Ducati engines.
Ducati Motor

Pantah (350/500/600/650 SL, 350/600 TL, 350 XL) 500 SL (1979-83)

The first 500 SL Pantah of 1979 was a pre-production model produced to gauge market acceptance.

Ducati Motor

After a 2-year development period, a small number of the first series of Pantah was produced to test the quality and market acceptance before regular production commenced. While the family connection was strong, the Pantah differed in a number of details to the bevel-drive twins. Retaining vertically split crankcases, the swingarm pivoted on bearings within the gearbox casing, bringing the pivot as close as possible to the countershaft sprocket. To properly incorporate a left-side gearshift the Pantah was almost a mirror image of the bevel version. The crankshaft was still supported by axial thrust ball main bearings, with the helical primary drive gears on the right side and the alternator on the left. The cylinders were offset with the horizontal cylinder to the left on the bevel-drive twins, but in the interests of keeping the exhaust pipes more compact, this was also reversed on the Pantah. Also, unlike the big twin, the flywheel with ignition trigger sat inside the alternator. The starter motor fitted under the

When the 500 SL went into production in 1980, there were a number of updates, but the fairing shape was retained.

Ducati Motor

front cylinder, and the toothed belts and valve gear were driven off a jackshaft running between the cylinders. As a result, the engine was considerably narrower (776mm) than the bevel-drive.

The cylinder heads were designed only for desmodromic valves, and the included valve angle was reduced to a more modern 60 degrees. As the engine was initially envisioned

to have a maximum of 500cc, the valves were quite small (37.5mm intake and 33.5mm exhaust) A helical-geared primary drive drove a standard Ducati-style wet multi-plate clutch, but this, too, was the reverse of the larger twins, with the six springs clamping the driving and driven plates from the inside outward of the alloy clutch drum and hub. A forged one-piece crankshaft included two-piece 124mm connecting rods with plain bearing big-ends, an 18mm wristpin and 40mm crankpin. The lubrication system was higher pressure, and finally included a full-flow oil filter. Unlike the larger twin, maintaining a short wheelbase wasn't such a problem, so the gearbox was the indirect type, with separate input and output shafts. Consequently, the engine rotated forward, not backward as the bevel-drive twins did. The cylinder barrels were also Gilnisil.

Supporting this engine was a trellis-type frame with two pairs of parallel tubes running from the rear cylinder to the steering head meeting another pair of tubes running up from the rear of the crankcases. The engine hung below the trellis at six mounts. The suspension on early examples was by Marzocchi. The wheels where aluminum FPS models. The brakes were Brembo drilled discs, with small 05-series calipers. The Nippon Denso instruments and instrument panel were similar to the Darmah SSD, and

Production	1979	1980	1981	1982	1983	Total
500 SL	163	1,459	1,804	408	1	3,835

500 SL 1979-83

Engine	Twin cylinder four-stroke, air-cooled	**Ignition (degrees)**	Bosch BTZ electronic, 6 static, 32 total	**Tires**	3.25 x 18, 3.50 x 18 or 4.00 x 18
Bore	74mm	**Battery**	Yuasa 12V 14Ah	**Wheelbase**	1,450mm (57.1 in.)
Stroke	58mm	**Primary drive**	2.226:1 (31/69)	**Length**	2,150mm (84.6 in.)
Displacement	499cc	**Clutch**	Wet multiplate	**Height**	1,160mm (45.7 in.)
Compression ratio	9.5:1	**Gear ratios**	0.900 (0.931 from 660901), 1.074, 1,333, 1.714, 2.500	**Width**	670mm (26.4 in.)
Valve actuation	Belt driven desmodromic overhead camshaft	**Final drive**	2.533:1 (15/38), 2.786:1 (14/39 from 1981)	**Seat height**	760mm (30 in.)
Valve timing (degrees)	50, 80, 75, 45	**Front suspension**	35mm Marzocchi (605mm) or Paioli fork	**Dry weight**	180 kg (396.5 lbs.)
Carburetion	Dell'Orto PHF36 A	**Rear suspension**	Three-way adjustable 310mm Marzocchi or Paioli twin-shock swingarm	**Top speed**	196 km/h (121.8 mph)
Power	45 horsepower at 9.050 rpm			**Colors**	1979: Black frame, red and silver 1980-83): Blue 1981: White
Spark plugs	Champion L81A, L82Y or Bosch W7B	**Front brake**	260mm dual disc (10.2 in.)	**Engine numbers**	From DM 500L.I 600001
Generator	12v/200W	**Rear brake**	260mm disc (10.2 in.)	**Frame numbers**	From DM 500 SL 660001

By 1981, the 500 SL had the 600 SL fairing, but retained the earlier colors. A few 1981 500 SLs were white.

the half fairing, clip-on handlebars, and rear set footpegs accentuated the café racer image.

For 1980, the Pantah received new colors, a revised fifth gear ratio, and a number of internal engine and gearbox updates. The shape of the fairing was the same as the earlier model, but for 1981 the fairing was the 600

SL type. The crankcases were also standardized with the 600 SL after engine number 601654, effectively making the 500 SL a sleeved-down 600. From engine number 603246 on the gearbox was also the stronger three-dog 600 type. The 170mm Aprilia headlight was also replaced by a 154mm Bosch unit for 1981 (from frame number 661763). Paioli suspension was sometimes fitted to 500 SL Pantahs during 1981, along with oleo-pneumatic Paioli shock absorbers.

Although it immediately set new standards for performance in the 500cc category, the 500 Pantah was limited by restrictive air filters, extremely quiet Conti mufflers, and ridiculously high gearing. And to those used to the torque of the larger twins the Pantah felt anemic. The frame and suspension provided quite a loose feeling for a Ducati, and the Pantah wasn't a particularly good-handling model. But the engine was very smooth and oil tight, and could be revved to 10,000 rpm without fear of self destruction. The unremarkable performance, and bland styling, has prevented the 500 SL from reaching classic status, and it has always been overshadowed by the 600 and 650 SL.

600 SL (1980-85)

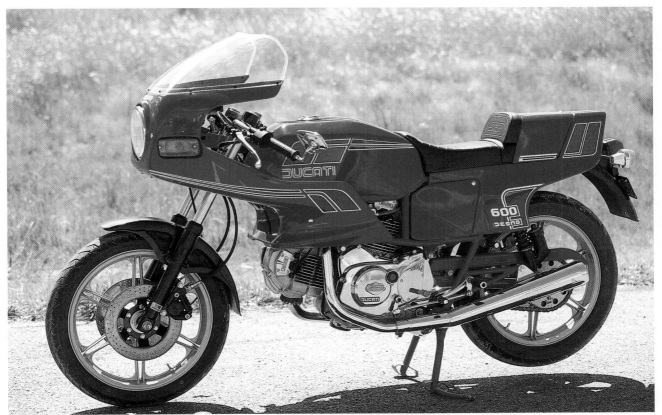

By 1983, the 600 SL came in MHR colors, and the clutch was cable-operated.

For 1981, the 500 SL was joined by a larger 600 SL. Apart from the extra capacity, the only change to the engine specification from the 1981 series 500 SL was a set of stronger clutch springs and hydraulic operation via a handlebar-mounted master cylinder. While the 600 SL frame was also identical to the 500, there were different brakes and suspension. Most early 600s came with Paioli forks and oleo-pneumatic Marzocchi shock absorbers. The front brakes included larger 08 Brembo calipers. The bodywork was identical to the 1981 500, except for a silver ABS front mudguard. The 600 SL was one of the more attractive Ducatis of this period, and the additional capacity provided a welcome torque increase.

During 1982 (from engine number 701650), the 600 SL received a new clutch that was cable operated rather than hydraulic. This included a larger-diameter clutch drum, steel rather than aluminum, and a new clutch engine side cover. Further small refinements continued during the year. From engine number 702388 on the ignition flywheel was altered, providing a three-stage rather than two-stage advance. Updates included a black front fender, a Marzocchi front fork and Mike Hailwood Replica colors.

All 600 SLs had MHR colors from 1983, and the transmission included a lower fifth gear. Some 1983 600 SLs were fitted with a Conti two-into-one exhaust system exiting on the left, and the taillight and turn signal indicators were the larger CEV type that were also fitted to the 900 MHR. The wheels, too, were Oscam, accepting tubeless tires. Electrical upgrades included a three-wire regulator, which replaced the six-wire type that had first been featured on the 860 GT. The final 600 SLs also featured a 170mm Carello H4 headlight and black-anodized dogleg brake and clutch levers.

Production	1980	1981	1982	1983	1984	1985	Total
600 SL	1	1,094	1,251	551	32		2,929
600 SL Police			99			1	100
Total	1	1,094	1,350	551	32	1	3,029

600 SL 1980-85

Engine	Twin cylinder four-stroke, air-cooled
Bore	80mm
Stroke	58mm
Displacement	583cc
Compression ratio	10.4:1
Valve actuation	Belt-driven desmodromic overhead camshaft
Valve timing (degrees)	50, 80, 75, 45
Carburetion	Dell'Orto PHF36 A
Power	61 horsepower at 9,100 rpm
Spark plugs	Champion L81A, L82Y or Bosch W7B
Generator	12v/200W

Ignition (degrees)	Bosch BTZ electronic, 6 static, 32 total (5, 33 from 1983)
Battery	Yuasa 12V 14Ah
Primary drive	2.226:1 (31/69)
Clutch	Wet multiplate
Gear ratios	0.931 (0.966 from 1983), 1.074, 1.333, 1.714, 2.500
Final drive	2.400:1 (15/36), 2.600:1 (15/39)
Front suspension	35mm Marzocchi (605mm) or Paioli fork
Rear suspension	Three-way adjustable 310mm Marzocchi or Paioli twin-shock swingarm
Front brake	260mm dual disc (10.2 in.)
Rear brake	260mm disc (10.2 in.)

Tires	3.25 x 18, 4.00 x 18
Wheelbase	1,450mm (57.1 in.)
Length	2,150mm (84.6 in.)
Height	1,280mm (50.4 in.)
Width	660mm (26 in.)
Seat height	760mm (29.9 in.)
Dry weight	187 kg (411.9 lbs.)
Top speed	201 km/h (124.9 mph)
Colors	1981: Black frame, silver 1982-85: Red frame, red white and green
Engine numbers	From DM 600L 700001
Frame numbers	From DM 600 SL 700001

Only produced during 1983, the 650 SL was the rarest, and most desirable, Pantah.

This final sporting Pantah before the advent of the 750 F1 was also arguably the best, and certainly one of the rarest. The 650 was produced to homologate a longer stroke for the racing 750 TT1, but the 650 SL received a moderate bore increase at the same time. Valve sizes remained for the same as the 500 and 600: 37.5mm inlet and 33.5mm exhaust. Although the stroke was lengthened 3.5mm, the same 124mm con-rods were used, and in all other respects the engine was identical to the 1983-84 600 SL. Conti mufflers were the same restrictive type as on the first 500 SL.

The chassis and bodywork, too, was essentially identical to that of the 1983 600 SL. All 650 SLs came with Marzocchi suspension, Oscam wheels, and large rectangular CEV indicators and taillight. The most noticeable departure for the 650 was a new instrument panel and instruments. The Nippon Denso instruments were only used on the 650 SL, and they were surrounded by an ugly plastic support, with three warning lights on the right. Although short-lived, the 650 SL is undoubtedly the most desirable Pantah. The 650 engine also lived on in the Alazzurra.

PRODUCTION	1983	TOTAL
650 SL	288	288

650 SL 1983

Engine	Twin cylinder four-stroke, air-cooled	**Ignition (degrees)**	Bosch BTZ electronic, 5 static, 33 total	**Tires**	100/90 x 18, 110/90 x 18
Bore	82mm	**Battery**	Yuasa 12V 14Ah	**Wheelbase**	1,450mm (57.1 in.)
Stroke	61.5mm	**Primary drive**	2.226:1 (31/69)	**Length**	2,150mm (84.6 in.)
Displacement	649cc	**Clutch**	Wet multiplate	**Height**	1,280mm (50.4 in.)
Compression ratio	10:1	**Gear ratios**	0.966, 1.074, 1,333, 1.714, 2.500	**Width**	700mm (27.6 in.)
Valve actuation	Belt-driven desmodromic overhead camshaft	**Final drive**	2.733:1 (15/41)	**Seat height**	770mm (30.3 in.)
Valve timing (degrees)	50, 80, 75, 45	**Front suspension**	35mm Marzocchi fork	**Dry weight**	180 kg (396.5 lbs.)
Carburetion	Dell'Orto PHF36 A	**Rear suspension**	Three-way adjustable Marzocchi twin-shock swingarm	**Colors**	Red frame, red and yellow
Power	63 Horsepower at 8,500 rpm	**Front brake**	260mm dual disc (10.2 in.)	**Engine numbers**	From DM 650L 610001
Spark plugs	Champion L82Y	**Rear brake**	260mm disc (10.2 in.)	**Frame numbers**	From DGM 650 SL 065001
Generator	12v/200W				

Ducati Motor

Although a pleasant machine to ride and easy to live with, the 600 TL was one of Ducati's more unremarkable models.

Occasionally Ducati releases a model that is a triumph of styling over function, and one of those was the 600 TL. Along with the Giugiaro-designed 860 GT of 1974, the 600 TL has earned a place as one of Ducati's ugliest. Unlike the 860 GT, though, underneath the extreme bodywork of the 600 TL was a reliable and competent motorcycle. In many ways it was a superior all-round machine to the SL.

The engine and five-speed gearbox (with the later lower fifth gear) of the 600 TL was shared with the 600 SL of the same period, and all 600 TLs featured the larger

cable-operated 15-plate wet clutch. Either Silentium or Conti exhaust systems as for the SL were fitted, most TLs having Silentium on the TL. The 600 TL featured a number of unique electrical components. A rectangular Carello halogen headlight was mounted in the small fairing, along with rectangular CEV indicators on stalks. The Nippon Denso instruments were shrouded by a large black plastic dashboard with a dazzling arrangement of warning lights.

The basic Pantah frame was retained for the 600 TL, but now had a provision for a side-stand on the left, underneath the lower engine mount. The dual seat was thickly padded and locked to the seat base. Along with the steering lock and ignition, the TL included four keys. Completing the bodywork was a small handlebar-mounted fairing. Unlike the 600 SL, the TL had a front brake with twin 05 Brembo calipers, and the wheels were six-spoke FPS, becoming Oscam during 1983.

The colors of the 600 TL were changed for 1983, but the styling was still unusual.

Production	1982	1983	Total
600 TL	288	513	801

600 TL 1982-83

Engine	Twin cylinder four-stroke, air-cooled	**Ignition (degrees)**	Bosch BTZ electronic, 5 static, 33 total	**Tires**	100/90 x 18, 110/90 x 18
Bore	80mm	**Battery**	Yuasa 12V 14Ah	**Wheelbase**	1,450mm (57.1 in.)
Stroke	58mm	**Primary drive**	2.226:1 (31/69)	**Length**	2,160mm (85 in.)
Displacement	583cc	**Clutch**	Wet multiplate	**Width**	760mm (29.9 in.)
Compression ratio	10.4:1	**Gear ratios**	0.931 (0.966 from 1983), 1.074, 1,333, 1.714, 2.500	**Seat height**	820mm (32.3 in.)
Valve actuation	Belt-driven desmodromic overhead camshaft			**Dry weight**	177 kg (389.9 lbs.)
Valve timing (degrees)	50, 80, 75, 45	**Final drive**	2.600:1 (15/39)	**Top speed**	183 km/h (113.7 mph)
Carburetion	Dell'Orto PHF36 A	**Front suspension**	35mm Paioli fork	**Colors**	1982: Black frame, white / 1983: Black frame, gray
Power	58 horsepower at 8,700 rpm	**Rear suspension**	Three-way adjustable Paioli twin shock swingarm	**Engine numbers**	From DM 600L 650001
Spark plugs	Champion L81A, L82Y or Bosch W7B	**Front brake**	260mm dual disc (10.2 in.)	**Frame numbers**	From DM 600 TL 060001
Generator	12v/200W	**Rear brake**	260mm disc (10.2 in.)		

350 XL, 350 TL, 350 SL

Alongside the 500, 600, and 650 Pantahs, was a range of 350s specifically produced for the Italian market to accommodate a tax break for motorcycles below 350cc. The 350 XL was one of Ducati's parts-bin specialties and was essentially a 500 SL with a 600 TL handlebar fairing and higher handlebars. More was sourced from the SL than the TL, including instruments, instrument panel, and rear-set footpegs.

The 350 engine was a downsized 500 SL with smaller valves (33.5mm inlet and 30.5mm exhaust). The carburetors were smaller and there were new camshafts. The lower end, including the five-speed gearbox and wet cable-operated clutch, was identical to the later 500 SL, and the exhaust system was Silentium. The 350 XL chassis

The 350 SL was a downsized 500 SL, and only produced during 1983.

Ducati Motor

was also very similar to the 500 SL, with Paioli suspension and small 05 series Brembo front brake calipers.

The 350 TL and 350 SL also arrived in 1983. The 350 TL was ostensibly a smaller 600 TL, with a Marzocchi fork, Oscam wheels, and XL Nippon Denso instruments. The 350 SL looked similar to the red 600 SL, except for silver FPS wheels and smaller brake calipers. Suspension was Paioli and mufflers were Conti. Ostensibly larger motorcycles with small engines, this trio of 350s was another unremarkable series.

Ducati Motor

A parts bin model created primarily for the Italian market, the 350 XL was more attractive than the TL.

Production	1982	1983	1985	Total
350 XL	749	191		940
350 TL		275	1	276
350 SL		211		211
Total	749	677	1	1,427

350 XL, TL, SL

Engine	Twin cylinder four-stroke, air-cooled	**Ignition (degrees)**	Bosch BTZ electronic, 5 static, 33 total	**Wheelbase**	1,450mm (57.1 in.)	
Bore	66mm	**Battery**	Yuasa 12V 14Ah	**Length**	XL, TL: 2,160mm (85 in.) SL: 2,150mm (84.6 in.)	
Stroke	51mm	**Primary drive**	2.226:1 (31/69)	**Width**	XL, TL: 710mm (28 in.) SL:670mm (26.4 in.)	
Displacement	349cc	**Clutch**	Wet multiplate			
Compression ratio	10.3:1	**Gear ratios**	0.931, 1.074, 1,333, 1.714, 2.500	**Seat height**	XL, TL: 760mm (29.9 in.) SL: 740mm (29.1 in.)	
Valve actuation	Belt-driven desmodromic overhead camshaft	**Final drive**	3.143:1 (14/44)	**Dry weight**	177 kg (389.9 lbs.) 176 kg SL (387.7 lbs.)	
Valve timing (degrees)	46, 65, 76, 37	**Front suspension**	35mm Paioli or Marzocchi fork	**Top speed**	XL, TL: 170 km/h (105.6 mph) SL: 180 km/h SL (111.9 mph)	
Carburetion	Dell'Orto PHF30 A	**Rear suspension**	Three-way adjustable Paioli twin-shock swingarm			
Power	40 horsepower at 9,600 rpm	**Front brake**	260mm dual disc (10.2 in.)	**Colors**	XL: Black frame, red and black TL: Red (350 TL) SL: Red frame, red	
Spark plugs	Champion L82Y	**Rear brake**	260mm disc (10.2 in.)	**Engine numbers**	From DM 350L 030001	
Generator	12v/200W	**Tires**	3.00 x 18, 3.50 x 18			

Closely patterned on the factory TT2, the catalog TT2 racer was a beautiful diminutive racer.

Continuing a tradition of customer racers available only in limited numbers were the TT2 and later TT1. These spectacular machines were similar to Tony Rutter's four-time World TT2 Championship-winning TT2 racers. Modeled closely after the factory TT2, the production version also featured a 597cc engine using special two-ring Borgo pistons (weighing only 408 grams). Valve sizes were 41mm and 35mm, and racing camshafts provided 11mm of intake valve lift and 10.5mm of exhaust valve lift. The crankshaft and con-rods were highly polished, with a new steel clutch and straight-cut primary gears. The clutch was a cable-operated wet type similar to the street bike. All TT2s were fitted with an oil cooler—the 1982 version had a cylinder head bypass, while the 1983 TT2 received a full-flow cooling system with stainless-steel lines. 1983 TT2s also had a steering damper. All TT2s came with an electric start. Ignition was the usual Bosch BTZ, with the battery situated in the tailpiece.

The compact Verlicchi frame with cantilever rear suspension was shared with the factory bikes, as was the racing Marzocchi fork with magnesium fork legs and adjustable rebound damping. The Marzocchi rear shock had a remote reservoir and adjustment for both compression and rebound damping. Wheels were magnesium Campagnolo, 2.15 x 18-inch and 2.50 x 18-

inch in 1982, with a wider 3.50 x 16-inch front and 3.50 x 18-inch rear for 1983. Brakes were 05 Brembo Gold Series with fully floating disc rotors.

For 1984, a factory 750 kit was available to transform the TT2 into a 750 before a limited run of TT1 replicas was constructed. These were basically the earlier TT2 fitted with a 748cc engine. The valve sizes were identical. These catalog racers were heavily based on the Tony Rutter 1984 TT1. The Verlicchi frame was the same except for

Only a few TT1s were produced in 1984, and they are so rare they don't even figure in the production data.

a wider aluminum cantilever swingarm to accommodate the wider wheels. The Marzocchi fork and Brembo brakes were shared with the TT2, but an outboard countershaft sprocket allowed for the larger-section 18-inch rear tire, with an endurance-style quick-change assembly. This allowed the disc and caliper to stay in the swingarm as the wheel and sprocket were removed. The front wheel was still a 16-inch.

While largely unappreciated, except by the cognoscenti, the diminutive TT2 and TT1 were among the finest of all catalog Ducatis. In many ways they epitomized Taglioni's philosophy of maximum performance through light weight and simplicity. There was nothing superfluous on the TT, with function determining the form of every component.

PRODUCTION	1982	1983	1984	TOTAL
600 TT2	20	30		50

600 TT2 AND 750 TT1

Engine	Twin cylinder four-stroke, air-cooled	Power	1982 TT2: 76 horsepower at 10,500 rpm	Front suspension	35mm Marzocchi magnesium fork
Bore	600: 81mm 750: 88mm		1983 TT2: 78 horsepower at 10,500 rpm TT1: 80 horsepower	Rear suspension	Marzocchi PVS 1 single-shock cantilever swingarm
Stroke	600: 58mm 750: 61.5mm	Generator	12V 200 W	Front brake	280mm dual disc (11 in.)
Displacement	600: 597mm 750: 748mm	Ignition (degrees)	Bosch BTZ electronic	Rear brake	260mm disc (10.2 in.)
Compression ratio	10.2:1	Battery	12V 14Ah	Tires	Michelin 14/68 x 18 slick (1982)
Valve actuation	Belt-driven desmodromic overhead camshaft	Primary drive	1.944:1 (36/70)	Seat height	762mm (30 in.)
Valve timing (degrees)	74, 92, 100, 64	Clutch	Wet multiplate	Dry weight	130 kg (286.3 lbs.)
Carburetion	Dell'Orto PHF36 A (1982) Dell'Orto-Malossi 41mm (1983)	Gear ratios	0.966, 1.074, 1.333, 1.714, 2.500	Colors	TT2: Red frame, red and yellow TT1: Red frame, red and blue
		Final drive	3.15:1 (13/40) 520 DID chain		

750 F1 1985-86

With the factory TT2 continuing to win World Championships, it was inevitable that the TT2 would eventually become a production road model. Unfortunately, serious economic problems during the early 1980s saw the production model delayed for several years. But when it did arrive for 1985 as the 750 F1, it was worth the wait. The 750 F1 almost came too late, and its release coincided with the sale of Ducati to Cagiva. One of Cagiva's initial changes was to scale down the production of the traditional

Ducati bikes (like the F1) to concentrate on more dubious models (like the Paso). The F1 thus represents the end of the pre-Cagiva era. There were two versions of the F1, the 1985 and 1986 examples, with minor variations of both. It is common, and incorrect, to describe these bikes as F1A, F1B, or F1S, as no official factory literature ever distinguished the various models like this.

750 F1 1985

The black engine of the F1 was still basically that of a Pantah, except for a few modifications to allow for the larger capacity and corresponding increase in power. The cylinder head was largely unchanged from the 650 SL, retaining the small 37.5mm inlet and 33.5mm exhaust valves. There were new camshafts and aluminum timing

pulleys, and higher-ratio straight-cut primary gears. The crankshaft and 124mm con-rods were the same as other Pantahs. There was also a change to the wet clutch layout with 16 clutch plates and hydraulic actuation. For the second 1985 series, the clutch was changed to a hydraulic multi-plate dry type. An oil cooler was mounted under the

The 1985 750 F1 was descended from the TT1 and TT2, but the styling of the seat was compromised.

headlight with a takeoff point from the pressure switch and two return lines to each cylinder head. Carburetion was the same as the 650 SL, but the F1 frame provided no room for an air filter. There was a black-chrome Conti two-into-one exhaust system exiting on the left.

The frame was modeled on the TT2, but required modification to adapt it for street use. The racing TT2 frame was so compact that there was no room for

timing belt covers, essential on a street motorcycle, and no provision for either a side or center stand. A loop was added to the rear of the F1 subframe to support the battery and seat, and the frame extended below the engine, providing an additional engine support as well as a center stand mount.

The aluminum fuel tank followed the lines of the TT2, fitting inside the frame tubes with grooves underneath for the front carburetor cables. The 1985 750 F1 was the final Ducati (until Pierre Terblanche's Mike Hailwood Evoluzione of 1998) to feature the distinctive Giugiaro graphics. While the tank was an attractive design, the same couldn't be said of the large tail section that kicked up at the rear.

The earliest F1s had non-floating Brembo cast-iron discs with aluminum centers, along with a solid rear disc. However, most 1985 F1s featured fully floating front and rear discs. The wheels were Oscam: an MT 2.50 x 16-inch on the front, and MT 3.00 x 18-inch on the rear. The instruments and electrical equipment came from the Mille MHR, except for the headlight, which was a rectangular H4 55/60-watt CEV. Although it didn't offer tremendous engine performance, the 750 F1 was a commendably light and compact motorcycle, befitting a machine descended from a pure racer.

With the bodywork removed, the 1985 750 F1 was a thinly disguised racer.

The final 1986 750 F1 no longer featured "elephant" graphics on the fairing. There was also a dual seat and Montjuich front fender.

Ducati Motor

An updated 750 F1 was produced for 1986 to overcome many of the shortcomings of the 1985 version. The crankcases were strengthened, and for the first time the engine was no longer an oversized 500. There was additional webbing between the drive-side main bearing and gearbox mainshaft bearing. Until engine number 7501494 these bearings were the same as before; after engine number 7501495 the F1 engine was standardized with that of the Montjuich. These later engines had the larger gearbox bearings, a different gearbox mainshaft, and second driving gear.

There were also several changes in the cylinder head. The casting was new, with more metal around the ports, and there were larger 41mm and 35mm valves. There were new higher-lift camshafts, and higher-compression pistons. The 124mm con-rods were thicker around the little end, while the forged crankshaft carried more metal around the big-end journal. The transmission was stronger with gears 30 percent wider. The dry clutch, too, was new, with a steel inner clutch drum and 14 plates. Another improvement over the 1985 model was in the oil cooling system, It had more durable oil lines and supplied cooling to the entire oil supply, not just to the cylinder head.

For 1986, the instrument panel was revised, with white-faced Veglia instruments and a set of eight LED warning lights mounted in a gray foam surround. There was no longer the usual external steering head lock as this was now incorporated with the ignition key. While in many respects the 1986 750 F1 was an improvement on the earlier model, thea steel gas tank was not. The tailpiece was still large, but was probably more attractive because it was lower at the rear.

An improvement for 1986 was the fitting of a Forcelle Italia (formerly Ceriani) front fork. Though not featuring air-assistance, these excellent units provided adjustment for compression damping at the base of the fork leg, and rebound damping by a knob on the top of the fork. The Brembo braking system was identical to that of the previous year, but with a solid cast-iron disc at the rear instead of floating. Also unchanged were the Oscam wheels, but they were now painted red.

The final batch of 750 F1s was constructed towardst the end of 1986, and for the first time there was a specific F1 for the U.S. market. These final F1s sold slowly and were still available well into 1988. The engines were standardized with the Laguna Seca, including crankcases, gearbox, clutch, and entire lower end. They all had Kokusan ignition, (including pick-ups, coils and ignition amplifiers), which was was generally a more reliable setup. U.S. examples also came with a heavier and quieter two-into-two exhaust system. Only a sidestand was fitted to these final F1s. Other bodywork updates included a two-piece Montjuich front fender and a dual seat with grab handles and a replaceable solo seat cowling.

750 F1 1985-86

Engine	Twin cylinder four-stroke, air-cooled	**Ignition (degrees)**	Bosch BTZ electronic, 5 static, 33 total	**Wheelbase**	1,400mm (55.1 in.)
Bore	88mm		Kokusan (from 7501496)	**Length**	2,110mm (83 in.)
Stroke	61.5mm	**Battery**	Yuasa 12V 14Ah	**Height**	1,130mm (44.5 in.)
Displacement	748cc	**Primary drive**	1.972:1 (36/71)	**Width**	690mm (27.2 in.)
Compression ratio	1985: 9.3:1	**Clutch**	Wet (later dry) multiplate	**Seat height**	750mm (29.5 in.)
	1986: 10:1	**Gear ratios**	0.966, 1.074, 1.333,	**Dry weight**	175 kg (385.5 lbs.)
Valve actuation	Belt-driven desmodromic overhead camshaft		1.714, 2.500	**Top speed**	200 km/h (124.3 mph)
Valve timing (degrees)	29, 90, 70, 48	**Final drive**	2.666:1 (15/40)	**Colors**	Red frame, red white and green
	39, 80, 80 ,38 (1986)	**Front suspension**	1985: 38mm Marzocchi fork	**Engine numbers**	1985: 7500001-7500594
Carburetion	Dell'Orto PHF36 A		1986: 40mm Forcella Italia		1986: From 7500595
Power	1985: 62.5 horsepower at 7,500 rpm	**Rear suspension**	Marzocchi PVS 4 single-shock cantilever swingarm		Final series: From 7501505
	1986: 75 horsepower at 9,000 rpm	**Front brake**	280mm dual disc (11 in.)	**Frame numbers**	1985: ZDM 750R 7500001-7500594
Spark plugs	Champion L82YC	**Rear brake**	260mm disc (10.2 in.)		1986: From ZDM 750R 7500595
	Champion RA6YC	**Tires**	120/80V16, 130/80V18		Final series: From ZDM750R 7501505
Generator	12v/300W				

Production	1985	1986	Total
750 F1 (7/85)	591		591
750 F1 (12/85)	33	793	826
750 F1 (12/85) US		84	84
750 F1 Kokusan		250	250
750 F1 Kokusan US		50	50
Total	624	1,177	1,801

The 1986 750 F1 had Cagiva graphics, including elephant logos, but was an improved model over the 1985 version.

Montjuich, Laguna Seca, Santamonica

Although Cagiva was committed to replacing the existing model lineup, it released the limited edition Montjuich for 1986. This extraordinary motorcycle was a race replica in the traditional Ducati fashion, supplied with racing tires, no turn signal indicators, and an extremely loud Verlicchi exhaust.

Only an extremely loud competition Verlicchi exhaust was fitted to the Montjuich, and there were no turn signals.

Named after one of Ducati's happiest racing hunting grounds—the Montjuich Park circuit in Barcelona, Spain—the Montjuich was a development of the 750 F1. While similar to the 750 F1, the Montjuich engine included different crankcases to accept larger gearbox mainshaft bearings, along with a different mainshaft and second driving gear. The outer clutch drum was aluminum and the external cover vented. Although the valve sizes were unchanged, the Montjuich cylinder heads had larger inlet ports, much hotter cams, and larger carburetors. All Montjuichs came with Kokusan ignition.

But for an aluminum swingarm, the frame was the same as the F1. There was no centerstand, and the gas tank was aluminum. To provide for the wider front tire, there was a two-piece front fender, and the suspension included a higher-quality rear Marzocchi shock absorber with adjustable damping. The biggest changes in specification occurred in the wheels and brakes. The wheels were composite Marvic/Akront magnesium/aluminum: a 3.50 x 16-inch on the front, and 4.25 x 16-inch on the rear.

The Montjuich front end was impeccable. The four-piston gold series Brembo brakes were the best available in 1986, and the Marvic/Akront wheels were extremely light. *(Cycle World)*

With polished aluminum rims and three red-painted magnesium spokes, these were much lighter than the Oscams of the F1. The rear brake disc was now fully floating, and the front brakes were significantly upgraded to include racing Brembo P 432 D "Gold series" with four-piston calipers.

Each Montjuich came with a numbered plaque on the fuel tank. They were loud and uncompromising machines. Although they could have been more effective if they were more closely related to the factory TT1 racers of 1984 and 1985 (with a rising-rate rear suspension), they remain beautiful and highly desirable. In every respect, the Montjuich was a considerably faster and more effective sports motorcycle than a stock 750 F1.

Cycle World

One of the most exotic production Ducatis was the limited edition 750 F1 Montjuich of 1986.

Laguna Seca

Although similar to the Montjuich, the Laguna Seca had 750 Paso wheels and brake rotors, along with a rear wheel hugger.

Marco Lucchinelli's success in the Battle of the Twins race at Laguna Seca in 1986 prompted Ducati to name the next series of limited edition 750 F1 the Laguna Seca. Each Laguna Seca also came with a Marco Lucchinelli decal autograph on the gas tank.

Except for slightly different cylinder heads, the engine of the Laguna Seca was identical to that of the Montjuich. There was a steel, rather than aluminum, inner clutch drum, and small changes to the clutch actuation system. There was a new clutch slave cylinder and bearing, although the vented clutch cover was retained. In an effort to reduce noise levels, the Laguna Seca featured a new muffler, with a larger canister and riveted aluminum cover. U.S. versions received a different muffler again; a Conti similar to that on the 1986 750 F1.

The frame was identical to that of the Montjuich, except for a revised footpeg and exhaust brackets, and a Verlicchi alloy swingarm that included a plastic rear fender. There was some evidence of cost cutting as the hand-beaten aluminum fuel tank made way for a normal 18-liter steel type, and the wheels and brake discs came straight off the 750 Paso. These aluminum Oscam wheels had wider rims. The 3.75 x 16-inch on the front and 5.00 x 16-inch on the rear allowed the fitting of wider and lower-profile Pirelli radial tires. The same four-piston Brembo racing "Gold series" front brake calipers as the Montjuich were fitted, but with a rectangular handlebar master cylinder. To go with the Paso wheels, the rear P2108N brake caliper was also shared with the Paso. It was unfortunate that the

The oil cooler intake in the Laguna Seca fairing was a one-piece unit, and narrower than that of the Montjuich.

Laguna Seca was burdened with these few Paso items, because they detracted from the purity of the Montjuich, and compromised the performance and handling.

The red and silver fairing, too, was revised slightly, with a narrower front oil cooler air intake and lower screen. While most Laguna Secas came with a solo seat, a number were also produced with a dual seat. All Laguna Secas came with a new front fender that was also shared with the 750 Paso.

Santamonica

All Santamonicas were dual seat, but the wheels and brakes were now those of the Montjuich, rather than Laguna Seca.

Ducati Motor

By 1987, the racing days of the F1 were almost over for the air-cooled two-valve engine. However, one of the most astounding victories late in its racing life was at Misano at the Autodromo Santamonica in April 1986. Lucchinelli won the opening round of the World TT Formula 1 Championship, prompting Ducati to name their final limited edition 750 F1, the Santamonica. Built primarily for the Japanese market (at that time Ducati's most important), the engine was identical to the Laguna Seca, but there were some changes to the chassis components.

Everything was similar to the Laguna Seca, except for the wheels and brakes. The Marvic/Akront wheels of the Montjuich returned, along with fully floating cast-iron brake calipers. The front brake calipers were the new black P4 type, and the brake lines braided steel. All Santamonicas had a dual seat. While the Santamonicas were offered as a 1988 model, they were very much relics of past under the new Cagiva regime. This certainly doesn't detract from

their desirability, and all members of the limited edition series of the 750 F1 are among the most classic production Ducatis of the 1980s.

Production	1986	1987	Total
750 Montjuich	180		180
750 Montjuich US.	20		20
750 Laguna Seca monoposto		150	150
750 Laguna Seca 1987 US		50	50
750 Laguna Seca biposto		96	96
750 Santamonica		204	204
Total	200	500	700

750 Montjuich, Laguna Seca, Santamonica

Engine	Twin cylinder four-stroke, air-cooled	Battery	Yuasa 12V 14Ah	Wheelbase	1,400mm (55.1 in.)
Bore	88mm	Primary drive	1.972:1 (36/71)	Length	2,110mm (83.1 in.)
Stroke	61.5mm	Clutch	Wet (later dry) multiplate	Height	1,130mm (44.5 in.)
Displacement	748cc	Gear ratios	0.966, 1.074, 1,333, 1.714, 2.500	Width	690mm (27.2 in.)
Compression ratio	10:1	Final drive	2.866:1 (15/43)	Seat height	750mm (29.5 in.)
Valve actuation	Belt driven desmodromic overhead camshaft	Front suspension	40mm Forcella Italia	Dry weight	155 kg (341.4 lbs.)
Valve timing (degrees)	67, 99, 93, 70	Rear suspension	Marzocchi single-shock cantilever swingarm	Colors	Red frame, red and silver / Red frame, red and white (Santamonica)
Carburetion	Dell'Orto PH 40 N	Front brake	280mm dual disc (11 in.)	Engine numbers	From 7500595
Power	95 horsepower at 10,000 rpm	Rear brake	260mm disc (10.2 in.) 270mm Laguna Seca (10.6 in.)	Frame numbers	ZDM750M 001-200 (Montjuich) / From ZDM750LS 750001 (Laguna Seca) / From ZDM750LS 750303 (Santamonica)
Spark plugs	Champion RA6YC	Tires	Montjuich: 12/60-16, 18/67-16 Laguna Seca, Santamonica: (130/60 x 16, 160/60 x 16.		
Generator	12v/300W				
Ignition (degrees)	Kokusan 5 static, 33 total				

350/400 F3 1986-88

A 350 and 400 F3 based on the F1 were also built during 1986, primarily for the Italian and Japanese markets. Although now painted black, the 350 F3 engine was similar in specification to the final 350 SL. This included the smaller valves, a cable-operated wet clutch, and Bosch ignition, but with different camshafts. The 400 F3 used the same engine, but with larger pistons. It also included a bypass oil cooler like the 1985 750 F1.

The 350 and 400 F3 frame was shared with that of the 750F1, but the 400 featured different brackets for the muffler. The first series also included the 22-liter aluminum gas tank of the Montjuich, and the 350 F3 the same instrument panel with white-faced Veglias. The warning lights and instruments on the 400 were the Nippon Denso setup from the 1985 750 F1. The biggest difference between the 750 and its smaller brothers was

The 1987 Japanese-market 400 F3 was very much a downsized 750 F1.

in the brakes and suspension. Non-adjustable Marzocchi forks were fitted, and the brakes were non-floating cast-iron front and rear, with Brembo P2F05N calipers.

There were only a few developments for the F3 for 1987. An 18-liter steel F1 fuel tank replaced the earlier aluminum one, and the 400 (Edition 9/86) included white Veglia instruments and 260mm fully floating cast-iron front discs. Towards the end of 1988, a final series of six-speed 400 F3s was produced for the Japanese market. These were styled as a mini-Santamonica with a dual seat. Half had a red gas tank, and half a white gas tank. This

series of F3 was the final traditional Ducati with forward-facing exhausts.

PRODUCTION	1986	1987	1988	TOTAL
350 F3 1986	470			470
400 F3 1986	300			300
400 F3 Ed. 9/1986	206	94		300
400 F3 6 6-sp. red tank			150	150
400 F3 6 6-sp. white tank			150	150
Total	976	94	300	1,370

350 F3, 400 F3 1986-88

Engine	Twin cylinder four-stroke, air-cooled
Bore	350: 66mm 400: 70.5mm
Stroke	51mm
Displacement	350: 349mm 400: 398mm
Compression ratio	350: 10.3:1 400: 10.4:1
Valve actuation	Belt-driven desmodromic overhead camshaft
Valve timing (degrees)	40, 80, 57, 43
Carburetion	1986-87: Dell'Orto PHF30 M 1988: PHF 36

Power	350: 42 horsepower at 9,700 rpm 400: 47 horsepower at 10,000 rpm (1988)
Spark plugs	Champion L82YC
Generator	12v/200W
Ignition (degrees)	Bosch BTZ electronic, 5 static, 33 total
Battery	Yuasa 12V 14Ah
Primary drive	2.226:1 (31/69)
Clutch	Wet multiplate
Gear ratios	1986-87: 0.931, 1.074, 1.333, 1.714, 2.500 1988: Six speed
Front suspension	35mm Marzocchi fork
Rear suspension	Boge single-shock cantilever swingarm

Front brake	260mm dual disc (10.2 in.)
Rear brake	260mm disc (10.2 in.)
Tires	100/90 x 18, 120/80 x 18
Wheelbase	1,400mm (55.1 in.)
Length	2,050mm (80.7 in.)
Height	900mm (34.4 in.)
Width	670mm (26.4 in.)
Seat height	750mm (29.5 in.)
Dry weight	180 kg (396.5 lbs.)
Top speed	175 km/h (108.7 mph)
Colors	Red frame, red and white
Engine numbers	From DM 350 034001

CHAPTER 7

CAGIVA BELT-DRIVE TWO-VALVE TWINS

CAGIVAS, PASO and SUPERSPORT

A new era for Ducati began in 1985 with the transfer of control from the Italian Government EFIM Group to Cagiva, based in Varese in Northern Italy. Cagiva was owned by the Castiglioni brothers and they initiated a change in direction, with an emphasis on widening the appeal of Ducati beyond that of the sports bike for the enthusiast. They also endeavored to make production more profitable, and instigated a program of new model development that was largely absent in early 1980s.

Two years before it purchased Ducati in 1985, Cagiva entered an agreement with Ducati to supply engines for the Cagiva Ala Azzurra (blue wing) and Elefant trail bike. Although there were delays before the design made the production line, from 1985 the Cagiva Ducatis played an integral role in Ducati's lineup. These Cagivas were assembled in Varese, but the engines were always manufactured in Bologna, and the Alazzurra and Elefant can be considered Ducatis. The Alazzurra also shared many components with the Pantah.

650 Alazzurra

Cagiva restyled the 650 Pantah for 1985 and put its name on the Alazzurra. Underneath it was still very much a Ducati.

The first Alazzurra was a 650, and while still officially titled the Ala Azzurra, the name was simplified to Alazzurra on the side-covers. The engine was essentially that of the 650 SL, with the higher fifth gear of the earlier 500, and a hydraulically operated dry clutch and the higher primary drive of the 750 F1. The engine was black from engine number 611554 (frame number 3M000789), and there were several more alterations to the engine specification. This included new crankcases, pistons and cylinders, cylinder heads, timing belt covers, engine and valve covers, and a new starter gear assembly. Only the Silentium exhaust system was fitted to the Alazzurra. It was initially chrome plated, but with the black engine the exhaust system was black chrome.

The Veglia instruments and switches were also new for the Alazzurra, and while the frame was similar to the Pantah, nearly all the cycle parts were different. The styling may have been rather bland, but the Alazzurra was an improvement over its predecessor, the 600 TL. A frame-mounted fairing provided increased protection and superior handling. The wheels were five-spoke Oscam, similar to those on the final 600 and 650 SL. The brakes were shared with the 600 TL having twin drilled cast-iron front discs and P2F05N Brembo calipers.

For 1986, the 650 Alazzurra was joined by the GT 650, also known as the SS 650 because of the SS decals on the side covers. This took the sport-touring idea further by

During 1985, the Alazzurra gained a black engine and exhausts.

incorporating a full fairing that merged with the gas tank. There were no engine changes for 1986, except the clutch was standardized to that of the 1986 750 F1. The GT featured a full fairing and a new two-piece front fender patterned on that of the 750 F1 Montjuich. The wheels were now three-spoke Oscam, a 2.50 x 18-inch on the front and 3.00 x 18-inch on the rear. Although intended to compete with the BMW K75S and Moto Guzzi V65 Lario, the Alazzurra 650 GT, like those motorcycles, was quite expensive for the modest performance offered.

350/400 Alazzurra

Following the Ducati 350 TL and 350 XL, the Cagiva Alazzurra 350 was essentially the 350 SL engine slotted into the regular Alazzurra chassis. As with other 350s, it was created for the Italian market. Compared to earlier 350s there were a number of changes in engine specification. This included the camshaft and higher fifth gear of the 650 Alazzurra. For 1986, the 350 Alazzurra was joined by a 400cc version for Japan. It was identical to the 350, except forthe crankshaft, cylinder and pistons.

PRODUCTION	1985	1986	TOTAL
Cagiva 350 Ala Azzurra			
	270		270
Cagiva 400 Ala Azzurra			
		100	100
Cagiva 650 Ala Azzurra			
	276		276
fairing		380	380
(Health Rescue)		10	10
US	453	47	500
Total	999	537	1,536

650, 350, 400 ALAZZURRA 1985-86

Engine	Twin cylinder four-stroke, air-cooled	**Ignition (degrees)**	Bosch BTZ electronic, 6 static, 32 total	**Length**	650: 2,100mm (82.7 in.) 350: 2,090mm (82.3 in.)
Bore	650: 82mm 400: 70.5mm 350: 66mm	**Battery**	Yuasa 12V 14Ah	**Height**	1,220mm (48 in.)
		Primary drive	650: 1.972:1 (31/71) 350: 31/69; 350	**Width**	790mm (31.1 in.)
Stroke	650: 61.5mm 400, 350: 51mm	**Clutch**	650: Dry multiplate 350: Wet	**Seat height**	800mm (31.5 in.)
Displacement	650: 649cc 400: 398cc 350: 349cc	**Gear ratios**	0.931, 1.074, 1.333, 1.714, 2.500	**Dry weight**	650: 191 kg (420.7 lbs.) 350: 190 kg (418.5 lbs.)
Compression ratio	10:1 (10.3:1)	**Final drive**	650: 2.733:1 (15/41) 350: (14/46)	**Colors**	650: Black frame, silver and red, red and silver GT: Dark blue and silver 400, 350: Black frame, gray
Valve actuation	Belt-driven desmodromic overhead camshaft	**Front suspension**	35mm Marzocchi fork		
Valve timing (degrees)	40, 70, 67, 43 (39, 80, 80, 38; 650 from #612550)	**Rear suspension**	Marzocchi twin-shock swingarm	**Engine numbers**	650: From DM 650L 610365 350: From DM 350L 032503
Carburetion	650: Dell'Orto PHF36 M 400, 350: PHBH 28 A)	**Front brake**	260mm dual disc (10.2 in.)		
Power	650: 56.5 horsepower at 8,400 rpm 350: 40 horsepower at 9,600 rpm	**Rear brake**	260mm disc (10.2 in.)	**Frame numbers**	650: From 3M000001 (1986: From 3M001024) GT: From 3ME000066 350, 400: From 2M000001 (1986 350, 400: From 2M002503)
		Tires	650: 100/90 x 18, 120/80 x 18 350: 90/90 x 18, 110/90 x 18)		
Spark plugs	Champion L82Y	**Wheelbase**	1,460mm (57.5 in.)		
Generator	12v/300W Ducati or Saprisa				

Indiana

Now gone and forgotten, most Indianas were produced during 1986, but this 750 was primarily a 1987 model. Indianas had a number of unusual features, including Bing carburetors, and chrome-plated engine and timing belt covers.

While they did much to preserve Ducati's heritage and future, Cagiva was also responsible for several dubious models, in particular the Indiana cruiser. Though the earlier Americano provided a historical precedent for this type of motorcycle, the Indiana was totally misguided in conception and application. In an endeavor to recapture a lost U.S. market, the Indiana was intentionally named after a U.S. state, but its execution was extremely flawed. The cruiser exterior looked impressive, but the desmodromic engine was unsuitable for a cruiser, and the model was tarred with an extremely poor-quality finish and chrome plating.

650 Indiana

The primary model for the U.S. was the 650 Indiana, and despite its usual Ducati rear twin-shock absorber setup, the Indiana shared more with the Paso and Elefant than the Pantah-derived Alazzurra. Like the Paso, the Indiana engine featured a reversed rear cylinder head, and the frame was a full cradle type constructed of square-section steel tubing, although with a large hollow backbone.

Quite a bit of development went into the 650 Alazzurra engine to adapt it to the different requirements of a cruiser. While the engine specification was similar, the Indiana received a wider ratio five-speed gearbox with the same hydraulically activated dry clutch as 1986 650 Alazzurra and 750 F1. There were Bing constant-vacuum carburetors. All the external alloy engine covers, including the clutch cover and timing belt covers, were chrome plated. This finish was disastrous and suffered frequently from pitting and corrosion.

When it came to the chassis, the Indiana broke new ground for Ducati. The frame, although obviously inspired by the Elefant, was all new, and was constructed of square-section steel tubing. This full cradle frame supported the engine rigidly at the rear in two positions, and also by two alloy arms at the front. An aluminum cross brace connected the front downtubes, with the lower right frame tube unbolting for engine removal. The cast-aluminum swingarm was box-section, pivoting only in the engine cases. The extreme steering geometry included 32.8 degrees of rake from the frame and another 7 degrees from the triple clamps.

There was also new cruiser-style bodywork, notably a 12-liter gas tank and scalloped saddle. Very high and rearward sweeping handlebars, along with forward footpegs, provided a strange riding position. While the front Oscam alloy wheel was similar to the Alazzurra, the suspension, rear wheel and brakes were new. Rim widths were generous: a 2.50 x 18-inch on the front and 3.50 x 15-inch on the rear. The suspension looked impressive, although the action was exceedingly harsh. Another evolutionary development was the use of a single four-piston Brembo PA 32C front brake caliper.

350 Indiana

Produced simultaneously for the Italian market, the 350 Indiana was identical to the 650, except for the engine. This was also the first 350 to receive a reversed rear cylinder head, and featured a few differences from other 350s. The five-speed gearbox was the same as the 650 Indiana, but for a lower fifth gear, while the cable-operated wet clutch was shared with the final 350 Alazzurra. Unlike the 650 Indiana, the primary gears were helical, and carburetion was Dell'Orto. Even in Italy the Indiana was a failure, and the 350 was discontinued after only one year.

750 Indiana

Alongside the 650 was a 750cc version—ostensibly the 650 Indiana with a 750 Paso engine. Many of the 650 Indiana features were retained, including the five-speed gearbox, and Bing carburetors. Valve sizes were also the smaller 37.5mm inlet and 33.5mm exhaust of the 650 rather than the 750 Paso's larger type. The 750 primary drive gears were helical rather than straight cut, and the clutch was still dry, and hydraulically actuated. In other respects the 750 Indiana was similar to the Paso. The exhaust system was a larger diameter than the 650, with an expanded and redesigned collector under the engine. The 750 Indiana received a new dashboard, headlight and taillight (not shared with any other model of Ducati). The Veglia instruments were from the 650, but the instrument

650, 350, 750 Indiana 1986-90

Engine	Twin cylinder four-stroke, air-cooled	Power	650: 53 horsepower at 7,000 rpm	Front brake	260mm disc (10.2 in.)
Bore	650: 82mm 350: 66mm 750: 88mm		350: 38 horsepower at 9,250 rpm	Rear brake	280mm disc (11 in.)
			750: 53.6 horsepower at 7,000 rpm	Tires	110/90 x 18, 140/90 x 15.
Stroke	650, 750: 61.5 350: 51mm	Spark plugs	Champion L82Y	Wheelbase	1,530mm (60.2 in.)
Displacement	650: 649cc 350: 349cc 750: 748cc	Generator	12v/300W Ducati or Saprisa	Length	2,024mm (79.7 in.)
		Ignition (degrees)	Kokusan electronic, 6 static, 32 total	Height	1,400mm (55.1 in.)
Compression ratio	10:1	Battery	Yuasa 12V 14Ah	Width	930mm (36.6 in.)
Valve actuation	Belt-driven desmodromic overhead camshaft	Primary drive	1.972:1 (31/71), (31/69; 350)	Seat height	760mm (29.9 in.)
Valve timing (degrees)	650: 39, 80, 80, 38 350: 19, 62, 53, 33 750: 31, 88, 72, 46	Clutch	750, 650: Dry multiplate 350: Wet	Dry weight	180 kg (396.5 lbs.)
		Gear ratios	0.931, (350: 0.966), 1.074, 1.333, 1.850, 3.071	Colors	650: Black, blue 350: Black frame, black, red, purple 750: Black, silver
Carburetion	650: Bing 64-32/375 350: Dell'Orto PHF 30 DD 750: Bing 64-32/379	Final drive	750, 650: 3.066:1 (15/46) 350: 14/48; 350		
		Front suspension	40mm Marzocchi P.A. 185/40	Frame numbers	650: From ZDM 650 C 650001 350: From ZDM 350 C 350001 750: From ZDM 750 C 750001
		Rear suspension	Marzocchi A 84 twin-shock swingarm		

holder was new. The 750 chassis was virtually identical to the 650, but for polished aluminum fork legs and a new seat. The Indiana was short lived and wasn't one of Ducati's memorable models. Cagiva was responsible for some of the greatest ever Ducatis, but also some of the most horrendous. The Indiana fell firmly in the latter category.

While Cagiva showed its intent on broadening the appeal of Ducati with the Alazzurra, a much more radical model was the Paso. This was its first all-new model and represented a significant departure for Ducati. Here was a Ducati designed to have a broader appeal. Cagiva realized that for Ducati to survive and sell more than a few of its hard-edged sportbikes, a new generation of Ducatis was required. These needed to have a broader appeal and be more user friendly. An attempt was made to simplify servicing and create a balanced motorcycle. Unfortunately, while the concept was sound, the execution left something to be desired and the Paso didn't achieve any of the goals Cagiva set. As the first Ducati with the engine completely covered, it was almost too radical. While it may have come under criticism from the traditional Ducati enthusiast, the Paso was really an important step forward for the company.

Production	1986	1987	1988	1989	1990	Total
350 Indiana						
Black	511					511
Red	115					115
Purple	174					174
650 Indiana						
Black	382					382
Blue	318					318
Black U.S.	3	249				252
Police			36	14	12	62
750 Indiana						
Black	250			1		251
Silver	61	189		1		251
Police				2		2
Total	1,814	438	36	18	12	2,318

Designed by one of the greatest modern motorcycle designers, Massimo Tamburini, the name Paso was derived from the Italian racer Renzo Pasolini, who was killed at Monza in 1973. Pasolini had a long association with Aermacchi, a company acquired by Cagiva in 1978.

750 Paso

The 350 Paso wasn't produced, but the white color scheme was used on the "Limited" for the U.S.

Using the 1986 750 F1 engine as a basis, the 750 Paso incorporated a number of significant changes. Among these was a reversed rear cylinder head to allow the installation of a dual-throat automotive-style Weber carburetor and large single air cleaner. The design of the cylinder head was similar to the F1, (still with 41mm and 35mm valves), and the camshaft timing was retarded 8 degrees to improve top-end power, although at the expense of the mid-range. A significant development occurred after March 1988, when the opening rocker system of the desmodromic valve layout was redesigned to allow for easier servicing. Here, Taglioni's assistant Luigi Mengoli designed a removable clip that allowed a shortened rocker to be slid sideways to allow access to the opening cap. The opening rocker pin didn't need to be removed for the adjustment of valve clearances. Engines with this system received gold-anodized rocker covers. While most 750 Pasos used Kokusan ignition, California models received the Marelli Digiplex MED 441-442 ignition system of the 906 Paso.

Due to the increased heat generated from the rear exhaust valve, the oil cooling system on the Paso included twin oil radiators, one on either side of the engine in the fairing. In an effort to obtain almost-straight, equal-length inlet tracts, and to be able to incorporate the large single air filter, the Paso was fitted with a single twin-choke downdraft automotive-style Weber carburetor. The Weber, though theoretically a suitable carburetor for the Ducati engine, never worked as well as the individual Dell'Ortos, despite several factory updates. They also required a fuel pump that often provided excessive pressure, causing richness and flooding. The exhaust system was also very complex, with a large four-way swirl-type collector underneath the engine. Until number 750130, the final drive was by a 3/8 x 5/8-inch chain. It was a narrower 1/4 x 5/8-inch chain after number 750131.

Much of the electrical system was also derived from the 750 F1, but it was more complex. The headlight, handlebar switches and instrument panel were completely new, the instrument panel featuring a plastic cover and Veglia

Production	1986	1987	1988	Total
750 Paso				
Red 1986/87	1,023	828		1,851
Red Ed. 7/87		450		450
White Ed. 7/87		50		50
Red 1986 US	2	390		392
Red 1987/88 Cal.			350	350
Blue 1987/88 Cal.		150	100	250
Red 1987/88 US		1,010	55	1,065
Blue 1987/88 US		250	55	305
White 1987/88 US		50		50
1987/88 US uprated		50		50
1987/88 Cal. Uprated		50		50
Total	1,025	3,278	560	4,863

750 Paso

Engine	Twin cylinder four-stroke, air-cooled	**Ignition (degrees)**	Kokusan 6 static, 32 total	**Wheelbase**	1,450mm (57.1 in.)
Bore	88mm	**Battery**	Yuasa 12V 14Ah	**Length**	2,032mm (80 in.)
Stroke	61.5mm	**Primary drive**	1.972:1 (36/71)	**Height**	1,150mm (42.3 in.)
Displacement	748cc	**Clutch**	Dry multiplate	**Width**	655mm (25.8 in.)
Compression ratio	10:1	**Gear ratios**	0.966, 1.074, 1.333, 1.714, 2.500	**Seat height**	780mm (30.7 in.)
Valve actuation	Belt-driven desmodromic overhead camshaft	**Final drive**	2.533:1 (15/38)	**Dry weight**	195 kg (429.5 lbs.)
Valve timing (degrees)	31, 88, 72 ,46	**Front suspension**	42mm Marzocchi M1R	**Top speed**	210 km/h (130.5 mph)
Carburetion	Weber 44DCNF 107	**Rear suspension**	Öhlins CA 508 or Marzocchi Supermono rising-rate swingarm	**Colors**	Red, white, blue
Power	72.5 horsepower at 7,900 rpm	**Front brake**	280mm dual disc (11 in.)	**Engine numbers**	From ZDM 750 LP 750001 / 751081-751480 (US)
Spark plugs	Champion RA6YC	**Rear brake**	270mm disc (10.6 in.)	**Frame numbers**	From ZDM 750 P 750001 / 751081-751480 (US) / From 752608 (1988)
Generator	12v/300W	**Tires**	130/60 x 16, 160/60 x 16		

instruments. These included fuel level and oil temperature gauges, and an analogue clock. New handlebar switches were used on the Paso, and would be featured on the next generation of Ducatis.

When it came to the chassis and running gear the Paso was also unlike any previous model of Ducati. The frame was a traditional double downtube, full cradle design, leaving the rear cylinder head exposed for easier servicing. The rake was much steeper than was normal for a Ducati (25 degrees), and the weight distribution was altered with a longer swingarm. The three Pantah engine mounting bosses were used as stiffening members, and the lower cradle tubes were unbolted to aid servicing. It was in the design of the rear suspension that the Paso exhibited most advances over the F1. The aluminum swingarm (with eccentric chain adjusters) no longer pivoted solely in bronze bushes in the engine crankcases. It was additionally supported on outside frame plates by two needle roller bearings. Three linkages operated the single shock absorber, these also supported by needle roller bearings. This "Soft Damp" system was considerably more sophisticated and effective than that of the F1, although it did contribute some to the bike's weight and complexity.

The early 750 Paso also came with high-quality suspension components. Front suspension came from the new racing-inspired Marzocchi M1R forks. These used the left fork leg to control compression damping and the right to control rebound damping. The first 979 750 Pasos were fitted with an Öhlins shock absorber, with an external hydraulic spring pre-load adjuster along with adjustable rebound damping. After frame number 750980, an inferior Marzocchi Supermono shock absorber

With its full coverage bodywork and solid screen, the 750 Paso was unlike any other Ducati and took some getting used to.

was fitted. Integral to the design of the 750 Paso were the 16-inch Oscam wheels fitted with radial tires. The brakes were Brembo P2F08N on the front and a P2108N on the rear. The Paso had new footpegs and levers, and enclosed fiberglass bodywork. With its solid screen and integral mirror/indicators, the 750 Paso was such a radical departure it was difficult for traditional Ducatisti accept it. In the U.S. there was also a limited edition white model sold at a premium price. It was identified by "Limited" decals on either side of the fairing. In all guises, the 750 Paso was never very successful in America, with many being re-exported to Europe in 1991.

906 Paso

The evolution of the 750 Paso continued for 1989 with the liquid-cooled 906 Paso.

Like the 750, the 906 Paso has become a somewhat neglected and unloved model.

The evolution of the 750 Paso continued in late 1988 with the 906. Most of the changes between the 750 and the 906 occurred in the engine, which was now based on the new 851 "large crankcase" four-valve engine, but with two valves. Because of the six-speed gearbox, it was titled the 906—the "6" to indicate the six speeds and not the capacity. The other development was liquid cooling.

The new engine was an evolutionary development of the 750. There were larger valves (43mm inlet and 38mm exhaust), higher-lift camshafts (11.10mm inlet and 10.56mm exhaust), and a "tri-spherical" combustion chamber machined in three stages by centering milling machines. The flat-topped three-ringed pistons used a 19mm wrist pin, and the piston crowns were cooled with oil sprayed from nozzles underneath. Con-rod length

grew to 130mm, and big-end bearing size increased to 42mm (from 40mm).

The crankcases, primary drive and gearbox were shared with the 1989 series 851. In every respect these were stronger than those of the 750, particularly around the cylinder base. There were also larger ball bearings fitted to both primary and secondary shafts in the gearbox. These were increased to 62mm (from 52mm), and the gears of the six-speed gearbox were wider. There were higher ratio straight-cut primary drive gears, but the hydraulically operated dry clutch (14 plates) was the same as the 750 Paso. For 1990, the actuation assembly was moved to the left side of the engine (as with the 1989 851). Also new with the larger engine were timing belt covers that allowed for the adjustment and checking of belt tension without

Production	1988	1989	Total
906 Paso			
Red 1988	502		502
Red 1989		400	400
U.S. Red 1988	250		250
Switz. Red 1988	100		100
Blue 1988	200		200
Black 1989		100	100
Black 1988	100		100
U.S. Blue 1988	100		100
Switz. Blue 1988	50		50
Total	1,302	500	1,802

906 Paso, 1988-89

Engine	Twin cylinder four-stroke, liquid-cooled	**Ignition (degrees)**	Marelli Digiplex variable advance	**Tires**	130/60 x 16, 160/60 x 16
Bore	92mm	**Battery**	12V 19Ah	**Wheelbase**	1,450mm (57.1 in.)
Stroke	68mm	**Primary drive**	2.000:1 (31/62)	**Length**	2,032mm (80 in.)
Displacement	904cc	**Clutch**	Dry multiplate	**Height**	1,150mm (45.3 in.)
Compression ratio	9.2:1	**Gear ratios**	0.857:1, 0.958, 1.091, 1,350, 1.764, 2.466	**Width**	665mm (26.2 in.)
Valve actuation	Belt-driven desmodromic overhead camshaft	**Final drive**	2.666:1 (15/40), 2.533 (15/38)	**Seat height**	780mm (30.7 in.)
Valve timing (degrees)	20, 60, 58, 20	**Front suspension**	42mm Marzocchi M1R	**Dry weight**	205 kg (451.5 lbs.)
Carburetion	Weber 44DCNF 116	**Rear suspension**	Marzocchi Duoshock (Supermono from 001303) rising-rate swingarm	**Top speed**	225 km/h (139.8 mph)
Power	88 horsepower at 8,000 rpm			**Colors**	Red, blue, black
Spark plugs	Champion RA6YC	**Front brake**	280mm dual disc (11 in.)	**Engine numbers**	From ZDM 904SC 000001
Generator	12v/350W	**Rear brake**	270mm disc (10.6 in.)	**Frame numbers**	From ZDM 906 PC 000001

removing the complete cover. The belts and pulleys, too, were stronger, with round teeth instead of square.

The cooling system came from the 851, with the water pump driven off the left side of the camshaft driveshaft. Another development was Digiplex Magneti Marelli digital electronic ignition. Ignition advance was monitored by crankshaft rpm, inlet manifold vacuum and throttle valve opening, with five mapped ignition advance curves programmed into an EPROM inside the Digiplex electronic unit.

Despite an increase in engine length and height of 10mm, the 906 engine still fitted the 750 Paso frame. An increase in fork offset ensured the front wheel didn't hit the front cylinder with the forks on full compression. The Marzocchi fork was also 20mm longer. Like the 750 Paso, the 906 should have been successful, but it wasn't. Not only was the styling radical, the low profile tires and 16-inch wheels provided unusual steering and handling. The Weber carburetor was problematic, and the manufacturing quality was lacking. These were idiosyncratic motorcycles that haven't stood the test of time. Tamburini made amends with his next effort: the 916.

750 SPORT, 900 SUPERSPORT, 400 SUPERSPORT JUNIOR

With the 750 F1 phased out, and the 750 Paso becoming the sport-touring model in Cagiva's new Ducati lineup, there was room for another sporting Ducati in 1988 to complement the expensive 851. Replacing the 750 F1, the 750 Sport was named to create an association with the delectable round-case bevel-drive 750 Sport. This was a very spurious association as the nuovo 750 Sport suffered from insufficient development and was beset with small problems throughout its production life, from gas tanks splitting from vibration, to swingarms cracking.

750 Sport 1988-89

A 1988 750 Sport with the model it replaced, the 750 F1.

The 750 Sport was another Ducati conceived as an amalgam of existing models—in this case a 750 Paso engine, wheels, and brakes—in a modified 750 F1 steel trellis frame with a Verlicchi aluminum swingarm. The instrument layout also came from the F1, while the suspension was more budget. The black-painted engine and exhaust system was shared with the 750 Paso, with all 750 Sports featuring the new valve adjusting arrangement and gold valve covers. The oil-cooling system was different, with a single 750 F1-style radiator located in the fairing under the headlight. For 1989, some 750 Sports incorporated an air-oil cooling system where jackets around the bore liners allowed additional oil to circulate.

While the frame was an adaptation of the 750 F1 type, the top tubes were wider to accommodate the large airbox and Weber carburetor. Steering geometry was more traditional, with a 28-degree fork angle. The battery was also located in a more satisfactory position between the airbox and steering head. One weakness was the aluminum Verlicchi swingarm that frequently suffered from cracks in the welding around the suspension unit mount. In November 1989, the factory supplied a new swingarm pin, rear axle, rear mudguard and chain cover under warranty. All the bodywork was new for the 750 Sport, including a steel fuel tank, full fairing and seat with detachable cover. The Oscam wheels and Brembo brakes came directly from the 750 Paso. As with the 750 Paso, Californian versions also featured the Marelli Digiplex ignition. Although more widely accepted than the 750 Paso, the 750 Sport was seen as a budget parts bin model and a poor substitute for the 750 F1. Flawed and ugly, this wasn't one of Ducati's better efforts.

Most of the second series of 750 Sport was red and silver to replicate the Montjuich and Laguna Seca.

PRODUCTION	1988	1989	TOTAL
750 Sport			
5/1988	568		568
Oil 1988 Red/Blue	151		151
Oil 1988 Red/Silver	34	715	749
Oil 1989 Red/Silver		100	100
US Oil 1989 Red/silver		300	300
Calif. Oil 1989 Red/Silver		100	100
Ed. 9/88 Black/Silver	95		95
Ed. 9/88 Red/Silver	393		393
Switz. 1989 Red		50	50
Switz.1989 Red/Silver	1	100	101
Total	**1,242**	**1,365**	**2,607**

750 SPORT 1988-89

Engine	Twin cylinder four-stroke, air-cooled	**Ignition (degrees)**	Kokusan 6 static, 36 total	**Wheelbase**	1,450mm (57.1 in.)
Bore	88mm	**Battery**	Yuasa 12V 14Ah	**Length**	2,000mm (78.7 in.)
Stroke	61.5mm	**Primary drive**	1.972:1 (36/71)	**Height**	1,160mm (45.7 in.)
Displacement	748cc	**Clutch**	Dry multiplate	**Width**	670mm (26.4 in.)
Compression ratio	10:1	**Gear ratios**	0.966, 1.074, 1.333, 1.714, 2.500	**Seat height**	750mm (29.5 in.)
Valve actuation	Belt-driven desmodromic overhead camshaft	**Final drive**	2.533:1 (15/38)	**Dry weight**	195 kg (649.8 lbs.)
Valve timing (degrees)	31, 88, 72 ,46	**Front suspension**	40mm Marzocchi M1BB	**Top speed**	210 km/h (130.5 mph)
Carburetion	Weber 44DCNF 113	**Rear suspension**	Marzocchi PBS1R cantilever swingarm	**Colors**	Red frame, red and blue, red and silver (after 751052)
Power	72 horsepower at 8,500 rpm	**Front brake**	280mm dual disc (11 in.)		Black frame, black and silver
Spark plugs	Champion RA6YC	**Rear brake**	270mm disc (10.6 in.)	**Engine numbers**	From ZDM 750 LS 750001
Generator	12v/300W	**Tires**	130/60x16, 160/60x16	**Frame numbers**	From ZDM 750 S 750001

900 Supersport (1990)

During 1989, the "large crankcase" six-speed 906 engine was adapted for another Supersport: the 900 Supersport. Like the 750 Sport, this was intentionally titled a 900 Supersport to create a link with the classic bevel-drive Super Sport of 1975-82. Although the spirit of the new Supersport did recall much that had made the earlier version so appealing, it was a tenuous link. The theme was still a large-capacity air-cooled V-twin engine in a lightweight sporting package, but the execution was flawed. Installed in a 750 Sport frame, with 17-inch wheels and larger brakes, the 900 Supersport addressed some of the problems of the 750 Sport but, unfortunately, Ducati persevered with the Weber carburetor.

Apart from air cooling, the engine was very similar to that of the 906 Paso. It shared the same cylinder head design, crankshaft with 130mm con-rods, primary drive, six-speed gearbox and hydraulically operated dry clutch with the actuation system on the right. Though the camshaft timing was the same, the valve lift was increased to 11.76mm on the inlet and 10.56mm on the exhaust. A new Weber carburetor didn't solve any problems and there was a severe flat spot around 4,000 rpm and it suffered severely icing in cold weather as the air ducts were in the front of the fairing. The exhaust system featured the canister-style aluminum mufflers of the 1989 851 Strada.

Using a development of the air-oil system of the 1989 750 Sport, the 900 Supersport featured oil passages

The 17-inch wheels provided improved steering and handling, but the 1990 900 Supersport was still a flawed motorcycle.

between the bore and outer cylinder wall. Oil drained via two external lines on the left side of the cylinders and was cooled by a radiator fitted underneath the headlight.

Production	1988	1989	Total
900 Supersport			
1990	1,471	460	1,931
1990 Switzerland		70	70
Total	1,471	530	2,001

900 Supersport 1990

Engine	Twin-cylinder four-stroke, air-cooled	**Ignition (degrees)**	Marelli Digiplex variable advance	**Tires**	120/70 ZR17 or 130/60ZR17 180/55ZR17 or 170/60ZR17
Bore	92mm	**Battery**	12V 19Ah		
Stroke	68mm	**Primary drive**	2.000:1 (31/62)	**Wheelbase**	1,450mm (57.1 in.)
Displacement	904cc	**Clutch**	Dry multiplate	**Length**	2,040mm (80.3 in.)
Compression ratio	9.2:1	**Gear ratios**	0.857:1, 0.958, 1.091, 1,350, 1.764, 2.466	**Height**	1,140mm (44.9 in.)
Valve actuation	Belt-driven desmodromic overhead camshaft	**Final drive**	2.600:1 (15/39)	**Width**	670mm (26.4 in.)
Valve timing (degrees)	20, 60, 58, 20	**Front suspension**	40mm Marzocchi M1BB	**Seat height**	620mm (24.4 in.)
Carburetion	Weber 44DCNF 118	**Rear suspension**	Marzocchi PBS1R cantilever swingarm	**Dry weight**	185 kg (407.5 lbs.)
Power	83 horsepower at 8,400 rpm	**Front brake**	300mm dual disc (11.8 in.)	**Max speed**	220 km/h (136.7 mph)
Spark plugs	Champion RA6YC	**Rear brake**	245mm disc (9.6 in.)	**Colors**	Red frame, red and white
Generator	12v/350W			**Engine numbers**	From ZDM 904 A 2C 000001
				Frame numbers	From ZDM 900 SC 000001

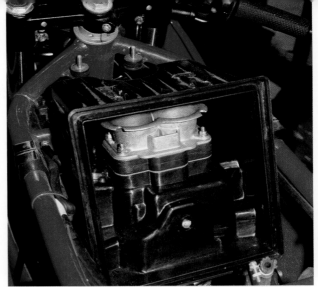

The frame was derived from the 750 Sport, but was stronger around the swingarm pivot that was supported in needle roller bearings inserted in the larger crankcases. The steeper steering head angle was slightly steeper (27 degrees), but the 900 Supersport was afflicted with the same basic Marzocchi suspension of the 750 Sport. An improvement over the Sport, though, was the wheels and brakes. The white-painted Brembo wheels (3.50 x 17-inch front; 5.50 x 17-inch rear) came from the 1989 851 Strada The brakes were upgraded with twin black Brembo P4 32A calipers on the front and larger-diameter discs. Early 900 Supersports also suffered from splitting fuel tanks and while this short-lived model represented an improvement over the 750 Sport it was still flawed. The real successor to the bevel-drive Super Sport came a year later.

Ducati persevered with the troublesome Weber automotive carburetor on the 1990 900 Supersport.

400 Supersport Junior 1990

Another specific Japanese market model was the 400 Supersport Junior of 1990. This was an unusual model, incorporating features not seen on previous Ducatis. The engine was essentially the same six-speed wet-clutch unit of the final 400 F3, but with a reversed rear cylinder head. The valve sizes were 33.5 and 30.5mm, and there were new camshafts providing inlet valve lift of 9.35mm and exhaust valve lift of 8.50mm. New for a Ducati were the twin Mikuni constant vacuum carburetors.

The cycle parts of the 400 SS Junior were an amalgam of various parts from several models. The frame and

aluminum swingarm were shared with the new 900 Supersport, as was the basic Marzocchi suspension. The Marvic/Akront composite 16-inch wheels and fully floating brakes were leftovers from the 1988 851 Strada and Santamonica. The front Brembo calipers were the larger 08 type. All the other equipment was from the 1990 900 Supersport.

Production	1988	1989	Total
400 Supersport			
1990 Junior Jpn.	301	340	641

400 Supersport 1990

Engine	Twin cylinder four-stroke, air-cooled	**Generator**	12v/300W	**Tires**	130/60 x 16, 160/60 x 16
Bore	70.5mm	**Ignition**	Kokusan	**Wheelbase**	1,450mm (57.1 in.)
Stroke	51mm	**Battery**	12v/16Ah	**Length**	2,000mm (78.7 in.)
Displacement	398cc	**Primary drive**	2.264:1 (34/77)	**Height**	1,160mm (45.7 in.)
Compression ratio	10.5:1	**Clutch**	Wet multiplate	**Width**	670mm (26.4 in.)
Valve actuation	Belt-driven desmodromic overhead camshaft	**Gear ratios**	0.931, 1.074, 1,280, 1.590, 2.111, 3.071	**Seat height**	750mm (29.5 in.)
Valve timing (degrees)	31, 88, 72, 46	**Final drive**	3.142:1 (14/44)	**Dry weight**	174 kg (383.3 lbs.)
Carburetion	Mikuni CVK-V36	**Front suspension**	40mm Marzocchi M1BB	**Colors**	White frame, red
Power	50 horsepower at 11,000 rpm	**Rear suspension**	Marzocchi PBS1R cantilever swingarm	**Engine numbers**	From ZDM 400 L 000001
Spark plugs	NGK BP7HS	**Front brake**	280mm dual disc (11 in.)	**Frame numbers**	From ZDM 400 SS 000001
		Rear brake	260mm disc (10.2 in.)		

ELEFANT

Although not listed as Ducatis in official data, the dual-purpose Elefant was similar to the Alazzurra in that it used a Ducati engine, but was built at Varese. Later examples were also sold as Ducatis in America, so it is appropriate they are included in this catalog.

350/650 Elefant

Above: **The 650 Elefant full-cradle square-section steel frame included a removable lower section, and an air intake through the backbone. Regular Pantah features were the Dell'Orto carburetors and Bosch ignition.** *(Cycle World)*

Right: **Although it was quite a radical design, the 650 Elefant was very popular in Europe.**

Cycle World

While the Elefant initially seemed an unlikely recipient for the Pantah engine, it was one of the longest-running of the Cagiva/Ducati models. The Elefant built a loyal following in Europe and enjoyed a successful competition life in desert rallies like the Paris-Dakar. The first production Elefants rolled out of Cagiva's Schiranna plant at Varese in May 1985.

The engines of both the 350 and 650 Elefant were shared with the respective Indiana, though with black, rather than chrome-plated, engine cases. Other shared specifications included the gearbox ratios and primary drive, although the Elefant also had a kickstart in addition to the normal electric start. The 650 Elefant also had an oil cooler, which was mounted on the upper right frame downtube. Unlike the Indiana, the ignition was from Bosch, and in keeping with the trends of the mid-1980s, much of the equipment was square or rectangular. This included all the lights and Veglia instruments. During 1986, Elefants received a revised instrument panel with a more conventional set of warning lights combining with new hexagonal-shaped instruments. Very little of the electrical equipment was the same as on other Ducati twins.

The full-cradle frame layout followed that of the Indiana and was constructed square section steel tubing, with a rectangular backbone. A rectangular section aluminum swingarm was operated by Cagiva's own "Soft Damp" rising rate linkage suspension system. The bodywork was mostly plastic, including the headlight shield, high front fender and 17.5-liter gas tank. The equipment level of the Elefant was high, indicating Cagiva's intention to offer a quality product. This included an Öhlins shock absorber, and Akront aluminum wheels (1.85 x 21-inch and 2.75 x 17-inch). Continuing the high specification was the braking system, with a fully floating cast-iron Brembo disc with a four-piston Brembo P4 32C caliper on the front. Although heavy and tall, the Elefant proved an immediate success and the 650cc soon grow to 750cc. The 350 continued, in slightly revised form, until 1989.

650, 350, 750 ELEFANT (1985-89)

Engine	Twin cylinder four-stroke, air-cooled	Spark plugs	650, 350: Champion L82Y	Tires	90/90 x 18, 130/90 x 17
			750: Champion RA 6 YC	Wheelbase	1,520mm (59.8 in.)
Bore	650: 82mm	Generator	12v/300W Ducati or Saprisa	Length	2,290mm (90.2 in.)
	350: 66mm			Width	845mm (33.3 in.)
	750: 88mm	Ignition (degrees)	650, 350: Bosch BTZ electronic, 5 static, 33 total	Seat height	905mm (35.6 in.)
Stroke	650, 750: 61.5mm			Dry weight	650, 750 191 kg (420.7 lbs.)
	350: 51mm		750: Kokusan 6 static, 32 total		350: 189 kg (416.3 lbs.)
Displacement	650: 649cc	Battery	Yuasa 12V 14Ah	Colors	650: Red frame and seat, red and white (1986: Black and red, blue and white, black and white Explorer)
	350: 349cc	Primary drive	650, 750: 1.972:1 (31/71)		
	750: 748cc		350: 31/69		
Compression ratio	650: 10:1 350: 10.3:1	Clutch	Dry multiplate (wet; early 650, 350)		350: White frame, blue seat, blue and white (1987: Red and black)
	750: 9.3:1				
Valve actuation	Belt-driven desmodromic overhead camshaft	Gear ratios	0.931, (350: 0.966), 1.074, 1.333, 1.850, 3.071		750: Black frame, black and white
Valve timing (degrees)	650: 39, 80, 80, 38	Final drive	2.733:1 (15/41); (350: 14/46)	Frame numbers	350: From 5N000001
	350: 19, 62, 53, 33	Front suspension	41.7mm Marzocchi fork		650: From 1N000001
	750: 31, 88, 72, 46				650: From 6N000001
Carburetion	650: Dell'Orto PHF36 M	Rear suspension	Öhlins rising rate swingarm		
	350: PHF 30 DD				
	750: Bing 64/32/375	Front brake	260mm disc (10.2 in.)		
Power	650: 52.4 horsepower at 7,500 rpm	Rear brake	240mm disc (9.4 in.)		
	350: 33 horsepower at 8,000 rpm				
	750: 60.5 horsepower at 8,000 rpm				

750 Lucky Explorer

In June 1987, the 750 Lucky Explorer replaced the 650 Elefant. The 350 Elefant continued much as before, incorporating the cosmetic changes of the 750, and was also available in Lucky Explorer colors. There was significantly more than an increase in capacity with the 750, with the entire motorcycle restyled and altered to improve its off-road appeal.

The lower end of the 750 Elefant engine was essentially the same as the 750 Indiana, but without the chromed engine covers. Most of the internal components were identical, including the dry clutch, helical primary drive and five-speed gearbox. The 750 Elefant received the cylinder heads of the 750 Paso, with larger (41mm and 37mm) valves, and there were Bing carburetors and Kokusan ignition. Starting was either kick or electric.

Although the essential frame and running gear was unchanged, there were a number of cosmetic alterations with the 750, including "Lucky Explorer" colors and decals of the 1987 works racers. There was a larger and wider (19-liter) gas tank, large white engine protection plate, and white plastic fork and brake shield. The gas tank now attached to an integral fairing. For 1989, the 750 Elefant continued basically unchanged, except for a new fairing, which now with a small Plexiglas screen, and the substitution of the rectangular headlight for twin round headlights. The rear 05 Brembo brake caliper was upgraded to a 28mm twin-piston type. Continual

900 I.E. Lucky Explorer, 900 I.E. GT

Patterned on the Paris-Dakar factory racers, the 900 I.E. was a much larger motorcycle than the earlier Elefant.

As the Cagiva "Lucky Explorer" Paris-Dakar racers were using 904cc engines based on the six-speed 851 crankcases by 1988, it was inevitable the Elefant would grow to 900cc. When the 900 I.E. appeared in 1990, much was new, and it was only available in "Lucky Explorer" colors.

Using the basic air-oil cooled 900 Supersport engine, the 900 I.E.'s main developments were the replacement of the Weber carburetor by Weber-Marelli electronic fuel injection, and lower-lift (9.35mm and 8.50mm) 750 camshafts. The 900 I.E. (Iniezione Elettronica) also featured a five-speed gearbox, rather than the usual 900 six-speed. Because the primary drive was shared with the 900 Supersport, the gearbox ratios were new and unique to the 1990 model 900 I.E. The 900 I.E. also received its

own 16-plate dry clutch setup with the hydraulic clutch actuation assembly incorporated in the right side clutch cover. Starting was now only electric. The 900 I.E. was the first production air-cooled Ducati to feature the Weber I.A.W. electronic ignition system. This was virtually identical to that of the 907 I.E. that appeared a few months later, with six sensors and one injector per cylinder.

The 900 I.E. had a new double-cradle frame constructed of a square section steel backbone with a detachable cradle of square section aluminum, with a rectangular section aluminum swingarm. The new model was patterned after the Paris-Dakar racers. The overall dimensions increased, accentuated by the large (24-liter) fuel tank that merged into the fairing. New suspension included a leading axle

Marzocchi fork and Öhlins shock absorber with "Soft Damp" linkage. The wheels featured aluminum rims designed for tubeless tires, laced to alloy hubs. Rims were 2.15 x 19-inch and 3.00 x 17-inch. Also new was the twin-piston floating Nissin front brake caliper.

The 900 I.E. Lucky Explorer continued with few changes for 1991 and was joined by the 900 I.E. GT.

While the Explorer continued with the five-speed gearbox, the 900 I.E. GT received the six-speed gearbox of other "large-crankcase" models. In other respects, the engine was unchanged from the Lucky Explorer. The GT also featured some new chassis components, reflecting more of a street orientation—notably a new larger-diameter front fork. Both models lasted with only small updates into 1992.

900 I.E., 900 I.E. GT 1990-92

Engine	Twin cylinder four-stroke, air-cooled	Ignition (degrees)	Marelli Digiplex variable advance	Tires	100/90 x 19, 140/80 x 17
Bore	92mm	Battery	12V 16Ah	Wheelbase	I.E.: 1,570mm (61.8 in.) GT: 1,150mm GT (45.3 in.)
Stroke	68mm	Primary drive	2.000:1 (31/62)	Length	I.E.: 2,295mm (90.4 in.) GT: 2,275mm GT (89.6 in.)
Displacement	904cc	Clutch	Dry multiplate	Height	970mm (38.2 in.)
Compression ratio	9.2:1	Gear ratios	I.E.: 0.88, 1.403, 1.238, 1.611, 2.466 GT: 0.857:1, 0.958, 1.091, 1,350, 1.764, 2.466	Width	860mm (33.9 in.)
Valve actuation	Belt-driven desmodromic overhead camshaft			Seat height	900mm (35.4 in.) 897mm GT (35.3 in.)
Valve timing (degrees)	31, 88, 72, 46	Final drive	I.E.: 3.286:1 (14/46) GT: 3.20:1 (15/48)	Dry weight	I.E.: 188 kg (414.1 lbs.) GT: 189 kg GT (416.3 lbs.)
Carburetion	Weber I.A.W. P7 electronic injection	Front suspension	I.E.: 42mm Marzocchi PA SD Nissin 298 GT: Marzocchi 45mm PA FD 298 Nissin	Top speed	190 km/h (118.1 mph)
Power	I.E.: 90 horsepower at 8,500 rpm GT: 67.7 horsepower at 8,000 rpm (at the rear wheel)	Rear suspension	Öhlins rising rate swingarm	Colors	Black frame, black and white
Spark plugs	Champion RA4HC	Front brake	296mm disc (11.7 in.)	Frame numbers	I.E.: From 1B000001 GT: From 1BE001011
Generator	12v/300W (350 W; 1991)	Rear brake	240mm disc (9.4 in.)		

Elefant 900 and 750

The final version of the Elefant appeared in early 1993, and was without electronic fuel injection. The engine was identical to the 900 Supersport, including carburetors, clutch, gearbox, crankshaft, pistons, and cylinder head. The E 900 was also fitted with a catalytic converter. Shared with the 900 I.E was the steel and aluminum dual cradle frame, but the suspension included an upside-down Showa fork and Boge rear shock absorber. Along with the new suspension came Brembo brakes with dual discs at the front and floating twin-piston calipers. One improvement was a much lower seat than earlier versions. U.S. versions of the Elefant 900 were called the Ducati E-900. The model lasted until 1998 with only minor updates.

For 1994, the 750 Elefant made a reappearance. It had the basic running gear of the earlier 900 I.E. GT, with the five-speed engine of the 750 Supersport. The Elefant 750 retained the earlier Marzocchi fork and single Nissin

Ducati Motor

The E750 was still available in Lucky Explorer colors for 1994.

front disc brake. A Nissin was also used at the rear, along with the E900's Boge shock absorber. The Elefant 750 continued through the 1996 season but, as with other Ducati models this year, suffered from a lack of supply of various components.

There were few changes to the E900 for 1994. It still retained a catalytic converter in the exhaust.

A revamped Elefant 900 for 1993 saw a return to carburetors, and new brakes and suspension.

ELEFANT 900, 750 1993-98

Engine	Twin cylinder four-stroke, air-cooled	**Ignition (degrees)**	Kokusan	**Rear brake**	240mm disc (9.4 in.)		
Bore	900: 92mm 750: 88mm	**Battery**	12V 16Ah	**Tires**	100/90 x 19, 140/80 x 17		
Stroke	900: 68mm 750: 61.5mm	**Primary drive**	2.000:1 (31/62)	**Wheelbase**	900: 1,555mm (61.2 in.) 750: 1,560mm (61.4 in.)		
Displacement	900: 904mm 750: 748mm	**Clutch**	900: Dry multiplate 750: Wet	**Length**	900: 2,200mm (86.6 in.) 750: 2,205mm 750 (86.8 in.)		
Compression ratio	900: 9.2:1 750: 9:1	**Gear ratios**	900: 0.857:1, 0.958, 1.091, 1,350, 1.764, 2.466	**Height**	1,360mm (53.5 in.)		
Valve actuation	Belt-driven desmodromic overhead camshaft		750: 0.966, 1.074, 1,333, 1.714, 2.500	**Width**	915mm (36 in.)		
Valve timing (degrees)	31, 88, 72, 46	**Final drive**	3.066:1 (15/46)	**Seat height**	835mm (32.9 in.)		
Carburetion	Mikuni BDST 38	**Front suspension**	900: Showa inverted 45mm 750: Marzocchi 45mm	**Dry weight**	900: 185 kg (407.5 lbs.) 750: 188 kg (414.1 lbs.)		
Power	900: 68 horsepower at 6,500 rpm 750: 60 horsepower at 6,500 rpm	**Rear suspension**	Boge rising-rate swingarm	**Top speed**	190 km/h (118.1 mph)		
		Front brake	900: 282mm dual disc (11.1 in.) 750: 296mm disc (11.7 in.)	**Colors**	900: Maroon and gold, dark blue 750: Red and silver		
Spark plugs	Champion RA 6 HC			**Frame numbers**	900: From 5B000001 750: From 6B000001		
Generator	12v/350W						

Although the 907 I.E. continued the style of the 906, it was an improved model.

After two years, the 906 Paso was replaced by the much improved 907 I.E. for 1991. This drew on the engine and chassis technological improvements of the 851, and the resulting 907 I.E. was finally a homogeneous sport-touring motorcycle that could compete with anything on offer from Germany or Japan.

The liquid-cooled engine of the 906 carried over to the 907 I.E., but there were stronger crankcases with more extensive internal webbing and ribbing, especially around the cylinder support base. The clutch was also revised for 1991, with the 907 I.E. (like the 1991 900 Supersport) having a new 16-plate type. The intake system was completely revised, with the air intakes re-positioned up by the steering head, drawing in cold, dense air. Adapting the single-injector Weber electronic fuel injection system of the 851 Strada to the two-valve 906 engine provided vastly improved engine operation. The 907 I.E. received more reliable Veglia instruments, but all other electrical equipment was shared with the 906 Paso.

While the rectangular-section steel double-cradle frame was that of the 906, the longer aluminum swingarm and axle

adjusters came from the 851 Strada. The front suspension was the same as before, but with 10mm-longer fork legs so that the larger wheel/tire combination would clear the engine on fork compression. There were also changes to the wheels and brakes, with three-spoke Brembo (3.50 x 17 and 5.50 x 17) wheels, and larger stainless-steel front discs with Brembo four-piston P4.32d calipers. At the rear the disc was reduced in size to that of the 851, with a smaller P2.105N Brembo caliper. The larger wheels (and longer swingarm) led to an increase in both wheelbase, but the steering and handling characteristics were vastly superior to those of the 906 Paso. While the style of the bodywork was similar to the 906, the solid 907 I.E. screen incorporated a NACA duct, supposedly to smooth the airflow.

The 907 I.E. continued for 1992 with only minor changes. There was a minor clutch update during the year, and the front brakes were upgraded with larger discs and gold Brembo P4.30-34 brake calipers. The 907 I.E. wasn't as popular as anticipated, although it offered improved power and reliability, plus more sophisticated rear suspension than the Supersport models. The 907 I.E.

was a very well-developed all-round motorcycle, with excellent handling and comfort, but it was discontinued during 1992. There wouldn't be a replacement sport touring Ducati until 1997.

The 1992 907 I.E. included larger-diameter front disc brakes, but it was otherwise unchanged.

Ducati Motor

Production	1989	1990	1991	1992	Total
907 I.E.					
1990	1	1052			1,053
1992			60	270	330
1992 black			110		110
US 1990		195			195
US 1992			146	140	286
US 1992 black			64		64
Cal. 1990		55			55
Cal. 1992			63	40	103
Cal. 1992 black			27		27
Ger. 1992			10	50	60
Ger. 1992 black			20		20
Total	1	1,302	500	500	2,303

907 I.E.

Engine	Twin cylinder four-stroke, liquid-cooled	**Generator**	12v/350W	**Tires**	120/70 x 17, 170/60 x 17
Bore	92mm	**Battery**	12V 19Ah	**Wheelbase**	1,490mm (55.7 in.)
Stroke	68mm	**Primary drive**	2.000:1 (31/62)	**Length**	2,090mm (82.3 in.)
Displacement	904cc	**Clutch**	Dry multiplate	**Height**	1,160mm (45.7 in.)
Compression ratio	9.2:1	**Gear ratios**	0.857:1, 0.958, 1.091, 1,350, 1.764, 2.466	**Width**	700mm (27.6 in.)
Valve actuation	Belt-driven desmodromic overhead camshaft	**Final drive**	2.666:1 (15/40)	**Seat height**	780mm (30.7 in.)
Valve timing (degrees)	20, 60, 58, 20	**Front suspension**	41.7mm Marzocchi M1R	**Dry weight**	215 kg (473.6 lbs.)
Carburetion	Weber I.A.W P7 CPU (42mm throttle bodies)	**Rear suspension**	Marzocchi Duoshock 38mm rising-rate swingarm	**Top speed**	230 km/h (142.9 mph)
Power	90 horsepower at 8,500 rpm	**Front brake**	300mm (11.8 in.) 320mm 1992 dual disc (12.6 in.)	**Colors**	Red, black
Spark plugs	Champion RA 4 HC	**Rear brake**	245mm disc (9.6 in.)	**Engine numbers**	From ZDM 904 W2 000001
				Frame numbers	From ZDM 906 PI 2 000001

900, 750, 600, 400, 350 SUPERSPORT, 900 SUPERLIGHT, FINAL EDITION

While most of Cagiva's early efforts after they bought Ducati were disappointing, they made amends with the carbureted Supersport of 1991-98. This was a brilliant model and has justifiably become one of the classic modern Ducatis. Although derived from the 1990 version, the 1991 Supersport looked fresh, and was functionally superior to its predecessor in nearly every respect. It was also a sales success and spawned the 750, 350, 400, and 600 Supersports, as well as the Superlight.

900 Supersport (1991-97)

For 1991, the 900 Supersport evolved into one of the classic modern models. There was an option of full or half-fairings, and the oil cooler was positioned close to the front wheel.

The engine for the 1991 900 Supersport was based on the 1990 model, but the crankcases were strengthened around the base of the cylinder. Clutch actuation was moved to the left, there was a new clutch arrangement, and a return to Kokusan ignition. Unchanged was the air-oil cooling system, although the oil radiator was now located in more vulnerable location on the front exhaust valve cover. The troublesome Weber carburetor was replaced by twin constant-vacuum Mikuni carburetors and, while not perfect, they were an improvement only hampered by the very long inlet tracts.

Most of the changes with the 1991 Supersport were to the chassis. The layout of the frame tubing was revised, there was a new rear subframe and the steering head angle was steeper. A shorter aluminum swingarm reduced the wheelbase and the new Supersport was considerably more agile than its predecessor. Front and rear suspension was also new, with an inverted 41mm Showa front fork and Showa rear shock absorber. The new bodywork was not only more attractive, but servicing was made easier as the 17.5-liter gas tank pivoted to allow access to the battery and airbox. There were two versions: full fairing, or half fairing.

While the white-painted 17-inch Brembo wheels were carried over from before, the front brakes were now standardized with the 851, with larger discs and Brembo P4 32d four-piston calipers. After frame number 001601

these were replaced by the newer P4 30/34 gold series with 34 and 30mm pistons. The riding position was completely revised. The higher-rise clip-on handlebars and lower footpegs gave a unique sport-touring riding position. This riding position, combined with the light weight and agreeable power characteristics, made the new Supersport an extremely competent all-round street motorcycle.

Although a relatively long-lived model, the 900 Supersport was subject to a number of small developments over its model life. For 1992, there was new clutch that lasted until 1998. From January 1992, the valve guides were changed from cast-iron to aluminum-bronze. All cylinder heads featuring these new valve guides were

The 1994 and 1995 900 Supersports were virtually indistinguishable. This is the 1995 version.

Ducati Motor

Some 1992 900 Supersports were black, with white wheels, but all had gold-series brake calipers and a rear seat cowling that year.

identified by a "V1" marking on the timing cover side. Black or red versions were both offered. The rear seat included a removable cowling. Following problems with the chain adjustment bolts bending, these were increased in size to 8mm from frame number 003306 (U.S. 002474-2505 and 002596-2605, California 002578-2595). The wheels were painted black on red models, and white on the black versions.

Cosmetic changes again predominated for 1993. There were new graphics with silver decals and a bronze frame. Wheels were still painted black. There were larger-diameter cylinder head studs (8.0mm from engine number 013833) in response to the problem of previous studs breaking. There were more updates for 1994, with the engine covers, cylinders and heads now painted silver, but still with black timing belt covers. Cosmetically, the 900 Supersport looked much as before, except for frame-matching bronze wheels, and black footpeg supports and foot levers. The biggest developments were with the

swingarm and suspension that came from the 1993 900 Superlight. The front fork was upgraded and strengthened with a larger (20mm) axle. The aluminum swingarm was also stronger (also from the 1993 900 Superlight). There were remote fluid reservoirs for the clutch and front brake master cylinders.

The 900 Supersport continued with minor developments for 1995. Most changes were cosmetic. The engine timing belt covers and rear sprocket cover were gray, and the frame was painted the gold of the 916. The instrument panel included an oil temperature gauge. The rear Brembo P2 105N brake caliper was positioned under the swingarm, as with the 900 Monster. By 1996, serious financial and production problems at Ducati saw the 900 Supersport continue with only a few updates. To reduce noise there were sound-absorbing panels in the full fairing, and a sound-absorbing clutch cover. The crankcases for 1996 were from new castings, and were without the boss originally intended for the kick start.

Cagiva formed an alliance with the Texas Pacific Group in September 1996, but a replacement Supersport was still some time away. In the meantime, the existing 900 Supersport continued for 1997. The Mikuni carburetors included a carburetor heating kit with a two-way valve directing engine oil from the oil cooler to the carburetor float bowls. The oil cooler was mounted under the lower triple clamp, as with the Monster, and the full fairing featured additional vents to the rear cylinder to improve cooling. Along with a carbon-fiber front fender, there were improved front brake calipers and both the clutch and brake lines were braided steel (except for the U.S. and Australia). The rear brake was now the Superlight fully floating setup. Although the 900 Supersport was still an extremely pleasant motorcycle, by 1997 many considered it antiquated and obsolete, and it was time for a change.

Ducati Motor

The 1993 900 Supersport had a bronze frame and new graphics.

Apart from new crankcases, the 1996 900 Supersport was very similar to previous years.

The final year for the old style classic Supersport was 1997. There were new graphics and a fully floating rear disc brake.

Produced only for America, the 900 CR of 1994-95 combined the chassis of the 750 SS with the 900 SS motor.

An oil temperature gauge was included in the 900 Supersport instrument panel from 1995.

900 Supersport CR

After the dismal failure of the 750 Supersport in the U.S., a new model mating the 900 Supersport engine with the more basic 750 Supersport chassis was created for 1994. Originally titled the 900 Supersport "Economy," this bike was only available with a half fairing. This U.S.-only budget Supersport featured a non-adjustable Showa front fork, narrower 4.50 x 17-inch rear wheel and a steel swingarm. For 1995, the 900 CR received the non-adjustable Marzocchi fork of the 750 Supersport, and Sachs-Boge shock absorber of the 600 Supersport. Yearly changes to colors and specification were shared with the 900 Supersport SP.

The 900 CRs built for the U.S. in late 1997 were the final Ducatis with the older "Cagiva"-style graphics. These had 1998 specification U.S. 900 Supersport Final Edition engines (new pistons and cylinders), but with the oil cooler mounted underneath the front cylinder as on the older versions. Unlike earlier examples, these final 900 CRs also featured a rear seat cowling.

900 SUPERSPORT 1991-97

Engine	Twin-cylinder four-stroke, air-cooled	Clutch	Dry multiplate
Bore	92mm	Gear ratios	0.857:1, 0.958, 1.091, 1,350, 1.764, 2.466
Stroke	68mm	Final drive	2.466:1 (15/37)
Displacement	904cc	Front suspension	41mm inverted Showa GD 011
Compression ratio	9.2:1		From 1994: GD 021
Valve actuation	Belt-driven desmodromic overhead camshaft		900 CR 1994: GD 031)
Carburetion	Mikuni BDST 38-B67 (B73; CR)		900 CR from 1995: 40mm USD/E Marzocchi
Power	73 horsepower at 7,000 rpm (rear wheel)	Rear suspension	Showa GD 022-007-OX cantilever swingarm
	80 horsepower at 7,000 rpm (crankshaft)		900 CR from 1995: Sachs-Boge
Spark plugs	Champion RA6YC (RA6HC from 1993)	Front brake	320mm dual disc (12.6 in.)
Generator	12v/300W (350 W from 1993)	Rear brake	245mm disc (9.6 in.)
Ignition (degrees)	Kokusan; 6 static, 32 total	Tires	120/70 x 17, 170/60 x 17 (160/60 x 17; 900 CR)
Battery	12V 16Ah	Wheelbase	1,410mm (55.5 in.)
Primary drive	2.000:1 (31/62)	Length	1991-93: 2,020mm (79.5 in.)
			From 1994: 2,000mm (78.7 in.)

Height	1991-93: 1,110mm (43.7 in.)
	From 1994:1,125mm (44.3 in.)
Width	1991-93: 710mm (28 in.)
	From 1994:730mm (28.7 in.)
Seat height	780mm (30.7 in.)
Dry weight	1991-93: 183 kg (403.1 lbs.)
	From 1994: 186 kg (409.7 lbs.)
Max speed	220 km/h (136.7 mph)
Colors	1991-92: White frame, red or black
	1993-94: Bronze frame, red
	From 1995: Gold frame, red or yellow
Engine numbers	Continuing ZDM 904 A 2C 000001 series
Frame numbers	From ZDM 900 SC 2 000001

PRODUCTION	1990	1991	1992	1993	1994	1995	1996	1997	TOTAL
900 Supersport									
1991 Half fairing		462							462
1991 Fairing	3	1107							1,110
1992 Half fairing		271	172						443
1992 Half fairing black		42							42
1992 Fairing		839	740						1,579
1992 Fairing black		108							108
1993 Half fairing			90	455					545
1993 Fairing			700	1,482					2,182
USA 1991 Fairing		190							190
USA 1992 Half fairing		56	40						96
USA 1992 Half fairing black		14	10						24
USA 1992 Fairing		112	100						212
USA 1992 Fairing black		28	40						68
USA 1993 Fairing			360	250					610
Cal. 1991 Fairing		65							65
Calif. 1992 Half fairing		24	30						54
Calif. 1992 Half fairing black		6							6
Calif. 1992 Fairing		48	60						108

PRODUCTION	1990	1991	1992	1993	1994	1995	1996	1997	TOTAL
Calif. 1992 Fairing black	12	20							32
Calif. 1993 Fairing			240						240
Switz. 1991 Fairing		140							140
Switz. 1992 Fairing		80	60						140
Switz. 1993 Fairing			200	70					270
Aus. 1992 Fairing			10						10
Aus. 1993 Half fairing				20					20
Aus. 1993 Fairing			30	70					100
Ger. 1991 Fairing		341							341
Ger. 1992 Half fairing		90	20						110
Ger. 1992 Half fairing. Black		10							10
Ger. 1992 Fairing		220	180						400
Ger. 1992 Fairing black		40							40
Ger. 1993 Half fairing			50	180					230
Ger. 1993 Fairing			150	420					570
1994 Half fairing				125	94				219
1994 Fairing				396	612				1,008

PRODUCTION	1990	1991	1992	1993	1994	1995	1996	1997	TOTAL
Switz. 1994 Fairing				60	80				140
Aus. 1994 Half fairing				10					10
Aus. 1994 Fairing				10	50				60
Ger. 1994 Half fairing					40	100			140
Ger. 1994 Fairing					100	200			300
USA 1994/95 Economy					125	890	300		1,315
USA 1996 C.R.						510	80		590
USA 1997 C.R.							50		50
USA 1997 C.R. Yellow								100	100
USA 1998 C.R.									100
USA 1998 C.R. Yellow									100
Cal. 1994/95 Economy					40	240	100		380
Cal. 1996 C.R.						160			160
Cal. 1997 C.R. Yellow								150	150
1995 Half fairing					20	160			180
1995 Fairing					279	825			1,104
1996 Fairing						79	551		630
1997 Fairing							262	171	433
1997 Fairing Yellow								156	156
1997 Half fairing								25	25
1997 Half fairing Yellow								5	5
Switz. 1995 Fairing						110			110
Switz. 1997 Fairing								30	30
Switz. 1997 Fairing Yellow								30	30
Aus. 1995 Half fairing						35			35

PRODUCTION	1990	1991	1992	1993	1994	1995	1996	1997	TOTAL
Aus. 1995 Fairing					35	205			240
Aus. 1996 Fairing						40			40
Aus. 1997 Fairing							100	99	199
Aus. 1997 Fairing Yellow								23	23
Jpn. 1996 Fairing						40			40
Jpn. 1997 Fairing							40	37	77
Jpn. 1997 Half fairing							20	62	82
Ger. 1995 Half fairing						240			240
Ger. 1995 Fairing					140	460			600
Ger. 1996 Fairing						40	60		100
Ger. 1997 Fairing							35	333	368
Ger. 1997 Fairing Yellow								60	60
Eng. 1995 Fairing					76	265			341
Eng. 1996 Fairing							90		90
Eng. 1997 Fairing							40	60	100
Eng. 1997 Fairing Yellow								70	70
Total	3	4,305	3,302	3,853	2,816	3,569	1,328	1,411	20,787

KEY

Australia	= Aus.	Germany	= Ger.
California	= Cal.	Japan	= Jpn.
England	= Eng.	Singapore	= Sng.
France	= Fra.	Switzerland	= Switz.

900 Superlight

Following the immediate success of the 1991 900 Supersport, Ducati unveiled a limited edition 900 Superlight for 1992. While the engine and chassis were unchanged from the 1992 900 Supersport, there were a few details that set the Superlight apart. These included a vented clutch cover, fully floating cast-iron front disc rotors, and larger-diameter mufflers (from the 888 SP4) stepped down to fit the standard 900 SS collector. Each Superlight came with a carbon-fiber front fender, solo seat and numbered plaque on the top triple clamp. A considerable number were produced and it was hardly a true limited edition. 1992 models featured lightweight

The 1993 900 Superlight had regular Brembo wheels and didn't feature the fully floating cast-iron discs, as in this publicity photo.

(Ducati Motor)

There was little to differentiate the 1994 and 1995 900 Superlight. Both received an upgraded front fork and full-floating front discs. This is the 1995 version.

17-inch Marvic/Akront composite wheels, and of all the Superlights, the 1992 version epitomized the concept of minimum weight the most effectively. All the U.S. examples were yellow.

Following the success of the 1992 version, the Superlight specification was downgraded for 1993. The most expensive components were replaced by regular items, which also resulted in an increase in weight. The wheels were regular Brembo (although painted bronze), and the front disc rotors the usual Supersport stainless steel. Apart from the solo seat and upswept mufflers, it was only a fully floating rear brake linkage and carbon-fiber front fender that set the Superlight apart from the Supersport. The vented clutch cover disappeared, but the Superlights continued with the rectangular numbered plaque on the top triple clamp.

Some amends for the disappointing specification of the Superlight II were made for the Superlight III of 1994. Along with a return to cast-iron discs, there was an upgraded front fork and a stronger aluminum swingarm. Other changes shared between the 1994 900 SS incuded the gray engine covers, black footpeg brackets and levers, a larger-diameter front wheel axle, and remote reservoirs for the brake and clutch master cylinders. Only detail

updates were apparent on the Superlight IV for 1995 and Superlight V of 1996. Most were shared with the 900 Supersport and included the 916-gold painted frame and a new windshield. Except for the oil temperature gauge on the dashboard, the Superlight IV was almost indistinguishable from the Superlight III. By now the Superlight was selling slowly, with less production every year, but the Superlight V was still offered for 1996. Updates included sound-absorbing panels in the full fairing, and revised crankcases.

One of the most desirable Ducatis of the 1990s was the 1992 900 Superlight with Marvic/Akront wheels. U.S. examples were yellow.

900 Supersport SP (Sport Production)

After 1992, there were no more Superlights for the U.S., but 1994 saw the introduction of the 900 SS SP (Sport Production). The 900 SS SP was an amalgam of the Supersport and the Superlight, and was essentially a fully faired Superlight with a dual seat and lower exhaust pipes. Like the Superlight, it carried numbered plaques on the top triple clamp, and shared the refinements of the Superlight III. These included a carbon-fiber clutch cover and front and rear fenders, fully floating rear disc brake, and floating cast-iron front disc rotors.

The 900 SS SP was offered again in 1995 with a new number sequence. Basically, this machine was identical to the earlier version, but for the usual changes that appeared on the Supersport and Superlight IV that year. The 900 SS SP continued for 1996 and 1997 with all the changes applying to the regular 900 Supersport. Changes for 1997 included the relocation of the oil cooler and carburetor heating kit.

The 900 Supersport SP was a U.S-only model and included a numbered plaque on the top triple clamp.

900 Supersport Final Edition

Continuing the Superlight tradition, the 900 Supersport FE was the last of the carbureted Supersports.

With the release of the new Supersport imminent, a Final Edition was offered for 1998. Harking back to the days of the silver and blue 900 Super Sports, the 900 FE had silver bodywork with new graphics, accentuated by black wheels. There were no gas tank decals. Two 900 FE versions were produced—one for Europe and one for the U.S. The European FEs used 1997 specification engines with silver engine covers and external cylinder oil lines. They also had a carbon-fiber clutch cover and braided-steel clutch and brake lines. U.S. 900 FEs included 1998 specification engines (similar to the Monster 900 S) with gray engine covers and clutch cover. The new Tecnol cylinders were neater looking as the oil lines were now internal.

As usual for the U.S., the FE had rubber brake and clutch lines, but much of the rest of the FE specification was for the same as the earlier Superlight. There was a solo seat with upswept Termignoni exhausts, cast-iron fully floating front brake discs, and carbon-fiber mudguards. Carbon fiber extended to the chainguard and simplified dashboard (without a battery warning light). The full fairing was the same as that on the 1997 900 Supersport, with additional air intakes. All 900 SS FEs carried a numbered plaque.

900 SUPERLIGHT, SP, FINAL EDITION 1992-98

Engine	Twin-cylinder four-stroke, air-cooled	Ignition (degrees)	Kokusan; 6 static, 32 total	Length	2,030mm (79.9 in.)
Bore	92mm	Battery	12V 16Ah	Height	1,125mm (44.3 in.)
Stroke	68mm	Primary drive	SP: 2.000:1 (31/62); FE: 1.84:1 (32/59)	Width	730mm (28.7 in.)
Displacement	904cc			Seat height	780mm (30.7 in.)
Compression ratio	9.2:1	Clutch	Dry multiplate	Dry weight	1992: 176 kg (387.7 lbs.) 1993-98: 182 kg (400.9 lbs.)
Valve actuation	Belt-driven desmodromic overhead camshaft	Gear ratios	0.857:1, 0.958, 1.091, 1,350, 1.764, 2.466		
Carburetion	Mikuni BDST 38-B67 (B73; SP)	Final drive	2.466:1 (15/37)	Top speed	220 km/h (136.7 mph)
Power	73 horsepower at 7,000 rpm (rear wheel) 80 horsepower at 7,000 rpm (crankshaft) 75 horsepower at 7,000 rpm (900 FE)	Front suspension	1992-93: 41mm inverted Showa GD 011 1994-98: GD 021	Colors	1992: White frame, red or yellow 1993-94: Bronze frame, red or yellow 1995-96: Gold frame, red or yellow FE: Gold frame, silver
		Rear suspension	Showa GD 022-007-OX cantilever swingarm		
		Front	320mm dual disc (12.6 in.)		
Spark plugs	1992: Champion RA6YC 1993-98 RA6HC from 1993	Rear brake (mm)	245mm disc (9.6 in.)	Engine numbers	Continuing ZDM 904 A 2C 000001 series
Generator	1992: 12v/300W 1993-98: 12v/350 W	Tires	120/70 x 17, 170/60 x 17	Frame numbers	From ZDM 900 SC 2 004456-023636
		Wheelbase	1,410mm (55.5 in.)		

PRODUCTION	1992	1993	1994	1995	1996	1997	1998	TOTAL
900 Superlight								
1992	522							522
1993	325	250						575
1994 Yellow		136	202					338
1995 Yellow			128	220				348
1996 Yellow					1	7		8
1994 red		50	148					198
1995 Red				220				220
1996 Red					112			112
U.S.A. 1992 Yellow	200							200

PRODUCTION	1992	1993	1994	1995	1996	1997	1998	TOTAL
Cal. 1992 Yellow	100							100
Aus. 1992	30							30
Aus. 1993		20						20
Aus. 1995 Yellow				12				12
Aus. 1996 Yellow					3			3
Aus. 1996 Red					13			13
Jpn. 1996 Red					88			88
Ger. 1992	100							100
Ger. 1993	40	120						160
Ger. 1994 Yellow		80	80					160

PRODUCTION	1992	1993	1994	1995	1996	1997	1998	TOTAL
Ger. 1994 red		40	20					60
1995 Red Ger.			144	126				270
1996 Red Ger.					40			40
1996 Red Eng.					45			45
900 Supersport								
USA 1994/95 Special		125	390	340				855
USA 1996 Special				280	240			520
USA 1997 Special					80			80
Cal. 1994/95 Special		40	160	60				260

Production	1992	1993	1994	1995	1996	1997	1998	Total
Cal. 1996 Special				80	80			160
Cal. 1997 H.T.					40			40
Cal. 1997 H.T. Yellow						180		180
Final Edition 1998 Silver						148		148
Final Edition 1998 Cal. Silver							300	300

Production	1992	1993	1994	1995	1996	1997	1998	Total
Final Edition 1998 Aus. Silver						22		22
Final Edition 1998 Jpn. Silver						96		96
Final Edition 1998 German Silver						154		154

Production	1992	1993	1994	1995	1996	1997	1998	Total
Final Edition 1998 Eng. Silver							80	80
Total	1,317	861	1,272	1,338	748	680	300	6,516

750 Supersport

The 1991 750 Supersport was a budget version of the 900. There was a hydraulic dry clutch that year, and the oil cooler was an option.

Shortly after the release of the 900 Supersport came the 750 Supersport. This was essentially the small-crankcase engine of the earlier 750 Sport, with Mikuni constant vacuum carburetors, installed in a similar chassis to the 900. The five-speed engine was painted black and shared its hydraulically operated dry clutch of the 750 Sport. As a budget model, the 750 SS, received a non-adjustable front fork, a different aluminum swingarm, and a single stainless-steel front disc brake with a gold P4

There were few changes to the 750 Supersport for 1992, apart from black wheels and a standard oil cooler.

Two Wheels

1993 750 Supersports still featured a single front disc brake and black-painted wheels. There was always an option of full or half-fairing.

Ducati Motor

Color changes for 1995 mirrored those of the 900 Supersport, and included the 916-gold frame and gray timing belt covers. During the year there was a Marzocchi 40mm front fork, still with the double-front disc setup. Apart from the sound deadening panels in the fairing, there were no changes to the 750 Supersport for 1996. This was a difficult year for production and only a few 750s were produced.

For its final year with carburetors, the 750 Supersport received a new fairing with an air intake, new graphics, bimetallic inlet and exhaust valves, and carburetor heating kit. The oil cooler was now mounted above the front cylinder. The carbureted 750 Supersport finished during 1997, but it was more than a year before the replacement fuel injected 750 Supersport appeared.

30/34 Brembo brake caliper. The rear wheel was narrower, with a 4.50 x 17-inch rim. Updates for 1992 included a hydraulically operated wet clutch, the 900 oil cooler and higher primary drive ratio, and black-painted wheels (on red examples). From frame number 001210 on there were stronger chain adjusters bolts.

While the only change to the 750 Supersport engines for 1993 were silver-painted crankcases, but there were a number of cosmetic alterations to the motorcycle. These included a bronze-painted frame and new decals. 1993 models still featured a single front disc brake but the introduction of the 600 Supersport in 1994 saw the 750 upgraded with dual front disc brakes. The non-adjustable Showa front fork continued, but had a larger 20mm, front axle. The wheels were painted bronze. The previous aluminum swingarm was also replaced by a steel unit.

Ducati Motor

The 750 Supersport for 1995 included a gold frame and gray timing belt covers. The wet clutch and dual front discs were carried over from the earlier models.

The final carbureted 750 Supersport of 1997 had a rear seat cover, and looked similar to the 900 of the same year.

750 SUPERSPORT 1991-97

Engine	Twin cylinder four-stroke, air-cooled	Primary drive	1991: 1.972:1 (36/71) 1992-97: 2.0:1 (31/62) from 1992	Height	1991-93: 1,110mm (43.7 in.) 1994-97: 1,125mm (44.3 in.)
Bore	88mm	Clutch	Dry multiplate (wet from # 001275)	Width	1991-93: 710mm (28 in.) 1994-97: 730mm (28.7 in.)
Stroke	61.5mm	Gear ratios	0.966, 1.074, 1.333, 1.714, 2.500	Seat height	780mm (30.7 in.)
Displacement	748cc	Final drive	2.466:1 (15/37)	Dry weight	1991-93: 173 kg (381.1 lbs.) 1994-97: 176 kg (387.7 lbs.)
Compression ratio	9:1	Front suspension	41mm inverted Showa GD 031 Marzocchi 40 USD/E (from # 007707)	Max speed	1991-93: 210 km/h (130.5 mph) 1994-97: 200 km/h (124.3 mph)
Valve actuation	Belt-driven desmodromic overhead camshaft	Rear suspension	Showa GD 022-007-OX cantilever swingarm	Colors	1991-92: White frame, red or black 1993-94: Bronze frame, red 1995-97: Gold frame, red or yellow
Valve timing (degrees)	31, 88, 72 ,46	Front brake	320mm disc [dual discs from 1994] (12.6 in.)		
Carburetion	Mikuni BDST 38-B70	Rear brake	245mm disc (9.6 in.)		
Power	60 horsepower at 8,500 rpm 66 horsepower at 8,500 rpm (crankshaft)	Tires	120/60 x 17, 170/60 x 17		
Spark plugs	Champion RA6HC	Wheelbase	1,410mm (55.5 in.)	Engine numbers	From ZDM 750 A 2C 000001
Generator	12v/300W	Length	1991-93: 2,020mm (79.5 in.) 1994-97: 2,000mm (78.7 in.)	Frame numbers	From ZDM 750 SC 000001
Ignition (degrees)	Kokusan 6 static, 32 total				
Battery	Yuasa 12V 14Ah				

PRODUCTION	1990	1991	1992	1993	1994	1995	1996	1997	TOTAL
750 Supersport									
Switz. 1990 Fairing	150								150
1991 Half fairing	3	851	1						855
1992 Half fairing		265	111						376
1992 Fairing		205	859						1,064
1993 Half fairing			73	100					173
1993 Fairing			529	385					914
Italy 1993 Half fairing				30					30
Italy 1993 Fairing			350	190					540
U.S.A. 1992 Half fairing		80	60						140
U.S.A. 1993 Half fairing			210						210
Calif. 1992 Half fairing		35	25						60
Calif. 1993 Half fairing			120						120
Switz. 1992 Half fairing		25	25						50
Switz. 1992 Fairing		50							50
Switz. 1993 Half fairing				50					50
Switz. 1993 Fairing			40	35					75
Aus. 1992 Fairing			20						20
Aus. 1993 Fairing			20	20					40
Ger. 1991 Fairing		301							301

PRODUCTION	1990	1991	1992	1993	1994	1995	1996	1997	TOTAL
Ger. 1992 Half fairing		40	170						210
Ger. 1992 Fairing		20	110						130
Ger. 1993 Half fairing			180	190					370
Ger. 1993 Fairing			70	160					230
1994 Half fairing				158	14				172
1994 Fairing				789	122				911
1995 Half fairing					45	60			105
1995 Fairing					270	390			660
1996 Fairing						110			110
1997 Fairing							60	450	510
1997 Fairing Yellow								87	87
1997 Half fairing								1	1
1997 Half fairing Yellow								3	3
Switz. 1994 Fairing				5					5
Aus. 1994 Half fairing					10				10
750 Aus. 1994 Fairing					44				44
Aus. 1995 Fairing					30	30			60
Aus. 1996 Fairing							40		40
Aus. 1997 Fairing red								109	109
Aus. 1997 Fairing Yellow								61	61

Production	1990	1991	1992	1993	1994	1995	1996	1997	Total
Ger. 1994 Half fairing				40	120				160
Ger. 1994 Fairing				200	198				398
Ger. 1995 Half fairing					40	240			280
Ger. 1995 Fairing					60	390			450
Ger. 1996 Fairing						120			120
Ger. 1997 Fairing red								185	185
Ger. 1997 Fairing Yellow								30	30

Production	1990	1991	1992	1993	1994	1995	1996	1997	Total
Eng. 1995 Fairing					55	140			195
Eng. 1996 Fairing						30			30
Eng. 1997 Fairing Red								140	140
Eng. 1997 Fairing Yellow								80	80
Total	153	1,872	2,973	2,352	1,008	1,550	60	1,146	8,762

350, 400, and 600 Supersport

The 350 and 400 Supersports were produced primarily for the Italian and Japanese markets. This is the 1992 350 Supersport.

Ducati Motor

Joining the 750 Supersport in 1991 was a Japanese market 400 Supersport Junior. The engine and six-speed transmission was similar to that of the earlier 400 F3, but there was a two-into-one exhaust system, and the smaller dry clutch was carried over from the 750 Sport. The specification was similar to the 750 Supersport, including the non-adjustable front fork, single front disc brake, narrower rear wheel, and aluminum swingarm. There was also the option of either a full or half fairing. For the 1992 model year, the 400 Supersport was joined by a 350 Sport for the Italian market.

Unlike the 750 and 900 Supersports that received black wheels for 1992, the smaller versions still used white-painted wheels.

Both the 350 and 400 continued largely unchanged for 1993. The frame was now painted bronze, the swingarm steel, and the wheels painted black. For 1994, the 350 was discontinued, with the 400 available as 27 horsepower for Europe and 42 horsepower for Japan. Apart from the six-speed transmission, the engine and chassis were standardized with the new 600 Supersport. This model was produced until 1998.

The 600 Supersport was new for 1994. While the crankcases, five-speed gearbox and cylinders were similar to the earlier 600 SL Pantah, the 600 Supersport used 400 cylinder heads with 33.5mm and 30.5mm valves. There was no oil cooler, and the hydraulically actuated wet clutch was the same as of the 750 Supersport. There were two versions (33 and 53 horsepower), both with a two-into-one exhaust. The first 600 Supersports were fitted with Showa suspension, but this soon changed to a Marzocchi fork and Sachs Boge shock absorber. There were only a few updates between 1995 and 1997. Constructed to fill niches in particular markets, the baby Supersports were never serious performance alternatives to the larger models.

Ducati Motor

The 600 Supersport was released for 1994, with a single front disc brake and the option of full or half-fairing.

Ducati Motor

There was a steel swingarm and black wheels for the 350 Supersport of 1993.

350, 400, 600 SUPERSPORT 1991-98

Engine	Twin cylinder four-stroke, air-cooled	**Generator**	12v/300W	**Rear brake**	245mm disc (9.6 in.)
Bore	600: 80mm 400: 70.5mm 350: 66mm	**Ignition (degrees)**	Kokusan, 6 static, 32 total	**Tires**	120/60 x 17, 160/60 x 17
		Battery	12V/16Ah	**Wheelbase**	1,410mm (55.5 in.)
Stroke	600: 58mm 400, 350: 51mm	**Primary drive**	600, 400 (1994-98): 2.28:1 (32/73) 400, 350: 2.264:1 (34/77) 600 (from 001853): 2:1 (31/62)	**Length**	2,020mm (79.5 in.)
				Height	1,110mm (43.7 in.)
Displacement	600: 583cc 400: 398cc 350: 349cc			**Width**	730mm (28.7 in.)
				Seat height	770mm (30.3 in.)
Compression ratio	400: 10:1 600, 350: 10.7:1	**Clutch**	1991: Dry multiplate 1992-98: Wet multiplate	**Dry weight**	600: 172 kg (378.9 lbs.) 400: 173 kg (381.1 lbs.) 350: 169 kg (372.2 lbs.)
Valve actuation	Belt-driven desmodromic overhead camshaft	**Gear ratios**	600: 0.966, 1.074, 1.333, 1.714, 2.500 400, 350: 0.931, 1.074, 1.280, 1.590, 2.111, 3.071	**Top speed**	600: 190 km/h (118.1 mph) 400, 350: 180 km/h (111.9 mph)
Valve timing (degrees)	31, 88, 72, 46				
Carburetion	Mikuni BDST 38 B156 (600) B79 (400) B100 (350)	**Final drive**	600: 2.4:1 (15/36) 600 (from 001853): 2.73:1 (15/41) 400, 350: 3.21:1 (14/45)	**Colors**	1991-92: White frame, red 1993-94: Bronze frame, red 1995-98: Gold frame, red or yellow
Power	600: 53 horsepower at 8,250 rpm 600: 33 horsepower at 7,500 rpm 400: 42 horsepower at 10,000 rpm 350: 36 horsepower at 10,500 rpm	**Front suspension**	350: 41mm Showa GD031 600, 400 (1995-98) Marzocchi 40USD/E		
		Rear suspension	400: Marzocchi PBS1R cantilever swingarm 350: Showa GD 022-007-OX (350) 600, 400 (from 1995): Sachs-Boge	**Engine numbers**	600: From at ZDM 600 A 2C 000001
Spark plugs	400, 350: Champion L82YC (400 1994-98): RL82Y 600: RA 4 HC	**Front brake**	320mm disc (12.6 in.)	**Frame numbers**	600: From ZDM 600 S 000001

By 1997, the 600 Supersport was still very similar to the first version.

Ducati Motor

PRODUCTION	1989	1990	1991	1992	1993	1994	1995	1996	1997	TOTAL
350 Supersport										
Italy 1992 Half fairing			1	501						502
Italy 1993 Half fairing				250	100					350
400 Supersport										
1990 Junior Jpn.	301	300								601
1990 Junior Jpn.		40								40
1991 Junior Jpn.			199							199
1991 Junior Jpn. Half fairing			295							295
1992 Junior Jpn.				1						1
1992 Half fairing				5						5
1993 Half fairing				130	50					180
Aus. 1993 Half fairing				20						20
Jpn. 1993 Half fairing					80					80
Jpn. 1993 Fairing				150	70					220
1994 Half fairing					200					200
Italy 1994 33 HP					200					200
Jpn. 1994 Fairing					80					80
Jpn. 1994 Half fairing					170					170
Jpn. 1995 Fairing						100				100
Jpn. 1995 Half fairing						50				50
Jpn. 1996/98 Fairing Red							120	130		250
Jpn. 1998 Fairing Yellow								10		10
Jpn. 1996/98 Half fairing Red							80	50		130
Jpn. 1998 Half fairing Yellow								10		10
600 Supersport										
1994 Half fairing					2	210				212
1994 Fairing						1,013				1,013
1995 Half fairing						35				35
1995 Fairing						219	125			344
Italy 1995 Fairing 33 hp							160			160
1996 Fairing							147	161		308

PRODUCTION	1989	1990	1991	1992	1993	1994	1995	1996	1997	TOTAL
1996 Fairing 33 HP							10	15		25
1997 Fairing Red									218	218
1997 Fairing Yellow									114	114
1997 Half fairing Red									23	23
1997 Half fairing Yellow									2	2
Italy 1997 Half fairing 33 hp Red									47	47
Italy 1997 Half fairing 33 hp Yellow									44	44
Switz 1995 Fairing						1	80			81
Aus. 1995 Fairing							20			20
Aus. 1996 Fairing							20	50		70
Aus. 1997 Fairing Red									63	63
Aus. 1997 Fairing Yellow									20	20
Aus. 1997 Half fairing								1		1
Ger. 1994 Half fairing						100				100
Ger. 1994 Fairing						267				267
Ger. 1995 Half fairing						30				30
Ger. 1995 Fairing						90	60			150
Ger. 1996 Fairing							30	100		130
Ger. 1997 Fairing Red									95	95
Ger. 1997 Fairing Yellow									25	25
Eng. 1994 Fairing						260				260
Eng. 1995 Fairing						125	55			180
Eng. 1996 Fairing							30	136		166
Eng. 1997 Fairing Red									100	100
Eng. 1997 Fairing Yellow									50	50
Total	301	340	501	1051	952	2,500	737	663	1001	8,046

CHAPTER 8

851 & 888

Although many of Cagiva's initial decisions following the company's purchase of Ducati in 1985 were dubious, its commitment to the development of a more modern engine design with a long service life was inspired. This engine, known as the Desmoquattro, would eventually achieve more racing success than any other Ducati design, and lead the renaissance of the company during the 1990s. The first production Desmoquattro was the 851 of 1988, and this early engine was very much a developed Pantah, with four-valve desmodromic cylinder heads, 40-degree included valve angle, liquid cooling, and Weber Marelli electronic fuel injection.

851 Strada and Superbike Kit 1988

Ducati Motor

To homologate the 851 for Superbike Racing, the 851 Kit was produced. It had racing wheels and brakes, but also a headlight and taillight.

Only a small number of 851s were produced during 1988. The only two models built were the 851 Strada and 851 Superbike Kit. The Superbike Kit was a homologation model for World Superbike racing. The motors on the two bikes were quite similar, with the same 32 and 28mm valves, and Weber fuel-injection system with twin injectors per cylinder. The pair shared Pankl con-rods, but the Strada had a wider ratio six-speed transmission. The 851s were considerably more powerful than the air-cooled 750 and 900, but the output on these early models was still quite conservative.

The tubular steel frame was derived from the F1, but with an aluminum swingarm and a rising rate linkage rear suspension setup similar to the Paso. The wheels on the Strada were the 16-inch Marvic/Akront composite models previously fitted to the Montjuich, while those of the Superbike Kit were Marvic 17-inch racing magnesium. The wheels were shod with Michelin racing slicks, yet the Superbike Kit came with an electric start and a headlight and taillight. The front brakes on both 851s were fully floating cast-iron with Brembo P4.32B front brake calipers.

Because these bikes were limited production models, many components were individually crafted on the first series, including the 20-liter aluminum fuel tank and rear suspension rocker linkage. Unfortunately, while the quality of execution was high, the 1988 851 Strada was a flawed motorcycle and the 16-inch wheels provided idiosyncratic steering and handling. The Superbike Kit was also too heavy and slow to be a competitive Superbike racer.

Production	1987	1988	1989	Total
851 Superbike				
Ed. 11/1987	7			7
4/1988		304		304
Kit 1/1988			152	1	153
Kit 1/1988 U.S.A.		54		54
Total	7	510	1	518

The first production Desmoquattro was the 851 Strada of 1988. The mirrors were incorporated in the fairing like the Paso, and there were 16-inch wheels.

851 Strada, Superbike Kit 1988

Engine	Twin-cylinder four-stroke, liquid-cooled	**Spark plugs**	Champion A59G	**Front brake**	280mm dual disc (11 in.)
Bore	92mm	**Generator**	12v/350W	**Rear brake**	260mm disc (10.2 in.)
Stroke	64mm	**Battery**	12V/14Ah	**Tires**	Strada: 130/60 x 16, 160/60 x 16
Displacement	851cc	**Primary drive**	2:1 (31/62)		Kit: 12/60 x 17, 18/67 x 17
Compression ratio	Strada:10.2:1 Kit: 10.6:1	**Clutch**	Dry multiplate	**Wheelbase**	1,460mm (57.5 in.)
Valve actuation	Belt-driven desmodromic double overhead camshafts	**Gear ratios**	Strada: 0.857, 0.958, 1.091, 1.35, 1.765, 2.466 Kit: 0.958, 1.043, 1.182, 1.40, 1.765, 2.466	**Length**	2,050mm (80.7 in.)
				Height	1,130mm (44.5 in.)
Valve timing (degrees)	Strada: 11, 70, 62, 18 Kit: 44, 73, 77, 42	**Final drive**	2.60:1 (15/39)	**Width**	700mm (27.6 in.)
Injection	Weber I.A.W. CPU P7	**Front suspension**	42mm Marzocchi M1R	**Seat height**	760mm (29.9 in.)
Power	Strada: 102 horsepower at 9,000 rpm Kit: 120 horsepower at 10,000 rpm	**Rear suspension**	Marzocchi Supermono rising-rate swingarm	**Dry weight**	Strada: 185 kg (407.5 lbs.) Kit: 165 kg (363.4 lbs.)
				Colors	Silver frame, red, white, green

851 Strada 1989-92

Although no longer a limited production model, and showing evidence of cost cutting, the 851 Strada was significantly improved for 1989. Apart from a slight increase in the compression ratio, and a single fuel injector per cylinder, there were few engine updates. But the chassis was improved. White-painted aluminum Brembo 17-inch wheels replaced the earlier 16-inch wheels, and the steering head angle on the frame was reduced to 24 1/2

degrees. The front brake disc diameter was also increased, and the rear disc reduced. These thinner discs were made of stainless steel and were inferior to the floating cast-iron type.

For 1990, the 851 gained a dual seat with stronger rear subframe, and the engine included Macchi forged conrods instead of the Pankl H-section. There were more

The 851 for 1990 got a new dual seat, but there were few other changes.

851 Strada 1989-92

Engine	Twin-cylinder four-stroke, liquid-cooled	**Generator**	1989-90: 12v/350W 1991-92: 12v/300W	**Tires**	120/70 x 17, 180/55 x 17	
Bore	92mm	**Battery**	12V/16Ah	**Wheelbase**	1,430mm (56.3 in.)	
Stroke	64mm	**Primary drive**	2:1 (31/62)	**Length**	1989-91: 2,000mm (78.7 in.) 1992: 2,030mm (79.9 in.)	
Displacement	851cc	**Clutch**	Dry multiplate			
Compression ratio	1989-90: 11:1 1991-92: 10.5:1	**Gear ratios**	0.857, 0.958, 1.091, 1.35, 1.765, 2.466	**Height**	1989-91: 1,120mm (44.1 in.) 1992:1,130mm (44.5 in.)	
Valve actuation	Belt-driven desmodromic double overhead camshafts	**Final drive**	2.60:1 (15/39)	**Width**	1989-91: 670mm (26.4 in.) 1992: 780mm (30.1 in.)	
Valve timing (degrees)	11, 70, 62, 18	**Front suspension**	1989-90: 42mm Marzocchi M1R 1991-92: Showa inverted 41mm GD011	**Seat height**	1989-91: 760mm (29.9 in.) 1992: 790mm (31.1 in.)	
Injection	Weber I.A.W. CPU P7	**Rear suspension**	1989-90: Marzocchi Duoshock rising rate swingarm 1991: Öhlins DU 0060 1992: Showa GD 012-007-OA	**Dry weight**	1989: 190 kg (418.5 lbs.) 1990: 192 kg (422.9 lbs.) 1991: 199 kg (438.3 lbs.) 1992: 202 kg (444.9 lbs.)	
Power	105 horsepower at 9,000 rpm 91 horsepower at 9,000 rpm (rear wheel 1991) 95 horsepower at 9,000 rpm (rear wheel 1992)	**Front brake**	320mm dual disc (12.6 in.)	**Max speed**	240 km/h (149.1 mph)	
Spark plugs	Champion A59G	**Rear brake**	245mm disc (9.6 in.)	**Colors**	White frame, red	

significant updates for 1991, when the front fork became a Showa and the rear shock an Öhlins. However, there was no longer a provision for ride height adjustment. By 1992, the 851 Strada was beginning to look slow and dated, so Pierre Terblanche provided a facelift.

The 851cc engine was also updated, with Sport Production cylinder heads with 33 and 29mm valves. The redesigned cooling system included a curved radiator. Changes to the white-painted frame saw single bent outer frame tubes, rather than individually welded sections, and new footpeg brackets. The rear shock absorber was also Showa. The braking system included Brembo "Gold Series" P4.30/34 front brake calipers with a gold P2.105N on the rear. Terblanche's bodywork was quite different, particularly the pivoting steel (rather than aluminum) 19-liter fuel tank. A restyled seat unit and new front fender accompanied the tank, and there were recess-mounted handles for the passenger.

PRODUCTION	1989	1990	1991	1992	TOTAL
851 S Monoposto					
Red 1989	751				751
851 S Biposto					
1990	430	596			1,026
1991		495	315		810
U.S.A. 1990	124				124
U.S.A. 1991		190			190
Cal. 1990	41				41
Cal. 1991		65			65
Switz. 1990	50	125			175
Switz. 1991			60		60
Switz. 1992				50	50
Ger. 1991			75		75
1992			133	758	891
U.S.A. 1992				180	180
Cal. 1992			50	25	75
Ger. 1992			42	158	200
888 S Biposto					
Italy 1993				500	500
Total	1,396	1,471	675	1,671	5,213

For 1989, the 851 was considerably improved, although it was no longer a limited-production motorcycle.

Although the engine was largely unchanged, the 1991 851 Strada received a Showa upside-down front fork.

888 Strada 1993-94

As the official factory racers and the Sport Production series were already displacing 888cc, it was inevitable that the production Superbike Strada would follow suit. This occurred for 1993, with the series also becoming a generic "888" rather than "851." The 888 also featured Pierre Terblanche's 851 styling facelift of 1992.

The European 888 Strada was very similar to that of the 1992 851 Strada and, except for an 888cc engine, most of the specifications were shared. They had the same valves, camshafts gearbox, and a single fuel injector per cylinder. To set the 1994 versions apart from the almost identical 1993 model there were new decals. The final 888s also featuring bronze-painted wheels.

The 888 for 1993 looked similar to the 1992 851, with new styling by Pierre Terblanche.

888 SPO (Sport Production Omologato) 1993-94

The U.S. 888 was called the SPO, with a solo seat, and 888 Strada motor and front end.

The 888 was sold as the 888 SPO in the U.S. market, an amalgam of the limited production high-performance SP5, and the European-specification 888 Strada. As the SP5 was unable to pass U.S. DOT requirements for registration, the SPO was created to homologate the 888 for AMA Superbike competition. While they were titled a Sport Production, they were more closely related to the 888 Strada than the SP5.

The SPO engine was identical to that of the 888 Strada, but many chassis components were shared with the SP5. The stainless-steel front discs and Showa fork were shared with the 888 Strada, but the SPO had a single seat, upswept exhaust pipes, and an Öhlins shock absorber with eccentric ride height adjustment. Even though it was a Monoposto, there wasn't an aluminum rear subframe as on other Sport Production models. There were only detail changes for the 1994 Model Year. Updates included a carbon fiber front fender, bronze wheels, a larger-diameter front axle, and a numbered plaque on the top triple clamp. Although overshadowed by the 916, the 888 was a well-developed, and largely underappreciated, model..

PRODUCTION	1992	1993	1994	TOTAL
888 S Biposto				
Italy 1993		500		500
Aus. 1993	20			20
Switz 1993	20	110		130
Switz 1994		60		60
Ger. 1993	120	40		160
Europe 1993	154	316		470
888 S Europe 1994		610	300	910
888 S Aus. 1994		30		30
888 S Ger. 1994		200		200
888 SPO				
USA 1993	169	1		170
USA 1994		75		75
Cal. 1993	120			120
Cal. 1994		25		25
Total	1,103	1,467	300	2,870

888 STRADA, SPO 1993-94

Engine	Twin-cylinder four-stroke, liquid-cooled	Generator	12v/350W	Tires	120/70 x 17, 180/55 x 17
Bore	94mm	Battery	12V/16Ah	Wheelbase	1,430mm (56.3 in.)
Stroke	64mm	Primary drive	2:1 (31/62)	Length	2,040mm (80.3 in.) 2,000mm SPO (78.7 in.)
Displacement	888cc	Clutch	Dry multiplate	Height	1,140mm (44.9 in.) 1,120mm (44.1 in.)
Compression ratio	11:1	Gear ratios	0.857, 0.958, 1.091, 1.35, 1.765, 2.466	Width	780mm (30.7 in.) 670mm (26.4 in.)
Valve actuation	Belt-driven desmodromic double overhead camshafts	Final drive	2.466:1 (15/37)	Seat height	805mm (31.7 in.) 760mm (29.9 in.)
Valve timing (degrees)	11, 70, 62, 18	Front suspension	Showa inverted 41mm GD011	Dry weight	202 kg (444.9 lbs.) 188 kg (414.1 lbs.)
Injection	Weber I.A.W. CPU P7 (P8 after 000508)	Rear suspension	888: Showa GD 012-007-OA rising rate swingarm SPO: Öhlins DU 8071	Top speed	250 km/h (155.4 mph) 260 km/h (161.6 mph)
Power	100 horsepower at 9,000 rpm	Front brake	320mm dual disc (12.6 in.)	Colors	Bronze frame, red
Spark plugs	Champion A59GC	Rear brake	245mm disc (9.6 in.)		

851 and 888 Sport Production 1989-93

Produced for the 1989 Italian Sport Production series that pitted production 750cc fours against twins of up to 1,000cc, the first 851 Sport Production was virtually indistinguishable from the Strada. These machines were still 851cc, with 851 Superbike Kit updates, but a more serious homologation model appeared for 1990: the 851 SP2.

Although still titled an 851, the 851 SP2 displaced 888cc. There was a return to two injectors per cylinder, and the SP retained the H-section Pankl con-rods and 300-watt alternator. The transmission was the closer-ratio unit of the earlier 851 Superbike Kit, as were the camshafts. The valve sizes were 33 and 29mm, and the exhaust a 45mm Termignoni. Chassis improvements included an upside-down Öhlins front fork, Öhlins shock absorber, and fully floating Brembo cast-iron front disc brakes. The Öhlins fork was a high-quality unit, but it suffered from premature fork seal failure. There was an aluminum rear subframe. Although it was an expensive limited production model, the SP2 provided unparalleled handling and performance in 1990.

Compared to other 851s, the specification of the 851 SP2 of 1990 was considerably higher.
Not only was the displacement 888cc, but the suspension was Öhlins.

851 AND 888 SPORT PRODUCTION 1989-93

Engine	Twin-cylinder four-stroke, liquid-cooled	**Spark plugs**	SP, SP1-4: Champion A59GC SPS-SP5: A55V	**Wheelbase**	1,430mm (56.3 in.)
Bore	1989: 92mm 1990-93: 94mm	**Generator**	12v/300W	**Length**	2,000mm (78.7 in.)
Stroke	64mm	**Battery**	12V/16Ah	**Height**	1,120mm (44.1 in.)
Displacement	1989: 851 1990-93: 888	**Primary drive**	2:1 (31/62)	**Width**	670mm (26.4 in.)
Compression ratio	SP (1989):11.5:1 SP2: 10.7:1 SP3: 11:1 SP4: 11.2:1 SPS: 11.7:1	**Clutch**	Dry multiplate	**Seat height**	760mm (29.9 in.)
		Gear ratios	0.958, 1.043, 1.182, 1.40, 1.765, 2.466	**Dry weight**	188 kg (414.1 lbs.) 185 kg SPS (407.5 lbs.)
Valve actuation	Belt-driven desmodromic double overhead camshafts	**Final drive**	SP 1989: 2.6:1 (15/39) SP2-3: 2.466:1 (15/37) SP4, SPS, SP5: 2.4:1 (15/36)	**Top speed**	SP2-3: 250 km/h (155.4 mph) SP4: 255 km/h (158.5 mph) SPS, SPO: 260 km/h (161.6 mph)
Valve timing (degrees)	SP- SP4: 44, 73, 77, 42 SPS, SP5: 55, 71, 77, 42			**Colors**	White frame, red Bronze frame, red (SP5)
Injection	SP- SP4: Weber I.A.W. CPU P7 SP5: P8	**Front suspension**	1989 SP: 42mm Marzocchi M1R) SP2-SPS: 42mm Öhlins FG 9050 SP5: 41mm Showa GD 061		
Power	SP (1989): 122 horsepower at crank at 10,000 rpm at crank SP2: 109 horsepower at rear wheel at 10,500 rpm SP3-4: 111 horsepower at 10,500 rpm SPS: 120 horsepower at 10,500 rpm SP5: 118 horsepower at 10,500 rpm)	**Rear suspension**	Öhlins DU 8070 rising rate swingarm SP3, SP4, SPS: DU 8070 SP5: DU 8071		
		Front brake	320mm dual disc (12.6 in.)		
		Rear brake	245mm disc (9.6 in.)		
		Tires	120/70 x 17, 180/55 x 17		

The SP3 for 1991 was very similar to the SP2, but the exhausts were more upswept.

There was new bodywork for the 1992 SP4, but internally much was the same as the SP3.

A similar 851 SP3 appeared 1991, identified by louder and more upswept Termignoni exhaust pipes. Higher-compression pistons and a forced air intake contributed to a slight power increase. There were stronger crankcases this year, and an updated clutch. The Brembo wheels were painted black, and the brake and clutch master cylinders included remotely mounted fluid reservoirs. As with the SP2, each SP3 received a numbered plaque.

For 1992, there were two listed 888 Sport Production models: the SP4, and SPS (Sport Production Special). Sharing the bodywork of the 1992 851 Strada, they were both Monoposto, and while the SP4 retained the engine specifications of the earlier SP3, the SPS was almost a Corsa with lights. Except for a revised cooling system and curved radiator, the engine for the 888 SP4 was much the same as that of the SP3. The higher-specification SPS engine included 34 and 30mm valves, with the higher lift inlet camshaft of the 888 Corsa. The SPS also featured a Termignoni racing exhaust system with carbon fiber mufflers. The cooling system was from the Corsa, with a lightweight curved radiator and no electric fan.

Both the 888 SP4 and SPS featured the frame of the 1992 851 Strada, with revised footpeg mounts and bent outer tubes. The front brakes included Brembo "Gold Series" P4.30/34 calipers. Also from the 1992 851 Strada came the pivoting gas tank—steel on the SP4, and quick-release carbon fiber on the 888 SPS. While the SP4 was certainly impressive, the SPS was undoubtedly the most exotic production motorcycle available in 1992. More than a decade later it remains unique, and the closest Ducati came to putting lights on a Corsa. It was also one of the rarest of all the limited edition models.

The final 888 Sport Production was the 888 SP5 of 1993. With the higher-performance SPS engine, but with an SP4 cooling system, this continued to set the performance standard for twin-cylinder motorcycles. All the usual SP features were retained, including twin injectors, Pankl con-rods and close-ratio gearbox. There were a few updates on the chassis. The frame and wheels were painted bronze, and a Showa front fork replaced the expensive Öhlins. There were Termignoni carbon-fiber mufflers, a fully floating rear disc brake and braided-steel brake lines.

Although there have been annual limited higher-performance series since the 888, the 888 SPs were different. These machines were loud, hard-edged race replicas offering considerably more performance than an 851 or 888 Strada. They were also built in fewer numbers than later SPs, and their rarity has resulted in diminished appreciation of their qualities.

Production	1990	1991	1992	1993	Total
851 Sport Production					
1990	380				380
1991	350	184			534
851 SPS 1991		16			16
851 SP4 1992			500		500
888 Sport Production					
888 SPS 1992			101		101
888 SP5 1993				500	500
Total	730	200	601	500	2,031

While the SP5 of 1993 lost the Öhlins front fork, the engine was upgraded to that of the 888 SPS.

888 Corsa (Racing) 1989-94

The Lucchinelli Replica of 1989 was very much a developed 888 Superbike Kit, and not very competitive.

Continuing a tradition of providing over-the-counter racers, a Lucchinelli Replica was offered for 1989. This 888cc racer was basically undeveloped and uncompetitive, but led to the 1990 851 Corsa, or Roche Replica. Most updates were aimed at improving reliability, but the engine was much as it had been on the Lucchinelli Replica. The valve sizes were 34 and 30mm, and there was a new inlet camshaft providing 11mm of valve lift. Chassis improvements saw Öhlins upside-down front forks and 320mm front disc brakes.

Following the success of the factory Superbike during 1990, more 851 Corsas were produced for 1991. Chassis updates included wider wheels (3.75 x 17 and 6.00 x 17-inch), Brembo P4 30/34 front brake calipers, and a number of carbon-fiber body parts. As with past examples, the 1991 851 Corsa was still somewhat removed from the official factory machines and privateers struggled to be competitive. The cataloged racing 888 for 1992 was based on the 1991 SP3, rather than the SP4. It retained the earlier frame, gas tank shape and seat. Except for a new camshaft and exhaust system, the engine was very similar to that of the 1991 Corsa, although more attention was paid to weight saving. There was a new carbon fiber and Kevlar fuel tank.

For 1993, the 888 Racing shared the newly homologated frame and bodywork with the factory bikes. The valves were increased to 36mm and 31mm. There was a new exhaust camshaft (with 10.5mm of valve lift), and a larger airbox. Along with a closer-ratio gearbox, there was an improved clutch, and differential mapping for the two cylinders. Although the factory raced the new 916 during 1994, the customer 888 Racing was similar to the 1993 926cc factory racer. The valve sizes were now 37mm and 31mm, and there were titanium con-rods and an improved crankcase design. The frame was altered, too, with the steering head angle reduced to 22 1/2 degrees. Other updates extended to five-spoke Marchesini wheels (3.50 x 17, and 6.00 x 17-inch), and new disc rotors.

888 CORSA 1989-94

Engine	Twin-cylinder four-stroke, liquid-cooled	**Spark plugs**	1989-92: Champion A506V (A55V; 1993-94: Champion A55V	**Tires**	1989-93: S 1016 x 17, S 1423 x 17
Bore	1988-93: 94mm 1994: 96mm	**Generator**	12v/180W		1994: 12/60-17SC1275, 18/67-17SC 1866 Michelin
Stroke	64mm	**Battery**	12V/5Ah	**Wheelbase**	1,430mm (56.3 in.)
Displacement	1989-93: 888cc 1994: 926cc	**Primary drive**	2:1 (31/62)	**Length**	2,000mm (78.7 in.)
Compression ratio	12:1	**Clutch**	Dry multiplate	**Height**	1,120mm (44.1 in.)
Valve actuation	Belt-driven desmodromic double overhead camshafts	**Gear ratios**	1989-92: 0.958, 1.043, 1.182, 1.40, 1.765, 2.466 1993: 1.00, 1.091, 1.19, 1.35, 1.61, 2.0	**Width**	670mm (26.4 in.)
				Seat height	760mm (29.9 in.)
Valve timing (degrees)	1989-91: 53, 71, 77, 42 1992-94: 53, 71, 71, 45	**Final drive**	2.466:1 (15/37)	**Dry weight**	1990: 158 kg (348 lbs.) 1991: 155 kg (341.4 lbs.) 1992: 150 kg (330.4 lbs.) 1993-94: 145 kg (319.4 lbs.)
Injection	1989-93: Weber I.A.W. CPU P7 1994: Weber I.A.W. CPU P8	**Front suspension**	42mm Öhlins		
Power	1989-92: 128 horsepower at 11,000 rpm 1993: 135 horsepower at 11,500 rpm 1994: 142 horsepower at 11,500 rpm	**Rear suspension**	Öhlins rising rate swingarm	**Colors**	1989-92: White frame, red 1993-94: Bronze frame, red
		Front brake	320mm dual disc (12.6 in.)		
		Rear brake	1989-91: 210mm disc (8.3 in.) 1992-94: 190mm (7.5 in.)		

PRODUCTION	1990	1991	1992	1993	1994	1995	TOTAL
851 Racing							
1990	20						20
1991		42	8				50
888 Racing							
1992			30	1	3	1	35
1993				42	4		46
1994					32		32
Total	62	8	30	43	39	1	183

By 1991, the Roche Replica was closer to the factory bikes, but still not close enough to win Superbike races.

Although the factory raced the 916 during 1994, the catalog racer for 1994 was still the 888, but with a 926cc motor.

The 1993 888 Corsa highly developed machine, and similar to the factory 888 Superbike racers of the previous year.

Supermono

One of the most beautiful Ducatis of all was the Supermono. Every component was superbly crafted.

One of the most interesting machines produced by Ducati was the Supermono racer of 1993-95. This combined the horizontal cylinder of an 888 Corsa with a counterbalancing system consisting of the second con-rod attached to a lever pivoting on a pin fixed in the crankcase. Titled the doppia bielletta (double con-rod), it provided the perfect primary balance of a Vee-twin. As it was a racing-only motorcycle, many of the features of the Supermono were inherited from the 888 Racing. There were two fuel injectors per cylinder, a 50mm throttle body, and 37 and 31mm valves. But there were some important departures from the 888 in the design. These included 49mm plain main bearings, a dry alternator, and the water pump driven off the exhaust camshaft. As with the 888 Racing, the two 124mm con-rods were titanium Pankl,

with a 21mm wristpin, and a 42mm big-end. The 50mm exhaust exited on the right into either a Termignoni single- or dual-outlet muffler.

Housing this remarkable engine was a tubular steel frame of ALS500, with an aluminum swingarm. Weight distribution placed 54.5 percent of the load on the front wheel. All the chassis components were of the highest quality. This included Marchesini three-spoke magnesium wheels (3.50 x 17 and 5.00 x 17 inches), Brembo fully floating iron front discs, and racing P4.30-34 calipers. To minimize weight, every body part was made of carbon-fiber, with the carbon-fiber seat also acting as the rear subframe. The spectacular styling was by Pierre Terblanche. The Supermono remains his finest effort.

Following the first series of 1993, plus a few more in 1994, the second Supermono series included a slightly larger engine and revised suspension, including a 10mm-longer rear shock absorber. But by this time the engine wasn't large enough to provide victory in Supermono racing. Although possessing an exceptionally low center of gravity, and brilliant handling and power characteristics, the Supermono couldn't emulate the success of the 888. A production Supermono was always promised, but remains an unfulfilled dream.

Production	1992	1993	1994	1995	1998	Total
Supermono						
550 Racing	1	30	10	25		66
900 Supersport frame					1	1
Total	1	30	10	25	1	67

SUPERMONO 1993-95

Engine	Single-cylinder four-stroke, liquid-cooled	**Spark plugs**	Champion A55V	**Tires**	310/480R17440, 155/60R17622 Dunlop
Bore	1993-94: 100mm 1995: 102mm	**Generator**	12v/180W	**Wheelbase**	1,360mm (53.5 in.)
Stroke	70mm	**Battery**	12V/5Ah	**Length**	1,960mm (77.2 in.)
Displacement	1993-94: 550cc 1995: 572cc	**Primary drive**	2:1 (31/62)	**Height**	1,060mm (41.7 in.)
		Clutch	Dry multiplate	**Width**	670mm (26.4 in.)
Compression ratio	11.8:1	**Gear ratios**	1.095, 1.2, 1.32, 1.5, 1.81, 2.33	**Seat height**	760mm (29.9 in.)
Valve actuation	Belt-driven desmodromic double overhead camshafts	**Final drive**	2.4:1 (15/36)	**Dry weight**	122 kg (268.7 lbs.)
Valve timing (degrees)	73, 91, 90, 70	**Front suspension**	42mm Öhlins FG 9311	**Colors**	1993-94: Bronze frame, red 1995: Gold frame, red
Injection	Weber I.A.W. CPU P8	**Rear suspension**	1993-94: Öhlins DU2041 cantilever swingarm 1995: DU 2042		
Power	1993-94: 78 horsepower at 10,500 rpm 1995: 81 horsepower at 10,000 rpm	**Front brake**	280mm dual disc (11 in.)		
		Rear brake	190mm disc (7.5 in.)		

The Supermono engine was basically the horizontal cylinder setup of the 888 Corsa, and the center of gravity was extremely low.

CHAPTER 9

MONSTERS

Although many of Cagiva's new ideas for Ducati were ill-conceived and poorly executed, the Monster was one of the company's most brilliant. Designer Miguel Angel Galluzzi cleverly created a new niche motorcycle, a naked and minimalist street bike unlike anything else available, with all the sporting credentials expected of a Ducati. The Monster has been an enormous success for Ducati, growing to encompass a bewildering number of variants. It continues to maintain strong sales more than a decade after it was introduced.

Monster M900 (1993-99)

Ducati Motor

The 1997 900 Monster had a detuned motor and handlebar fairing.

As with some earlier efforts, the 900 Monster was a synthesis of components of various existing models, but concocted into a considerably more effective package than previous endeavors. The engine was basically that of the 900 Supersport, with slightly different carburetor, the oil radiator positioned above the front cylinder, and a different twin exhaust system. The chassis though was derived from the 851/888 rather than the Supersport, with rising-rate rear suspension. The swingarm was aluminum and the suspension relatively unsophisticated, with a non-adjustable front fork and Boge shock absorber. The instruments and bodywork were new, and the minimalist instrument panel was without a tachometer. Production commenced during 1993, and the 1994 models were virtually unchanged.

There was also little to distinguish the 1995 Monster from earlier models. Most updates were cosmetic. The frame was now 916-gold, with matching wheels and gray timing belt covers and sprocket cover. To improve ground

With the 900 Monster of 1993, Ducati successfully created a new niche in the market. The Monster has been so successful the same basic style continues more than a decade later.

clearance, the mufflers were chamfered underneath. New crankcases appeared for 1996, but the biggest update included a fully adjustable Marzocchi front fork with a 20mm axle.

While all the improvements incorporated in the Supersport (such as bimetallic valves and a carburetor heating kit) were also included in the Monster for 1997. The biggest change was the de-tuning of the 900 engine. In an effort to improve torque at low rpm, the valve sizes were reduced to that of the 750 (41mm inlet and 35mm exhaust), and there were new camshafts. These retained the 11.76mm and 10.56mm valve lift of the 900 Supersport, but shared timing figures with the 600 and 750 Monster. Also differentiating the 1997 Monster was a standard handlebar fairing.

By 1998, the TPG influence was more obvious and there were more annual updates and model proliferation. This year saw the return of the larger valve engine in the M 900 S, while the regular M 900 continued with the smaller valve engine. Engine updates for 1998 (shared with both 900 Monsters and the 900 Supersport) included new cylinders (Tecnol) and pistons (Asso). The redesigned cylinders incorporated the oil return internally, making external oil lines unnecessary. Another update was the 41mm adjustable Showa fork of the 900 Supersport FE. The brake and clutch lines were now braided steel (except for the U.S. and Australia), and the regular M 900 lost the handlebar fairing, exhaust heat shields, and lower rear fender. By 1999, the Monster was the only model left in Ducati's lineup with carburetors. Three versions used the higher output engine this year: the M 900 S, California, and the Cromo. All other Monster 900s featured the lower-output motor.

By 1996, the 900 Monster had a Marzocchi front fork, but was little changed.

Ducati Motor

Monster 900 S, 900 Cromo, City/Dark/City Dark

The 1998 900 Cromo had a chrome-plated gas tank, but the model wasn't particularly popular.

In response to complaints about the reduced engine performance of the 1997 M 900, the M 900 S was released for 1998. It was powered by the carbureted 900 Supersport engine. The front discs were fully floating cast-iron, and there was a floating rear brake caliper. Carbon fiber extended to the front and rear fenders, side panels, and exhaust heat shields. The Cromo was another variation of the M 900 offered for 1998. This took the standard low-power M 900, but added a chrome-plated fuel tank, black frame and wheels, and carbon fiber fenders, side panels, and seat cover. Both the Cromo and M 900 S for 1999 were similar to the previous year, although the M 900 S now included a steering damper and an Öhlins rear shock absorber.

The M 900 City was a further attempt to broaden the appeal of the Monster. It had a new seat, windshield, saddlebags and higher handlebars. The City was obviously designed more for city use, while the 900 Dark was a no-frills Monster designed as a platform for customization with Ducati Performance accessories. It had a black frame and wheels, and matte black tank and fenders without any clear lacquer. By combining the features of the 900 City

The Monster 900 City for 1999 included a screen and small saddlebags. *(Ducati Motor)*

and 900 Dark, a budget 900 City called the 900 City Cark was also created. This was essentially a 900 City with the higher handlebars, windshield, and bags, but with the Dark black frame and wheels, matte black tank and fenders.

The M900S for 1998 had higher-specification brakes, and the 900 Supersport motor.

M 900 I.E. and Monster 900 Special (2000-2002)

The final 900 Monster was the 900 I.E. of 2002. It featured a new frame and CPU.

Ducati Motor

For 2000, the Monster received its first stylistic revision since its inception. The changes were relatively minor. Pierre Terblanche introduced a new rear license plate bracket, taillight assembly, and front fender. Replacing the Cromo was the Monster Metallic, derived from the Dark and inspired by the metalflake fashion of the 1960s and 1970s

All 900 Monsters for 2000 used an engine based on that of the post-1998 900 Supersport. The camshafts were the same, and there was 11.8mm of inlet and 11.4mm of exhaust valve lift. Unlike the Supersport, there was no oil circulation of the cylinders. Jets directed oil underneath the piston crowns, and there was a larger oil cooler to cope with the increased temperatures. The electronic fuel injection system was the same Marelli 1.5 unit as the

900 Supersport, with single injectors. The new six-speed gearbox was the closer-ratio unit used on the 748.

While the basic frame was unchanged, there was a non-adjustable 43mm Showa inverted front fork, with a 25mm diameter axle contributing to increased front end rigidity. A Sachs-Boge shock absorber was featured on all 900 Monsters (except the 900 S), and there was now a steel, instead of aluminum, swingarm. Like the other bikes in the series, the front discs were updated with aluminum carriers, with new Brembo brake calipers and a PSC 16mm master cylinder. The Brembo wheels were similar to those of the ST2, stronger, and 400 grams lighter than before. To improve the riding position the gas tank was narrowed and reshaped where it met the more thickly padded seat. This saw a slight reduction in the capacity to

M900 MONSTER 1993-02

Engine	Twin cylinder four-stroke, air-cooled	Ignition (degrees)	1993-1999: Kokusan; 6 static, 32 total	Length	2,090mm (82.3 in.) 2,100mm from 2002 (82.7 in.)
Bore	92mm	Battery	1993-2000: 12V/16Ah 2001-2002: 10Ah sealed from	Height	1,060mm (41.7 in.) 1,058mm from 2002 (41.7 in.)
Stroke	68mm	Primary drive	1993-1999: 2.000:1 (31/62)	Width	770mm (30.3 in.) 794 mm from 2002 (31.3 in.)
Displacement	904cc		2000-2002: 1.84:1 (32/59)		
Compression ratio	9.2:1	Clutch	Dry multiplate	Seat height	770mm (30.3 in.) 800mm from 2002 (31.5 in.)
Valve actuation	Belt-driven desmodromic overhead camshaft	Gear ratios	0.857 (0.958), 0.958 (1.043), 1.091 (1.182), 1.350 (1.40), 1.764, 2.466		
Valve timing (degrees)	1993: 20, 60, 58, 20 1994-99: 43, 85, 82, 46 M900 from 037728: 31, 88, 72, 46 2000-2002: 25, 75, 66, 28	Final drive	1993-1999: 2.6:1 (15/39) 2000-2002: 2.533:1 (15/38)	Dry weight	184 kg (405.3 lbs.) 187 kg City (411.9 lbs.) 189 kg from 2002 (416.3 lbs.)
Carburetion	1993-1999: Mikuni BDST 38-B129 (B132; US) B 222 from 037728. 2000-01: Marelli 1.5 Electronic injection 45mm throttle bodies 2002: Marelli CPU 5.9M	Front suspension	1993-1997: 41mm inverted Showa GD 041 From 009915: Marzocchi 40 USD/REG 1998-99: 41mm inverted Showa GD 021 2000-2002: 43mm inverted Showa	Top speed	190 km/h (118.1 mph) 210 km/h from 2000 (130.5 mph) City, City Dark: 200 km/h (124.3 mph)
Power	73 horsepower at 7,000 rpm (rear wheel) 80 horsepower at 7,000 rpm (crankshaft) 66.6 horsepower at 7,000 rpm (1997) 78 horsepower at 8,000 rpm (from 2000)	Rear suspension	1993-1998: Boge rising-rate swingarm 1999-2002: Öhlins	Colors	Red 473.101 (PPG) Yellow 473.201 (PPG) Met. Gray 291.601 (PPG) Met. black 291.500 (PPG) Met. Blue 291.800 (PPG)
		Front brake	320mm dual disc (12.6 in.)	Engine numbers	Continuing ZDM 904 A 2C 000001 series
		Rear brake	245mm disc (9.6 in.)	Frame numbers	From ZDM 900 M 000001 From ZDM 1LC4N XB 000001 (USA)
Spark plugs	Champion RA6HC	Tires	120/70 x 17, 170/60 x 17		
Generator	12v/350W (520W from 1998)	Wheelbase	1,430mm (56.3 in.) 1,440mm from 2002 (56.7 in.)		

The Monster was restyled for 2000, and the 900 Dark was the most basic model.

Ducati Motor

There was also a new M 900 S for 2000 with an upgraded suspension. The Showa fork was fully adjustable. There was an aluminum swingarm and Öhlins shock absorber. There were only a few updates for 2001. The chassis included larger mounting bolts (12mm), and the rear brake caliper was positioned above the swingarm. Engine updates were also minor and included more rigid timing belts and split timing belt rollers, to a new oil pump and KTM oil cooler. For 2002, the M900 I.E. and M900 I.E. Dark were the only 900 Monsters in the lineup, with the M900 I.E. replacing the 900 S. It also featured an adjustable front fork and aluminum swingarm. All Monster frames were now derived from the S4 (claimed to be 30 percent stiffer). The S4 frame allowed for a new airbox, and there was a new Marelli 5.9 CPU. Engine updates for this final year of the 900 included new case-hardened rocker arms, timing belt covers without inspection openings, and an additional oil jet in the left crankcase to supply oil to the vertical cylinder.

16 liters, and the handlebars were raised 10mm. Cosmetic updates included a small fairing that incorporated a more complete instrument panel, which included a tachometer.

PRODUCTION	1993	1994	1995	1996	1997	1998	1999	2000	2001	TOTAL
900 Monster										
Italy 1993	1,521									1,521
1994/95	987	1,240	1,222							3,449
1996			82	449						531
1997				210	526					736
1998					137	248				385
1999						89	425			514
2000							133	262		395
2002									101	101
1994/95 Black	434	405	528							1,367
1996 Black			37	252						289
1997 Black				119	480					599
1998 Black					149	235				384
1999 Black						20	132			152
2000 Black							75	40		115
2002 Black									33	33
1996 Yellow			150	216						366
1997 Yellow				201	180					381
1998 Yellow					154	117				271
1999 Yellow						59	141			200
2000 Yellow							112	130		242
2002 Yellow									19	19
1998 Silver					39	70				109
1999 Silver						72				72
2000 Silver							25	62		87
1999 Blue						138	63			201
2000 Blue							52	80		132
USA 1993	190									190
USA 1994/95	80	75	190							345
USA - Cal. 1999						156				156
USA 1994 Black	120	250								370

PRODUCTION	1993	1994	1995	1996	1997	1998	1999	2000	2001	TOTAL
USA - Cal. 1999 Black						72				72
USA 1995 Yellow		75								75
USA - Cal. 1999 Yellow						72				72
Cal. 1993	120									120
Cal. 1994/95	25	25	60							110
Cal. 1996			140	80						220
Cal. 1997				30	80					110
Cal. 1998					49	84				133
Cal. 2000							300			300
Cal. 2002									50	50
Cal. 1994 Black	55	95								150
Cal. 1996 Black			110	60						170
Cal. 1997 Black				26	70					96
Cal. 1998 Black					51	83				134
Cal. 1995 Yellow		25								25
Cal. 1996 Yellow			96	74						170
Cal. 1997 Yellow				25	70					95
Cal. 1998 Yellow					133					133
Cal. 2000 Yellow							100			100
Cal. 2002 Yellow									60	60
Switz. 1993	40									40
Switz. 1994/95	120	165	155							440
Switz. 1996			30	20						50
Switz. 1997				1	60					61
Switz. 1999						10	30			40
Switz. 1994/95 Black		55	95							150
Switz. 1996 Black			30	30						60
Switz. 1997 Black					20					20
Switz. 1996 Yellow			20	30						50
Switz. 1997 Yellow					40					40
Switz. 1999 Yellow							20			20

Left table:

PRODUCTION	1993	1994	1995	1996	1997	1998	1999	2000	2001	TOTAL
Switz. 2000 Yellow							20			20
Switz. 1999 Blue						10	20			30
Switz. 2000 Blue							29			29
Switz. 2000 Silver							20			20
Aus. 1993	40									40
Aus. 1994/95	60	65	45							170
Aus. 1996			30	45						75
Aus. 1997				10	21					31
Aus. 1998					3					3
Aus. - Jpn. 1999						31	55			86
Aus. 2000							5	13		18
Aus. 2002									5	5
Aus. 1994/95 Black	10	20	15							45
Aus. 1996 Black			30	25						55
Aus. 1997 Black					18					18
Aus. 1998 Black					1					1
Aus. - Jpn. 1999 Black						18	3			21
Aus. 2000 Black							5	8		13
Aus. 2002 Black									5	5
Aus. 1996 Yellow			20							20
Aus. 1997 Yellow					15					15
Aus. - Jpn. 1999 Yellow						19	25			44
Aus. 2000 Yellow							4	12		16
Aus. - Jpn. 1999 Silver						4	9			13
Aus. - Jpn. 1999 Blue							25			25
Aus. 2000 Blue							7	8		15
Jpn. 1996			30	21						51
Jpn. 1997				20	60					80
Jpn. 1998					7	11				18
Jpn. 2000							18			18
Jpn. 2002									150	150
Jpn. 1996 Black			30	20						50
Jpn. 1997 Black					10					10
Jpn. 1996 Yellow			20							20
Jpn. 1997 Yellow					10					10
Jpn. 1998 Yellow					3	6				9
Jpn. 2000 Yellow							6			6
Jpn. 2002 Yellow									103	103
Jpn. 1998 Silver					2	3				5
Jpn. 2000 Blue							3			3
Jpn. 2002 Blue									25	25
Sng. 2000 Red								2		2
Jpn. 2000 Yellow								2		2
Jpn. 2000 Silver								4		4
Ger. 1993	251									251
Ger. 1994/95	291	224	227							742
Ger. 1996			30	60						90
Ger. 1997				20	220					240
Ger. 1998						95				95
Ger. 1999						10	53			63
Ger. 1994/95 Black	80	116	110							306
Ger. 1996 Black			20	20						40

Right table:

PRODUCTION	1993	1994	1995	1996	1997	1998	1999	2000	2001	TOTAL
Ger. 1997 Black				20	220					240
Ger. 1998 Black					10	37				47
Ger. 1999 Black							35			35
Ger. 1996 Yellow				70						70
Ger. 1997 Yellow					40					40
Ger. 1998 Yellow						18				18
Ger. 1999 Yellow							19			19
Ger. 1998 Silver						10				10
Ger. 1999 Silver							5			5
Ger. 1999 Blue							22			22
Eng. 1996			15	41						56
Eng. 1997					60					60
Eng. 1998					30	10				40
Eng. 1999							60			60
Eng. 1996 Black				20						20
Eng. 1997 Black					50					50
Eng. 1998 Black						20				20
Eng. 1996 Yellow			15							15
Eng. 1998 Yellow					10	30				40
Police	3		1							4
1996 Special		3								3
1996 Club Italia		2	37							39
1998 CROMO				1	155					156
1999 CROMO					2	73				75
2000 CROMO							110			110
2001 CROMO								4	30	34
1999 CROMO USA – Cal.						101				101
2001 CROMO Cal.								101		101
1998 CROMO Switz					39					39
1999 CROMO Switz						5				5
2000 CROMO Switz							40			40
1998 CROMO Aus.					1					1
1999 CROMO Aus.						72				72
1998 CROMO Jpn.					4					4
2001 CROMO Jpn.								1		1
1998 CROMO Ger.					24					24
Special 1998					252	287				539
Special 2000							185	471		656
Special 1999 Black							538			538
Special 2000 Black							669	150		819
Special 2000 Yellow							140	260		400
Special 2001								448	187	635
Special 2001 Black								284	167	451
Special 2001 Yellow								80	124	204
Special 2001 Blue								40	29	69
Special 2001 Silver								15	33	48
Special 1999 USA						101				101
Special 1999 Cal. Black							50			50
Special 2000 Cal. Red								100		100
Special 2000 Cal. Black							150			150
Special 2000 Cal. Yellow								100		100

PRODUCTION	1993	1994	1995	1996	1997	1998	1999	2000	2001	TOTAL
Special 2001 Cal. Red								76	100	176
Special 2001 Cal. Black								50	49	99
Special 2001 Cal. Yellow								75	100	175
Special 1998 Switz.						45				45
Special 2000 Switz.							40	20		60
Special 1999 Switz. Black							25			25
Special 2000 Switz. Black							35			35
Special 1998 Aus.					19	15				34
Special 1998 Aus. Red					15	15				30
Special 1999 Aus. Black							87			87
Special 2000 Aus. Red								9		9
Special 2000 Aus. Black							25			25
Special 2000 Aus. Yellow								5		5
Special 2001 Aus. Red								20	4	24
Special 2001 Aus. Black								18		18
Special 2001 Aus. Yellow								15	5	20
Special 1998 Jpn.					45	20				65
Special 2000 Jpn.							45	20		65
Special 1998 Jpn. Black						10				10
Special 2000 Jpn. Black							38			38
Special 2000 Jpn. Yellow							10	10		20
Special 2001 Jpn.								91	50	141
Special 2001 Jpn. Black								5		5
Special 2001 Jpn. Yellow								47	35	82
Special 2001 Jpn. Blue								37		37
Special 2001 Jpn. Silver								1		1
Special 1998 Ger.					50	145				195
Special 1998 Eng.					60	40				100
Special 2000 Eng. Red								60		60
Special 2000 Eng. Black								10		10
Special 2000 Eng. Yellow								15		15
Special 2001 Eng. Red									20	20
Special 2001 Eng. Black									20	20
Special 2001 Eng. Yellow									20	20
1997 EU Black " Solo				3						3
2000 I.E. Red						4				4
DARK 1999 Black						231	1,555			1,786
DARK 2000 Black							372	1,268		1,640
DARK 2001 Black								1,024	669	1,693
DARK 2002 Black									288	288
DARK 2000 Cal. Black								252		252

PRODUCTION	1993	1994	1995	1996	1997	1998	1999	2000	2001	TOTAL
DARK 2001 Cal. Black								101	100	201
DARK 2002 Cal. Black									50	50
DARK 1999 Switz. Black						20	85			105
DARK 2000 Switz. Black							32			32
DARK 1999 Aus. Black							166			166
DARK 2000 Aus. Black							27	37		64
DARK 2001 Aus. Black								31		31
DARK 2002 Aus. Black									10	10
DARK 2000 Jpn. Black							96	11		107
DARK 2001 Jpn. Black								81		81
DARK 2002 Jpn. Black									41	41
DARK 1999 Ger. Black					100	35				135
DARK 1999 Eng. Black					40	100				140
DARK 2001 Eng. Black								40	40	80
CITY 1999 Blue							58			58
CITY 1999 Cal. Blue							150			150
CITY 1999 Aus. Red							42			42
CITY 1999 Aus. Yellow							12			12
CITY 1999 Aus. Black							6			6
CITY 1999 Aus. Silver							6			6
CITY 1999 Aus. Blue							6			6
CITY 1999 Ger. Red							11			11
CITY 1999 Ger. Yellow							2			2
CITY 1999 Ger. Black							3			3
CITY 1999 Ger. Blue							4			4
DARK CITY 1999 Black							10			10
DARK CITY Switz. 1999 Black							20			20
DARK CITY Ger. 1999 Black							20			20
Metallic 2000 Red								1		1
Metallic 2001 Red								10		10
Metallic 2001 Black								10		10
Metallic 2000 Blue Black								1		1
Metallic 2001 Blue Black								6	5	11
Metallic 2001 Blue								5	5	10
Metallic 2001 Silver								9		9
Metallic Cal. 2001 Blue								50	50	100
Metallic Eng. 2001 Blue								30		30
Metallic Eng. 2001 Silver								15		15
Total	4,424	2,838	3,657	2,186	3,357	3,297	7,133	6,393	2,782	36,067

600, 600 DARK, 620 I.E., and 400 MONSTER (JAPAN)

Although a relatively unexciting model, the 600 Monster was extremely popular.

Ducati Motor

A lightweight Monster, the 600, became available during 1994. It used the five-speed engine from the newly introduced 600 Supersport in a chassis similar to the 900 Monster. There was a steel swingarm, non-adjustable Marzocchi fork, and a single front disc brake. The 600 Monster was an exceptionally popular model in Europe, where it was offered with a lower-output engine for specific insurance categories. There were only detail updates until 1998 when the motor received new crankcases (with less external finning), a higher primary drive ratio, and a new clutch and timing belt covers. The hydraulic clutch actuation was moved to the left.

One of the more significant new models for 1998 was a budget 600 Monster: the Dark. Primarily intended for the Italian market, the Dark was promoted as an entry level Ducati, La Tua Prima Ducati (Your first Ducati), and was extremely successful. The Dark came with a plain painted fuel tank with no lacquer, unpainted front mudguard, and no seat cover. There were few updates to the 600 Monster and 600 Dark for 1999, but the 600 Monster model range expanded to include the City and City Dark.

For 2000, the 600 Monster received a Showa front fork and new Brembo wheels. There were automatic electric carburetor float bowl heaters in the Metallic, Dark and City. The Monster 600 was available in the U.S. for the first time for 2001. The U.S. version receive a 35mm lower seat. All 600 Monsters now had the 900 instrument panel. For 2002, the 600 Dark was the only 600 Monster remaining, and it was unchanged from the previous year.

Ducati Motor

One of Ducati's sales success stories of the late 1990s was the 600 Dark. It appeared for 1998 with a revised engine.

Ducati Motor

New for 2003 was the 620 Dark, with dual front discs for the U.S., as shown here.

New for 2002 were the 620 I.E. and 620 S I.E. Monster. Although the engine of the 620 was derived from the 600 (the additional capacity coming from a 750 stroke), there were a number of updates. The valve sizes were larger—41mm intake and 35 mm exhaust—and there was a new camshaft. Only two ball bearings (instead of three) supported the new shorter camshaft, and a Marelli 5.9 CPU took care of the fuel injection and ignition. The lubrication was updated with an internal duct, rather than a pipe, from the left casing to the clutch located in the right casing. Further updates included a rubber damper at the front sprocket to reduce drive chain noise.

The 620 frame was now derived from the S4, as was the rear suspension layout. The swingarm was steel on the 620 I.E., and aluminum on the 620 S I.E. Both 620s featured dual front disc brakes, and the 620 S included a headlight fairing, different mufflers, carbon fiber side covers and heat shields, ride height adjustment, and a taller seat. For 2003, the 620 I.E. was available as a Dark, and for 2004 was updated with an APTC (Adler Power Torque Plate Clutch) to reduce back torque during deceleration. The clutch disc diameter was also reduced from 150mm to 140mm. While the 620 Dark retained the five-speed gearbox, the regular 620 received a six-speed transmission this year with the same ratios as the 800 I.E. There was also a special Monster Matrix 620 I.E. for 2004, inspired by the movie The Matrix Reloaded, which featured a road chase on a 998. Another variation on the 620 S for 2004 was the Capirossi, in honor of the factory MotoGP rider. For 2005, there were three 620 Monsters: the 620 Dark single disc (with five-speed gearbox), the 620 and the 620 Dark.

Ducati Motor

The 620 S I.E. for 2002 had an updated engine, dual front disc brakes, and a small screen.

Ducati Motor

Another variant of the 620 Monster for 2004 was the Capirossi, complete with the rider's #65.

400 Monster

The 400 Monster was produced solely for the Japanese market, and was essentially a 400 Supersport engine in a 600 Monster chassis. From 1996, the engine was the five-speed 400 Supersport unit, and this was basically unchanged through until 2003. During that time, the 400 Monster received the same annual updates as the 600 Monster, and after the introduction of the 620 I.E. was the only Monster to retain the earlier frame and Mikuni carburetors.

Ducati Motor

A 400 Monster was produced for the Japanese market, and for several years was unchanged from this 1995 version.

600, 400, 620 I.E. Monster

Engine	Twin cylinder four-stroke, air-cooled	**Generator**	1994-97: 12v/300W 1998-2003: 520W from 1998	**Wheelbase**	1994-2001: 1,430mm (56.3 in.) 2002-2004: 1,440mm (56.7 in.)
Bore	600, 620: 80mm 400: 70.5mm	**Ignition (degrees)**	400, 600: Kokusan, 6 static, 32 total	**Length**	400, 600: 2,090 mm (82.3 in.)
Stroke	600: 58mm 400: 51mm 620: 61.5mm	**Battery**	1994-2000: 12V/16Ah 2001-2004: 10Ah sealed		620:2,100 mm (82.7 in.)
Displacement	600: 583cc 400: 398cc 620: 618cc	**Primary drive**	2.28:1 (32/73) until 002961 2:1 (31/62) from 002962 1.85:1 (33/61) from 1998	**Height**	400, 600: 1,060mm (41.7 in.) 620: 1,058mm (41.7 in.)
Compression ratio	600: 10.7:1 400: 10:1 620: 10.5:1			**Width**	400, 600: 770mm (30.3 in.)
Valve actuation	Belt-driven desmodromic overhead camshaft	**Clutch**	Wet multiplate		620: 794 mm (31.3 in.)
Valve timing (degrees)	600, 400 (1994-99): : 31, 88, 72, 46 (2000-2003): 11, 70, 50, 30 620: 12, 55, 58, 24	**Gear ratios**	400, 600, 620 (1994-2003): 0.966, 1.074, 1.333, 1.714, 2.500 620: (2004): 0.923, 1.0, 1.13, 1.333, 1.666, 2.466	**Seat height**	400, 600: 770mm (30.3 in.) 620 S: 795mm (31.3 in.)
Carburetion	400: Mikuni BDST 38 B159 B190 620: Marelli 5.9 Electronic injection	**Final drive**	2.6:1 (15/39) 2.866:1 (15/43) 3.06:1 (15/46) from 1998	**Dry weight**	400, 600: 174 kg (383.3 lbs.) 620: 177 kg (389.9 lbs.)
Power	600: 51 horsepower at 8,000 rpm 600: 33 horsepower at 7,500 rpm 400: 43 horsepower at 10,500 rpm 620: 60 horsepower at 9,500 rpm	**Front suspension**	400, 600 (1994-99): Marzocchi 40USD/E 400, 600 (2000-04): 43mm Showa 620: 43mm Marzocchi	**Top speed**	400, 600: 175 km/h (108.7 mph) 620: 185 km/h (115 mph)
		Rear suspension	Boge rising-rate swingarm	**Colors**	Red 473.101 (PPG) Yellow 473.201 (PPG) Black 248.514 (PPG) Silver gray 0022 (PPG) 620 Dark
		Front brake	320mm disc (12.6 in.) 620: dual disc	**Engine numbers**	600: Continuing ZDM 600 A 2C 000001
Spark plugs	400, 600, 620 (1994-99): RA 4 HC (also 620) 600 (2000-04): RA 6 HC	**Rear brake**	245mm disc (9.6 in.)	**Frame numbers**	600: From ZDM 600 M 000001
		Tires	120/60 x 17, 160/60 x 17		620 USA: From ZDM 1RA2K XB 000001

600 Monster

PRODUCTION	1993	1994	1995	1996	1997	1998	1999	2000	2001	TOTAL
1994	7	892								899
1994 Red		823								823
1994 33 hp	1									1
1995 Yellow			289	520						809
1995 Red			291	910						1,201
1995 Yellow 33 hp			137	210						347
1995 Red 33 hp			110	115						225
1996 Yellow				244	313					557
1996 Red				233	164					397
1996 Yellow 33 hp				47						47
1996 Red 33 hp				32						32
1997 Yellow				224	756					980
1997 Red				230	761	1				992
1997 Yellow 33 hp				20	202					222
1997 Red 33 hp				20	147					167
1998 Red					1	85				86
1998 Black						31				31
1998 Yellow						78				78
1998 Silver						18				18
1999 Red						124	283			407
1999 Black						11	59			70
1999 Yellow						78	233			311
1999 Silver						24	58			82
1999 Blue						15	106			121
2000 Red							121	270		391
2000 Black							35	40		75
2000 Yellow							141	107		248
2000 Silver							60	20		80
2000 Blue							55	40		95
2001 Red								288	333	621
2001 Black								20	47	67
2001 Yellow								49	265	314
2001 Silver								6	84	90
2001 Blue								25	97	122
Italy 33 hp 1998 Red						12				12
Italy 33 hp 1998 Black						5				5
Italy 33 hp 1998 Yellow						8				8
Italy 33 hp 1998 Silver						1				1
Italy 33 hp 1999 Red						1	9			10
Italy 33 hp 1999 Black						1	1			2
Italy 33 hp 1999 Yellow						7	5			12
Italy 33 hp 1999 Silver							3			3
Italy 33 hp 1999 Blue							4			4
Italy 33 hp 2001 Red									10	10
Italy 33 hp 2001 Black									5	5
Italy 33 hp 2001 Yellow									5	5
Italy 33 hp 2001 Blue									5	5
Switz 1994 Yellow			80							80
Switz 1994 Red			80							80

PRODUCTION	1993	1994	1995	1996	1997	1998	1999	2000	2001	TOTAL
Switz 1995 Yellow			110							110
Switz 1995 Red		20	125							145
Switz 1996 Yellow			40	31						71
Switz 1996 Red			40	20						60
Switz 1997 Yellow				40						40
Switz 1997 Red				40						40
Switz 1999 Red						10	33			43
Switz 1999 Yellow						12	18			30
Switz 1999 Silver						8	9			17
Switz 2000 Red							10			10
Switz 2000 Yellow							10	5		15
Switz 2000 Blue							10			10
Aus. 1995 Yellow		20	5							25
Aus. 1995 Red		20	20							40
Aus. 1996 Yellow			10							10
Aus. 1996 Red			15	15						30
Aus. 1997 Yellow				25	10					35
Aus. 1997 Red				25	10					35
Aus. 2000 Red							6	6		12
Aus. 2001 Red								10	10	20
Aus. 2000 Yellow							4	7		11
Aus. 2001 Yellow								10	4	14
Aus. 2000 Black							5			5
Aus. 2000 Blue							5			5
Aus. 2001 Blue								5		5
Aus. 2000 Silver							5			5
Aus. 2001 Silver								5		5
Jpn. 1998 Red						1				1
Jpn. 1998 Yellow						1				1
Ger. 1994 Yellow		183								183
Ger. 1994 Red		199								199
Ger. 1995 Yellow		120	40							160
Ger. 1995 Red		140	340							480
Ger. 1996 Yellow			60	40						100
Ger. 1996 Red			80	40						120
Ger. 1997 Yellow				120						120
Ger. 1997 Red				240						240
Ger. 1998 Red					8					8
Ger. 1998 Yellow					9					9
Eng. 1994 Yellow		80								80
Eng. 1994 Red		150								150
Eng. 1995 Yellow		45	65							110
Eng. 1995 Red		45	170							215
Eng. 1996 Yellow			35	30						65
Eng. 1996 Red			51	31						82
Eng. 1997 Yellow				15	75					90
Eng. 1997 Red				15	75					90
Eng. 2000 Red							20			20
Eng. 2001 Red								45	30	75
Eng. 2001 Yellow								25	10	35
Eng. 2001 Silver								5		5
Eng. 2000 Black							5	10		15
Eng. 2000 Blue							5			5
Eng. 2001 Blue								5	10	15

Production	1993	1994	1995	1996	1997	1998	1999	2000	2001	Total
Police Saudi Arabia		162								162
Police Bologna			1	35						36
Police Turin			1							1
City 1999 Italy 33 hp Red							1			1
City 1999 Red							56			56
City 1999 Black							40			40
City 1999 Blue							125			125
City 1999 Silver							133			133
City 1999 Yellow Silver							45			45
City 2000 Sng. Red							5			5
City Dark 1999 Black							365			365
City Dark 2000 Black								10		10
City Dark 1999 Switz. Black							40			40
Metallic 2000 Silver								65		65
Metallic 2001 Silver								29	10	39
Metallic 2000 Blue								51		51
Metallic 2001 Blue								5	10	15
Metallic 2000 Blue Black								50		50
Metallic 2001 Blue Black								15	10	25
Metallic 2000 Black								50		50
Metallic 2001 Black								30	10	40
Metallic 2000 Red								51		51
Metallic 2001 Red								5	5	10
Metallic 2001 USA Red								50		50
Metallic 2001 Eng. Silver									10	10
Metallic 2001 Eng. Blue									20	20
Metallic 2001 Eng. Red									10	10

600 Monster DARK

Production	1993	1994	1995	1996	1997	1998	1999	2000	2001	Total
1998 frame Bronze					119	254				373
1998 frame Black					989	836				1,825
1998 frame Yellow						370				370
1998 frame Red						100				100
1998 frame Silver						100				100
1998 frame Bronze 33 hp						55				55
1998 frame Black 33 hp					20	167				187
1998 frame Yellow 33 hp						124				124
1998 frame Red 33 hp						20				20
1998 frame Silver 33 hp						40				40
1999 frame Bronze						273	956			1,229
1999 frame Black						1,106	1,888			2,994
1999 frame Yellow						175	450			625
1999 frame Red						55	168			223
1999 frame Silver						226	860			1,086
1999 frame Blue						1				1
2000 frame Bronze							151	770		921
2000 frame Black							565	1,838		2,403
2000 frame Yellow							61	293		354
2000 frame Silver							90	871		961

Production	1993	1994	1995	1996	1997	1998	1999	2000	2001	Total
2001 frame Bronze								375	703	1,078
2001 frame Silver								450	820	1,270
2001 frame Black								1,052	2,207	3,259
2001 Metallic									1,090	1,090
2001 USA frame Black								250	200	450
1999 Italy 33 hp frame Bronze						87	62			149
2001 Italy 33 hp frame Bronze								5		5
1999 Italy 33 hp frame Black						157	134			291
2000 Italy 33 hp frame Black							45			45
2001 Italy 33 hp frame Black							8			8
1999 Italy 33 hp frame Yellow						33	16			49
1999 Italy 33 hp frame Red						32	5			37
1999 Italy 33 hp frame Silver						76	40			116
2000 Italy33 hp frame Silver							15			15
2001 Italy 33 hp frame Black								160		160
2001 Italy 33 hp frame Bronze								70		70
2001 Italy 33 hp frame Silver								80		80
2001 Italy 33 hp Metallic								95		95
1998 Switz. frame Bronze						30				30
1998 Switz. frame Black					40	20				60
1999 Switz. frame Black						30	55			85
2000 Switz. frame Black							10			10
2000 Switz. frame Silver							10			10
1998 Aus. frame Black					72	50				122
1998 Aus. frame Yellow						10				10
1999 Aus. frame Black						15				15
1999 Aus. frame Yellow						5				5
2000 Aus. frame Black						31	39			70
2001 Aus. frame Black							34	13		47
1998 Jpn. frame Black					12	1				13
2001 Jpn. frame Black								10		10
2001 Jpn. frame Bronze								7		7
1998 Ger. frame Bronze						23				23
1998 Ger. frame Black					31	132				163
1998 Ger. frame Yellow						145				145
1998 Ger. frame Red						30				30
1998 Ger. frame Silver						10				10
1999 Ger. frame Black						25				25
1999 Ger. frame Yellow						11				11

PRODUCTION	1993	1994	1995	1996	1997	1998	1999	2000	2001	TOTAL
1998 Eng. frame Bronze					60	30				90
1998 Eng. frame Black					118	60				178
1999 Eng. frame Black						43	80			123
2000 Eng. frame Black							20	15		35
2001 Eng. frame Black								40	70	110
2002 Eng. frame Black									30	30
1999 Eng. frame Bronze						30				30
2000 Eng. frame Bronze								20		20
2001 Eng. frame Bronze								20		20
2001 Eng. Metallic								20	30	50
1998 Eng. frame Yellow					90					90
1999 Eng. frame Yellow							10			10
2002 Red									251	251
2002 Black									49	49
2002 Yellow									46	46
Aus. 2002 Red									15	15
Aus. 2002 Yellow									15	15
Aus. 2002 Black									5	5
Jpn. 2002 Red									2	2
Eng. 2002 Red									30	30
Eng. 2002 Yellow									10	10

PRODUCTION	1993	1994	1995	1996	1997	1998	1999	2000	2001	TOTAL
620 I.e. Monster Dark										
2002 frame Black									107	107
2002 frame metallic									43	43
2002 frame Silver									31	31
2002 frame Bronze									15	15
2002 Cal. frame Black									445	445
2002 Italy frame Silver									49	49
2002 Italy frame Bronze									40	40
2002 Italy frame metallic									109	109
2002 Italy frame Black									202	202
620 le Monster										
Metallic 2002 Blue Black									4	4
Metallic 2002 Black									3	3
S 2002 Red									40	40
S 2002 Black									26	26
S 2002 Yellow									35	35
S 2002 Gray Senna									162	162
S 2002 Aus. Gray Senna									4	4
S 2002 Eng. Gray Senna									20	20
S 2002 Eng. Red									20	20
Total	8	3,886	3,430	1,462	3,858	5,596	7,805	7,579	8,373	41,997

PRODUCTION	1994	1995	1996	1997	1998	1999	2000	2001	TOTAL
400 Monster									
Police Saudi Arabia	300								300
Jpn. 1995 Red	1	200							201
Jpn. 1995 Yellow		40							40
Jpn. 1996 Red			60						60
Jpn. 1996 Yellow			240						240
Jpn. 1998 Red				235					235
Jpn. 1998 Yellow				113					113
Jpn. 1998 Black				16					16
Jpn. 2002 Black								10	10
Jpn. 1998 Silver				36					36
Jpn. 2000 Red						3	160		163
Jpn. 2002 Silver								10	10
Jpn. 2001 Red							80		80
Jpn. 2002 Red								150	150
Jpn. 2000 Blue							20		20

PRODUCTION	1994	1995	1996	1997	1998	1999	2000	2001	TOTAL
Jpn. 2001 Blue							50		50
Jpn. 2002 Blue								50	50
Jpn. 2000 Yellow							70		70
Jpn. 2001 Yellow							70		70
Jpn. 2002 Yellow								90	90
Jpn. 2000 Metallic Silver							50		50
Jpn. 2001 Metallic Silver							70		70
Jpn. 2002 Metallic Black								20	20
Jpn. 2002 Metallic Blue Black								20	20
Jpn. 2001 CROMO							30		30
Jpn. 2001 Dark frame Black							70		70
Jpn. 2001 Dark frame Silver							30		30
Total	301	240	300	400	0	3	600	450	2,294

The first 750 Monster of 1996 included the basic chassis of the 600 Monster, along with the 750 Supersport motor.

Ducati Motor

Following the success of the 600 Monster, the Monster range expanded to include a 750. This appeared for 1996, derived from the 600 Monster, and was the only new model that year. While the motor was similar to the 750 Supersport, the chassis was that of the 600 Monster, with a single front disc brake, non-adjustable Marzocchi front fork, and a 4.50 x 17-inch rear wheel. There were only minor updates for 1997, but many more changes for 1998. The redesigned engine now included smoother finished crankcases, and there was a new wet clutch, with the actuation moved to the left as on the 900. The camshaft drive belt covers were now the 900-style, allowing the checking of belt tension without removing the entire cover. While the chassis specifications were much as before, the 750 Monster also received twin front disc brakes (except for the U.S). There were more 750 Monsters for 1999, the range expanding to include the City, Dark, and City Dark—all very similar to their respective 900 counterparts.

For 2000, the 750 Monster was restyled. The engine received a new clutch and timing belt covers in 1998. *(Ducati Motor)*

750 MONSTER, 750 I.E. 1996-2002

Engine	Twin cylinder four-stroke, air-cooled	**Battery**	1996-2000: 12V/16Ah 2001-02: 12V/10Ah sealed	**Width**	1996-2001: 800mm (31.5 in.) 2002: 794mm 2002 (31.3 in.)
Bore	88mm	**Primary drive**	1996-97: 2.0:1 (31/62) 1997-2002: 1.85:1 (33/61)	**Seat height**	1996-2001: 770mm (30.3 in.) 2002: 795mm (31.3 in.)
Stroke	61.5mm	**Clutch**	Wet multiplate		
Displacement	748cc	**Gear ratios**	0.966, 1.074, 1,333, 1.714, 2.500	**Dry weight**	1996-2001: 178 kg (392.1 lbs.) City: 180 kg (396.5 lbs.) 2002: 179 kg (394.3 lbs.)
Compression ratio	9:1	**Final drive**	1996-97: 2.533:1 (15/38) 1998-2002: 2.73:1 (15/41)		
Valve actuation	Belt-driven desmodromic overhead camshaft	**Front suspension**	1996-1999: Marzocchi 40 USD/E 2000-01: 43mm Showa 2002: 43mm Marzocchi	**Top speed**	1996-2001: 190 km/h (118.1 mph) 2002 195 km/h (121.2 mph)
Valve timing (degrees)	1996-99: 31, 88, 72 ,46 2000-01: 11, 70, 50, 30 2002: 12, 70, 56, 25	**Rear suspension**	Sachs-Boge rising rate swingarm		
Carburetion	1996-01: Mikuni BDST 38 B 216A 2002: Marelli CPU 5.9M Electronic injection	**Front brake**	320mm disc (12.6 in.) (dual discs from 1998)	**Colors**	Red 473.101 (PPG) Yellow 473.201 (PPG) Met. Gray 291.601 (PPG) Met. black 291.500 (PPG) Met. Blue 291.800 (PPG) Met. Dark blue 0013 (PPG) Met. Dark gray 653.6047 (PPG) (750 S USA)
		Rear brake	245mm disc (9.6 in.)		
		Tires	120/60 x 17, 160/60 x 17		
Power	1996-97: 64 horsepower at 8,000 rpm (crankshaft) 1998-2001: 62 horsepower at 7,500 rpm 2002: 64 horsepower at 8,750 rpm	**Wheelbase**	1996-2001: 1,430mm (56.3 in.) 2002: 1,440mm (56.7 in.)		
		Length	1996-2001: 2,080mm (81.9 in.) 2002: 2,100mm (82.7 in.)	**Engine numbers**	Continuing ZDM 750 A 2C 000001
Spark plugs	Champion RA6HC			**Frame numbers**	From ZDM 750 M 000001 From ZDM 1RA3L XB 000001 (USA)
Generator	1996-97: 12v/300W 1998-2002: 12v/520W	**Height**	1996-2001:1,030mm (40.6 in.) 2002:1,058mm (41.7 in.)		
Ignition (degrees)	1996-2001: Kokusan 6 static, 32 total				

A Metallic 750 joined the lineup for 2000, and all 750s featured the styling revisions of this year. Like the 600, the 750 retained carburetors, but they now incorporated electrical heaters in the float bowls that were automatically activated at temperatures lower than 3 degrees Celsius. There was a non-adjustable Showa front fork, and the wheels were the new lighter three-spoke Brembo. The rear wheel was still 4.50 x 17 inches. There were only minor updates for 2001 (shared with the 600), but a redesigned 750 Monster (the 750 I.E.) appeared for 2002, similar to the 620 I.E. Along with electronic fuel injection, the motor shared the other updates of the two-valve engine this year, and the chassis was the S4 type with a Marzocchi front fork. There was also a 750S I.E. for the U.S., based on the 620S I.E., with an aluminum swingarm, higher seat, and headlight fairing. The 750 I.E. Dark continued with only a single front disc brake.

Ducati Motor

The 750 I.E. was new for 2002. It had electronic fuel injection, but this model only lasted for a year.

750 Monster

PRODUCTION	1995	1996	1997	1998	1999	2000	2001	TOTAL
1996 Red	3							3
1996 Yellow	1							1
1996 Silver		211						211
1997 Red			339					339
1997 Yellow			199					199
1997 Black			98					98
1997 Silver		689	289					978
1998 Red			80	50				130
1998 Black			30	50				80
1998 Yellow			30	35				65
1998 Silver			115	5				120
1999 Red				160	268			428
1999 Black				62	40			102
1999 Yellow				100	60			160
1999 Silver				69	60			129
1999 Blue				119	36			155
2000 Red					15	252		267
2000 Black					5	61		66
2000 Yellow					15	100		115
2000 Silver					12	55		67
2000 Blue					12	55		67
2001 Red						56	129	185
2001 Black						14	41	55
2001 Yellow						24	90	114
2001 Silver						17	42	59
2001 Blue						5	28	33
2002 Red							64	64
2002 Yellow							5	5
USA 1997 Silver			100					100
Cal. 1997 Silver			400					400
Cal. 1998 Red			50	100				150
Cal. 1998 Yellow			50	100				150
USA - Cal. 1999 Red				108	50			158
USA - Cal. 1999 Yellow				108	50	171		329
Cal. 2000 Red					196	29		225
Cal. 2000 Yellow					54			54
Cal. 2001 Red						50	162	212
Cal. 2001 Yellow						29	100	129
Switz 1997 Red			35					35
Switz 1997 Yellow			35					35
Switz 1997 Silver			50					50
Switz 2000 Red						10		10
Switz 2000 Black						10		10
Aus. 1998 Red			30					30
Aus. 1998 Black			19					19
Aus. 1998 Silver			23					23
Aus. / Jpn. 1999 Red				20	20			40
Aus. / Jpn. 1999 Black				6	18			24
Aus. / Jpn. 1999 Yellow				12	20			32
Aus. / Jpn. 1999 Silver				2	19			21
Aus. 2000 Red					20	5		25
Aus. 2000 Yellow						16		16
Aus. 2000 Black						11		11
Aus. 2000 Blue						12		12
Aus. 2001 Red						8	5	13
Aus. 2001 Yellow						8	5	13
Aus. 2001 Black							5	5
Aus. 2001 Silver						2	5	7
Aus. 2001 Blue						9		9
Jpn. 1997 Red			5					5
Jpn. 1997 Yellow			5					5
Jpn. 1997 Silver			10					10
Jpn. 2001 Red						1		1
Jpn. 2002 Red							15	15
Jpn. 2002 Yellow							15	15
Ger. 1996 Red	1							1
Ger. 1996 Silver		80						80
Ger. 1997 Red			210					210
Ger. 1997 Silver		160						160
Ger. 1998 Red				45				45
Ger. 1998 Black			5					5
Ger. 1998 Yellow			5					5
Ger. 1998 Silver			5					5
Eng. 1996 Silver		60						60
Eng. 1997 Red			81					81
Eng. 1997 Yellow			22					22
Eng. 1997 Silver		101						101
Eng. 1998 Red			32					32
Eng. 1998 Yellow			15					15
Eng. 2000 Red						28		28
Eng. 2000 Black						5		5
Eng. 2000 Yellow						15		15
Eng. 2000 Blue						15		15
Eng. 2001 Red						5	10	15
Eng. 2001 Yellow						3	5	8
Eng. 2001 Blue							5	5
Eng. 2001 Silver							5	5
Eng. 2002 Red							20	20
Eng. 2002 Yellow							21	21
Dark 1999 Black				258	797			1,055
Dark 2000 Black					259	877		1,136
Dark 2001 Black						742	325	1,067
Dark 2002 Black							171	171
Dark City 1999 Black					230			230
Dark USA 1999 Black				335				335
Dark Cal. 1999 Black					400			400
Dark Cal. 2000 Black					196	471		667
Dark Cal. 2001 Black						351	250	601
Dark Cal. 2002 Black							398	398
Dark Switz. 1999 Black					45			45
Dark Aus. 2000 Black					5	58		63
Dark Aus. 2001 Black						23		23
Dark Jpn. 2000 Black						72		72
Dark Jpn. 2001 Black						40		40

PRODUCTION	1995	1996	1997	1998	1999	2000	2001	TOTAL
Dark Eng. 2000 Black						50		50
Dark Eng. 2001 Black						40	20	60
Dark Eng. 2002 Black							30	30
City 1999 Red					15			15
City 1999 Black					15			15
City 1999 Yellow					10			10
City 1999 Silver					60			60
City 1999 Blue					80			80
Metallic 2000 Silver						1		1
Metallic 2001 Silver						2		2
Metallic 2000 Black						1		1

PRODUCTION	1995	1996	1997	1998	1999	2000	2001	TOTAL
Metallic 2001 Black						5		5
Metallic 2002 Blue Black							1	1
Metallic Cal. 2001 Silver						100		100
Metallic Jpn. 2001 Silver						1		1
S Cal. 2002 Gray Senna							1	1
Total	5	1,301	2,352	1,804	3,037	3,910	1,978	14,387

Monster S4, Fogarty S4

The Foggy Monster S4 was a limited edition Monster S4 offered for sale over the Internet during 2001.

After years of expectation, the Desmoquattro engine made it into the Monster for 2001. The Monster S4 was a new design, sharing the engine and frame architecture with the sport-touring ST4. From the ST4 came the 916cc Desmoquattro engine with lowered exhaust camshafts and more compact cylinder heads that enabled the engine to be positioned further forward. The engine was re-tuned to provide a broader powerband, with 40mm exhaust header pipes, a larger airbox, and a Marelli 5.9 M CPU. Valve sizes were 33 and 29mm. In an endeavor to create a more aesthetically pleasing engine layout, designers moved the battery above the rear cylinder. The frame was based on that of the ST4, with thicker tubing, a 24-degree steering head angle, and the engine positioned 20mm higher than the 900 IE Monster. Also separating the S4 from other Monsters were the five-spoke Marchesini wheels. As the Monster S4 was less popular than anticipated, there were no changes for 2002 and 2003. It was replaced by the S4R for 2004.

In June 2001, the Monster S4 Fogarty was offered for sale on the Internet. Created in honor of Carl Fogarty, Ducati's most successful racer, the "Foggy" S4 was a limited edition Monster S4 designed by Aldo Drudi for Ducati Performance. The gas tank was reshaped, and there were many additional carbon-fiber components. The front fork was upgraded, and while Desmoquattro engine remained unchanged internally, there was a high level exhaust system with oval carbon fiber Termignoni mufflers.

Ducati Motor

The Moster S4 used the 916cc Desmoquattro motor, and was virtually unchanged from 2001 until the 2003 model, shown here.

Monster S4, Fogarty S4 2001-03

Engine	Twin cylinder four-stroke, liquid-cooled	**Generator**	12v/520W	**Length**	2,080mm (81.9 in.)
Bore	94mm	**Battery**	12V/10Ah sealed	**Height**	1,030mm (40.6 in.)
Stroke	66mm	**Primary drive**	1.85:1 (32/59)	**Width**	800mm (31.5 in.)
Displacement	916cc	**Clutch**	Dry multiplate	**Seat height**	803mm (31.6 in.)
Compression ratio	11.0:1	**Gear ratios**	0.958, 1.043, 1.182, 1.40, 1.764, 2.466	**Dry weight**	Monster: 193 kg (425.1 lbs.)
Valve actuation	Belt-driven desmodromic double overhead camshafts	**Final drive**	Monster: 2.466:1 (15/37) Fogarty: 2.6:1 (15/39)		Fogarty: 189 kg (416.3 lbs.)
Valve timing (degrees)	11, 61, 62, 18	**Front suspension**	43mm inverted Showa	**Top speed**	225 km/h (139.8 mph)
Injection	Marelli CPU 5.9M (50mm throttle bodies)	**Rear suspension**	Boge rising-rate swingarm	**Colors**	Red 473.101 (PPG) Yellow 473.201 (PPG) Black 248.514 (PPG) Dark gray 653.6047
Power	Monster: 101 horsepower at 8,750 rpm	**Front brake**	320mm dual disc (12.6 in.)	**Engine numbers**	From ZDM 916 W 4 000001
	Fogarty: 110 horsepower at 9,750 rpm	**Rear brake**	245mm disc (9.6 in.)	**Frame numbers**	From ZDM S1 00AA 1B 000001
Spark plugs	Champion RA59GC	**Tires**	120/70 x 17, 180/55 x 17		From ZDM 1RB8S1B 000001 (USA)
		Wheelbase	1,440mm (56.7 in.)		

Production	1999	2000	2001	Total
916 HyperMonster				
2000	5			5
Monster S4				
2001 Red		241	1,505	1,746
2002 Red			133	133
2001 Black		115	890	1,005
2002 Black			11	11
2001 Yellow		85	398	483
2002 Yellow			3	3
2001 CROMO		30	19	49
2001 S Gray Senna		385	1,582	1,967
2002 Gray Senna			1	1
2001 Cal. Red		52	56	108
2002 Cal. Red			75	75
2002 Cal. Black			75	75
2001 Cal. Yellow		50	50	100
2001 S Cal. Gray Senna		22	178	200

Production	1999	2000	2001	Total
2002 Cal. Gray Senna			150	150
2001 Aus. Red		28	30	58
2002 Aus. Red			16	16
2001 Aus. Black		6	22	28
2002 Aus. Black			5	5
2001 Aus. Yellow		6	18	24
2001 S Aus. Gray Senna			23	23
2002 Aus. Gray Senna			26	26
2001 Jpn. Red		116	134	250
2002 Jpn. Red			181	181
2001 Jpn. Black		90	25	115
2002 Jpn. Black			45	45
2001 Jpn. Yellow		105	60	165
2002 Jpn. Yellow			130	130
2001 S Jpn. Gray Senna			147	147
2002 Jpn. Gray Senna			144	144
2001 Eng. Red		81	55	136

Production	1999	2000	2001	Total
2002 Eng. Red			44	44
2001 Eng. Black		15	44	59
2002 Eng. Black			10	10
2001 Eng. Yellow		45	18	63
2002 Eng. Yellow			10	10
2001 Eng. CROMO			11	11
2001 S Eng. Gray Senna		20	145	165
2002 Eng. Gray Senna			15	15
2002 Fogarty Red			51	51
2002 Fogarty Cal. Red			100	100
2002 Fogarty Jpn. Red			35	35
2002 Fogarty Eng. Red			11	11
2002 Fogarty Aus. Red			5	5
Total	5	1,492	6,686	8,183

Monster 1000, 1000 S 1000 Cromo

Ten years after its release, in 2003, the continual evolution of the Monster resulted in the Monster 1000 and 800. Powering the 1000 was the next generation air-cooled two-valve engine—the 1000 DS (Dual Spark)—that would also power the Multistrada and 1000 Supersport. In the cylinder head the included valve angle was reduced from 60 to 56 degrees, with larger valves (45mm intake and 40mm exhaust) with thinner stems (7mm). The camshaft was supported by plain bearings in the head, and ignition was by dual spark plugs. The cylinder heads were sealed by metal gaskets rather than O-rings as before. The exhaust ports were 40 percent shorter, and there were an additional two fins to support the cylinder. Other engine developments extended to thinner con-rods, timing belt gears with 20 teeth instead of 18, an aluminum clutch basket, a double-row bearing on the transmission output shaft, and a higher-pressure lubrication system. The chassis for the M1000 was similar to the final 900 I.E. The suspension was adjustable, as was the rear ride height, and while the M1000 had a steel swingarm, the 1000 S swingarm was aluminum. The 1000 S also included the S4R fairing, and a number of carbon-fiber body parts.

M1000, M1000S M1000 Cromo 2003-

Engine	Twin cylinder four-stroke, air-cooled	**Battery**	12V/10Ah
Bore	94mm	**Primary drive**	1.84:1 (32/59)
Stroke	71.5mm	**Clutch**	Dry multiplate
Displacement	992cc	**Gear ratios**	0.857, 0.958, 1.091, 1,350, 1.764, 2.466
Compression ratio	10:1	**Final drive**	2.6:1 (15/39)
Valve actuation	Belt-driven desmodromic overhead camshaft	**Front suspension**	43mm inverted Showa
Injection	Marelli CPU 5.9M (45mm throttle body)	**Rear suspension**	Sages Boge rising rate swingarm
Power	84 horsepower at 8,000 rpm	**Front brake**	320mm dual disc (12.6 in.)
Spark plugs	Champion RA6HC, NGK DCPR8E	**Rear brake**	245mm disc (9.6 in.)
Generator	12v/520W	**Tires**	120/70 x 17, 180/55 x 17

Wheelbase	1,440mm (56.7 in.)
Length	2,105mm (82.9 in.)
Height	1,060mm (41.7 in.)
Width	794mm (31.3 in.)
Seat height	803mm (31.6 in.)
Dry weight	189 kg (416.3 lbs.)
Max speed	220 km/h (136.7 mph)
Colors	Red 473.101 (PPG) Yellow 473.201 (PPG) Black 248.514 (PPG) Dark Gray 0017 (PPG) M1000S
Frame numbers	From ZDM 1RABP XB 000001 (USA)

**After 10 years, the highly successful M900 was replaced by the Monster 1000 for 2003.
This is the Monster 1000 Dark. The larger motor gave the Monster a new lease on life.**

Ducati Motor

Also new for 2003 were the Monster 800 and 800S. The 800S shown here had a small fairing and aluminum swingarm.

The Monster 800 replaced the 750 for 2003, the updated engine now including a six-speed transmission. The crankcases were identical to the 620 except for the displacement increase, the clutch including an aluminum clutch basket and plates. A rubber cushion drive with cylindrical springs joined the clutch housing to the primary drive. This featured dual teeth with a cushion to reduce play in the coupling with the clutch housing. In all other respects the 800 was identical to the previous 750. This year also saw the M800 S, with aluminum swingarm, but this only lasted a year, with the Monster 800 the only 800 for 2004.

M800, M800 S 2003-

Engine	Twin cylinder four-stroke, air-cooled	**Generator**	12v/520W	**Tires**	120/60 x 17, 160/60 x 17
Bore	88mm	**Battery**	12V/10Ah	**Wheelbase**	1,440mm (56.7 in.)
Stroke	66mm	**Primary drive**	1.85:1 (33/61)	**Length**	2,100mm (82.7 in.)
Displacement	803cc	**Clutch**	Wet multiplate	**Height**	1,058mm (41.7 in.)
Compression ratio	10.4:1	**Gear ratios**	0.923, 1.000, 1.13, 1,333, 1.66, 2.462	**Width**	794mm (31.3 in.)
Valve actuation	Belt-driven desmodromic overhead camshaft	**Final drive**	2.8:1 (15/42)	**Seat height**	770mm (30.3 in.)
Injection	Marelli CPU 5.9M (45mm throttle body)	**Front suspension**	43mm inverted Showa	**Dry weight**	179 kg (394.3 lbs.)
Power	73 horsepower at 8,250 rpm	**Rear suspension**	Sages Boge rising-rate swingarm	**Top speed**	210 km/h (130.5 mph)
Spark plugs	Champion RA4HC, NGK DCPR8E	**Front brake**	320mm dual disc (12.6 in.)	**Colors**	Red 473.101 (PPG) Yellow 473.201 (PPG) Black 248.514 (PPG)
		Rear brake	245mm disc (9.6 in.)	**Frame numbers**	From ZDM 1RAAN XB 000001 (USA)

Released during 2003, the Monster S4R was the most powerful and best handling Monster yet. Powered by the 996cc Desmoquattro motor, there was a new exhaust system with distinctive high-rise mufflers with aluminum covers, and a moderate power increase. Chassis improvements included a tubular aluminum single-sided swingarm, and an adjustable Showa front fork with TIN-coated legs. Individual touches extended to special mirrors, forged footpeg brackets and an electronic instrument panel. Carbon-fiber parts included the front fender, side covers, and timing belt covers. The wheels were five-spoke Marchesini, and the rear disc was slightly thicker (6mm).

For 2005, the S2R and S2R Dark joined the S4R. Similar in design to the S4R, this was powered by the six-speed 800cc air-cooled two-valve engine of the earlier Moster 800 I.E., but now included the wet APTC clutch of the 620 I.E. The chassis was shared with the S4R, with the single-sided aluminum swingarm and dual exhausts on the right. The front fork was a 43mm Marzocchi, and the rear shock absorber was from Sachs.

The most exciting of all Monsters was the S4R, introduced during 2003, with a 996cc Desmoquattro engine.

MONSTER S4R 2004-

Engine	Twin cylinder four-stroke, liquid-cooled	Battery	12V/10Ah	Length	2,121mm (83.5 in.)
Bore	98mm	Primary drive	1.85:1 (32/59)	Height	1,030mm (40.6 in.)
Stroke	66mm	Clutch	Dry multiplate	Width	790mm handlebar (31.1 in.)
Displacement	996cc	Gear ratios	0.958, 1.043, 1.182, 1.40, 1.764, 2.466	Seat height	806mm (31.7 in.)
Compression ratio	11.6:1	Final drive	2.8:1 (15/42)	Dry weight	193 kg (425.1 lbs.)
Valve actuation	Belt-driven desmodromic double overhead camshafts	Front suspension	43mm inverted Showa	Top speed	240 km/h (149.1 mph)
Injection	Marelli CPU 5.9M (50mm throttle bodies)	Rear suspension	Showa rising rate mono swingarm	Colors	Red 473.101 (PPG) Yellow 473.201 (PPG) Black 248.514 (PPG) Dark Gray 0017 (PPG) Blue 291.800 (PPG)
		Front brake	320mm dual disc (12.6 in.)		
Power	113 horsepower at 8,750 rpm	Rear brake	245mm disc (9.6 in.)		
Spark plugs	Champion RA59GC, NGK DCPR9EVX	Tires	120/70 x 17, 180/55 x 17	Frame numbers	From ZDM 1RB5T3B 000001 (USA)
Generator	12v/520W	Wheelbase	1,440mm (56.7 in.)		

CHAPTER 10

916, 996, 998, AND 748

Ducati has produced many great motorcycles, and one of the greatest was the 916. This was a landmark motorcycle, setting new standards for performance and aesthetics for nearly a decade. The result of 6 years of intensive work by Massimo Tamburini and his team at the Cagiva Research Center, the 916 broke from the earlier tradition of evolution, and apart from the engine, was a new design.

916 Strada (1994-98)

The 916 style was so distinctive that it has become one of the icons of modern motorcycling. All 1994 916s like this were Monoposto.

Apart from a longer stroke, and steel Pankl 124mm con-rods, with a 20mm wristpin, the 916 motor was much the same as the 888. Tamburini created a structure around the Desmoquattro engine that included a stronger frame with an additional lower engine support, a sealed airbox that included the lower part of the gas tank, and a single-sided cast-aluminum swingarm. Chain adjustment was by an eccentric at the hub. Another feature of the frame was an exceptionally strong steering head structure with ellipsoidal bearings. A non-adjustable Sachs-Boge steering damper was mounted transversely near the top triple clamp, its symmetrical action providing a neutral response to steering input. Nearly every component was

unique to the 916, including the Brembo hollow elliptical spoked wheels, and all the fasteners. A special headlight support contained unique twin poly-ellipsoidal headlights, and there were specifically styled twin taillights. The exhaust system exited under the seat and was designed to aid aerodynamics more than ultimate power. The design was extremely compact, and immediately became a benchmark for motorcycle style and function. Production was also initially slow due to a fire at the factory at Bologna and most 1994 916s were assembled at Varese.

Updates for the 1995 Model Year saw the 916 Strada became a Biposto (dual seat) in all markets except the

For 1995, the 916 was a Biposto in Europe. It was largely unchanged through 1997.

United States. U.S. versions also received an Öhlins rear shock absorber. The most significant update this year was a new Weber electronic injection system called the 1.6 M. To improve low-speed running, this system featured a single sensor for phase and rpm from the timing belt jackshaft. Other updates for 1995 included forged Macchi con-rods, instead of the previous Pankl. For 1996, there were new crankcases without the kickstart boss. The 916 Biposto was available in the U.S. for 1997 (with a Showa rear shock absorber), but was largely unchanged.

By the 1998 Model Year the 916 remained virtually as before, with only small details setting it apart from earlier examples. There were new Vignelli logos, and updates included Kevlar reinforced timing belts, additional baffles in the crankcases, and braided steel brake and clutch lines.

U.S. 916s were still either Monoposto or Biposto for 1998. The Monoposto had an Öhlins rear shock absorber.

The Senna I of 1995 was virtually a standard 916, with some SP equipment.

The great Brazilian Formula One driver Ayrton Senna was a friend of the Castiglioni brothers, and an owner of an 851. Only a few months before his death in 1994 Senna agreed to the production of a limited edition 916 Senna, with the profits going to the Senna Foundation. The Senna 1 appeared for 1995, and setting it apart from the regular 916 was the black and gray color scheme with red wheels. Apart from steel Pankl con-rods, the engine specification was that of the 916 Strada, while the chassis was similar to the 916 SP. This included the solo seat, aluminum rear subframe, Öhlins shock absorber, and fully floating cast-iron front brake discs. Also shared with the SP were adjustable brake and clutch levers, stainless-steel brake lines, and carbon-fiber front fender, clutch cover, chain guard, and exhaust pipe insulating panel.

Because of production difficulties there was no Senna for 1996, but another series, the Senna II, was produced for 1997. These were virtually identical to the earlier version, but were painted a lighter gray. The final series was produced for the 1998 Model Year. These bikes were painted black and featured a carbon-fiber airbox and exhaust heat shield. The Senna missed the mark as a limited edition model because it was not quite as exclusive as anticipated, and only provided the performance of a 916 Strada.

A virtually identical Senna II was produced for 1997.

The final 916 Senna appeared for 1998. It was mostly unchanged apart from colors and graphics.

916 STRADA AND SENNA (1994-98)

Engine	Twin cylinder four-stroke, liquid-cooled	**Generator**	12v/350W	**Tires**	120/70 x 17, 180/55 x 17 or 190/50 x 17
Bore	94mm	**Battery**	12V/16Ah	**Wheelbase**	1,410mm (55.5 in.)
Stroke	66mm	**Primary drive**	2:1 (31/62)	**Length**	2,050mm (80.7 in.)
Displacement	916cc	**Clutch**	Dry multiplate	**Height**	1,090mm (42.9 in.)
Compression ratio	11:1	**Gear ratios**	0.857, 0.958, 1.091, 1.35, 1.765, 2.466	**Width**	685mm (27 in.)
Valve actuation	Belt-driven desmodromic double overhead camshafts	**Final drive**	2.40:1 (15/36)	**Seat height**	790mm (31.1 in.)
Valve timing (degrees)	11, 70, 62, 18	**Front suspension**	43mm Showa GD051 GD131 from 1998	**Dry weight**	Strada, Senna: 198 kg (436.1 lbs.) Biposto: 204 kg (449.3 lbs.)
Injection	1994: Weber I.A.W. CPU P8 1995-98: 1.6 50mm throttle bodies	**Rear suspension**	Showa GD052-007-02 rising-rate mono swingarm (Bipesto: Showa GD052-007-50) (U.S. and Senna: Öhlins DU 3420)	**Top speed**	260 km/h (161.6 mph)
				Engine numbers	From ZDM 916 W4 000001
Power	114 horsepower at 9,000 rpm	**Front brake**	320mm dual disc (12.6 in.)	**Frame numbers**	1994-96: From ZDM 916 S 000001 1997: From ZDM 916 S B 000001
Spark plugs	Champion RA59GC	**Rear brake**	220mm disc (8.7 in.)		

916 Sport Production (1994-96), 916 SPS (1997-98)

Continuing where the 888 SP5 left off, the 1994 916 SP offered exclusivity and improved performance.

Following the success of earlier Sport Production series, the 916 was also offered as an SP for 1994. Inside the engine were titanium Pankl con-rods, and the injection system included twin fuel injectors for each cylinder (still with the P8 CPU). The cylinder heads were based on those of the 916 Racing, without the cast "DESMO 4V DOHC" lettering, to provide additional front wheel clearance. Another feature of the SP was forced lubrication to the piston wristpins through a gallery in the con-rod.

As with the earlier SP5, the 916 SP had larger valves (34mm inlet and 30mm exhaust), and more radical camshaft timing. Unlike the earlier SP, the 916 SP shared its gearbox with the 916 Strada. There was also a larger-diameter exhaust system, with 45mm header pipes and a 50mm collector box and mufflers.

Although the basic chassis was similar to that of the 916 Strada, the SP featured an Öhlins rear shock absorber and a number of carbon-fiber body parts. Some 1994 916 SPs also came with a carbon-fiber airbox and, as with all previous SPs, the front disc rotors were fully floating cast-iron. For 1995, the 916 SP was virtually unchanged, and almost indistinguishable from the 1994 version, except that the fairing was retained by screws rather than

For 1997, the 916 SP grew to 996cc and became the 916 SPS. It was visually similar to the 916 SP, but provided considerably more performance.

916 SP, SPS (1994-98)

Engine	Twin cylinder four-stroke, liquid-cooled	**Spark plugs**	1994: Champion RA59GC 1995-98: Champion A55V	**Wheelbase**	1,410mm (55.5 in.)
Bore	SP: 94mm SPS: 98mm	**Generator**	12v/350W	**Length**	1994-96: 2,050mm (80.7 in.) 1997-98: 2,030mm (80 in.)
Stroke	66mm	**Battery**	12V/16Ah		
Displacement	SP: 916cc SPS: 996	**Primary drive**	SP: 2:1 (31/62) SPS: 1.84:1 (32/59)	**Height**	1994-96: 1,090mm (42.9 in.) 1997-98: 1,080mm (42.5 in.)
Compression ratio	SP: 11.2:1 SPS: 11.5:1	**Clutch**	Dry multiplate		
Valve actuation	Belt-driven desmodromic double overhead camshafts	**Gear ratios**	0.857, 0.958, 1.091, 1.35, 1.765, 2.466	**Width**	1994-96: 685mm (27 in.) 1997-98: 780mm (30.7 in.)
		Final drive	2.57:1 (14/36)		
Valve timing (degrees)	SP: 53, 71, 77, 42 SPS: 14, 73, 57, 23	**Front suspension**	43mm Showa GD051 GD131 from 1998	**Seat height**	790mm (31.1 in.)
Injection	Weber I.A.W. CPU P8	**Rear suspension**	Öhlins DU 3420 rising-rate mono swingarm	**Dry weight**	SP: 192 kg (422.9 lbs.) SPS: 190 kg (418.5 lbs.)
Power	SP: 131 horsepower at 10,500 rpm SPS: 134 horsepower at 10,500 rpm	**Front brake**	320mm dual disc (12.6 in.)	**Top speed**	270 km/h (167.8 mph)
		Rear brake	220mm disc (8.7 in.)	**Engine numbers**	From ZDM 916 W4 000001
		Tires	120/70 x 17, 180/55 x 17 or 190/50 x 17	**Frame numbers**	From ZDM 916 S 000001

rivets. For 1996, the 916 SP became the SP3, now with a numbered plaque on the top triple clamp. The engine included the new series of crankcases, and 102mm (up from 100mm) cylinder mouths to allow the easy installation of 96mm pistons to give 955cc. Also during 1996, a small number of 955cc SPAs (Sport Production America) were manufactured as homologation specials for AMA Superbike racing. These featured 96mm pistons and Pankl titanium con-rods. The SPA was the only production street Ducati to feature a 955cc engine.

There was a major update to the Sport Production series for 1997 with the 916 SPS (Sport Production Special). Although it still carried the generic "916" title, the 916 SPS was 996cc and had new crankcases for World Superbike homologation. Other updates included 36mm inlet valves, larger intake ports, new camshafts, a lighter crankshaft, a higher primary gear ratio, and 50mm exhaust header pipes. The 916 SPS was offered again for 1998, with new logos, titanium con-rods, and a lighter frame constructed of thinner 25CrMo4 steel. The Showa front fork had wider front brake caliper mounts, and there was an Öhlins steering damper.

Also during 1998 a limited run of Fogarty Replica 916 SPSs were built to homologate an updated frame for World Superbike. This featured a change to the rear bracing tube to increase the airbox volume. Only available in England, the Fogarty Replica was virtually identical to the regular 916 SPS, except for graphics and black five-spoke Marchesini wheels.

Minimalist decals distinguished the 1998 916 SPS from the 1997 version, but the performance didn't change.

996, 996 S, and 996 SPS (1999-2001)

The 996 replaced the 916 for 1999. It had a larger engine and improved brakes.

The 996 replaced the 916 for 1999, and there was more to the 996 than simply a displacement increase. From the 916 SPS came the stronger crankcases, 36mm inlet and 30mm exhaust valves, and a higher primary drive ratio. New was the 1.6 M.B1 Weber injection system, incorporating twin injectors per cylinder, with both injectors triggered simultaneously. The airbox featured improved sealing and shorter intakes, while the 45mm exhaust header pipes were oval-section.

Chassis improvements included wider mount Brembo brake calipers, a PSC 16mm front master cylinder derived from the Brembo racing radial type, and thicker semi-floating stainless-steel discs. Also new were the lighter lower silicon content three-spoke Brembo wheels. While the 996 was generally a Biposto, the United States received Biposto and Monoposto versions. There was a hybrid 996 S (Special) made specifically for California. This combined the chassis of the 996 SPS with the regular 996 engine. The specification included an Öhlins rear shock absorber and steering damper, and Marchesini five-spoke wheels. There were only detail updates to the 996 for 2000. From

the 996 SPS came five-spoke Marchesini wheels, and the Showa fork had gold TiN-coated (titanium nitride) fork legs. The 996 S was offered specifically for the U.S. again and was much the same as before.

The second series of the Fogarty Replica 996 SPS, for 1999, was the first model to feature gold TiN-coated fork legs.

The 996 SPS for 1999 was similar to the 1998 916 SPS, but was the first model with the five-spoke Marchesini wheels.

Updates to the 996 SPS for 1999 saw a few engine improvements (mainly to the lubrication system), plus the closer-ratio 748 gearbox and five-spoke Marchesini wheels patterned on the type used by the factory racers. Later in 1999 there was a second series of the 996 SPS produced to homologate new cylinder heads for the World Superbike program, and a further series of 996 SPS Factory Replicas. These were ostensibly 996 SPSs with decals patterned on Fogarty's Ducati Performance World Superbike racer. This time the frame was a standard 996 SPS and, while the Showa fork was from the 996 SPS, the 1999 Factory Replica was the first to feature the gold-colored TiN-coated fork legs. The 996 SPS was upgraded yet again for 2000. The engine specifications were as before. There was a sealed-for-life battery, but the chassis received some development. Most significant was the Öhlins front fork

The final 996 arrived for 2001 with an Öhlins rear shock absorber. The five-spoke wheels first appeared for 2000.

with TiN-coated fork legs. The final series of 996 SPS Factory Replicas was also produced for 2000, the 996 Factory Replica 2, or "Pista" (circuit).

While the 996 SPS was replaced by the Testastretta 996R for the 2001, the 123-horsepower engine lived on in the European specification 996 S, but with the 1.6 M B1 twin simultaneous injector setup, rather than the now-ancient P8. The injectors were positioned inside the 50mm throttle bodies. In other respects the engine specifications were the same as the 996 SPS. The 2001 U.S. 996 was only Monoposto, retained the stock 996 motor, and came with an Öhlins (rather than Boge) steering damper and some carbon fiber body parts. The front suspension included a TiN-coated Showa fork. All 996s for 2001 received the Öhlins rear shock absorber. This was the final year for the 996 Superbike, although the engine would live on in the ST4S.

Annual updates to the SPS brought an Öhlins front fork for 2000.

996, S, SPS 1999-01

Engine	Twin cylinder four-stroke, liquid-cooled	**Battery**	12V/16Ah (SPS 2000: 10Ah)	**Wheelbase**	1,410mm (55.5 in.)
Bore	98mm	**Primary drive**	1.84:1 (32/59)	**Length**	2,030mm (79.9 in.)
Stroke	66mm	**Clutch**	Dry multiplate	**Height**	1,080mm (42.5 in.)
Displacement	996cc	**Gear ratios**	996, S, SPS: 0.857, 0.958, 1.091, 1.35, 1.765, 2.466 SPS (2000-01) 0.958, 1.043, 1.182, 1.40, 1.765, 2.466	**Width**	780mm (30.7 in.)
Compression ratio	11.5:1			**Seat height**	790mm (31.1 in.)
Valve actuation	Belt-driven desmodromic double overhead camshafts			**Dry weight**	996: 198 kg (436.1 lbs.) S: 195 kg (429.5 lbs.) SPS: 190 kg (418.5 lbs.) SPS (2000-01): 187 kg (411.9 lbs.)
Valve timing (degrees)	996, S: 11, 70, 62, 18 SPS: 14, 73, 57, 23	**Final drive**	2.4:1 (15/36)		
Injection	996, S: Weber I.A.W. CPU 1.6 SPS: MB1 (P8)	**Front suspension**	996, S, SPS: 43mm Showa SPS (2000-01): Öhlins	**Top speed**	996, S: 260 km/h (161.6 mph) SPS: 270 km/h (167.8 mph)
Power	996, S: 112 horsepower at 8,500 rpm SPS: 123 horsepower at 9,500 rpm	**Rear suspension**	996, S, SPS: Showa rising rate mono swingarm SPS (2001): Öhlins		
				Colors	Red 473.101 Yellow 473.201
Spark plugs	996, S: Champion RA59GC SPS: A55V	**Front brake**	320mm dual disc (12.6 in.)	**Engine numbers**	From ZDM 996 W4 000001
		Rear brake	220mm disc (8.7 in.)	**Frame numbers**	From ZDM 996 S 9B 000001 From ZDM 1H B7RHPB 000001 (USA)
Generator	12v/520W	**Tires**	120/70 x 17, 190/50 x 17		

The Pista of 2000 was the last of several limited edition series of the 996 SPS.

Ducati Motor

The 916 Corsa from 1995 until 1997 looked very similar, but underneath there were considerable annual updates. This is the 1996 Corsa.

For 1995 the catalogue factory racer was the 916 Racing, closely patterned on Fogarty's 1994 factory bike. Also displacing 955cc, this had identical camshaft timing and valve sizes (37 and 31mm), while the chassis included a 10mm longer swingarm, and a larger carbon-fiber fuel tank (22 liters). Racing specification brakes included twin 320mm cast-iron discs with P4.32-36mm calipers and a 19mm master cylinder. The five-spoke Marchesini wheels were 3.50 x 17- and 6.00 x 17-inch.

The 1996 955 Racing was visually identical to the 1995 version, but there were a number of updates. Engine developments included new crankcases and aluminum engine covers. The camshafts were patterned on those of the 1995 factory racers, while the exhaust system was enlarged to 52mm.

For 1997, the crankcases were the newly homologated 916 SPS type, and many of the developments to the factory bikes during 1996 were included. The fuel pressure was

increased to 5 bar, there was a larger capacity airbox, a larger oil radiator, and 54mm exhaust headers. It was a similar scenario for 1998, with the injection system featuring huge 60mm throttle bodies, although still with the twin-injector P8 system. New for 1998 was a 25CrMo4 frame using 1.5mm tubing and a longer magnesium swingarm to improve the weight distribution. Smaller 290mm discs were available, and there was a larger, and reshaped, 24-liter fuel tank.

As more emphasis was now placed on winning national Superbike championships, a higher-specification 996 Racing Special was offered to selected teams for 1999. This incorporated the MF3-S electronic injection system (with three injectors), and the revised frame with larger airbox of the 1998 factory racers. There were 39mm and 32mm titanium valves, shorter inlet tracts and a higher-lift inlet camshaft (13mm). A sump extension in the crankcase improved lubrication, and upgraded brakes featured four-pad Brembo calipers. Also new for 1999 was a slightly lower-specification 996 Racing, retaining the twin-injector P8 CPU, but the RS was the most successful.

A further batch of 996 Racing Specials was produced for 2000. The specification included the revised single injector MF3-S Marelli injection system and a 57mm stainless-steel exhaust system. The 996 RS 2000 was surprisingly close in performance to the official Team Ducati Infostrada machines. The customer 996 RS also retained the earlier 996cc engine for 2001. It was essentially the same as the works bikes of the previous year; the power was increased, the front fork was a 42mm Öhlins, and it had radial caliper Brembo front brakes. This year 16.5-inch wheels were fitted front and rear. Again, these proved surprisingly competitive against the new-generation factory machines.

916, 996 CORSA, RS 1995-2001

Engine	Twin cylinder four-stroke, liquid-cooled	Spark plugs	Champion A55V	Tires	Front: 12/60-17SC 12/75, (1998: 12/60 17SC 12/95) Rear: 18/76-17SC 18/76 (1998: 18/60 17SC 18/86) Michelin
Bore	1995-96: 96mm 1997-2001: 98mm	Generator	12v/180W		
		Battery	12V/2.5Ah (1996-98: 12V/4Ah)		
Stroke)	66mm	Primary drive	1995-96: 2:1 (31/62) 1997-2001: 1.84:1 (32/59)	Wheelbase	1,420mm (55.9 in.) 1998: 1,430mm (56.3 in.)
Displacement	1995-96: 955 1997-2001: 996			Length	2,050mm (80.7 in.) 1998: 2,030mm (79.9 in.)
Compression ratio	1995, 1997-98: 12:1 1996: 11.8:1	Clutch	Dry multiplate		
Valve actuation	Belt-driven desmodromic double overhead camshafts	Gear ratios	1.00, 1.091, 1.19, 1.35, 1.61, 2.0	Height	1,090mm (42.9 in.) 1998: 1,080mm (42.5 in.)
Valve timing	1995: 31, 78, 71, 45 1996: 36, 72, 71, 45 1997-98: 36, 72, 69, 47	Final drive	2.466:1 (15/37) (1996-98: 2.4:1 (15/36))	Width	685mm (27 in.)
				Seat height	790mm (31.1 in.)
Injection	916, Corsa: Weber I.A.W. CPU P8 RS: MF3-S	Front suspension	916, Corsa (1995-2000): Öhlins 46mm FG 9650 fork 916, Corsa (2001): Öhlins 42mm RS: Öhlins 46mm FG 8750S fork	Dry weight	1995: 154 kg (339.2 lbs.) 1996: 160 kg (352.4 lbs.) 1997: 162 kg (356.8 lbs.) 1998: 155 kg (341.4 lbs.)
Power	1995: 155 horsepower at 11,500 rpm 1996: 153 horsepower at 11,000 rpm 1997: 155 horsepower at 11,000 rpm 1998: 151 horsepower at 11,000 rpm 2001: 168 horsepower at 12,000 rpm) RS: 162 horsepower at 12,000 rpm	Rear suspension	916, Corsa: Öhlins DU 5360 rising rate mono swingarm RS: Öhlins DV 7290		
		Front brake	1995-98: 320mm (12.6 in.) 1999-2001: 290mm dual disc (11.4 in.)		
		Rear brake	200mm (7.9 in.)		

996 R, 998, 998 R, 998 S, Bostrom, Bayliss, Matrix, FE

Soon after TPG acquired control of Ducati the company initiated the development of a replacement engine for the Desmoquattro. Although the Desmoquattro was still a competitive Superbike racer, ultimate development was limited by the combustion chamber design. Retired Formula One Ferrari engineer Ing. Angiolino Marchetti was hired to create a new engine, albeit an evolution of the existing Desmoquattro. Marchetti decided on a flatter 25-degree included valve angle, and a larger bore and shorter stroke. To place the valve stems closer together required a redesign of the existing Desmoquattro rocker layout, locating opening rocker arms outwards, while keeping the closing rockers inside. The camshafts rotated directly in plain bearings in the cylinder head, while a central cast-steel sleeve was inserted for the smaller (10mm) spark plug, with the ignition coils incorporated on the top of each spark plug cap. The engine was called the Testastretta, because the cylinder head was narrower and slimmer.

The first model with the new Testastretta motor was the 2001 996 R. It was initially sold over the Internet.

The first Testastretta was the limited-production 996 R. With 40 and 33mm valves, higher-lift (11.7mm inlet and 10.1mm exhaust) camshaft, and more downdraft ports, the shorter-stroke engine was noticeably more powerful than the 996. The redesigned crankcases were sand-cast and incorporated a coppa bossa deep sump—a feature of the racing engines since 1998. In addition to the regular spin-on type oil filter, there was now a vertically mounted cylindrical gauze filter in the base of the sump. Also new was the 5.9 M Marelli electronic ignition and injection control unit, with a single, centrallypositioned, external raindrop spray-type injector per cylinder.

Initially the Testastretta engine was placed in the 996 SPS chassis as the 996 R. Most components were shared with the 996 SPS, although the front braking system was upgraded with thinner discs and four-pad Brembo front brake calipers with four 34mm pistons. The carbon-fiber fairing no longer incorporated side vents for a reduced drag coefficient. Most 996 R's were sold immediately over the Internet on its release on September 12, 2000, and all U.S. examples came without lights and stands, although the wiring remained in place.

The 998 Testastretta replaced the 996 Desmoquattro in the Superbike lineup for 2002. The crankcases were still the die-cast low sump, without the sump extension. With milder and lower-lift camshafts (10.15 and 9.1mm) the engine made less power than the 996 R. The 998cc 996 R motor now made its way into the 998 S for Europe, but not America. The 998 S for America included the base 998 engine. This year also saw a 999cc shorter stroke-engine for the 998 R. Apart from the engine, the 998

R was similar to the earlier 996 R, but the Marchesini wheels were lighter, and there was a carbon-fiber tailpiece without air intakes.

There were also two series of limited-edition 998s in addition to the 998 R for 2002: the Bostrom and Bayliss. Celebrating the two factory World Superbike riders, these were 998 S's, but with an Öhlins front fork and colors replicating the racers. The Bostrom was built in three series of 155 (his racing number), while the Bayliss was initially sold over the Internet. Although the 999 was released for 2003, the 998 continued, only as a standard version with the 123-horsepower engine. For 2004, the 998 was offered as a Final Edition and Matrix. Produced "on request," the 998 FE was a red Monoposto, and included the 136-horsepower Testastretta engine and Öhlins suspension front and rear. The Matrix , celebrating the use of the 998 in the movie Matrix Reloaded, was Biposto, with the 123-horsepower engine.

The 998 R for 2002 had a shorter-stroke 999cc Testastretta engine.

Ducati Motor

Ducati Motor

The 998 replaced the 996 for 2002. It was available as the 998, or higher-specification 998 S, shown here.

996 R, 998, R, S, Bostrom, Bayliss, FE, Matrix

Engine	Twin-cylinder four-stroke, liquid-cooled	**Spark plugs**	Champion RG4HC	**Width**	780mm (30.7 in.)	
Bore	100mm (998 R: 104 mm)	**Generator**	12v/520W	**Seat height**	790mm (31.1 in.)	
Stroke	63.5mm (998 R: 58.8mm)	**Battery**	12V/10Ah	**Dry weight**	996 R: 185 kg (407.5 lbs.)	
Displacement	998cc (998 R: 999cc)	**Primary drive**	1.84:1 (32/59)		998 R: 183 kg (403.1 lbs.)	
Compression ratio	11.4:1 (998 R: 12.3:1)	**Clutch**	Dry multiplate		Bostrom U.S.: 185 kg (407.5 lbs.)	
Valve actuation	Belt-driven desmodromic double overhead camshafts	**Gear ratios**	0.958, 1.043, 1.182, 1.40, 1.765, 2.466		998 S, Bostrom, Bayliss: 187 kg (411.9 lbs.)	
Valve timing (degrees)	996 R, 998 S: 16, 60, 60, 18 998: 4, 56, 53, 11	**Final drive**	2.4:1 (15/36)		998: 198 kg (436.1 lbs.)	
Injection	Weber Marelli CPU 5.9 M 54mm throttle bodies	**Front suspension**	996 R, 998 R, Bostrom, Bayliss: 43mm Öhlins 998 S: 43mm Showa	**Top speed**	998 R: 280 km/h (174 mph) 998 S: 270 km/h (167.8 mph)	
Power	996 R: 135 horsepower at 10,200 rpm 998 R: 139 horsepower at 10,200 rpm 998 S, FE: 136 horsepower at 10,200 rpm 998, 998 S U.S.)123 horsepower at 9,750 rpm	**Rear suspension**	Öhlins rising-rate mono swingarm	**Colors**	Red 473.101 (PPG) Yellow 473.201 (PPG) Matrix: Green 0030 (PPG)	
		Front brake	320mm dual disc (12.6 in.)	**Engine numbers**	From ZDM 998 A 2 000001	
		Rear brake	220mm disc (8.7 in.)	**Frame numbers**	996 R: From ZDM V1 00 AA 1B 000001 998 U.S.: From ZDM 1SB5V XB 000001	
		Tires	120/70 x 17, 190/50 x 17			
		Wheelbase	1,410mm (55.5 in.)			
		Length	2,030mm (79.9 in.)			
		Height	1,080mm (42.5 in.)			

Another limited edition 998 S of 2002 was the Bayliss, decked out in full Superbike replica colors.

PRODUCTION	1993	1994	1995	1996	1997	1998	1999	2000	2001	TOTAL
955 Racing 1995			60							60
955 Racing 1996				31						31
996 Racing 1997					20					20
996 Racing 1998						24				24
916 Monoposto 1994	4	1,443	3	1						1,451
916 S.P. 1994/95		310	401							711
916 S 1994 Monoposto		199								199
916 Biposto 1995		9	791							800
916 Biposto 1996			163	550						713
916 Sport Production 1996				497						497
916 Monoposto USA 1994/95		470	323							793
916 Monoposto USA 1996			120	80						200
916 Monoposto Cal. 1994/95		171	89							260
916 Monoposto Cal. 1996			80							80
916 Biposto Switz. 1994		120								120
916 Biposto Switz. 1995			220							220
916 Biposto Switz. 1996			30	70						100
916 Biposto Aus. 1994		65								65
916 Biposto Aus. 1995			85							85
916 Biposto Aus. 1996			50	50						100
916 Biposto Jpn. 1994		60								60
916 Biposto Jpn. 1995			68							68
916 Biposto Jpn. 1996			15	103						118
916 Biposto Ger. 1995			340							340
916 Biposto Ger. 1996			41	154						195
916 Biposto Eng. 1994		193								193
916 Biposto Eng. 1995			258							258
916 Biposto Eng. 1996			30	128						158

PRODUCTION	1993	1994	1995	1996	1997	1998	1999	2000	2001	TOTAL
916 Biposto France 1994	141									141
916 Biposto France 1995		360								360
916 Biposto France 1996		40	140							180
916 Senna Brazil 1995		31								31
916 Senna 1995	1	149								150
916 Senna Switz. 1995		10								10
916 Senna Jpn. 1995		35								35
916 Senna Ger. 1995		30								30
916 Senna Eng. 1995		15								15
916 Senna France 1995		30								30
916 Senna 1997				151						151
916 Senna Switz. 1997				20						20
916 Senna Jpn. 1997				70						70
916 Senna Ger. 1997				30						30
916 Senna Eng. 1997				30						30
916 Senna 1998				56	35					91
916 Senna Aus. 1998				34						34
916 Senna Jpn. 1998				41						41
916 Senna Ger. 1998				50						50
916 Senna Eng. 1998				70	14					84
916 Official Team 1994		14								14
955 Endurance 1995		2								2
916 Factory 1995		6								6
916 Factory 1996			6							6
916 Factory 1997				8						8
916 Factory 1998					18					18
996 Factory 1999						1				1
996 R 1999						6				6
996 R 2001 Testastretta Red Internet								2	189	191
996 R 2001 Testastretta Red									120	120

Production	1993	1994	1995	1996	1997	1998	1999	2000	2001	Total
998 R 2002 Testastretta Red Internet									5	5
996 RS 1999							11			11
916 S.P.A. 1996				54						54
916 S.P.S. 1997 996 Cc.				4	400					404
916 S.P.S. 1998					550	408				958
996 S.P.S. 1999						167	158			325
996 S.P.S. 2 1999							150			150
996 S.P.S. 2000							314	261		575
916 S.P.S. 1998 USA					50	50				100
996 S.P.S. 1999 USA Solo						56				56
996 S.P.S. 2000 USA							80			80
996 S.P.S. 1999 Aus.						38	13			51
996 S.P.S. 2000 Aus.							30	9		39
996 S.P.S. 1999 Jpn.						72	79			151
996 S.P.S. 2000 Jpn.							108	40		148
916 S.P.S. 1998 Fogarty Replica Eng.						202				202
996 S.P.S. 1999 Eng.							40			40
996 S.P.S. 2000 Eng.								80		80
996 S.P.S. 1999 France						15	20			35
996 S.P.S. 2000 France							20	30		50
916 Biposto 1997				240	853					1,093
916 Biposto 1998					311	634				945
916 Biposto 1998 Yellow					147	245				392
916 Monoposto Cal. 1997				189	111					300
916 Biposto Cal. 1997				34	216					250
916 Monoposto Cal. 1998					100	200				300
916 Monoposto Cal. 1998 Yellow					100					100
916 Biposto Cal. 1998					100					100
916 Biposto Cal. 1998 Yellow						100				100
916 Biposto Switz. 1997				60	140					200
916 Biposto Switz. 1998					22	28				50
916 Biposto Switz. 1998 Yellow						20				20
916 Biposto Aus. 1997				80	61					141
916 Biposto Aus. 1998					41	45				86
916 Biposto Aus. 1998 Yellow						22				22
916 Biposto Jpn. 1997					25					25
916 Monoposto Jpn. 1997				45	119					164
916 Biposto Jpn. 1998						12				12
916 Biposto Jpn. 1998 Yellow						6				6
916 Monoposto Jpn. 1998					16	14				30
916 Monoposto Jpn. 1998 Yellow						15				15
916 Biposto Ger. 1997				120	570					690
916 Biposto Ger. 1998						205				205
916 Biposto Ger. 1998 Yellow						45				45
916 Biposto Eng. 1997				120	460					580
916 Biposto Eng. 1998					114	121				235
916 Biposto Eng. 1998 Yellow					40	101				141

Production	1993	1994	1995	1996	1997	1998	1999	2000	2001	Total
916 Biposto France 1997				140	131					271
916 Monoposto France 1997					100					100
916 Biposto France 1998						80				80
916 Biposto France 1998 Yellow						27				27
916 Monoposto France 1998 Yellow						8				8
996 Biposto 1999						966	898			1,864
996 Biposto 1999 Yellow						190	402			592
996 Biposto 2000							1,060	706		1,766
996 Biposto 2000 Yellow							351	72		423
996 Biposto 2001								715	739	1,454
996 Biposto 2001 Yellow								176	145	321
998 Testastretta Biposto Red 2002									559	559
998 Testastretta Biposto Yellow 2002									90	90
996 Monoposto 2000							56	96		152
996 Monoposto 2000 Yellow							18	20		38
996 Monoposto 2001								52	80	132
996 Monoposto 2001 Yellow								16	20	36
998 Testastretta Monoposto Red 2002									57	57
998 Testastretta Monoposto Yellow 2002									11	11
996 Biposto USA - Cal. 1999						303	165			468
996 Biposto USA - Cal. 1999 Yellow						150	50			200
996 Biposto Cal. 2000							302	103		405
996 Biposto Cal. 2000 Yellow							150	208		358
996 Biposto Cal. 2001								250	46	296
996 Biposto Cal. 2001 Yellow								200	101	301
998 Testastretta Biposto Cal. Red 2002									233	233
998 Testastretta Biposto Cal. Yellow 2002									17	17
996 Monoposto Cal. 1999							125			125
996 Monoposto Cal. 1999 Yellow							75			75
996 Monoposto Cal. 2000							120	94		214
996 Monoposto Cal. 2000 Yellow							80	95		175
996 Monoposto Cal. 2001								150	120	270
996 Monoposto Cal. 2001 Yellow								100	75	175
998 Testastretta Monoposto Cal. Red 2002									100	100
998 Testastretta Monoposto Cal. Yellow 2002									75	75
996 R USA 2001 Testastretta Red									60	60
996 S USA 1999 Red						1				1
996 S Cal. 1999 Red							200			200
996 S 2001 Red								136	507	643
996 S 2001 Yellow								37	80	117
998 Testastretta S 2002 Red									163	163

PRODUCTION	1993	1994	1995	1996	1997	1998	1999	2000	2001	TOTAL
998 Testastretta S 2002 Yellow									1	1
996 S Monoposto 2001 Red								12	308	320
996 S Monoposto 2001 Yellow								1	50	51
998 Testastretta S Monop. 2002 Red									44	44
998 Testastretta S Monop. 2002 Red									17	17
996 S Cal. 2000 Red							200			200
996 S Cal. 2001 Red								180		180
996 S Aus. 2001 Red								8	22	30
996 S Aus. 2001 Yellow								7	8	15
998 Testastretta S Aus. 2002 Red									18	18
998 Testastretta S Aus. 2002 Yellow									5	5
998 Testastretta S Monop. Aus. 2002 Red									7	7
996 S Jpn. 2001 Red									7	7
996 S Jpn. 2001 Yellow									10	10
996 S Monoposto Jpn. 2001 Red								25	30	55
996 S Monoposto Jpn. 2001 Yellow								25	30	55
998 Testastretta S Monop. Jpn. 2002 Red									51	51
998 Testastretta S Monop. Jpn. 2002 Yellow									29	29
996 S Eng. 2001 Red								40	180	220
996 S Eng. 2001 Yellow								10	70	80
998 Testastretta S Eng. 2002 Red									46	46
996 Testastretta S Eng. 2002 Yellow									10	10
996 S Monoposto Eng. 2001 Red									15	15
996 S Monoposto Eng. 2001 Yellow									5	5
998 Testastretta S Monop. Eng. 2002 Red									10	10
996 S France 2001 Red									137	137
996 S France 2001 Yellow									11	11
998 Testastretta S France 2002 Red									35	35
998 Testastretta S Monop. France 2002 Red									2	2
996 Biposto Switz. 1999						60	70			130
996 Biposto Switz. 1999 Yellow						10	40			50
996 Biposto Switz. 2000							60	42		102
996 Biposto Aus. 1999						96	40			136
996 Biposto Aus. 1999 Yellow						22	27	26		75
996 Biposto Aus. 2000							40	48		88
996 Biposto Aus. 2000 Yellow								10		10
996 Biposto Aus. 2001							60	44		104
996 Biposto Aus. 2001 Yellow								19	15	34
998 Testastretta Biposto Aus. Red 2002									40	40
998 Testastretta Biposto Aus. Yellow 2002									5	5

PRODUCTION	1993	1994	1995	1996	1997	1998	1999	2000	2001	TOTAL
996 R Aus. 2001 Testastretta Red									40	40
996 Monoposto Jpn. 1999						132	32			164
996 Monoposto Jpn. 1999 Yellow						47	5			52
996 Monoposto Jpn. 2000							126	50		176
996 Monoposto Jpn. 2000 Yellow							36	5		41
996 Monoposto Jpn. 2001								80		80
996 Monoposto Jpn. 2001 Yellow								50		50
998 Testastretta Monoposto Jpn. Red 2002									45	45
998 Testastretta Monoposto Jpn. Yellow 2002									10	10
996 Biposto Jpn. 2000							14	6		20
996 Biposto Jpn. 2000 Yellow							6			6
996 Biposto Jpn. 2001								26	21	47
996 Biposto Jpn. 2001 Yellow								12	14	26
996 R Jpn. 2001 Testastretta Red Internet									113	113
996 R Jpn. 2001 Testastretta Red									50	50
996 Biposto Sng. 2000							5			5
996 Biposto Sng. 2000 Yellow							5			5
996 Biposto Eng. 1999						180	342			522
996 Biposto Eng. 1999 Yellow						80	40			120
996 Biposto Eng. 2000							100	115		215
996 Biposto Eng. 2000 Yellow							30	20		50
996 Biposto Eng. 2001								130		130
996 Biposto Eng. 2001 Yellow								30		30
998 Testastretta Biposto Eng. Red 2002									100	100
998 Testastretta Biposto Eng. Yellow 2002									14	14
996 R Eng. 2001 Testastretta Red Internet									56	56
996 R Eng. 2001 Testastretta Red									30	30
996 Monoposto Eng. 2000								20		20
996 Monoposto Eng. 2000 Yellow								20		20
996 Monoposto Eng. 2001									2	2
996 Monoposto Eng. 2001 Yellow									1	1
996 Biposto France 1999						90	135			225
996 Biposto France 1999 Yellow						30	29			59
996 Biposto France 2000							110	160		270
996 Biposto France 2000 Yellow							45	35		80
996 Biposto France 2001								75	97	172
996 Biposto France 2001 Yellow								5	33	38
998 Testastretta Biposto France Red 2002									88	88

Production	1993	1994	1995	1996	1997	1998	1999	2000	2001	Total
996 R France 2001 Testastretta Red Internet									13	13
996 R France 2001 Testastretta Red									25	25
996 Factory Replica 1999 Red							100			100
996 Factory Replica 2 2000 Red								147	2	149
996 Factory Replica 1999 France Red							20			20
996 Factory Replica 1999 Jpn. Red							20			20

Production	1993	1994	1995	1996	1997	1998	1999	2000	2001	Total
996 Factory Replica 1999 Aus. Red							10			10
998 Strada 2000							3	8		11
998 Testastretta Bostrom Cal. 2002									155	155
998 Testastretta Bostrom 2002									1	1
Total	4	3,196	3,875	2,896	5,281	5,460	6,929	5,000	5,762	38,403

748 Strada, Biposto, SP, SPS, S, R (1995-2002)

The 748 Biposto of 1995 was visually similar to the 916, but the power characteristics were quite different.

Because the Desmoquattro started its life as a 748, and the cylinder heads were designed around a smaller bore, it wasn't surprising to see the 748 introduced for 1995. There were initially three versions: the Strada, Biposto, and Sport Production. The 748 SP was a homologation machine for the expanding Supersport racing category in Europe, where the 748cc twin could compete against 600cc four-cylinder machines.

The engine dimensions were the same as the earlier 748 (and all other Pantah 750s), but were based on the larger crankcase six-speed engine. The 33 and 29mm valves were shared with the 916, as was the single-injector 1.6 M, although the throttle body was reduced in line with Supersport regulations. The crankshaft featured regular Macchi forged con-rods with a lighter flywheel, and the gearbox was the closer-ratio model of the 888 SP. The power characteristics were quite different than the 916; the 748 needed to be revved harder. The chassis was identical to the 916, but there was a lower-profile front tire and a narrower (5/8 x 1/4-inch) drive chain. Many believed the combination of less internal reciprocating engine weight,

The 1999 748 Biposto was little changed from the 1995 version.

SP. The SPS was almost identical in specification to the SP and also proved relatively unsuccessful. A silver limited edition 748L was produced for the U.S. and sold through the Neiman Marcus mail order catalog of men's accessories. The 748 wasn't particularly popular in America, but in Europe it accounted for nearly 40 percent of Desmoquattro sales in 1998. 1999 updates mirrored those of the 996, and the 748 lineup included three versions for 2000.

At the bottom of the range was the 748 Economy, featuring a frame without adjustable caster, chrome-plated fork legs, three-spoke Brembo wheels, and a Sachs-Boge shock absorber. Filling out the 748 lineup for 2000 was the 748 S, which was essentially the 1999 748 with

For 2000, a basic economy 748 was offered, with a less-sophisticated chassis.

a lower profile front, and narrower rear tire, provided superior steering and handling to the 916.

Alongside the 748 Strada and Biposto was the striking yellow 748 Sport Production. Apart from new camshafts, the 748 SP engine was very similar to the 748 Strada and Biposto. The con-rods were steel Pankl, and there was an external oil cooler. The 748 SP chassis was similar to the 916 SP, with an aluminum rear subframe, an Öhlins rear shock absorber, and fully floating cast-iron front discs. The 748 SP continued for two more years, but wasn't especially popular.

There were few changes to the 748 Biposto for 1996, 1997, and 1998, and this year the 748 SPS replaced the

Joining the 748 Biposto were the slightly higher-performance 748 SP and SPS. This is the 1998 748 SPS.

five-spoke Marchesini wheels and gold TiN-coated fork legs. There were only detail updates to the 748 for 2001. The 748 Economy now had a "gun metal gray" frame and wheels, and for 2002 the 748 was the only Ducati Superbike to retain the earlier Desmoquattro engine. All 748s now sported the smoother fairing (from the 2001 996 R) and slightly revised decals.

The 748 S for 2002 was available in titanium gray with red wheels.

Ducati Motor

748 R (2000-02)

The 748 R for 2000 incorporated many features previously reserved for racing-only machines.

Replacing the 748 SPS as a Supersport homologation machine for 2000 was the considerably higher-specification 748 R. This featured the Superbike racing frame that allowed for a larger, 14-liter, airbox and throttle body, with a single "shower" injector above the butterflies. The engine was based on the 996, with 36 and 30mm valves. The timing belts were wider (19mm, up from 17mm), and the camshafts were shorter duration and higher lift (12.5 and 10.5mm) than other Desmoquattros. There was also a racing slipper clutch. The chassis was similar to the 748 S, including the rather low-spec Showa shock absorber.

For 2001, there were a few updates to the 748 R. Included was a carbon-fiber airbox, a lighter frame, and Öhlins suspension as on the 996 SPS. The brakes were improved, and while European specification models received a Boge steering damper, U.S. versions featured an Öhlins unit. The 748 R continued unchanged for 2002, but for the new fairing and revised decals.

The 748 R of 2001 included higher-specification Öhlins suspension, but was otherwise unchanged.

748 STRADA, BIPOSTO, SP, SPS, S, ECONOMY, R 1995-2002

Engine	Twin cylinder four-stroke, liquid-cooled	**Battery**	1995-2000: 12v/16Ah 2001-02 12v/10Ah	**Width**	1995-96: 685mm (27 in.) 1997-2002: 780mm (30.7 in.)
Bore	88mm	**Primary drive**	2:1 (31/62)	**Seat height**	790mm (31.1 in.)
Stroke	61.5mm	**Clutch**	Dry multiplate		
Displacement	748cc	**Gear ratios**	0.958, 1.043, 1.182, 1.40, 1.765, 2.466	**Dry weight**	Strada: 200 kg (440.5 lbs.) Biposto: 202 kg (444.9 lbs.) SP: 198 kg (436.1 lbs.) SPS: 194 kg (427.3 lbs.) Economy: 196 kg (431.7 lbs.) 748 R: 192 kg (422.9 lbs.)
Compression ratio	11.5:1 (SP, SPS: 11.6:1)	**Final drive**	2.71:1 (14/38) SP, SPS: 2.64: 1 (14/37)		
Valve actuation	Belt-driven desmodromic double overhead camshafts	**Front suspension**	1995-97: 43mm Showa GD051 1998-2002: Showa GD131 748 R (2000-02): 43mm Öhlins		
Valve timing (degrees)	Strada, Bipestso, Economy: 11, 70, 62, 18 SP: 44, 72, 77, 42 SPS: 44, 72, 74, 44 R: 20, 60, 62, 38			**Top speed**	Strada, Biposto, Economy: 240 km/h (149.1 mph) SP, SPS: 250 km/h (155.4 mph) 748 R: 255 km/h (158.5 mph)
		Rear suspension	Showa GD052-007-02 rising rate mono swingarm Showa GD052-007-50 (Biposto) Öhlins DU 3420 (SP, SPS, 748R from 2000) Sachs-Boge (Economy)		
Injection	Weber I.A.W. CPU 1.6M (44mm throttle bodies, (2000-02: 50mm (R: 54mm)			**Colors**	Red 473.101 Yellow 473.201 748 S: Titanium Gray 0017 (PPG)
		Front brake	320mm dual disc (12.6 in.)		
Power	Strada, Bipesto, Economy (1995-1999): 98 horsepower at 11,000 rpm 2000-2002: 97 horsepower at 11,000 rpm SP, SPS: 104 horsepower at 11,000 rpm 748 R: 106 horsepower at 11,000 rpm	**Rear brake**	220mm disc (8.7 in.)	**Engine numbers**	From ZDM 748 W4 000001 748 R: From ZDM 748 R 4 000001
		Tires	120/60 x 17, 180/55 x 17		
		Wheelbase	1,410mm (55.5 in.)	**Frame numbers**	From ZDM 748 S 000001 1997-02: From ZDM 748 S B 000001 (from 1997) 748 R: From ZDM 748 R 0B 000001 U.S. (1995-01): From ZDM 1HB7RHPB 000001 U.S. (2002): From ZDM 1SB3RXB 000001
		Length	1995-96: 2,050mm (80.7 in.) 1997-02: 2,030mm (79.9 in.)		
Spark plugs	Champion RA59GC (SP, SPS: A55V)				
Generator	1995-1998: 12v/350W 1999-02: 12v/520W	**Height**	1995-96: 1,090mm (42.9 in.) 1997-2002: 1,080mm (42.5 in.)		

748 Racing and Racing Special (1998-2001)

From 1998, the 748 Racing was available in limited quantities, but never achieved the success of the 996 Racing.

Sport Touring

748 RACING AND RACING SPECIAL

Engine	Twin cylinder four-stroke, liquid-cooled
Bore	88mm
Stroke	61.5mm
Displacement	748cc
Compression ratio	R: 11.6:1 RS: 12:1
Valve actuation	Belt-driven desmodromic double overhead camshafts
Valve timing (degrees)	R: 44, 72, 77, 42 RS: 30, 58, 74, 38
Injection	Marelli 1.6M electronic injection
Power	R: 108 horsepower at 11,500 rpm RS: 124 horsepower at 12,000 rpm

Spark plugs	R: Champion RA 59GC RS: QA55V
Generator	R: 12v/180W RS: 12v/280W
Battery	12V/4Ah Yuasa YT4L-BS
Primary drive	2:1 (31/62)
Clutch	Dry multiplate
Gear ratios	1.00, 1.091, 1.19, 1.35, 1.61, 2.0
Final drive	R: 2.64:1 (14/37) RS: 2.53:1 (15/38)
Front suspension	Showa 43mm fork
Rear suspension	Öhlins rising-rate mono swingarm
Front brake	320mm dual disc (12.6 in.)

Rear brake	220mm (8.7 in.)
Tires	120/60 x 17, 180/55 x 17
Wheelbase	R: 1,410mm (55.5 in.) RS: 1,415mm (55.7 in.)
Length	R: 2,030mm (79.9 in.) RS: 2,035mm (80.1 in.)
Height	1,080mm (42.5 in.)
Width	R: 685mm (27 in.) RS: 680mm (26.8 in.)
Seat height	R: 790mm (31.1 in.) RS: 830mm (32.7 in.)
Dry weight	R: 170 kg (374.4 lbs.) RS: 172 kg (378.9 lbs.)

A limited number of 748 Racing machines were also available from 1998 for selected teams in Supersport racing. World Supersport regulations limited modifications, and the 748 Racing retained the single injector Marelli 1.6 M CPU, but included a 916 Racing gearbox. More latitude was allowed in the modification of the chassis, and this included complete carbon-fiber bodywork, sump guard, chain guard and mufflers, front dashboard and electronic control unit mount. The 748 Racing continued for 1999, but results were disappointing, leading to the higher-specification 748 RS (Racing Special) being produced for 2000. Based on the production 748 R, the RS featured an injection system similar to that of the 996 Factory racer, with a single injector placed above the throttle valve. There were new camshafts and a 54mm racing titanium Termignoni exhaust system. Although Ducati Corse appeared to lose interest in pursuing the World Supersport Championship, the 748 RS was produced for 2001. Apart from the updated Öhlins forks and Brembo brakes, these were ostensibly identical to the previous year.

PRODUCTION	1994	1995	1996	1997	1998	1999	2000	2001	TOTAL
748 Biposto 1995	3	844							847
748 Biposto 1996		307	420						727
748 Biposto 1997			199	786					985
748 Biposto 1997 Yellow				44					44
748 Biposto 1998 Red					200	310			510
748 Biposto 1998 Yellow					200	207			407
748 Biposto 1999 Red						532	171		703
748 Biposto 1999 Yellow						341	97		438
748 Economy 2000 Red						430	842		1,272
748 Economy 2000 Yellow						223	430		653
748 Economy 2001 Red							786	456	1,242
748 Economy 2001 Yellow							386	228	614
748 Economy 2002 Red								244	244
748 Economy 2002 Yellow								52	52
748 Economy Monoposto 2000 Yellow							17		17
748 Biposto Cal. 1997			240						240
748 Biposto USA - Cal. 1999 Red						100			100
748 Biposto USA - Cal. 1999 Yellow					282	28			310
748 Monoposto USA - Cal. 1999 Red						100			100
748 Monoposto USA - Cal. 1999 Yellow					118	72			190
748 Biposto Cal. 1998 Red				90	50				140
748 Biposto Cal. 1998 Yellow				60	150				210
748 Biposto Cal. 1998 Silver				102					102
748 Monoposto Cal. 1998 Red					100				100
748 Monoposto Cal. 1998 Yellow				220	100				320
748 Economy Cal. 2000 Red						80	170		250
748 Economy Cal. 2000 Yellow						170	182		352
748 Economy Cal. 2001 Red							163	119	282
748 Economy Cal. 2001 Yellow							125	210	335
748 Economy Cal. 2002 Red								166	166
748 Economy Cal. 2002 Yellow								170	170
748 Econ. Monoposto Cal. 2000 Yellow						150	50		200
748 Econ. Monoposto Cal. 2000 Red							125		125
748 Econ. Monoposto Cal. 2001 Yellow							75	110	185
748 Econ. Monoposto Cal. 2001 Red							100	75	175
748 Econ. Monoposto Cal. 2002 Yellow								50	50
748 Econ. Monoposto Cal. 2002 Red								50	50

PRODUCTION	1994	1995	1996	1997	1998	1999	2000	2001	TOTAL
748 Biposto Switz. 1995		61							61
748 Biposto Switz. 1996		30							30
748 Biposto Switz. 1997				40					40
748 Biposto Switz. 1998					10				10
748 Biposto Switz. 1999 Red					5	10			15
748 Biposto Switz. 1999 Yellow					5	5			10
748 Economy Switz. 2000 Red						5			5
748 Economy Switz. 2000 Yellow						5	5		10
748 Biposto Aus. 1995		20							20
748 Biposto Aus. 1996		31	15						46
748 Biposto Aus. 1997			25	51					76
748 Biposto Aus. 1998				19	4				23
748 Biposto Aus. 1999 Red					34				34
748 Biposto Aus. 1999 Yellow					10	6			16
748 Economy Aus. 2000 Red						33	36		69
748 Economy Aus. 2000 Yellow						12	24		36
748 Economy Aus. 2001 Red							32	24	56
748 Economy Aus. 2001 Yellow							13	17	30
748 Economy Aus. 2002 Red								46	46
748 Economy Aus. 2002 Yellow								20	20
748 Biposto Jpn. 1996		10							10
748 Biposto Jpn. 1998 Red				5	11				16
748 Biposto Jpn. 1998 Yellow					8				8
748 Monoposto Jpn. 1998				5					5
748 Economy Jpn. 2000 Red						32			32
748 Economy Jpn. 2001 Red							64	5	69
748 Economy Jpn. 2001 Yellow							40	5	45
748 Economy Jpn. 2002 Yellow								10	10
748 Econ. Monoposto Jpn. 2000 Red						28			28
748 Econ. Monoposto Jpn. 2000 Yellow						12	18		30
748 Econ. Monoposto Jpn. 2001 Red							40		40
748 Econ. Monoposto Jpn. 2001 Yellow							30		30
748 Econ. Monoposto Jpn. 2002 Red								25	25
748 Econ. Monoposto Jpn. 2002 Yellow								15	15
748 Biposto Ger. 1995		210							210
748 Biposto Ger. 1996		80	80						160
748 Biposto Ger. 1997			60	245					305
748 Biposto Ger. 1998 Red					120				120
748 Biposto Ger. 1998 Yellow					45				45

PRODUCTION	1994	1995	1996	1997	1998	1999	2000	2001	TOTAL
748 Biposto Eng. 1995		145							145
748 Biposto Eng. 1996		60	45						105
748 Biposto Eng. 1997			40	220					260
748 Biposto Eng. 1997 Yellow				40					40
748 Biposto Eng. 1998				60	195				255
748 Biposto Eng. 1998 Yellow				41	125				166
748 Biposto Eng. 1999					36	189			225
748 Biposto Eng. 1999 Yellow					45	20			65
748 Economy Eng. 2000 Red						30	150		180
748 Economy Eng. 2000 Yellow						10	75		85
748 Economy Eng. 2001 Red							256	60	316
748 Economy Eng. 2001 Yellow							50	30	80
748 Economy Eng. 2002 Red								60	60
748 Economy Eng. Monoposto 2000 Yellow							15		15
748 S.P. 1995	1	600							601
748 S.P. 1996			400						400
748 S.P. 1997				305					305
748 S.P.S. 1998				88	267				355
748 S.P.S. 1999					152				152
748 S.P.S. 2000						3			3
748 S.P.S. Aus. 1998				14	30				44
748 S.P.S. Aus. 1999					11				11
748 S.P.S. Jpn. 1998				28	33				61
748 S.P.S. Jpn. 1999					18				18
748 S.P.S. Ger. 1998				30					30
748 S.P.S. Eng. 1998				40	40				80
748 S.P.S. Eng. 1999					20				20
748 Monoposto Fra. 1995		120							120
748 Monoposto Fra. 1996		40	30						70
748 Monoposto USA 1997			6						6
748 Monoposto Cal. 1997 Yellow				190					190
748 S Monoposto Cal. 2001 Red							75	69	144
748 S Monoposto Cal. 2001 Yellow							125	147	272
748 S Monoposto Cal. 2002 Gray Opaque								200	200
748 S Monoposto 1997 Red				25					25
748 S Monoposto 1997 Yellow				10					10
748 S Monoposto Ger. 1997 Red				32					32
748 S Monoposto Ger. 1997 Yellow				3					3
748 S Monoposto Eng. 1997 Red				20					20
748 S Monoposto Eng. 1997 Yellow				10					10
748 S Monoposto 2000 Red						2	65		67
748 S Monoposto 2000 Yellow						4	25		29
748 S Monoposto 2001 Red							21		21
748 S Monoposto 2001 Yellow							5		5
748 S Monoposto Jpn. 2001 Red							20		20
748 S Monoposto Jpn. 2001 Yellow							30		30
748 S Monoposto Jpn. 2002 Red								15	15
748 S Monoposto Jpn. 2002 Yellow								10	10
748 S Monoposto Jpn. 2002 Gray Opaque								25	25
748 S Monoposto Eng. 2000 Red							20		20
748 S Monoposto Eng. 2000 Yellow							10		10
748 S 2000 Red						3	420		423
748 S 2000 Yellow						1	255		256
748 S 2001 Red							387	40	427
748 S 2001 Yellow							359	40	399
748 S 2002 Red								60	60
748 S 2002 Gray Opaque								116	116
748 S Cal. 2000 Red							200		200
748 S Cal. 2000 Yellow							100		100
748 S Cal. 2001 Red							1		1
748 S Jpn. 2001 Red							1	5	6
748 S Jpn. 2001 Yellow								5	5
748 S Eng. 2000 Red							30		30
748 S Eng. 2000 Yellow							45		45
748 S Eng. 2001 Red							65		65
748 S Eng. 2001 Yellow							35		35
748 S Eng. 2002 Red								35	35
748 S Eng. 2002 Yellow								5	5
748 S Eng. 2002 Gray Opaque								30	30
748 R 2000 Yellow						139	551		690
748 R 2001 Red							136	259	395
748 R 2001 Yellow							106	67	173
748 R 2002 Red								177	177
748 R 2002 Yellow								89	89
748 R Eng. 2000 Yellow							150		150
748 R Eng. 2001 Red								60	60
748 R Eng. 2001 Yellow						1	20		21
748 R Eng. 2002 Red								64	64
748 R Eng. 2002 Yellow								15	15
748 R USA 2000 Yellow							70		70
748 R USA 2001 Yellow								100	100
748 R USA 2002 Yellow								15	15
748 R Aus. 2000 Yellow							12		12
748 R Aus. 2001 Red							15		15
748 R Aus. 2001 Yellow							20		20
748 R Aus. 2002 Red								10	10
748 R Aus. 2002 Yellow								12	12
748 R Jpn. 2000 Yellow						20	54		74
748 R Jpn. 2001 Red							12	71	83
748 R Jpn. 2001 Yellow							14	131	145
748 R Jpn. 2002 Red								50	50
748 R Jpn. 2002 Yellow								170	170
748 RACING 1998				20					20
748 RACING 1999					17	1			18
748 RACING 2000						37	15		52
748 RACING 2001							42		42
Total	4	2,558	1,560	3,243	3,431	2,228	7,791	4,359	25,174

CHAPTER 11

SPORT TOURING AND MULTISTRADA

Soon after TPG acquired control of Ducati, it added an additional family line to broaden the appeal of Ducati. This was the Sport Touring range, later expanded to include the Multistrada. The first Sport Touring though, the ST2, was a remnant of the Cagiva era, and styled by Miguel Galluzzi.

ST2

Two Wheels

The ST2 of 1997 initiated a new family of sport touring Ducatis that continues today.

While continuing where the 906 and 907 I.E. left off, the ST2 was more conventional in execution. The 944cc water-cooled two-valve engine (43 and 38mm valves) was an evolution of the previous 906 unit, with a higher primary drive ratio and a Marelli 1.6 M CPU. All the instruments and switches were new and, along with traditional analog instrumentation, there was a digital display indicating fuel consumption, fuel reserve, water temperature, and a clock. The frame was based on the 900 Monster rather than the Paso, with a steel swingarm and 916-style rear suspension linkage with adjustable ride height. The Showa suspension included an upside-down fork with wider mounts for the brake calipers, and the level of equipment was higher than earlier sport touring Ducatis. Side panniers were a factory option. To accommodate them, the mufflers could be lowered.

As the ST2 went into production during 1997, there were only a few changes for 1998. Apart from new graphics, there were improved brakes (shared with the new 900 Supersport). Updates for 1999 included lighter wheels, and the rear Brembo P 32 brake caliper upgraded to a P 34 (with 34mm pistons). The gradual refinement of the ST2 continued for 2000, with the elimination of the annoying automatically retracting sidestand, and a Kryptonite anti-theft padlock housed under the seat. An additional water passage was added near the exhaust valve for 2002. The ST2 entered 2003, its final year, unchanged.

ST2 1997-2003

Engine	Twin cylinder four-stroke, liquid-cooled	**Battery**	1997-2000: 12v/16Ah	**Length**	2,070mm (81.5 in.)
			2001-2003: 12v/10Ah	**Height**	1,320mm (52 in.)
Bore	94mm	**Primary drive**	1.84:1 (32/59)	**Width**	910mm (35.8 in.)
Stroke	68mm	**Clutch**	Dry multiplate	**Seat height**	820mm (32.3 in.)
Displacement	944cc	**Gear ratios**	0.857, 0.958, 1.091, 1.35, 1.765, 2.466	**Dry weight**	209 kg (460.4 lbs.)
Compression ratio	10.2:1	**Final drive**	2.80:1 (15/42)	**Top speed**	215 km/h (133.6 mph)
Valve actuation	Belt-driven desmodromic single overhead camshaft	**Front suspension**	43mm Showa GD081	**Colors**	Red 473.101
					Blue 291.800
Valve timing (degrees)	26, 72, 61, 34	**Rear suspension**	Showa GD082 rising rate swingarm		Gray 291.601
			Sachs Boge (from 2001)		Yellow 473.201
Injection	Marelli 1.6 M (45mm throttle body)	**Front brake**	320mm dual disc (12.6 in.)	**Engine numbers**	From ZDM 944 W2 000001
Power	83 horsepower at 8,500 rpm	**Rear brake**	245mm disc (9.6 in.)	**Frame numbers**	From ZDM S1 00AA 7 B 000001
Spark plugs	Champion RA 4 HC	**Tires**	120/70 x 17, 170/60 x 17		From ZDM 1TB9P WB 000001 (USA)
Generator	1997-98: 12v/420W	**Wheelbase**	1,430mm (56.3 in.)		
	1999-03: 12v/520W				

ST4

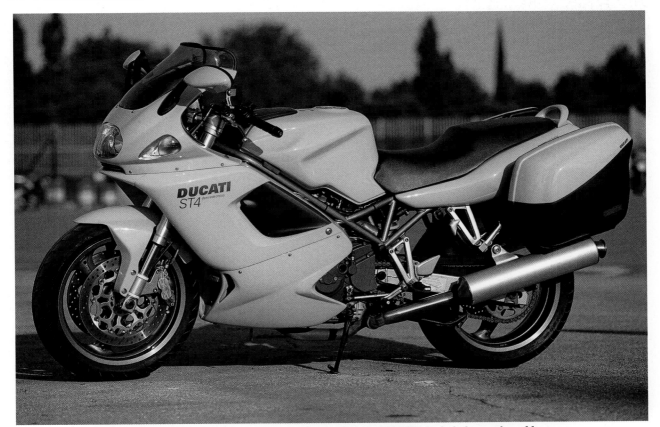

Although early ST4s looked almost identical to the ST2, the 2000 ST4 included a number of features to set it apart.

With the evolution of the 916 into the 996 for 1999, the 916cc engine made its way into the ST4. The ST4 was an amalgam of the Desmoquattro engine in the ST2 chassis, with the front cylinder head shortened to maintain adequate front wheel clearance. The exhaust camshaft was moved 10mm closer to the center of the engine. Otherwise the engine specifications were identical to the 916, with the same valve sizes, camshafts, clutch and gearbox. Unlike the 916, the ST had a separate airbox, and a similar exhaust system to the ST2. The Desmoquattro engine was noticeably smoother and more responsive than that of the ST2. The chassis was virtually identical to the ST2, and it was difficult to tell the early models apart. To overcome this there were revised decals for 2000, and a

number of chassis improvements on the ST4. The front brake disc rotors were thicker, and the brake lines were stainless steel. Further distinguishing the two models was the "gun metal gray" frame and wheels on the ST4. The ST2 retained the earlier bronze frame and wheels.

With the release of the higher-performance ST4S for 2001, the ST4 remained virtually unchanged. Engine updates included larger (12mm) engine mounts, while the rear shock absorber was now a Sachs-Boge. There were only minimal updates for 2002, with an aluminum clutch instead of steel, and for 2003 there was a revised shifting drum. This was the final year for the 916cc ST4.

ST4S

The ST4S was powered by the 996cc Desmoquattro motor, and included higher-quality chassis components. There were few differences between the 2001 and this 2003 example.

The 996cc Desmoquattro engine finally made it to the Sport Touring range for 2001. The Desmoquattro power unit, still with the ST4 lowered exhaust camshaft, was re-tuned to provide power midway between the 996 and the 996 S. The valve sizes were 36 and 30mm, and the injection was the new Marelli 5.9 M system that fired twin injectors simultaneously, like the 996. The chassis was almost identical to the ST4, except for an aluminum swingarm, a Showa fork with TiN-coated legs, and an

Öhlins rear shock absorber with a hydraulically operated remote spring pre-load adjuster. Completing the chassis improvement were lighter five-spoke Marchesini wheels. ABS was available on the ST4S for 2003, but the most significant updates were for 2004. A new taller fairing included a double curved headlight, and there was a fully electronic instrument panel. The handlebars were height adjustable, and there was a new seat. Updates for 2005 incuded a wet clutch and improved fairing fasteners.

Ducati Motor

ABS was an option on the ST4S from 2003, and for 2004 there was a new fairing.

ST4, ST4S (1999-)

Engine	Twin cylinder four-stroke, liquid-cooled	**Clutch**	Dry multiplate	**Width**	910mm (35.8 in.)	
Bore	ST4: 94mm ST4S: 98mm	**Gear ratios**	0.857, 0.958, 1.091, 1.35, 1.765, 2.466	**Seat height**	820mm (32.3 in.)	
Stroke	66mm	**Final drive**	ST4: ST4S: 2.53:1 (15/38)	**Dry weight**	ST4: 215 kg (473.6 lbs.) ST4S: 212 kg (467 lbs.) ST4S ABS: 217 kg (478 lbs.)	
Displacement	ST4: 916cc ST4S: 996cc	**Front suspension**	43mm Showa GD081			
Compression ratio	ST4: 11:1 ST4S: 11.5:1	**Rear suspension**	ST4 (1999-2000): Showa GD082 rising-rate swingarm ST4 (2001-04): Sachs Boge ST4S: Öhlins	**Top speed**	ST4: 245 km/h (152.2 mph) ST4S: 255 km/h (158.5 mph)	
Valve timing (degrees)	ST4: 11, 70, 62, 18 ST4S: 11, 61, 62, 18			**Colors**	Red 473.101 Blue 291.800 Yellow 473.201 ST4S: Iron gray 291.600 ST4S: Met. dark gray 653.6047	
Injection	ST4: Marelli 1.6 M (50mm throttle body) ST4S: 5.9 M	**Front brake**	320mm dual disc (12.6 in.)			
		Rear brake	245mm disc (9.6 in.)			
Power	ST4: 107 horsepower at 9,000 rpm ST4S: 117 horsepower at 8,750 rpm	**Tires**	ST4 (1999): 120/70 x 17, 170/60 x 17 ST4: (2000-04): 180/55 ZR17 ST4S: 190/50 x 17	**Engine numbers**	ST4: From ZDM 916W 4 000001	
Spark plugs	Champion RA59GC			**Frame numbers**	ST4: From ZDM S1 00A 9B 000001 ST4 U.S.: From ZDM 1TB8S XB 000001 ST4S: U.S.: From ZDM 1TB5T 3B 000001	
Generator	12v/520W	**Wheelbase**	1,430mm (56.3 in.)			
Battery	1999-2000: 12v/16Ah 10Ah from 2001-04: 12v/10Ah	**Length**	2,070mm (81.5 in.)			
Primary drive	1.84 (32/59)	**Height**	1999-2003: 1,180mm (46.5 in.) 2004: 1,274mm (50.2 in.)			

916 ST2

Production	1995	1996	1997	1998	1999	2000	2001	Total
Eng. 2000 Blue						20		20
Eng. 2000 Gray						10		10
Eng. 2000 Red					10	20		30
Eng. 2001 Blue							4	4
Eng. 2001 Gray							4	4
Eng. 2001 Red							35	35
Eng. 2001 Yellow							18	18
Eng. 2002 Red							10	10

916 ST4

Production	1995	1996	1997	1998	1999	2000	2001	Total
1996/97 - 1999 Red	3	1	3	365	526			898
1999 Black				15	84			99
1999 Blue				256	195			451
1999 Gray				19	127			146
2000 Blue					41	113		154
2000 Red					166	327		493
2000 Yellow					118	73		191
2001 Blue						28	89	117
2001 Red						123	77	200
2001 Yellow						257		257
2002 Blue							16	16
2002 Red							98	98
2002 Yellow							10	10
Aus. 1999 Black				14	14			28
Aus. 1999 Blue				7	12			19
Aus. 1999 Gray				13	11			24
Aus. 1999 Red				66	25			91
Aus. 2000 Blue					27			27
Aus. 2000 Red					15	13		28
Aus. 2000 Yellow					17	4		21
Aus. 2001 Blue						14		14
Aus. 2001 Red						17	11	28
Aus. 2001 Yellow						15	10	25
Aus. 2002 Red							10	10
Aus. 2002 Yellow							2	2
Cal. 2000 Red					150			150
Cal. 2000 Yellow					99	100		199
Cal. 2001 Blue						100		100
Cal. 2001 Red						95	61	156
Cal. 2001 Yellow						93	60	153
Eng. 1999 Blue				40	45			85
Eng. 1999 Red				60	162			222
Eng. 2000 Red						50		50
Eng. 2000 Yellow						20		20
Eng. 2001 Blue						5	5	10
Eng. 2001 Red						15	20	35
Eng. 2001 Yellow						20	5	25
Eng. 2002 Red							15	15
Eng. 2002 Yellow							5	5
Jpn. 2000 Blue					5			5
Jpn. 2000 Red					5	10		15
Jpn. 2000 Yellow					3			3
Jpn. 2001 Blue						10	3	13
Jpn. 2001 Red						28	8	36
Jpn. 2001 Yellow						27	7	34
Jpn. 2002 Blue							10	10
Jpn. 2002 Red							24	24
Jpn. 2002 Yellow							30	30
Sng. 2000 Blue					3			3
Sng. 2000 Red					2			2
Switz. 1999 Black					10			10
Switz. 1999 Red				10	10			20
Switz. 2000 Blue						5		5
Switz. 2000 Red					20			20
Switz. 2000 Yellow					10			10
USA 1999 Black				72				72
USA 1999 Red				428				428

944 ST2

Production	1995	1996	1997	1998	1999	2000	2001	Total
1996		4	4					8
1997 Black		364						364
1997 Gray		875						875
1997 Red		918						918
1998 Black		63	135					198
1998 Blue			2					2
1998 Gray		94	251					345
1998 Red		186	408					594
1999 Black				50				50
1999 Blue			2	100				102
1999 Gray			2	50				52
1999 Red			18	378				396
2000 Blue				77	137			214
2000 Gray				43	126			169
2000 Red				280	198			478
2001 Blue					9	90		99
2001 Gray						60		60
2001 Red					184	97		281
2001 Yellow						60	91	151
2002 Blue							85	85
2002 Gray							47	47
2002 Red							157	157
2002 Yellow							40	40
Aus. 1997 Black		26						26
Aus. 1997 Gray		56						56
Aus. 1997 Red		83						83
Aus. 1998 Black		13	17					30
Aus. 1998 Gray		14	12					26
Aus. 1998 Red		34	39					73
Aus. 1999 Black				12				12
Aus. 1999 Gray				12				12
Aus. 1999 Red				20				20
Aus. 2000 Blue				6	12			18
Aus. 2000 Gray				2	4			6
Aus. 2000 Red				17	10			27
Aus. 2001 Blue					2			2
Aus. 2001 Gray					2	6		8
Aus. 2001 Red					6	10		16
Aus. 2001 Yellow						20		20
Aus. 2002 Red							35	35

PRODUCTION	1995	1996	1997	1998	1999	2000	2001	TOTAL
Aus. 2002 Yellow							8	8
Aus. Ex - 1998 Red				30				30
Cal. 1998 Black			75					75
Cal. 1998 Gray			125					125
Cal. 1999 Gray					30			30
Cal. 1999 Red					170			170
Cal. 2000 Blue					100	20		120
Cal. 2000 Red					180	1		181
Cal. 2001 Blue						100		100
Cal. 2001 Red						100		100
Cal. 2001 Yellow						100		100
Cal. 2002 Blue							55	55
Cal. 2002 Red							54	54
Cal. 2002 Yellow							65	65
Eng. 1997 Gray			134					134
Eng. 1997 Red			230					230
Eng. 1998 Black			76					76
Eng. 1998 Gray			35					35
Eng. 1998 Red			90	40				130
Ex - 1998 Red				40				40
Jpn. 1997 Black			23					23
Jpn. 1997 Gray			54					54
Jpn. 1997 Red			52					52
Jpn. 1998 Black			1	4				5
Jpn. 1998 Gray			32					32
Jpn. 1998 Red			19	2				21
Jpn. 2000 Blue					5			5
Jpn. 2000 Gray					5			5
Jpn. 2000 Red						2		2
Jpn. 2001 Blue						11	19	30
Jpn. 2001 Gray						11	15	26
Jpn. 2001 Red						26	35	61
Jpn. 2001 Yellow							2	2
Jpn. 2002 Blue							55	55
Jpn. 2002 Gray							45	45
Jpn. 2002 Red							73	73
Switz. 1998 Black			15	23				38
Switz. 1998 Gray			15	39				54
Switz. 1998 Red			10	65				75
Switz. 1999 Blue					5			5

PRODUCTION	1995	1996	1997	1998	1999	2000	2001	TOTAL
Switz. 2000 Blue						5		5
Switz. 2000 Red						20		20
USA 1998 Black			150					150
USA 1998 Gray			450					450
996 ST4 S								
2001 Gray							360	360
2001 Red						2	230	232
2001 Yellow							20	20
2002 Gray							108	108
2002 Red							109	109
2002 Yellow							38	38
Aus. 2001 Gray							5	5
Aus. 2001 Red							19	19
Aus. 2001 Yellow							9	9
Aus. 2002 Gray							2	2
Aus. 2002 Red							33	33
Aus. 2002 Yellow							15	15
Cal. 2002 Gray							200	200
Cal. 2002 Red							100	100
Eng. 2001 Gray							55	55
Eng. 2001 Red							50	50
Eng. 2001 Yellow							25	25
Eng. 2002 Gray							26	26
Eng. 2002 Red							87	87
Eng. 2002 Yellow							14	14
Fra. 2001 Gray							98	98
Fra. 2001 Red							22	22
Fra. 2002 Gray							30	30
Fra. 2002 Red							10	10
Fra. 2002 Yellow							10	10
Jpn. 2001 Gray							48	48
Jpn. 2001 Red							13	13
Jpn. 2001 Yellow							17	17
Jpn. 2002 Gray							96	96
Jpn. 2002 Red							41	41
Jpn. 2002 Yellow							33	33
Total	3	5	4,319	2,494	3,476	2,738	3,734	16,769

The style of the Multistrada was unique, and it successfully found a niche market.

MULTISTRADA

Engine	Twin-cylinder four-stroke, air-cooled	**Battery**	12V 10Ah	**Wheelbase**	1,462mm (57.6 in.)
Bore	94mm	**Primary drive**	1.84:1 (32/59)	**Length**	2,130mm (83.9 in.)
Stroke	71.5mm	**Clutch**	Dry multiplate	**Height**	1,280mm (50.4 in.)
Displacement	992cc	**Gear ratios**	0.857:1, 0.958, 1.091, 1,350, 1.764, 2.466	**Width**	830mm (32.7 in.)
Compression ratio	10.5:1	**Final drive**	2.8:1 (15/42)	**Seat height**	820mm (32.3 in.)
Valve actuation	Belt-driven desmodromic overhead camshaft	**Front suspension**	43mm inverted Showa	**Dry weight**	188 kg (414.1 lbs.)
Injection	Marelli CPU 5.9M (45mm throttle bodies)	**Rear suspension**	Showa rising-rate mono swingarm	**Top speed**	208 km/h (129.3 mph)
Power	84 horsepower at 8,000 rpm	**Front brake**	320mm dual disc (12.6 in.)	**Colors**	Red frame, Red 473.101 Two-tone Gray Black
Spark plugs	Champion RA6HC	**Rear brake**	245mm disc (9.6 in.)	**Frame numbers**	From ZDM 1VABP 3B 000001 (USA)
Generator	12v/520W	**Tires**	120/70 x 17, 180/55 x 17		

First displayed towards the end of 2001, the Multistrada endeavored to emulate the Monster as another new niche model. Another product of Pierre Terblanche, this continued where the Scramblers left off 30 years earlier. The Multistrada was designed for tight mountain passes like the famous Futa pass near Bologna, and was arguably the most practical model in the lineup. The riding position, power characteristics, and quality brakes and suspension provided exceptional handling and road manners.

Powering the Multistrada was the new air-cooled 1000 DS (Dual Spark) engine, shared with the Monster 1000 and Supersport 1000. The frame was the usual tubular steel type, but with additional support for the lower engine mounts as on the 916/996 frame. The aluminum single-side swingarm pivoted on the crankcases and frame, and the Showa fork provided increased travel (165mm). The Showa rear shock featured a remote pre-load adjuster, and independent ride height adjustment. New wheels saw the discs mount directly to hubs, without carriers. The design featured a slim, integrated fairing, with the windshield turning with the handlebars. Modern touches extended to the electronic/analog tachometer, LCD screen, and electronically adjustable headlight.

As something midway between a street bike and trail bike, the Multistrada of 2003 was a brilliant all-round motorcycle.

Ducati Motor

For 2004, the ST3 replaced the ST2, with a new fairing and three-valve engine.

A significant update to the Sport Touring lineup occurred for 2004 with the ST3, powered by a new three-valve Desmodromic engine (Desmotre). The crankcases, crankshaft, gearbox and clutch were shared with the 1000 DS, with a new cylinder head, con-rod and piston. The two 34mm inlet valves and a single 40mm exhaust valve were set at a 40-degree included valve angle, the dished shape facing the combustion chamber saving weight. With 7mm stems, the valves were controlled by a single six-lobe camshaft, supported by plain bearings in the head, like the 1000 DS. The ignition also had twin spark plugs. This engine combined the finest attributes of both the ST2 and ST4 and was eminently suited to the Sport Touring. The basic chassis was as on the previous ST2, and the new fairing and instrument panel were shared with the ST4S. The ST3 continued for 2005 largely unchanged, exept for a new wet clutch.

ST3 2004-

Engine	Twin cylinder four-stroke, liquid-cooled	**Primary drive**	1.84:1 (32/59)	**Length**	2,070mm (81.5 in.)
Bore	94mm	**Clutch**	Dry multiplate	**Height**	1,274mm (50.2 in.)
Stroke	71.5mm	**Gear ratios**	0.857, 0.958, 1.091, 1.35, 1.765, 2.466	**Width**	906mm (35.7 in.)
Displacement	992cc	**Final drive**	2.80:1 (15/42)	**Seat height**	820mm (32.3 in.)
Compression ratio	11.3:1	**Front suspension**	43mm Showa	**Dry weight**	214 kg (471.4 lbs.)
Valve actuation	Belt-driven desmodromic single overhead camshaft (three valves per cylinder)	**Rear suspension**	Sachs Boge rising-rate swingarm	**Top speed**	235 km/h (146 mph)
		Front brake	320mm dual disc (12.6 in.)	**Colors**	Red 473.101 Yellow 473.201 Light Gray PPG 0026
Injection	Marelli 5.9 M (50mm throttle body)	**Rear brake**	245mm disc (9.6 in.)		
Power	102 horsepower at 8,750 rpm	**Tires**	120/70 x 17, 180/55 x 17	**Frame numbers**	From ZDM 1TBBS XB 000001 (USA)
Spark plugs	Champion RG4HC	**Wheelbase**	1,430mm (56.3 in.)		

CHAPTER 12

SUPERSPORT AND SPORTCLASSIC

For 1998, the carbureted Supersport was replaced by a new fuel-injected model, ensuring the continuation of the Supersport lineage. Designed by Pierre Terblanche, it had many components carried over from existing models, and while the new Supersport continued where the previous one left off, one thing that did change was the riding position. This was now more aggressively sporting, in the style of the 916.

900 Supersport 1998-2002, 900 Sport 2002

The 900 Supersport introduced in 1998 looked very different than its predecessor, but continued the classic theme.

As the 900 Supersport was considered a traditional model, the engine remained air-cooled. The Marelli electronic fuel injection included a new 1.5 CPU, and there were new camshafts, providing more valve lift (11.8mm for the 43mm inlet valve and 11.4mm for the 38mm exhaust valve). Redesigned cylinders incorporated the oil return internally, and while the new 900 Supersport wasn't any more powerful than before, the injection eradicated the cold running problems of the Mikuni carburetors. While the frame and aluminum cantilever swingarm were essentially the same as before, a newer generation Showa suspension, with a larger diameter (25mm) axle, provided considerably improved steering and handling

Ducati Motor

New for 2002 on the 900 Supersport was a stronger aluminum swingarm and Öhlins shock absorber.

Ducati Motor

Also new for 2002 was the more basic 900 Sport.

900 SUPERSPORT 1998-2002, 900 SPORT 2002

Engine	Twin cylinder four-stroke, air-cooled	**Clutch**	Dry multiplate	**Height**	1,125mm (44.3 in.)
Bore	92mm	**Gear ratios**	0.857:1, 0.958, 1.091, 1,350, 1.764, 2.466	**Width**	780mm (30.7 in.)
Stroke	68mm	**Final drive**	2.666:1 (15/40)	**Seat height**	1998-2000: 800mm (31.5 in.)
Displacement	904cc	**Front suspension**	43mm inverted Showa GD 131		2001-02: 815mm (32.1 in.)
Compression ratio	9.2:1		43mm Marzocchi (900 Sport)	**Dry weight**	188 kg (414.1 lbs.)
Valve actuation	Belt-driven desmodromic overhead camshaft	**Rear suspension**	Supersport: Showa GD 132 cantilever swingarm	**Top speed**	225 km/h (139.8 mph)
Valve timing (degrees)	25, 75, 66, 28		2001 Supersport, 900 Sport: Sachs	**Colors**	Red 473.101
Injection	Marelli CPU 1.5		2002 Supersport: Öhlins		Yellow 473.201
Power	80 horsepower at 7,500 rpm (crankshaft)	**Front brake**	320mm dual disc (12.6 in.)		Met Gray 473.201
Spark plugs	Champion RA6HC				Senna Gray 0017 (PPG)
Generator	12v/520W	**Rear brake**	245mm disc (9.6 in.)		Sport: Matt black 248.514 (PPG)
Battery	1998-2000: 12v 16Ah	**Tires**	120/70 x 17, 170/60 x 17	**Engine numbers**	Continuing ZDM 904 A 2C 000001 series
	2001-02: 12v/10Ah	**Wheelbase**	1,395mm (54.9 in.)	**Frame numbers**	From ZDM U1 00AA 8 B 000001
Primary drive	1.84:1 (32/59)		1,405mm 2002 (55.3 in.)		From ZDM 1LC4N XB 000001 (USA)
		Length	2,030mm (79.9 in.)		

over the earlier version. The front Brembo brakes were from the ST2, with twin P4 30-34 calipers with wider mounts. Terblanche's bodywork was strikingly different to the earlier Supersport. The full fairing incorporated ducting to cool the rear cylinder, there was a parabolic headlight, and a half fairing version was available for 1999. Updates for 2000 saw a higher windscreen, and to improve rider comfort, the handlebars were raised 12mm. In line with the rest of the 2000 range, the brakes on the 900 Supersport were also upgraded and the front discs were given aluminum carriers. There was very little development to the 900 Supersport for 2001 and 2002. A Sachs rear shock absorber and five-spoke Marchesini wheels appeared for 2001, and a new aluminum swingarm and Öhlins shock arrived for 2002. The more basic 2002 900 Sport retained the earlier three-spoke wheels, and included a non-adjustable Marzocchi front fork and steel swingarm.

PRODUCTION	1997	1998	1999	2000	2001	TOTAL
900 SSport						
1998 Red	3	1,400				1,403
1998 Yellow		407				407
1999 Red Fairing		286	232			518
2000 Red Fairing			409	493		902
2001 Red Fairing				277	226	503
2002 Red Fairing					30	30
1999 Yellow Fairing		251	65			316
2000 Yellow Fairing			132	293		425
2001 Yellow Fairing				90	74	164
2002 Gray Senna Fairing					115	115
1999 Red Half Fairing		89	231			320
2000 Red Half Fairing			126			126
2001 Red Half Fairing				69	29	98
1999 Yellow Half Fairing		23	81			104
2000 Yellow Half Fairing			70			70
2001 Yellow Half Fairing				50	20	70
2002 Yellow Half Fairing					1	1
1999 Cal. Red Fairing		208	100			308
2000 Cal. Red Fairing			50	51		101
2001 Cal. Red Fairing				200		200
1999 Cal. Yellow Fairing		508				508
2000 Cal. Fairing			50	51		101
2001 Cal. Yellow Fairing				150		150
1999 Cal. Red Half Fairing			200			200
2000 Cal. Red Half Fairing			50			50
1999 Cal. Yellow Half Fairing		1				1
2000 Cal. Yellow Half Fairing			50			50
1998 Switz. Red Fairing		70				70
1999 Switz. Yellow Fairing		10				10
2000 Switz. Red Fairing			5			5
1998 Aus. Red Fairing		123				123
1998 Aus. Yellow Fairing		30				30
1999 Aus. Red Fairing		191	7			198
2000 Aus. Red Fairing			102	26		128
2001 Aus. Red Fairing				73	45	118
2002 Aus. Red Fairing					18	18
1999 Aus. Yellow Fairing		77	2			79
2000 Aus. Yellow Fairing			31	12		43
2001 Aus. Yellow Fairing				39	18	57
2002 Aus. Yellow Fairing					15	15
2002 Aus. Gray Senna Fairing					5	5
1999 Aus. Red Half Fairing		30	60			90

PRODUCTION	1997	1998	1999	2000	2001	TOTAL
2000 Aus. Red Half Fairing			55			55
1999 Aus. Yellow Half Fairing		16	12			28
2000 Aus. Yellow Half Fairing			20			20
1998 Jpn. Red Fairing		132				132
1998 Jpn. Yellow Fairing		51				51
2000 Jpn. Red Fairing			18	11		29
2001 Jpn. Red Fairing				105	47	152
2002 Jpn. Red Fairing					26	26
2000 Jpn. Yellow Fairing			15	13		28
2001 Jpn. Yellow Fairing				70	24	94
2002 Jpn. Yellow Fairing					25	25
2002 Jpn. Gray Senna Fairing					15	15
2000 Jpn. Red Half Fairing			18			18
2001 Jpn. Red Half Fairing				70	20	90
2002 Jpn. Red Half Fairing					4	4
2001 Jpn. Yellow Half Fairing				65	10	75
2002 Jpn. Yellow Half Fairing					15	15
1998 Ger. Red Fairing		99				99
1998 Ger. Yellow Fairing		13				13
1998 Eng. Red Fairing		160				160
1998 Eng. Yellow Fairing		100				100
1999 Eng. Red Fairing		38				38
2000 Eng. Red Fairing			12	50		62
2001 Eng. Red Fairing				35	15	50
1999 Eng. Yellow Fairing		50				50
2000 Eng. Yellow Fairing			2	40		42
2001 Eng. Yellow Fairing				5	10	15
2002 Eng. Gray Senna Fairing					20	20
1999 Eng. Red Half Fairing		30	30			60
1999 Eng. Yellow Half Fairing		10	25			35
2000 Sng. Red Fairing			3			3
2000 Sng. Yellow Fairing			2			2
900 Sport						
2002 Dark Fairing					258	258
2002 Dark Half Fairing					61	61
2002 Dark Cal. Fairing					200	200
2002 Dark Aus. Half Fairing					9	9
2002 Dark Eng. Fairing					60	60
2002 Dark Jpn. Fairing					60	60
2002 Dark Jpn. Half Fairing					40	40
Total	3	4,403	2,265	2,338	1,515	10,524

Joining the 900 Supersport for 1999 was the smaller 750, still with a five-speed gearbox. There was a choice of full or half fairing.

750 SUPERSPORT 1999-2002, 750 SPORT 2001-2002

Engine	Twin cylinder four-stroke, air-cooled	Gear ratios	0.966, 1.074, 1,333, 1.714, 2.500	Height	1999-00: 1,100mm (43.3 in.)
Bore	88mm	Final drive	2.66:1 (15/40)		2001-02: 1,125mm (44.3 in.)
Stroke	61.5mm	Front suspension	1999-01: 43mm inverted Showa GD141	Width	780mm (30.7 in.)
Displacement	748cc		2002: 43mm Marzocchi	Seat height	1999-00: 812mm (32 in.)
Compression ratio	9:1	Rear suspension	1999: Showa GD 132 cantilever swingarm		2001-02: 815mm (32.1 in.)
Valve actuation	Belt-driven desmodromic overhead camshaft		2000-02: Sachs Boge	Dry weight	Supersport: 183 kg (403.1 lbs.)
Valve timing (degrees)	1999-01: 12, 70, 56, 25	Front brake	Supersport: 320mm dual disc (12.6 in.)		Sport: 181 kg (398.7 lbs.)
	2002: 11, 70, 50, 30		Sport: 320mm single disc (12.6 in.)	Top speed	205 km/h (127.4 mph)
Injection	Marelli 1.5 CPU	Rear brake	245mm disc (9.6 in.)	Colors	Red 473.101
Power	64 horsepower at 8,250 rpm	Tires	120/70 x 17, 160/60 x 17		Yellow 473.201
Spark plugs	Champion RA6HC	Wheelbase	1,405mm (55.3 in.)		Met Gray 473.201
Generator	12v/520W		1,410mm from 2001 (55.5 in.)		Senna Gray 0017 (PPG)
Battery	1999-00: 12v 16Ah	Length	2,020mm (79.5 in.)		Sport: Matt black 248.514 (PPG)
	2001-02: 12v 10Ah		2,030mm from 2001 (79.9 in.)	Engine numbers	Continuing ZDM 750 A2 C 000001
Primary drive	1.85:1 (33/61)			Frame numbers	From ZDM U1 00AA 9B 000001
Clutch	Wet multiplate				From ZDM 1LA3K XB 000001 (USA)

For 1999, the 750 Supersport was resurrected as an entry-level model in two versions: a full fairing and half-fairing. Apart from the Marelli 1.5 CPU electronic fuel injection system, the five-speed 750cc engine was the same as that for the 750 Monster, and featured all the 1998 revisions to the crankcases, clutch, engine covers, and timing belt covers. The frame was similar to the 900 Supersport, but included a steel swingarm with a different chain adjustment setup. The rear wheel was a smaller 4.50 x 17-inch model. The front fork was non-adjustable, and early examples included the Showa shock absorber of the 900 Supersport. From 2000, this was a Sachs Boge. New for 2001 was the budget 750 Sport, with a single front disc brake. Both the 750 Sport and Supersport continued for 2002 virtually unchanged before they were replaced by the 800.

PRODUCTION	1998	1999	2000	2001	TOTAL
750 SSport					
1999 Fairing Red	105	328			433
2000 Fairing Red		194	158		352
2001 Fairing Red			80	71	151
2002 Fairing Red				24	24
1999 Fairing Yellow	33	210			243
2000 Fairing Yellow		81	105		186
2001 Fairing Yellow			5	43	48
2002 Fairing Yellow				33	33
1999 Half fFairing Red	235	96			331
2000 Half Fairing Red		62	58		120
2001 Half Fairing Red			3	21	24
2002 Half Fairing Red				7	7
1999 Half Fairing Yellow	130	75			205
2000 Half Fairing Yellow		52	37		89
2001 Half Fairing Yellow			3		3
2002 Half Fairing Yellow				5	5
2001 Fairing Red 34 hp				8	8
2002 Fairing Red 34 hp				2	2
2001 Half Fairing. Red 34 hp.				2	2
2001 Fairing Yellow 34 hp				4	4
2001 Half Fairing Yellow 34 hp				10	10
USA 1999 Fairing Red		150			150
Cal. 2000 Fairing Red		50	25		75
Cal. 2001 Fairing Red			42		42
Cal. 2000 Fairing Yellow			25		25
Cal. 2001 Fairing Yellow			60	1	61
USA 1999 Fairing Yellow	1	100			101
USA 1999 Half Fairing Red	199	50			249
Cal. 2000 Half Fairing Red			25	75	100
Cal. 2001 Half Fairing Red				50	50

PRODUCTION	1998	1999	2000	2001	TOTAL
USA 1999 Half Fairing Yellow	173	27			200
Cal. 2000 Half Fairing Yellow		25	75		100
Cal. 2001 Half Fairing Yellow				49	49
Switz. 1999 Half Fairing Red	2	8			10
Switz. 1999 Half Fairing Red		10			10
Aus. 1999 Fairing Red	47	27			74
Aus. 2000 Fairing Red		1	8		9
Aus. 2001 Fairing Red			10	3	13
Aus. 2002 Fairing Red				13	13
Aus. 1999 Fairing Yellow	13	6			19
Aus. 2000 Fairing Yellow		4	6		10
Aus. 2001 Fairing Yellow			18		18
Aus. 2002 Fairing Yellow				4	4
Aus. 1999 Half Fairing Red	4	1			5
Aus. 2002 Half Fairing Red			10		10
Aus. 1999 Half Fairing Yellow	2	3			5
Eng. 1999 Fairing Red		25			25
Eng. 2000 Fairing Red			25		25
Eng. 2001 Fairing Red			25		25
Eng. 2002 Fairing Red				25	25
Eng. 1999 Fairing Yellow		15			15
Eng. 2000 Fairing Yellow			25		25
Eng. 2001 Fairing Yellow			5		5
Eng. 2002 Fairing Yellow				10	10
Eng. 1999 Half Fairing Red	40	60			100
Eng. 1999 Half Fairing Yellow		40			40
Jpn. 2000 Fairing Red		10	28		38
Jpn. 2001 Fairing Red			42		42

PRODUCTION	1998	1999	2000	2001	TOTAL
Jpn. 2002 Fairing Red				30	30
Jpn. 2000 Fairing Yellow		10	14		24
Jpn. 2001 Fairing Yellow			5		5
Jpn. 2002 Fairing Gray Senna				10	10
Jpn. 2000 Half Fairing Red		21	18		39
Jpn. 2001 Half Fairing Red			10		10
Jpn. 2002 Half Fairing Red				12	12
Jpn. 2000 Half Fairing Yellow		10	13		23
Jpn. 2001 Half Fairing Yellow			5		5
Jpn. 2002 Fairing. Gray Senna				5	5
750 Sport Dark					
Fairing 2001			272	1,210	1,482
Fairing 2002				111	111
Fairing 2001 34 hp				133	133
Half Fairing 2001			70	524	594
Half Fairing 2002				77	77
Half Fairing 2001 34 hp.				75	75
Cal. Half Fairing 2001			200	100	300
Cal. Half Fairing 2002				146	146
Aus. Fairing 2002				10	10
Aus. Half Fairing 2001			45	15	60
Aus. Half Fairing 2002				5	5
Jpn. Fairing 2001				10	10
Jpn. Fairing 2002				3	3
Jpn. Half Fairing 2001				4	4
Jpn. Half Fairing 2002				6	6
Eng. Fairing 2001			30	40	70
Eng. Fairing 2002				30	30
Eng. Half Fairing 2001			80	5	85
Total	984	1,776	1,687	2,974	7,421

The distinctive MH900e was another Terblanche effort. While the engine was stock 900 Supersport, most components were unique to the MH900e.

Shown towards the end of 1998 as a concept motorcycle, the Mike Hailwood 900 Evoluzione drew reaction that was so positive it was adapted for limited production 2 years later. It was nnother product of Pierre Terblanche, whose idea was to recreate the NCR racers of the late 1970s. While based on the two-valve fuel-injected 900 Supersport, the engine was tidied externally with sump covers to hide the oil cooler and lines. The polished engine cases were reminiscent of the earlier "round-case" Ducatis. A new tubular steel frame was created for the

MH900e, with a 60mm backbone, while the swingarm was single-sided, also in tubular steel. There was single shock absorber, but without a rising rate linkage. The fairing was integrated with the gas tank, which was a similar shape to the NCR. A number of components were changed in the transition from concept to production machine, including the the non-adjustable front fork of the 750 SS. The MH900e was initially sold only on the Internet, with the first production machines becoming available in May 2000.

MH900e 2000-01

Engine	Twin cylinder four-stroke, air-cooled	**Generator**	12v/520W	**Tires**	120/65 x 17, 170/60 x 17 (120/70 x 17 or 180/55 x 17)
Bore	92mm	**Battery**	12v/6.6 Ah (two)	**Wheelbase**	1,410mm [± 10] (55.5 in.) [± .4]
Stroke	68mm	**Primary drive**	1.84:1 (32/59)	**Length**	2,040mm (80.3 in.)
Displacement	904cc	**Clutch**	Dry multiplate	**Height**	1,090mm (42.9 in.)
Compression ratio	9.2:1	**Gear ratios**	0.857:1, 0.958, 1.091, 1.350, 1.764, 2.466	**Width**	740mm (29.1 in.)
Valve actuation	Belt-driven desmodromic overhead camshaft	**Final drive**	2.53:1 (15/38)	**Seat height**	825mm (32.5 in.)
Valve timing (degrees)	25, 75, 66, 28	**Front suspension**	43mm inverted Showa	**Dry weight**	186 kg (409.7 lbs.)
Injection	Marelli CPU 1.5	**Rear suspension**	Paioli mono swingarm	**Top speed**	215 km/h (133.6 mph)
Power	75 horsepower at 8,000 rpm	**Front brake**	320mm dual disc (12.6 in.)	**Color**	Red frame, red and silver
Spark plugs	Champion RA6HC	**Rear brake**	220mm disc (8.7 in.)	**Frame numbers**	From ZDM 1LA3N 1B000001 (USA)

PRODUCTION	2000	2001	TOTAL
900 MHE			
Europe 2001	21	142	163
Europe 2002		434	434
Cal. 2001		147	147
Cal. 2002		443	443
Jpn. 2001		321	321
Jpn. 2002		359	359
Eng. 2001		12	12
Eng. 2002		53	53
Aus. 2001		22	22
Aus. 2002		56	56
Total	21	1,989	2,010

The MH900e gas tank and fairing was intentionally designed to create an association with the NCR racers of the late 1970s.

Supersport 1000 (2003-)

The entire lineup of Supersports evolved into new models for 2003, headed by the 1000 DS. The 1000 DS engine was the same as the Monster 1000 and Multistrada, while the chassis was updated from the 900 Supersport. The adjustable Showa front fork was 600 grams lighter, and the rear brake caliper had larger (34mm) pistons. The rear shock length was adjustable, the standard length of 336mm able to be reduced by 4mm, or increased by 8mm. Additional weight reduction was accomplished with new exhaust manifolds (saving 350 grams) and new footpeg brackets. Also new was the electronic and analog instrument panel. The instruments featured a white background instead of black. The headlight lens was polycarbonate instead of glass (saving 800 grams), allowing a lighter front subframe. The Supersport 1000 continued for 2004 unchanged. For 2005 it was only available full-faired.

Heading the Supersport lineup for 2003 was the 1000 DS. It had the same motor as the Multistrada and 1000 Monster.

SUPERSPORT 1000 (2003-)

Engine	Twin cylinder four-stroke, air-cooled	**Generator**	12v/520W	**Tires**	120/70 x 17, 180/55 x 17
Bore	94mm	**Battery**	12V/10Ah	**Wheelbase**	1,395mm (54.9 in.)
Stroke	71.5mm	**Primary drive**	1.84:1 (32/59)	**Length**	2,030mm (79.9 in.)
Displacement	992cc	**Clutch**	Dry multiplate	**Height**	1,110mm (43.7 in.)
Compression ratio	10:1	**Gear ratios**	0.857, 0.958, 1.091, 1.350, 1.764, 2.466	**Width**	780mm (30.7 in.)
Valve actuation	Belt-driven desmodromic overhead camshaft	**Final drive**	2.53:1 (15/38)	**Seat height**	820mm (32.3 in.)
Injection	Marelli CPU 5.9M (45mm throttle body)	**Front suspension**	43mm inverted Showa	**Dry weight**	185.2 kg (407.9 lbs.)
Power	85.5 horsepower at 7,750 rpm	**Rear suspension**	Öhlins cantilever swingarm	**Top speed**	230 km/h (142.9 mph)
Spark plugs	Champion RA6HC, NGK DCPR8E	**Front brake**	320mm dual disc (12.6 in.)	**Colors**	Red 473.101 (PPG) Yellow 473.201 (PPG) Dark Gray 0017 (PPG)
		Rear brake	245mm disc (9.6 in.)	**Frame numbers**	From ZDM 1LABP XB 000001 (USA)

Supersport 800, Sport 800 (2003-04)

The 800 Sport replaced the 750 Sport for 2003. It featured a six-speed transmission.

The 800 Supersport replaced the 750 Supersport for 2003, and was joined by a lower-specification 800 Sport. The motor for both was shared with the 800 Monster, also with a new six-speed transmission. Compared to the earlier 750, the 800 Supersport specification was upgraded, with an adjustable Showa fork, five-spoke wheels (the rear a 5.50 x 17-inch), and an aluminum swingarm. The 800 Sport retained a non-adjustable Marzocchi fork, three-spoke wheels, and steel swingarm. This model lasted only a single year, and for 2004 the 800 Supersport was much the same as the 2003 model 800 Sport, with three-spoke wheels, a steel swingarm, and non-adjustable fork. It was discontinued for 2005.

The 800 Supersport for 2004 was a more budget model than the earlier example, and replaced the 800 Sport.

SUPERSPORT 800, SPORT 800 (2003-04)

Engine	Twin cylinder four-stroke, air-cooled	**Battery**	12V/10Ah	**Tires**	120/70 x 17, 170/60 x 17
Bore	88mm	**Primary drive**	1.85:1 (33/61)	**Wheelbase**	1,405mm (55.3 in.)
Stroke	66mm	**Clutch**	Wet multiplate	**Length**	2,030mm (79.9 in.)
Displacement	803cc	**Gear ratios**	0.923, 1.000, 1.13, 1,333, 1.66, 2.462	**Height**	1,110mm (43.7 in.)
Compression ratio	10.5:1	**Final drive**	2.6:1 (15/39)	**Width**	780mm (30.7 in.)
Valve actuation	Belt-driven desmodromic overhead camshaft	**Front suspension**	2003: 43mm inverted Showa / 2004: 43mm Marzocchi	**Seat height**	815mm (32.1 in.)
Injection	Marelli CPU 5.9M (45mm throttle body)	**Rear suspension**	Sages Boge cantilever swingarm	**Dry weight**	182.3 kg (401.5 lbs.)
Power	74.5 horsepower at 8,250 rpm	**Front brake**	320mm dual disc (12.6 in.)	**Top speed**	210 km/h (130.5 mph)
Spark plugs	Champion RA4HC, NGK DCPR8E	**Rear brake**	245mm disc (9.6 in.)	**Colors**	Red 473.101 (PPG) / Yellow 473.201 (PPG) / Silver gray 0022 (PPG)
Generator	12v/520W			**Frame numbers**	From ZDM 1LAAN XB 000001 (USA)

The 620 Sport was available for 2003 only. It was virtually identical to the 800 Sport, except for the smaller-capacity five-speed engine.

The 620 Sport was available only for 2003 and used the same five-speed engine introduced in 2002 on the Monster limited-power version. The chassis was much the same as for the 800 Sport, but with a narrower 4.50 x 17-inch rear wheel.

SPORT 620 2003

Engine	Twin cylinder four-stroke, air-cooled	**Battery**	12V/10Ah	**Wheelbase**	1,405mm (55.3 in.)
Bore	80mm	**Primary drive**	1.85:1 (33/61)	**Length**	2,030mm (79.9 in.)
Stroke	61.5mm	**Clutch**	Wet multiplate	**Height**	1,110mm (43.7 in.)
Displacement	618cc	**Gear ratios**	0.966, 1.074, 1,333, 1.714, 2.500	**Width**	780mm (30.7 in.)
Compression ratio	10.5:1	**Final drive**	2.6:1 (15/39)	**Seat height**	815mm (32.1 in.)
Valve actuation	Belt-driven desmodromic overhead camshaft	**Front suspension**	43mm inverted Marzocchi	**Dry weight**	182 kg (400.9 lbs.)
Injection	Marelli CPU 5.9M (45mm throttle body)	**Rear suspension**	Sages Boge cantilever swingarm	**Top speed**	195 km/h (121.2 mph)
Power	61 horsepower at 8,750 rpm	**Front brake**	320mm dual disc (12.6 in.)	**Colors**	Matt black 248.514 (PPG) Silver 0022 (PPG)
Spark plugs	Champion RA4HC, NGK DCPR8E	**Rear brake**	245mm disc (9.6 in.)	**Frame numbers**	From ZDM 1LA2K 3B 000001 (USA)
Generator	12v/520W	**Tires**	120/70x17, 160/60x17		

SportClassics

The PS 1000 headed the SportClassic lineup, and evoked memories of the 1972 Imola race winner.

Ducati Motor

Continuing the retro theme introduced with the Mike Hailwood 900 Evoluzione, a series of three SportClassics was displayed at the end of 2003. These emulated the three round-case 750s (Super Sport, Sport, and GT) of 1971-74, and were headed by the Paul Smart 1000. Whereas the original 750 Super Sport was a production replica of Smart's 1972 Imola race bike, the PS 1000 was a modern machine designed to capture the spirit of the original. Complementing the PS 1000 was a Sport 1000, in yellow with black outer engine covers like the 1973 750 Sport, and a GT 1000, which imitated the 750 GT.

Powering each SportClassic was the 1000 DS motor of the Supersport 1000, with the PS and Sport featuring an individual exhaust system with twin mufflers on the right. The frame was the usual tubular steel type, and while the PS and Sport had a dual-sided swingarm with a single left-side Öhlins shock absorber, the GT 1000 had twin shocks. The adjustable front fork was from the Supersport 1000, but the SportClassics included wire-spoked 17-inch wheels. Considerable attention was paid to the details of these models. The taillight replicated the original small CEV, and the round-section swingarm including chain adjusters similar to the earlier Seeley type. Production is scheduled for November 2005 for the PS 1000, with the Sport and GT following during 2006. They are likely to be produced in larger quantities than the MH900e.

PS 1000, Sport 1000, GT 1000

Engine	Twin cylinder four-stroke, air-cooled	**Spark plugs**	Champion RA6HC, NGK DCPR8E	**Rear brake**	245mm disc (9.6 in.)
Bore	94mm	**Primary drive**	1.84:1 (32/59)	**Tires**	120/70 x 17, 180/55 x 17
Stroke	71.5mm	**Clutch**	Dry multiplate	**Wheelbase**	1,425mm (56.1 in.)
Displacement	992cc	**Gear ratios**	0.857, 0.958, 1.091, 1.350, 1.764, 2.466	**Length**	2,100mm (82.7 in.)
Compression ratio	10:1	**Front suspension**	43mm inverted Showa	**Dry weight**	PS: 193 kg PS (425.1 lbs.) Sport, GT: 192 kg (422.9 lbs.)
Valve actuation	Belt-driven desmodromic overhead camshaft	**Rear suspension**	Öhlins single-shock swingarm / Twin shock (GT 1000)	**Colors**	SP: Blue frame, metalflake silver Sport: Black frame, burnt yellow FT: Black frame, gray
Injection	Marelli CPU 5.9M (45mm throttle body)	**Front brake**	320mm dual disc (12.6 in.)		
Power	85.5 horsepower at 7,750 rpm				

Ducati Motor

With modern chassis components, the Sport 1000 was an updated version of the 1973 750 Sport .

CHAPTER 13

999 & 749

While the first stage in the evolutionary replacement of the landmark 916/996/748 range occurred with the introduction of the Testastretta engine in the 996 R and 998 of 2001, and 2002, it was inevitable that a new model would replace it. This was the 999, released during 2002, and joined by the similar 749 for 2003. Although still more evolutionary than revolutionary, the 999 was considerably updated over the 998. Along with completely new styling came adjustable ergonomics, and an updated electrical and electronic system. Pierre Terblanche was responsible for the bodywork, which was was quite different than the 998.

999, 999 S, 999 R, 999 Fila

The 999 R was the highest-specification model for 2003. It had the short-stroke 999cc Testastretta motor.

There were initially two 999s, the 999 and 999 S, both using the 998cc Testastretta engine of the 998. The 999 S was the higher-output version. Developments on both included a non-symmetrical exhaust system with a varying front pipe diameter (from 45 to 50mm), while the rear exhaust was kept at 45mm. Combined with a large single muffler, this was claimed to simulate equal length pipes and improve mid-range torque. Intake noise was also suppressed by increasing the airbox volume to 12.5 liters, and fitting a Helmholz resonator in the intake tracts. The coolant reservoir was also incorporated in the right intake duct. Unlike the 916, the airbox wasn't sealed by the lower part of the gas tank, allowing the frame width to be reduced to 345mm.

The frame was also evolutionary, retaining the adjustable fork rake. Particular attention was paid to centralizing the mass with the optimum weight bias. A departure from the 998 was the double-sided sand-cast aluminum swingarm with sliding chain adjusters that allowed chain adjustment without altering ride height. While the Showa front fork with TiN-coated legs was similar to the 998, the fork triple clamps were moved forward 36mm, with the upper triple clamp machined from billet aluminum. The braking system was also similar, except for thinner (4.5mm) front disc rotors and a slightly larger-diameter rear disc. The front discs were spaced further outboard. The Brembo brake calipers included four 34mm pistons with individual pads. The 999 S included Öhlins suspension. Both the 999 and 999 S were available as Monoposto or Biposto.

In order to provide a perfect interaction between the rider and machine, Terblanche incorporated five-way adjustable footpegs, and a fore-aft seat/tank adjustment on the Monoposto of 20mm. The steering lock was also increased substantially. Other advances of the 999 over the 998 included a reduction in the total number of components by 230 pieces (30 percent), and simplification

Although an evolution of the 998, the 999 looked radically different and was functionally superior. This is the 2003 999 R.

The racing-inspired Brembo radial front brake calipers set the 999 R apart.

of the electrical components and cooling system, located on the left side of the motorcycle.

In December 2002, the 999 R was released, with the short-stroke 999cc motor of the previous 998 R. Chassis improvements included lightweight forged-alloy racing wheels, an Öhlins fork with radial brake caliper mount, magnesium headlight support, and carbon-fiber fairing. For the premium price of 30,000 Euros the owner also received a 102 dbA non-catalytic exhaust with single

muffler, new CPU, rear paddock stand, and bike cover. The racing exhaust saved 3 kg. To celebrate 200 victories in the World Superbike Championship, a limited edition of 200 999 R Fila was also produced during 2003. With colors replicating the 2003 factory racers, these were otherwise identical to the regular 999 R.

Updates to the 999 for 2004 were few. The engine lubrication system was improved through increased oil

999, S, R, Fila

Engine	Twin cylinder four-stroke, liquid-cooled	**Generator**	12v/480W	**Height**	999, S: 1,090mm (42.9 in.)
Bore	S: 100mm	**Battery**	12v/10Ah		R: 1,110mm (43.7 in.)
	R: 104mm	**Primary drive**	1.84:1 (32/59)	**Width**	730mm (28.7 in.)
Stroke	S: 63.5mm	**Clutch**	Dry multiplate	**Seat height**	780mm (30.7 in.)
	R: 58.8mm	**Gear ratios**	0.958, 1.043, 1.182, 1.40, 1.765, 2.466	**Dry weight**	999, S: 199 kg (438.3 lbs.)
Displacement	S: 998cc				R: 193 kg (425.1 lbs.)
	R: 999cc)	**Final drive**	2.4:1 (15/36)		R (2004): 192 kg (422.9 lbs.)
Compression ratio	S: 11.4:1	**Front suspension**	43mm Öhlins (998 R, S)	**Top speed**	999: 265 km/h (164.7 mph)
	R: 12.3:1		43mm Showa (999)		R, S: 270 km/h (167.8 mph)
Valve actuation	Belt-driven desmodromic double overhead camshafts	**Rear suspension**	Showa rising-rate swingarm	**Colors**	Red 473.101 (PPG)
Valve timing (degrees)	999: 16, 60, 60, 18		Öhlins (999 S and R)		Yellow 473.201 (PPG)
Injection	Weber Marelli CPU 5.9 M (54mm throttle body)	**Front brake**	320mm dual disc (12.6 in.)		R: Red frame
Power	R: 139 horsepower at 10,500 rpm	**Rear brake**	240mm disc (9.4 in.)	**Frame numbers**	999: From ZDM 1UB5T XB 000001 S: From ZDM 1UB5V XB 000001
	S: 136 horsepower at 9,750 rpm	**Tires**	120/70 x 17, 190/50 x 17		999 R U.S.A: From ZDM 1UB5T 3B 000001
	999: 124 horsepower at 9,500 rpm	**Wheelbase**	1,420mm (55.9 in.)		
Spark plugs	Champion RG4HC	**Length**	2,095mm (82.5 in.)		

pressure, and the 999 R received a new aluminum alloy swingarm patterned on that of the 2003 Factory Superbike racer. A cast-aluminum structure housed the pivot, while the arms consisted of two box-sections welded together. The 999 R footpegs were mounted on smaller plates to allow for a larger-diameter exhaust and only offered two alternative positions instead of five. Also new were the Brembo Marchesini five Y-spoke wheels that saved 3.2 kg over those of the standard 999 and 999 S.

Only 2 years after its release, the 999 was updated. Along with a redesigned fairing aimed at making the produciton 999 resemble the race machines more closely, there were significant updates. The upper and lower fairings provided improved aerodynamics, with the larger and more rounded cockpit fairing no longer incorcporting upper ducts. The screen was also higher, but most development was spent on the engine. The base 999 engine received the deep sump crankcase previously reserved for the S and R models, with the output increasing to 140 horespower at 9,750 rpm. This was achieved through new cam profiles and a higher compresion ratio. The engine of the 999R was also upgraded for 2005, with the power increasing to 150 hp at 9750 rpm.

749, 749 Dark, 749 S, 749 R

The 749 replaced the 748 for 2003. The Testastretta motor featured a shorter stroke, and a number of updates.

Soon after the 999 arrived, the 749 was released for 2003 as a replacement for the 748. The 749 Testastretta engine shared the shorter stroke of the 999 R, and featured a revised cylinder head design with a slightly wider included valve angle of 27 degrees (12.5 degrees for the intake and 14.5 degrees for the exhaust). The valve sizes were 37 and 30.5mm (with valve lift of 10.1 and 9.1mm). Also different to the 999 were the water jackets and circulation ports. Unlike the 999, which used Wills sealing rings between the cylinder head and cylinder, the 749 included a four-layer metal gasket. As occurred with the earlier 748, in many respects the smaller model (particularly the later 749 S and R) was technologically more advanced than the larger version.

The 749 chassis was identical to the 999, but with a slightly different weight bias (101 kg on the front and 98 kg on the rear). The 749 and 749 S this year featured the same motor, but slightly different chassis specifications. The basic frame 749 didn't include adjustable caster, and the rear shock absorber was Boge. The Showa front fork for the 749 S included TiN-coated legs.

Ducati Motor

The 2005 999 S featured Öhlins suspension and Brembo radial front brake calipers.

An expansion of the lineup for 2004 saw the 749 Dark join the 749, with a new 749 S also included. This featured an engine with slightly more power and some updates. The lighter crankshaft had tapered cross-section counterweights, there were higher-lift camshafts (11.4mm intake and 10.2mm exhaust), larger intake valves (38mm), and racing-derived die-cast rocker arms with cast, rather than machined, grooves. The closing shim retaining system employed titanium collets instead of the standard split rings. The shallower grooves allowed for narrower-stemmed (6mm instead of 7mm) valves. In all other respects the 2004 749 S was the same as before, with the same Showa suspension and frame with adjustable rake.

Also released for 2004 was the most advanced production Superbike ever from Ducati: the 749 R. This incorporated many updates that hadn't even made it to the top-of-the-line 999 R. Like the earlier 748 R, the 749 R was designed as a homologation model for World Supersport, where few modifications were allowed, and was little more than a racer with street equipment.

Along with a larger bore and even shorter stroke, the engine of the 749 R featured a revised cylinder head, crankshaft, cylinder and special Asso forged racing pistons. The crankshaft incorporated machined flywheels and a special profile to minimize friction. The pressure die-cast crankcases were like the 999 S, with a deeper sump. Apart from the valve seats and manifolds, the cylinder head casing remained unmachined to allow racing tuners to optimize the ports. As the engine height was unchanged, the titanium Pankl con-rods were longer (128.5mm) than the 749. Along with larger titanium valves (39.5mm inlet and 32mm exhaust), the new camshafts had higher lift (13mm and 11.5mm). The titanium valves, with 6mm stems, required special sintered valve seats and guides in Berilbronz, while the valve closing setup was similar to the 749 S. The carbon fiber timing belt covers also incorporated cooling ducts. The camshaft covers were magnesium. There was a new primary drive, and a slipper clutch to control back torque.

Another update was to the ECU trigger on the camshaft drive gear. A phonic wheel machined on the gear provided a more accurate signal, and for racing an additional RPM sensor could be coupled to the flywheel, with the housing already provided in the alternator cover. The single Marelli IWPR2 injectors were also a special racing type

749, DARK, S (2004), R

Engine	Twin cylinder four-stroke, liquid-cooled	Spark plugs	749, Dark, S: Champion RG4HC, NGK CR9VX R: Champion RG59V	Tires	120/70 x 17, 180/55 x 17
Bore	749, Dark, S: 90mm R: 94mm			Wheelbase	1,420mm (55.9 in.)
		Generator	749, Dark, S: 12v/520W R: 12v/480W	Length	2,095mm (82.5 in.)
Stroke	749, Dark, S: 58.8mm R: 54mm	Battery	12v/10Ah	Height	749, Dark, S: 1,090mm (42.9 in.) R: 1,110mm (43.7 in.)
Displacement	749, Dark, S: 748.14cc R: 749.5cc	Primary drive	1.84:1 (32/59) 2.111:1 (27/57) 749 R		
Compression ratio	749: 11.7:1 S: 12.3:1 R: 12.7:1	Clutch	Dry multiplate	Width	730mm (28.7 in.)
				Seat height	780mm (30.7 in.)
		Gear ratios	0.958, 1.043, 1.182, 1.40, 1.765, 2.466	Dry weight	749, S: 199 kg (438.3 lbs.) R: 193 kg (425.1 lbs.)
Valve actuation	Belt-driven desmodromic double overhead camshafts	Final drive	2.78:1 (14/39) 2.71:1 (14/38) 749 S 2.33:1 (15/35) 749 R	Top speed	749: 240 km/h (149.1 mph) S, R: 250 km/h (155.4 mph)
Valve timing (degrees)	21, 53, 60, 20 (749 R)	Front suspension	749, Dark, S: 43mm Showa 749 R: 43mm Öhlins		
Injection	749, Dark, S: Weber Marelli CPU 5.9 M (54mm throttle body) R: IAW 5AM	Rear suspension	S: Showa rising-rate swingarm R: Öhlins 749, Dark: Boge	Colors	Red 473.101 (PPG) Yellow 473.201 (PPG) R: Red frame Dark: Dark black 291.501 (PPG)
Power	749: 103 horsepower at 10,000 rpm S: 110 horsepower at 10,500 rpm R: 118 horsepower at 10,250 rpm	Front brake	320mm dual disc (12.6 in.)	Frame numbers	749 U.S.: From ZDM 1UB3S 3B 000001 749 S U.S.: From ZDM 1UB3S XB 000001 749 R U.S.: From ZDM 1UB3T 3B 000001
		Rear brake	240mm disc (9.4 in.)		

that featured 12 small holes instead of a single hole. The ECU was a new Marelli 5AM.

While the 749 R frame was the same as the 749 S, the aluminum swingarm was shared with the 2004 999 R. The attachment of the Öhlins rear shock absorber was also the same as on the 749 and 749 S, but the suspension progression was more rigid, and the shock absorber stroke was reduced to 56mm (from 71mm). The rocker arm was positioned above the shock absorber with a different push-rod mount. All the other equipment was the same as the 999 R, including the forged aluminum wheels, radial front brake calipers, and carbon fiber fairing. One racing feature unique to the 749 R was an adjustable fork offset between the center of the fork tubes and steering axis. The 749 R included an eccentric steering pin that could be set in two positions, 36 and 30mm. This feature was disabled on other production 999s and 749s. All these features combined to make 749 R the most most race-oriented production Ducati available, at least until the Desmosedici Race Replica, scheduled for one-a-day production in 2006.

Ducati Motor photo on CD****

The 749 R was new for 2004. It offered the highest specification of any production Ducati.